CONFESSIONS

OF A SPEEDWAY PROMOTER!

CONFESSIONS

OF A SPEEDWAY PROMOTER!

JOHN BERRY reveals the truth about speedway in the 70s and 80s

Published November 2004 by
Retro Speedway
Tel: (01708) 379 079
www.retro-speedway.com

©Copyright John Berry & Retro Speedway

Printed by Lavenham Press Ltd, Lavenham, Suffolk

Distributed by Vine House Distribution Ltd
Waldenbury, North Common, Challey, East Sussex,
BN8 4DR, England.
Tel: (01825) 723398
Email: sales@vinehouseuk.co.uk

Set in Sans

ISBN 0 9548336 1 9

Cover photographs by Dave Kindred and Ken Rivers

PHOTOGRAPHIC ACKNOWLEDGEMENTS
All photographs supplied by Dave Kindred, Owen Hines, Ken Rivers and John Berry
with the exception of the following:
AW – Alf Weedon; KC – Ken Carpenter; JH – John Hipkiss; CC – Chris Convine; MP – Mike Patrick;
DF – Dave Fairbrother; RA – Ray Archer; JB – John Bolle; JHa – John Hall; SD – Scott Daloisio

TO RUBY WOODS

'Mum Witch' was there on Day One when we first reopened Ipswich Speedway in 1969. She is still there now.
Ruby represents everything about speedway supporters. They are loyal, patient, knowledgeable about their sport, and dedicated to it.
This book is for Ruby, and to all the other Rubies, at Ipswich and at speedways up and down the country.

Contents

Foreword

"Is that with you?" This was the opening line of what was to be my lifelong friendship with John Berry. He was referring to my girlfriend (now my wife) of around six months, Anne, who I had taken to the first ever practice day of the new era of speedway at Ipswich Speedway in the spring of 1969. Thirty-five years later the banter continues across the world by email.

We stood at the pit gate watching as a collection of has-beens and hopefuls showed their skills and otherwise around the new track built at Foxhall by speedway's answer to The Likely Lads, John Berry and Joe Thurley.

They were in my age group of early-to-mid-20s and I quickly became hooked on the idea of watching racing again at Foxhall. I had been a speedway fan since the Witches first started in 1951. My father was a keen motorcyclist all his life and my parents took on flag marshalling duties at scrambles meetings and road racing at Snetterton.

In the 50s I was too small to see over the huge crowds at speedway and had to stand on a stool to see my schoolboy heroes, the likes of Titch Reed, Sid Clarke and Bert Edwards, roar around the huge, old track at Foxhall. Like just about every schoolboy at the time, my cycle had the mudguards removed as we mimicked the Witches on a track built on waste ground near our homes.

I joined the East Anglian Daily Times Company as a photographer in 1963 and when the story broke, early in 1969, that speedway was about to resume at Foxhall, I was keen to get involved.

The great day came for Ipswich to stage its reopening meeting – Witches v Rochester. This was a situation only speedway could find itself in. There was no speedway track at Rochester, just a team. Ipswich was the other way round – they had a track, but not what you could call a team.

I was at the first meeting with fellow photographer and speedway fan, Owen Hines. There was an old man on the centre green who ushered us around like a couple of lost lambs. "No flash photography"; "Keep away from the start gate"; "Don't go near the first bend".

 The "Old Man" was Howdy Byford who, at the insistence of the speedway authorities, had been asked to keep an eye on John and Joe's new promotion. I tried to find images from that first meeting for this book but failed. The portable track lights John and Joe had erected were just patches of light with the riders going from dark to light as they roared round the circuit. With flash photography banned in those days, there was not much to work with. Maybe, like the Witches, we were unsuccessful that night. For the next 15 years of my life, through getting married, starting a home and family, my Thursday evening routine meant home from work, a quick bite and off to Foxhall Stadium.

When Joe Thurley moved away from Ipswich, I got to know "JB" both professionally and personally.

After a couple of years struggling to build a business and team around the likeable local character of Ron Bagley, John had the good fortune of "discovering" John Louis.

I had known JL for several years from his scrambling days and recall watching a meeting with him during the 1970 season, when I asked him if he fancied racing speedway? The answer involved sex and travel!

The persuasive words of Bagley and Berry saw John Louis "have a go". The rest, as they say, is history.

As local interest and crowds increased, JB set his sights on top flight racing. I was with the speedway reporter for the *East Anglian Daily Times* and *Evening Star*, Mike Horne, the evening JB phoned Mike to say he had negotiated a deal to buy West Ham's British League first division licence. Much celebration followed.

In the spring of 1972, 16-year-old Billy Sanders arrived at Foxhall from Australia. The first meeting of the first division saw Billy make himself accepted as a local boy in just two hours. Sadly it was that day I took the sequence of photographs of the dreadful first bend crash that saw Tony Davey lose part of his hand.

I still feel very sad when I think how Billy's time at Ipswich came to such a tragic end in 1985. He was everybody's kid brother. We saw him grow up, marry, buy a house near Ipswich and, tragically, take his own life within walking distance of the Speedway.

There were many laughs over the years, though. Howdy Byford telling fallen riders to go off on a stretcher so he could announce: "He's a brave boy, he will be in the re-run, folks! The trip to Bavaria on a bus with the team and supporters, only to have the meeting rained off! During that trip I shared Germany's longest hotel room with friend and travel agent, James Easter. I am sure it was a corridor!

Watching JB trying to win an argument in the pits and not get into a fight. Speedway in fog! One October night it got so bad, Billy Sanders strapped a torch to his helmet before the referee called the meeting off.

My job gave me a little more insight than the fans to all the events at Foxhall that shaped Ipswich Speedway. I saw JB change from a shy, unsure young businessman into somebody who would argue and thump desks in his fight for justice and to try and give the sport a more professional image.

John enjoys a good "debate" (he will argue that one with me!). If there is not one already on the go, he delights in starting one. He has strong views on everything, newspapers being one of them. Editors are not used to being criticised in print. John's weekly programme notes would often raise a storm in my employer's office. Time to keep my head down.

The Speedway Control Board, match referees, local authorities, councillors, MPs, national and local journalists (and photographers!) will all testify to "exchanges" they have had with John Berry.

That was how John made Ipswich Speedway so hugely successful during his time at Foxhall. Many of his team changes over the years came as a surprise to the fans. Despite the brief departures of both Louis and Sanders, there are few who would not have missed the era featuring Dennis Sigalos and John Cook for anything.

On the following pages JB gives us a fascinating insight into the background of all the major stories during his time at Foxhall.

The championship-winning side of the mid-70s is my fondest era of Ipswich Speedway. It is great to still see the likes of John Louis, Tony Davey, Ted Howgego and Mike Lanham around town. Sadly, one of the best friends I made through my career, JB, lives in Australia.

I am sure my former newspaper colleagues and fellow speedway fans, Mike Horne, Elvin King and Owen Hines, will, like me, read the stories behind the stories with fascination.

This book explains how and why – from the man whose name will forever be a major part of the history of Ipswich Speedway.

Dave Kindred, 2004

Thanks to Nigel Pickover, editor of the Evening Star, for the use of the pictures from the newspaper's archive files.

Introduction

Don't look so sad
I know it's over
But life goes on
And this old world
Will keep on turning
Let's just be glad
We had some time
To spend together
There's no need to watch the bridges
That we're burning...

I don't know how 'proper' authors write their books. Then again, I'm not a 'proper' author.

I enjoyed sharing memories and anecdotes with friends via email. I think it was Bob Radford who asked if I had thought of writing a book, and then John Chaplin said the same.

I jotted a few disconnected lines down onto my computer, and found I quite enjoyed stirring up the archives deep in the personal hard drive that Poirot calls 'little grey cells'.

There these jottings lay, on my virtual desktop, gathering technological dust: not backed up and due to crash and burn at the next major computing disaster.

Then Colin Barber and Dave Feakes released their brilliantly accurate and painstakingly researched and edited *Ipswich Speedway. The First Fifty Years*. I recommend it to all lovers of speedway, and Ipswich Speedway lovers in particular.

I could never produce such a style of book. My memories are far too disjointed and I have precious little by way of research information.

Reading their book showed clearly how time has a habit of readjusting memories and mixing dates, times, even people. Largely though, I found I agreed with most things, and could maybe have added some inside thoughts as to the why rather than just the when, where, who, and how.

And so a more serious idea emerged. Maybe, even after all this time, some people might like to have a glimpse behind speedway history of the seventies and eighties, and perhaps they might like to see things through the eyes of an 'insider'.

Needless to say, if I was to be that insider then Ipswich Speedway would be the main focus, but I hope enough of my thoughts involve a general look at speedway – and some of its main people, places, and events – to make it interesting for all those who can look back nostalgically on the last of the 'Golden Years' in speedway.

It was finally the introduction earlier this year of the retro speedway magazine, *Backtrack*, and Tony McDonald's faith in my untutored and clumsy writing style, and his continued enthusiasm ever since, that pushed me into trying to join the disconnected jottings and put them into some kind of logical order.

Believe me, this putting in order, along with reviewing and rewriting the odd piece here and there to keep Tony and I out of court and to include later thoughts, has taken far longer and produced a good deal more angst than the original writing, which was the fun part!

As I slaved over yet another re-write, with Johnny Mathis playing in the background, I realised what I had created was a love story.

This explains why I still get excited when the *Speedway Star* drops into the mailbox, why I still follow the odd speedway newsgroup, and why my emails to and from England are nearly all speedway orientated.

By the time you read this I shall be 60, so this is not a starry eyed teenage love affair, nor is

Dag Lovaas knows it must be Thursday.

love blind to all the faults and problems within the sport, both then and now. Nevertheless, it is the kind of love that will not let go despite the time and distance between then and now.

Maybe every generation thinks it, but I have no doubt us baby boomers were born at the perfect time. Rock and roll, free love, the pill, That Was The Week That Was, and the peace and prosperity so many of our fathers fought and died to give us.

Sadly, we also presided over the last chapters in the collapse and death of the British Empire, and abused our musical emancipation with the likes of Johnny Rotten and Gary Glitter, but then, nobody's perfect!

Here and there through the book you might find the odd musical reference. For me, and I suspect, for all of us, music was a substantial influence, especially in those fun days of youth and excitement. It still helps to drag us back to the time when we were indestructible...

For the good times

It was just uncanny how the sun could shine beautifully all day Monday, Tuesday and Wednesday, but it seemed that every summer Thursday the good people of Ipswich would awaken to leaden skies.

I expect, in the town or city where your favourite speedway is located, it always rains on your race day, too. Sod's law it's called.

Of course I don't suppose it does rain any more on Thursdays than any other day of the week in Ipswich but when your livelihood hangs on the vagaries of the weather it can certainly make it seem that way.

Such is the life of a speedway promoter. All you can do is prepare the stage, select the actors, put together the production team ... and cross your fingers, because at the end of the day you are in the lap of the weather gods.

Speedway promoting is not a good career move for those who like to start at nine and finish at five, and who look forward to a quiet life and a good superannuation scheme. Nor is it a good pastime for those of a nervous disposition.

Of course, legend has it that a speedway promoter turns up at the stadium on the afternoon of the meeting, collects the money in a wheelbarrow and goes home rich at the end of the night. Well, I don't doubt nor deny that speedway was very good to me financially. But I promise you, the money did not just fall into my lap, and for every promoter who 'made it', I can point to many who limped away from the sport bruised, and often broken physically, mentally and financially.

Hopefully, over the pages of this book, I can try to provide a bit of an insight into the world of a speedway promoter. There will be tales that will hopefully make you laugh and maybe some to make you think. There will be tales specific to me, and some specific to Ipswich, but hopefully there will be enough to interest those who care little for either but are, or were, just speedway people.

From my point of view, if I can make you laugh, or really just make you think a bit about the sport of speedway racing, I will be happy. Here and there, my version of events as they happened, and people as they seemed, might well differ from commonly held views. Partly this will be down to my having access to private information, partly down to my own prejudices, of which I have many, and partly down to the way time plays tricks on memory.

Often we recall things from times gone by in a slightly different way to what really happened. That might well be the case once or twice here, and I also suspect that in one or two cases I will have got dates and places wrong, or maybe will have combined separate memories into an amalgam. If I have the odd fact wrong, please forgive me. Everything on these pages is just how

I remember it and any errors will have not been through malice or in an effort to 'sex up' any stories.

When I emigrated to Australia in 1989, I left just about all of my speedway stuff behind. It was the deliberate act of someone looking to move forward in life. But once speedway has you by the throat, it tends not to let go, and so I find myself drawn back to the memories of those days, those people, and those events.

So if you are looking for a history book, can I refer you to 'Ipswich Speedway, The First Fifty Years', by Colin Barber and Dave Feakes, an excellent work, chronicling the events at Foxhall Heath over many more years than I was there.

My recollections are a haphazard and largely unresearched collection of personal thoughts and memories.

Over the following pages you will learn something about me, about my good points, such as they are, and my weaknesses, which I recognise even more than others do. This is not meant to be an autobiography, though, so I reckon we can dispense with the relevant introductory bits in a few paragraphs.

I was the youngest child of four, and the only boy, which was a sure-fire recipe for being spoiled, and I was. Ernest, my dad, was a cabinet-maker, and Elsie May, my mum, a part time factory worker when she was fit enough. We were raised in a two-bedroomed terraced house on the Edmonton side of the Edmonton/Enfield border, in North London, giving the benefits of London living, mixed with the relative closeness of the countryside. 29 Woodstock Crescent, N9, to be precise.

Our thin but reasonably long back garden used to back onto a plant nursery. The nursery, which I suppose would have been about three or four football pitches in size, was hemmed in on all sides by back yards, but has long since succumbed to housing development.

Behind the houses, on the other side of the road, were a railway branch line and then a light industrial area.

I was born at the rear end of the war, when it had moved back to the Continent, except for the odd V1 buzz bomb, better known as a doodlebug. One of those things managed to blow out all of our front windows, I am told.

The post-war years were neither a time of plenty nor a time when much emotion was shown. There was no doubt our parents loved us, but there was precious little outward sign. How did we ever manage to live without psychologists, counsellors and professional do-gooders and did the odd clip around the ear really turn us from angels to devils?

Being the youngest, the only boy, and the 'brainy' one, my elder sisters were expected to nursemaid and defer to me, and, it must be said, I became the epitome of a spoiled brat.

By the time I was old enough to start reading Health and Efficiency, the older two sisters, Sylvia and June, had married, both quite young. Maybe there was a hint of wishing to get away from the tiny, crowded, and un-Walton style household involved in their rush to the altar, although both are still happily married.

Pamela, three years my senior, was (perhaps reasonably) annoyed, because when I was around the age of around 11 I finally moved out of my parents' bedroom into the only other one, which meant Pam had to decamp and take over the other two sisters' put-you-up bed in the downstairs front room.

The problem with this room was that it also served as a walkway between the front door (and stairs) and the parlour.

Such was the way of life back then but we never considered ourselves to be 'poor'. Poor was not having to pay for your school dinners, and we were never reduced to that embarrassment.

Pam also married young, so by the time I was a teenager it was just me left at home and most of the financial pressure was off. I wanted for nothing, and didn't even realise or consider that just about everything in the house had to be bought on the never-never.

I was lucky enough to go to The Edmonton County Grammar School (situated on the A10 Great Cambridge Road, and with an Enfield postal address!), where I abused my ability and the overbearingly Dickensian teachers in equal measure. I loved the sports and the physical education and the 'mateship', though, and can cheerfully say my school years were the best years of my life.

I emerged finally from tertiary education with a degree in food technology but with no desire to become a food technologist. The rest of the family wanted me to become a doctor or similar but, as I say, I abused my intelligence.

I was also, by this time, courtesy of many years of weekend and holiday work, a fully qualified fishmonger, and could also hold my own in the grocery, greengrocery, butchery and provisions trades. Needless to say, I'd also done my bit as a Christmas postman and petrol pump attendant, and I had held motley other positions of note.

John Berry had, by then, developed a simple philosophy. If a thing did not come easily, it was not worth doing! Hence, I do not have a great grasp of calculus, Latin, or ballroom dancing, and the only musical instruments I can play are the triangle and record player. I am one of those dangerously annoying people who have a little knowledge of most things, but am master of none.

It wasn't until I had been a speedway promoter for some time that I suddenly realised what my best attribute really was, and still is. I am a very good spectator. I miss very little, be it watching sport or studying life in general.

I have been asked over the years, by non-promoters, what the requirements are to being a successful speedway promoter? I stress the bit about non-promoters, because whenever anyone is granted a promoter's licence, this immediately confers upon them the Wisdom of Solomon. Well at least, that's how it seems, because I have yet to hear of any promoters, individually or collectively, listen to, let alone act upon, any outside advice from mere mortals.

Anyway, I decided to try and draw up a list of the jobs I needed to perform on a fairly regular basis as part of my time as a promoter. In fairness, at various times I had other people who helped with some of these tasks, but I also had to handle them all myself at some stage.

Here are a few of the skills I would need to list if I was drawing up a job description for a capable speedway promoter:

- Receptionist
- Public Relations Officer
- Personnel (human resources) Manager
- Press Officer
- Programme Editor
- Commercial and Business Manager
- Accountant
- Statistician
- Advertising Manager
- Legal Clerk
- Purchasing Manager
- Retail Sales Manager
- Plant Operative
- Construction Supervisor
- Labourer
- Stage Manager
- Paramedic
- Psychotherapist
- Marriage Guidance Counsellor
- Transport and Travel Manager

Now that's a pretty eclectic list in anybody's terms, but it gives a rough idea of just how comprehensive a set of skills is needed.

You will note none of those requirements listed above include that of being a speedway expert. Such a skill is an optional extra.

Here is a little story showing the diverse nature of the job. This would have taken place around 1984.

My secretary had finished work for the day and gone home when the telephone at the track rang. It was the Ipswich Mayor's secretary. The Mayor was inviting some representatives from the world of professional sport in the Ipswich area to a lunch in recognition of the publicity and prestige we brought to the town. Would I like to go along and represent Ipswich Speedway?

Yes, I said I would be delighted. She gave me the date, asked if I would be free at that time, but explained she would send a formal invitation. This was just a courtesy call to make sure the day was free.

The actual invitation came to my house. Very posh it was, too.

A month or so later, I was on the tractor grading the track. It was a glorious day and I was trundling around in ever decreasing circles with the constant drone of the tractor in my ears. This noise, and watching the beautiful, almost artistic symmetry of the trail of dirt coming off of the back of the grader blade was hypnotic. Sometimes the simple tasks are the most rewarding.

My secretary, Pat Louis (soon to become Doncaster), shouting across to tell me the Mayor's secretary was on the phone, shook me from my daydreams. They must want to change the date of the lunch, I mused, as I strolled into the office.

"Where are you?" she said, "We are waiting to start the meal!"

Because the invitation had been sent to my home, Pat had not vetted it nor had the date been added to either the office wall planner or diary. Therefore, she had not been able to pre-warn me, and I had just forgotten. Not even forgotten, to be honest. The date had never properly registered in my brain.

I was standing there at the track in jeans and short-sleeved shirt, covered in shale dust. I had to drive home, shower, change into a suit, and get into town, all in minus 45 minutes.

It actually took about 25 minutes, and then only because it included some highly illegal driving, so, it is fair to say, I was well late.

The Mayor's rooms are on the first floor of the town hall. There is a large reception room, called the Committee Room, at the top of the stairs. It is used mainly for large Mayoral functions, and entry to the Mayor's offices and 'parlour' is through this room.

I dumped the Merc in the dropping off area outside the front doors, ran straight past the commissionaire standing in the entrance of the town hall, bounded up the stone stairs, still doing up my tie, and gently opened the Committee Room door. There were close to a hundred people sitting down eating lunch. I could see some spare places fairly handy to the door. The guests were all tucking in, so I was sure I could slide, fairly inconspicuously, into a seat without attracting too much notice.

I achieved my objective, breathed a sigh of relief, and wondered if there was any chance of getting a bite to eat. I looked across the table I was on, and noticed Jeremy Doncaster's dad, Tony, sitting opposite. A friendly face!

Tony smiled kindly, and leaned forward.

"It's very nice to have you as our guest, John, but are you really positive you want to be here at this Rotary Club lunch?"

Through the Committee Room and on the other side of the Mayor's offices was the Mayor's Parlour. I had been there before. It is the size of a reasonable family living area.

Again, my blood ran cold. I excused myself from the assembled throng, shuffled through the Mayor's office, and into the parlour. There were no more than 10 bodies sitting at the dining table, halfway through their main course. There was Bobby Robson and the Ipswich Town secretary, David Rose, Bob Spalding, the then world powerboat champion, and Mike Reid, who had recently set a record for swimming the English Channel. Then there was the Mayor and one or two Ipswich Borough Council bods.

As I crept in, each pair of eyes turned and glared. There was to be no escape from my embarrassment. The Mayor's secretary had spoken to me at the track. There was no hiding the fact that I had simply overlooked the event, and snubbed the town's leading citizen. There is just no amount of apology or excuse that can get you out of that one.

Even though the Mayor, Peter Gardiner, was very kind, there was to be no recovery of equilibrium for me during the short time the remaining part of the meal took. Even today I remain dismayed whenever I recall the day.

Despite the disaster, though, I still hold proud the plaque, with its Ipswich Borough crest, that was presented to each of the guests who had attended. I do not surround myself with trophies or souvenirs but that little plaque, and the fact that it represents an appreciation from the community of Ipswich, means a lot to me.

Speedway programmes always contain a piece from the home promoter. Generally it is a very stylised and rigidly formatted affair, beginning with a reference to the last home meeting, going on to comment on any away matches undertaken that week, and then giving an update on any injuries within the team.

The middle part covers any major happenings in the sport generally, and then the piece finishes with a mention of the following week's proposed meeting, and finally a welcome for the visiting team that night.

These columns had a variety of boring and obvious headings, such as 'From the Promoter's Desk'. The first season we ran at Ipswich, our piece was headed 'To you – hello from John and Joe'.

Cringe factor of 100.

As my notes became more 'interesting' over the years, with the top and tail pieces being condensed to a bare minimum, leaving my often off-centre views on speedway in general taking up more and more space, something a bit more original was needed.

I settled for 'Slightly Sideways'

To me, it conveyed my less than straightforward way of looking at things whilst providing an image of speedway bikes in mid-turn.

I liked it then and I like it now. Speedway racing, and my thoughts on the subject remain to this day, Slightly Sideways.

1 We've Only Just Begun

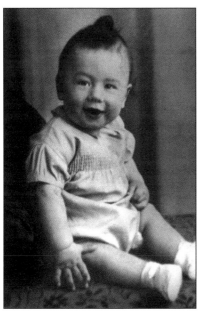

We've only just begun to live,
White lace and promises
A kiss for luck and we're on our way.
And yes, We've just begun.

Before the rising sun we fly,
So many roads to choose
We start out walking and learn to run.
And yes, We've just begun.

Sharing horizons that are new to us,
Watching the signs along the way,
Talking it over just the two of us,
Working together day to day
Together.

And when the evening comes we smile,
So much of life ahead
We'll find a place where there's room to grow,
And yes, We've just begun.

OK, hands up all the historians out there.
Here's the question:
Ready?
What happened on October 16, 1944?
Anyone who said it was the day Soviet troops first entered Germany on their way to Berlin, go to the top of the class. Those who added that the Allies had entered, and were about to take, Aachen, the first German city to fall, take full marks and a star.

Now if you were really good, you would also know that Lauren Bacall was on the front cover of that date's *Life Magazine*. She had just completed her first ever movie, co-starring alongside Bogie. No, the movie wasn't *Casablanca!* Maybe that was Ingrid Bergman?

Wow! A really exciting day. And in between all this heroics on the one part, and romance on the other, little Johnny Berry joined this world!

I was born in a hospital no less, something of a rarity in those days. It was the Westminster Hospital in London. I know that because it says so on my birth certificate.

I don't know the details. Well, there was a war on, and much more important things were filling the front pages of the *News Chronicle* and the *Daily Herald*.

None of my three sisters can add any more background to the birth. Sylvia and June, the eldest two, were evacuated away at the time because of the war, and Pam, three years my senior, was too young to be able to remember.

In fact, Sylv and June were disappointed to find the prune-like, real life dolly they had been told of, was quite a big boofer by the time they set eyes on him. Meantime Pam had decided the first name, William, from my official title of William John Berry, was too hard to pronounce and had settled for calling me by my middle name. Everyone else just followed suit.

So, to all officialdom, I am William John Berry but I am known as John. It could have been worse. I could have had to go through life labelled Billberry! In fact, nobody really bothered to stick a nickname on me at all. I recall a couple of pubescent girls trying to nail me with 'Pussy

'Cat Willum', after a kids' TV show of the time, and a group of speedway riders later tried on 'Chuck', but neither was original or offbeat enough to stick, and I'm not really a nickname kind of person anyway. I'll settle for 'JB'.

Meeting Joe

Joe Thurley keeping an eye on 'Diamond' John Berry.

First day at secondary school. You know, that horrible time when only a few of the kids know each other, and they huddle around in tight groups, leaving the non-aligned ones to wander around feeling lost and lonely and looking for a friendly face?

Well, that's when I first met Laurence Kenneth (aka Joe) Thurley. We were seated at opposite ends of the class but we became good pals. Even though Joe lived well outside of the normal catchment area for the school, and despite finding ourselves in different classes after the first year, we remained mates and served out our adolescence together.

We weren't a natural match. Me, skinny, manic and, even at that age, ready to answer back to anyone. I was always prone to sulking if I couldn't get my own way. Joe, barrel chested, easy going, laid back even, and generally non-confrontational unless really wound up.

That didn't make us of like mind on too many things, and it didn't make us bound up tightly together, but it did make us close mates. Mates worth falling out with your parents so you could meet up on Christmas Day type mates. Going to parties, sharing records, double-dating with, disclosing personal secrets to, and fixing the other up with girls, type mates.

Joe left school well before me, after having had several run-ins with the headmaster. After I left school, I went off to study at the National College of Food Technology, in Weybridge, Surrey, but, as mates do, we caught up with each other whenever we could.

We picked each other up and dusted each other off when either had girl trouble, and we enjoyed going to pop concerts and sporting events together. We were, as all other teenagers at the time, huge pop fans. Our era was the rock and roll years. We were the first of the baby boomers and the pioneers of pop culture. Joe and I were always one step in front of the crowd though. When our mates were still listening to Uncle Mac playing The Runaway Train on the BBC Light programme we were listening to Johnny Ray on Luxemburg. When they caught up with Luxemburg we had moved on to AFN (American Forces Network). We stuck with original American stars and records, rather than the UK released cover versions...

Joe was a motorbike lover. I rode motorbikes only until I could afford a car. Joe got caught up in speedway. I went along for something to do, to keep him company and to enjoy the beer and the birds.

Past his teens, Joe finally decided to try speedway himself. He was no natural but worked very hard at it. I would tag along when I could, pretending to be enjoying myself, up to my neck in shale and dirty, smelly motorbikes.

Being a keen road motorcyclist, Joe had an inbuilt resistance to sliding the back wheel of a bike. It went against all previous riding experience. Also, I expect, he did not have that lack of regard for his own safety that is a necessary requirement for making progress in the sport.

He struggled, along with such rookies as Ian Turner, Arthur Price, Russell Osbourne, John Ingamells and many others. At that stage, there was only the one British League and there were a million would-be world champions, all itching for a chance to prove themselves in second half junior races, or they would even settle just for a ride around the track after a speedway meeting.

Two things happened more or less at the same time in 1967. At 22 years of age, Joe conceded a career as a speedway rider was not going to happen for him (a fourth place finish in the Stars of Tomorrow meeting at King's Lynn was his best claim to fame) and the British League Division Two was formed.

We had not been the only ones to notice that there was an enormous surplus of young speedway talent just waiting for a chance to be harvested. A cartel of Division One promoters was busy putting together a second division, utilising those riders not able to hold down a Division One team place.

They opened either new venues or previously dormant speedway tracks on which to parade the new second division. Belle Vue and King's Lynn actually ran a 'junior' team as well as a senior team.

Joe pointed out that we could put together a team using the blokes we had come to know on the training track circuit. He had calculated that with the desperately low pay rates being offered in the second division, becoming a speedway promoter had to be a lot easier than being a rider and should also be an easy way to make money! All we needed was a venue.

So Joe started searching. He searched all around our North London/Hertfordshire home area (I had always lived in Edmonton whilst Joe's parents had recently sold a general store near Waltham Cross and the family had moved to Ware).

The search included Rye House, just around the corner from Joe's home. But Rye was going through one of its non-speedway periods and, in all honesty, we could not see the place becoming a successful venue again.

Then we spread our search area. We even looked at Stamford Bridge, where the majority of the old track was still evident, and the old Brafield track in Northamptonshire. Off the top of my head I recall examining possibilities in Hitchin, Kettering, Hertford and Harlow but none of these proposed venues, nor another 20 or more we ran the rule over, really fitted the bill..

The story about us driving up to Ipswich one Saturday late evening, and not being able to find anyone who had heard of the speedway stadium, has been told many times. Also has the fact that when we first looked at the place (a slight over-statement, given that it was pitch black and the nearest we had to a light was a box of matches) we dismissed it because the track had been re-laid with tarmac.

To be honest, at this stage, I thought Joe's pipedreams were just that. Although I paid lip service to his efforts, I was looking to expand from my East End fish and chip shop hidden away in the back streets of Poplar. This was real Eastenders country, where the pub on the corner was called the Ellesmere Arms but could just have easily been the Queen Vic.

I was negotiating to equip and open a state-of-the-art high street fish and chip shop in a new commercial development nearer my Edmonton home, and this took up most of my interest. Joe, meantime, was showing uncharacteristic resilience for the speedway idea and when my own plans hit local planning difficulties (smell rather than noise!), I gave his enthusiasm more time and attention.

Despite many more searches, we had drawn a collective blank in trying to find a suitable venue, so we popped up to Ipswich again in order to have a look in daylight. Joe figured it was possible to fit a new speedway track inside the original track, which was now a bitumen stock car circuit.

We made an appointment to see the boss of the stock car people, Spedeworth Ltd, who promoted at Foxhall. They kindly invited us down to Aldershot Stadium to meet them at their headquarters. Les Eaton was their main man. I've no doubt he had us summed up within 10 seconds of the interview beginning. A couple of young, wet behind the ears chancers who had not thought things through, and who were way out of their depth. He was right!

Nevertheless, Les hadn't got where he was without sticking his own neck out a few times and had a history of non-conformity himself. The 'official' stock car fraternity had given him a hard time, so he had simply set up his own rival national operation.

He was also no lover of speedway authorities, who were always giving him grief, and I think he quite fancied the idea of a couple of kids winding them up. Certainly, he had nothing to lose either way.

At the very worst, without any effort on his part, Les could enjoy being able to assist in giving the British Speedway Promoters' Association mob a kick. Also, I suppose he did consider the remote possibility that there might be something in it for him if, by some miracle, everything fell into place. I think he said something like: "You'll never break into that den of thieves but I'll support you if you want to try."

Building a track from scratch, especially one with removable safety fence and lighting, was going to be far more expensive than we had expected. Neither set of parents was well off – but both came to the rescue.

My dad was a cabinet-maker and worked for the same builder from before I was born until he retired. At best, mum had only worked the odd few hours part-time when I was young, so they had just about been able to make ends meet as I was growing up. So how could they possibly help financially?

We reckoned it would take about £5,000, or £2,500 each, to get things off the ground. That was a lot of money in the 60s – about 10 new Minis. I had £1,000 earned from the fish shop. Mum and dad had recently sold their house to the council and moved into a brand-new council flat.

The two-bedroomed flat had all mod cons, like under-floor heating and even a private balcony. Nobody knew then that this exercise in social engineering was going to become the notorious high-rise flats of the North London race riots, where firefighters lost their lives not too many years later.

Anyway, mum and dad had finished up with about £1,800 from the house sale, and this was stashed away in the 'Halifax' for their 'rainy day'. The speedway became the rainy day, as this was the money used to make up the difference between my £1,000 and the £2,500 needed. I presume Joe's parents funded his half from the sale of their shop in Waltham Cross. That £1,500 I borrowed was never formally repaid to mum and dad, although it is fair to say I looked after them financially further along the line.

So, armed with the venue and the money to develop it, we contacted the Speedway Control Board, in the shape of the then manager, a lovely man by the name of John McNulty. The Control Board offices were in the Dickensian world of Belgrave Square. On each side were embassies of this and that tinpot little country in some obscure corner of the world. In years gone by, the Bellamys might have lived here, upstairs and downstairs.

John's office had hospital cream walls and cast iron plumbing. Replace the electric light with a few candles or gas lamps and this quaint old place might easily have once been frequented by Mr Squeers, or the ever so 'umble Uriah Heap. It still had that dry and dusty byegone feel about it – and the present incumbents were tailor-made to fit.

John himself was a dapper man, nowhere near the first flush of youth. He wouldn't have looked too much out of place in those surroundings with a quill behind his ear. Conservative, if slightly dog-eared, business suit and immaculate grooming couldn't hide the many years he carried but it was interesting to hear that he still pottered around on a Triumph Tiger Cub when off duty. It goes without saying that John McNulty and Joe got on well!

His secretary, Ann Gillespie, was exactly what you would have expected as John McNulty's right hand. Correct, maybe even a bit prim, and with the air of a paid companion (continuing the Dickensian theme) rather than a technophile or petrol-head, Ann is a wonderful lady. How she ever became hooked up in speedway, when she seemed for all the world to have been made for a far more genteel life, is beyond me.

Our meeting with John was more like a visit to the Senior Master than a business appointment but he was most kind, explaining the differences between a track licence, a promoter's licence and membership of the BSPA.

He then pointed us in the direction, metaphorically, of far-flung Maidstone, where the BSPA had their office and where the sickly Dave Stevens was manager.

2 Happy Days

Sunday, Monday, Happy Days.
Tuesday, Wednesday, Happy Days.
Thursday, Friday, Happy Days.
Saturday, What a day,
Groovin' all week with you.

These days are ours,
Happy and Free.
These days are ours,
Share them with me.
Goodbye grey sky, hello blue.
There's nothing can hold me when I hold you.
Feels so right, it can't be wrong.
Rockin' and rollin' all week long.

These Happy Days are yours and mine, Happy Days.

Maybe I should backtrack a bit here.

I have always had a problem with Authority. Two of my many weaknesses are the inability to accept being 'told off' and the way I allow my thoughts and opinions to be easily interpreted by those around me. Sometimes this is called bad body language or 'attitude'.

I have since discovered there are times, even when you just know you are in the right and are being picked on, that it is better to at least appear to accept the situation with good grace. Discovering and putting that discovery into practice are two different things, though.

School was just one constant war between the vintage duffers of teachers and us bright eyed, bushy tailed post-war kids. These pre-war types still belonged to the 'little boys should be seen but not heard' era.

Not that school wasn't good fun and that I didn't enjoy playing Jack the Lad. Teacher-baiting was considered part of the fun, although, I have to say, the limits of tolerance in those days were decidedly tighter than today.

What I could never do was to accept the slings and arrows of the 'unfairness' of school life with good grace. Although I got away with heaps of stunts, there were times when I would be accused of things I did not do. This I could never cope with.

Whenever the finger was pointed wrongly at me I immediately reacted far too aggressively and felt very hard done by. Worse, I presented an open faced contempt for my inquisitors. Thus, my reputation as a troublemaker far outweighed my 'crimes'- certainly, the 'crimes' I was caught for anyway!

We were, however, fortunate that an entirely new breed of young teachers began replacing the old dinosaurs towards the end of our time at school. These young 20-odd-year old people treated us older students with something approaching respect. They even bothered to learn our first names – and sometimes even used them as well. In return, they were given the respect due from us.

In fact, as we moved through the school we became firm friends with many of this new brigade, and socialised with them away from school. One of our gang even had a reasonably long-term 'relationship' with the Botany mistress.

This didn't, of course, prevent me from maintaining a healthy disrespect for all those old codgers who were limited in ability and relied entirely on their positions of authority to protect themselves and their bad attitudes. They were fair game – and I enjoyed the challenge.

The die was cast, and although now trying to bring up my own handful of trouble (son), whilst approaching my dotage, I think I might be finally mellowing. Despite this, I have always answered a demand from anyone in authority with the simple question: why?

"Because I said so..."

"Because it's the law..."

"Because it's in the regulations..."

"Because I'm bigger than you..."

None of these answers has ever impressed as being reasonable and I daresay never will. I would like to think I try to explain the reasons for expecting my son to behave in a certain way. Sometimes, when he rejects the logic of those reasons, I admit to resorting to the "Cos I'm bigger than you" cop out, but I do try reasoning first.

I can feel an anecdote or two coming on. We are still nowhere near speedway yet but these two incidents help to explain what makes me tick, what I mean by unreasonable authority and the kind of things that formed me into the person I am, and perhaps influenced some of my attitudes and actions.

Story one. If you want to get ahead...

Even as 16-year old fifth-formers, we were required to wear the traditional school cap. Now we were all very proud of our school. We represented it at every conceivable sport and pastime, in our own time and at our own expense. Perhaps a little more time spent representing myself academically, rather than the school on the sporting scene, might not have hurt, but there you go.

We cheerfully accepted at that time, as I do now, the wearing of school uniform is a good thing. But our headmaster, one R L Hudson, was an unreasonable man. Forcing 16-year olds to wear a school cap demeaned and belittled us, causing resentment and bad feeling. School blazer, tie, flannels, white shirt and black shoes – no problem. But the cap was a plain insult.

Nevertheless, we were forced to pay lip service to the charade by each reaching our cap out of our schoolbag some 20 yards from the school entrance and balancing it carefully on the top of the Tony Curtis haircut as we passed through the school gates. The duty prefect would be lurking there to catch any miscreants. Once inside the gates, the offending cap would be stuck back in the bag and the Brylcreamed quiff restored.

It goes without saying that these items of headgear were not greatly cherished and were often mislaid. The procedure if a cap was lost was to go down to the boy's cloakroom after everyone had gone home and collect one of the guaranteed half dozen or so spares that were always kicking around in corners.

Thus it was that I was the 'owner' of one of these recycled chapeaux when we took our weekly trip to the local indoor baths for swimming lessons. Again, the charade of cap-balancing was required betwixt school doors and school bus, and then between bus and baths.

This particular performance was often lax, as I think the sports master felt much the same as us about the daft rule. Alas, obviously under orders, one morning he held a snap cap inspection.

Seven boys failed the test and I was genuinely surprised to be pulled out as one of the seven.

A speedway track, please!   **On parade at Galliard Road Infants.**   **With sisters Sylvia and Pam.**

After all, I had the cap, recently rescued from the smelly depths of the boys' cloakroom. Unfortunately, I had omitted to examine it properly. Had I done so, I would have realised it had no badge. I swear it was not until I was pulled out of the line that I had noticed. Of the seven rejects, two had no cap at all, whilst five had caps with 'defects'.

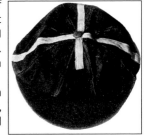

Wot, no badge!

Before I go any further, I should quickly describe the Edmonton County Grammar School cap. In its complete form it was black, quartered with yellowy-gold coloured ribbon, and had the school badge sewn on the front panel.

We less-than-magnificent seven were dragged up to see the headmaster, who had no doubt ordered the unexpected inspection. The two boys without caps were immediately allowed to leave with a warning. This struck the other five of us as not being really fair.

As it happens, the five lads left were part of a loose bunch of around seven or eight kids who were the mainstay of the school sporting and social sides, and were all close mates. This group had been known to brush with authority from time to time and although I never knew why, was often referred to as 'The Berry Gang'.

So the five of us stood in front of the headmaster, each with his offending article hanging from his index finger for the head to inspect. Bear in mind, these caps would by now (if they had been 'original equipment') have had five years of 'use'.

As I recall, the first cap had the rubber peak missing, where the covering cloth had frayed along the front edge and, no doubt, the rubber insert, once having become visible, had been 'helped out'.

The second, I believe, had the inside lining torn rather badly, whilst, as I have said, mine was missing its badge. Dave Sirrell's, however, had been given major surgery. The front peak had been removed completely, the yellow ribbons unpicked except where the central top button held them in place, and then they had been plaited around a pencil so the thing stuck up from the centre like an unfurled yellow maypole.

The badge on the front had been unpicked on the top and sides, so it hung upside down and back to front. The black lining had been carefully slit and pulled down, and had eye and nose holes cut, so when worn, the headgear would cover the head and face down past the chin. The whole thing was a customised classic work of art.

The headmaster had gone to each boy in turn.

"Why no rubber peak?"

"The cap is just worn out, sir?"

"Humph". Next one.

"Why is the lining torn?"

"I haven't looked after it properly, sir."

"You should have more respect for your uniform, blah, blah, blah..."

Then he moved on to me.

"Why does that cap not have a badge?"

Big sister June.

Jack the Lad.

The school under-16s basketball team, with me at No.12.

Now I could hardly tell him I had nicked it from the cloakrooms the week before and therefore didn't have a bloody clue, so I answered him as truthfully as I could.

"I did not realise it had no badge, sir, and have no idea how or why it was taken off."

This caused a whole torrent of unfounded and untrue abuse. I was told I had done it to insult the school. I was told I had no respect for the school or anything to do with it. I was told I was nothing but a troublemaker. The games master, who was witnessing all of this, was turning white, and I was giving the headmaster my full lip curl.

Then the inquisitor reached Dave Sirrell. The boy standing next to me on the other side, Peter Stetchman, was one of these uncontrollable gigglers. The headmaster, still red in the face from his attack on me, took one look at Dave's masterpiece and shouted: "WHAT IS THAT!"

Without changing his deadpan expression, Dave replied:

"It's all there, sir, but not quite in the right places."

I very gently nudged the compulsive giggler's arm with my elbow. He tried to stop himself but could not. The more he tried, the funnier the scene became, until all five of us boys ended up falling about, convulsed with laughter.

In seven years I never saw that headmaster crack a smile and he certainly didn't then. As I recall, we all got caned, but as the five of us and sports master were trailing out of the room, the head called me back. When the others had gone, he quietly said to me:

"Berry, if it's the last thing I do, I will have you thrown out of this school."

Story 2

My GCE 'O' level results were adequate, so rather than get a job I took the soft option of staying on in the sixth form and doing 'A' levels.

The morning I returned to school for the start of the new school year, I got as far as the front gates and was dragged into the headmaster's office. He told me he did not want me back. I told him I was coming back and that I really wasn't sure he had much option.

This must have been the case, because he kept me hanging around for the best part of an hour outside his office, whilst I presume he was trying to find a way to block my return.

However, Our form teacher, Mr Burridge, or 'Billy Bean' after a children's TV programme of the time, was very laid back and a nice bloke. There were about a dozen of us in the six form science class (all boys) and much the same number (mostly girls) on the arts side. 'Billy' more or less left us to organise ourselves. As time progressed, and more young teachers arrived, I became a prefect and House captain. I think I played a responsible role in the school – and managed generally to steer clear of the headmaster.

I like to think all us 'likely lads' made good responsible prefects. We continued to devote huge amounts of time to out-of-school-time activities and, when not representing the school, we were coaching the younger kids. We did more than our bit. Except academically, of course.

I don't know if things are the same these days but in my time, there was a three-week period during the 'A' level GCEs where the students were not required to attend school except to sit their exams. Then, there was a period of two or three weeks after the exams had finished before the end of year, when you were required to return to school. But, effectively, schoolwork had ceased. This was a pure fun period

At this time, my mum was in hospital. She had been born with a congenital heart condition, and the time had come when open-heart surgery was the only option left. 'Plastic valves' were in their infancy then, so mum was very much in the vanguard of being a recipient of such radical surgery.

The work was being carried out at the London Chest Clinic, not the local hospital. This specialist facility was in Hackney, maybe three quarters of an hour away from home by bus. Dad continued to work his normal hours, leaving the house at ten past seven in the morning, and getting back at twenty to seven in the evening. He then needed to grab some tea before we set off to visit mum. By the time we got back, it was quite late and well towards bed time.

So I was fending for myself and helping run the home, which, at nearly 19 years of age, was no big deal. I had been pretty well independent and more or less an unpaying lodger by the age of around 15.

My timekeeping was what suffered most whilst mum was in hospital. Invariably I would be late out of bed and then have to iron a shirt before leaving for school. Well, to be honest, my timekeeping had always been suspect. If speedway taught me one thing, it was the importance of timing.

I had heard that several of the lads were not going to report back to school on the first day they were due to return after the exam break. But missing the fun part of school seemed daft to me, so I decided to go, although I didn't rush. In fact, I wandered through the school gates about 25 minutes late.

Of the dozen boys who made up the Upper Sixth Science, less than half had bothered to show. The headmaster was going mad, he saw me arriving late, so I took the full brunt of his annoyance. Nothing new. He and I had a clear understanding – based on mutual hate.

Day two, I made a tactical error. I arrived late again. This was a mistake, for he was actually waiting for me. He gave me a "senior master's detention" even though sixth-formers did not receive detentions of any kind. I reported to the senior master, Sam Ellengorn, who fell about laughing and told me to consider my detention served.

The senior master was a wonderful man. His trousers were always held up with a tie and, out of class, he had a perennial pipe or cigarette in his mouth. He was a real teacher. Sadly, his subject was French, so he never actually taught me.

The third day, I arrived more or less on time. As organiser of the school Field Club, I was arranging a club angling competition for the following weekend, so during the morning break, I walked across to the shops near the school to buy a copy of Angling Times. This magazine always contained a section suggesting what might be the best stretches of local water for the following weekend.

You guessed! As I was coming back into school, the headmaster saw me again – and jumped to the conclusion I was just arriving. Up in front of him again, I showed the paper and told him if he didn't believe me, he should go downstairs and ask other people. He was crestfallen but still managed to berate me for leaving school premises during school time without permission.

Then, he had a brainwave. Us 'likely lads' had been having school dinners throughout our school lives but with only a couple of weeks to go, and bearing in mind we were all 18, had decided on a change. We would give up the school lunches and, instead, have bar snacks at a pub down the road for the last few weeks of our school life. Not entirely within the school rules, I suspect, but, then again, not unreasonable. There were about eight of us who decided to take this road.

The headmaster suddenly turned on me.

"What's this about you not having school dinners?" he said.

"That's correct, my mother is in hospital having heart surgery. I need the lunch times to go home and get things ready for my father's evening meal, so that he can get to hospital for visiting time." I lied.

"Well, the school rules state that if you wish to stop having school dinners, then you must bring a note to that effect from your parents."

Now, just bear in mind, none of the other lads had been required to do this.

I repeated what I had just said. That my mother was in hospital, I was having to run the household and that it was a bit unreasonable expecting me to bother to ask my father to stop and write a note, especially as I was nearly 19 anyway! Maybe I didn't phrase it as politely as I might but, clearly, the man was just out to get me.

He repeated that I would have to bring a note, so I told him clearly I had no intention of doing so, and why. I remember using the word 'piffling'.

Next morning I was late again. Not that it mattered in the overall course of things. The headmaster had actually positioned the deputy senior master, Mr Doubleday, a really nasty piece of work, who would have revelled in having a go at me, to await my arrival. I was escorted to the headmaster's office.

"Have you brought a note?"

"No, I told you I had no intention of doing so."

"You will leave the school premises immediately!"

"Explain?"

"YOU WILL LEAVE THE SCHOOL PREMISES IMMEDIATELY!" he repeated.

You might imagine, I had my say, but at the end of the day I had to go. He had finally carried out his threat. I had been expelled for not bringing a note to say I was stopping school dinners!

My two favourite school sports, basketball and cricket. Not that the school Head appreciated our efforts to fly the flag.
The basketball picture was taken after our defeat in the County finals at the US Airforce Base, Ruislip.

I discussed it with my dad, and with a few of the teachers who came round or telephoned offering sympathy. I wanted to take the matter to the school governors and the Local Education Authority but in doing so I would have involved my parents in a good deal of stress. In the end, dad and I decided we would let it go and not even tell mum.

R L Hudson was a nasty, vindictive, sad man.

What he failed to take into account at all was the pride we had in our school and the effort we put into representing it, especially in the sporting arena. I was never that good at football. Although I was extremely fast, I was a beanpole and never had enough power in my legs to kick the ball hard.

The best way to use my speed was as a goalkeeper. That got me into the school team in each year but I was never that good. The team did well through the years but it was in spite of my efforts and because we had several very good players.

My two favourite sports were cricket and basketball. My dad played cricket and from about eight onwards I was the scorer for his team, then filled in as a sub. By the age of 13 I was a full-time player.

Like kicking, though, my throwing was weak, and I soon realised wicketkeepers had more fun anyway, so keeper and opening bat I became.

I was better at cricket than football but my best sport was basketball. It was not a mainline sport back in the 50s but our sports master, Graham Briggs, was keen and so were we. Again, speed was my best attribute, along with effort and aggression, and these got me to the heady heights of the Middlesex County Schools squad.

Actually, that was a better achievement than it sounds, because Middlesex was the epicentre of basketball at that time and supplied most of the England players.

Again, it was grossly unfair for the headmaster to suggest we had no pride in our school. Middlesex is a big county but we would travel all over, on public transport, in our own time and at our own expense (and often at weekends and in the evenings where we would play against adult teams) to represent the school.

We weren't a bad team either. Throughout the years, we seemed to reach the final of the County competition. Sadly, we never won it. Our best chance was in our last year against a team we had beaten easily on their own court.

Their gym was quite small and I had the job of marking their star man, the England captain. Wherever he went, I went, and in the confines of that small gym I used a mixture of speed and, shall we say, physical tactics to keep him quiet.

The final, though, was in a huge indoor sports arena on the US Air Force base at Ruislip. The England skipper was used to playing under such conditions but our team got lost on the wide-open spaces and he beat us single-handed.

I received the usual bumps and bruises playing football and cricket but my worst injuries came playing the non-contact sport of basketball.

I remember a bad nosebleed from a stray elbow. We played in red shirts then and neither our coach nor the referees noticed for about five minutes, as I carried on playing and covered the whole area with claret. No AIDS to worry about then, though, so I managed to get back on later in the game, with shirt, shorts and socks still soaked in blood.

Perhaps my luckiest escape was in another school gym. As was common, the entrance to the gym was through double doors at one end, just under the backboard.

I was on a fast break; I dribbled down the court, launched myself for a spectacular lay up and braced myself for the crash into the doors. I wonder what the politically correct world these days would make of the fact that the doors had windows and the glass was not reinforced? I put each hand through a different window.

Both wrists had about half a dozen deep cuts; I still have the scars from them. Somehow, though, they managed to avoid veins or arteries and I was back playing in a week or so.

Touch wood, I,ve never been a hospital in-patient or broken anything important but whilst in the school fifth form I did give myself the worst injury I have ever suffered.

It was a Saturday morning. At that time, my parents and myself lived upstairs and my sister and family lived downstairs in a house dad had converted into two flats.

No central heating then, so as I usually did on cold winter mornings, I hopped out of bed, stuck on all four rings of the electric cooker in the kitchen, and hopped back into bed for 10 minutes to wait for the kitchen to warm up.

When I walked back in, clothes in hand, I found the chip pan that had been left on a ring, well alight, with flames licking the ceiling.

Instead of calmly putting the lid or a towel over it, I picked it up and ran downstairs with it, juggling it from hand to hand. I intended taking it through Pam's part of the house into the back yard, but her toddler was blocking the way, so I ended up going to the front door, throwing the pan down the front path, and closing the door on it.

At around that time, I realised my hands were hurting! I wrapped both hands in towels and went to the chemist. They gave me a dose of pain killing medicine and I caught a bus to the hospital.

I came out of there some time later with both arms in slings and decidedly the worse for wear. Dosed up with some stronger painkillers, I rested in the afternoon but there was a girl I had my eye on who I knew would be at a party that night, so I took a double dose of tablets and got picked up and taken.

I was having a great time, sitting there with people (including my target) fussing over me, until I made a bad error. I had half a pint of beer. With all the tablets, that was enough to send me over the edge. I was decidedly ill!

I won't go into the gory details of the damage to my hands. It took about three months but they are fine now – you can only see the scars when they are very cold. It meant I missed a great chunk of that year's basketball and football season, though.

I still feel bitter about R L Hudson. I might not have been a model student. But he was a bad headmaster.

I have since discovered there are times, even when you just know you are in the right and are being picked on, that it is better to at least appear to accept the situation with dignity, but I have always had a problem with doing such a thing. Even today I have fall-outs with people because I never sugar coat my opinions.

I rationalise it this way. If you have an issue with someone, it's better to talk to him rather than about him. Too many people I meet seem to take the latter option

Now I'm not advocating this as a way to make progress in life – such an attitude certainly ensured that my days in gainful employment in a big company were short and not very sweet. All I am saying is that there were (plenty of) times in speedway when such a simple philosophy of standing up for my beliefs was not all bad. It didn't make me the most popular guy on the block, but it did help to keep the scales at least level, and sometimes tipped just a touch my way.

For instance, when Joe and I were initially given the bums' rush by the BSPA following our first application to put Ipswich into Division Two.

I never actually made it to the BSPA's Maidstone office. I have a clear vision of it as being a couple of rooms over a shop in an old building, if not down a back street, then certainly not at the smooth end of town. Our application and all other dealings were handled by letter, though, so I never visited the BSPA's nerve centre.

We were invited to present ourselves at the Control Board offices (where the promoters held their meetings, because nobody other than Dave Stevens wanted to go to Maidstone!). Right up to this stage, I had treated the whole thing as having been something of an exercise in seeing how far Joe and I could get. I hadn't really believed we would go all the way with it.

But the attitude of our interviewers (the BSPA management committee) at that meeting was so annoyingly patronising and superior, it just got my back up – so I became really serious. I don't think that once in my life up until then (except in romance!) had I suffered a serious setback and this bunch of reprobates was not going to dish out the first.

They kept us hanging about for ages and then patently didn't take our application seriously, making wisecracks and generally making us feel small. They could clearly see we were neither ready for, nor capable of, running an existing speedway promotion, let alone building one from nothing.

The official knock-back came as a one-line letter in the post a couple of days later.

We appealed. At that stage, I'm not sure who we were appealing to, and about what, but after rattling repeatedly on SCB manager John McNulty's door, we got another hearing with the BSPA. This time it was with the full BSPA general council. And this time we didn't go in cap in hand, but ready to stand our ground.

We had done no pre-meeting lobbying. We were too green to understand what that entailed but we had done a bit more homework this time, and even laid out a few names we would be aiming to include in our team.

I can only think that this Star Chamber, or rather, some of the less miserable promoters in it, were impressed by our reluctance to go away. I would like to go on record here in thanking Len Silver for his contribution to our cause that day. He displayed genuine sympathy for our case and gave us the heart to keep talking.

Len spoke up, supporting our application, and he seemed to sway some of the clearly less sympathetic types. I recall the late Maurice Littlechild was also kind, and Wally Mawdsley as well, but Len was our trump card.

Given that he and I had many a set-to over the next best part of 20 years, I hope he doesn't feel too bad about things now. Drinking pals I don't think we would ever be, but I hope we both respect each other's love for, and contribution to, the sport. I surely do with him.

Eastbourne, in the shape of Charlie Dugard, was also applying for membership. I suspect the hearings must have been at an AGM, because this meeting was in a hotel and not at the SCB and I well recall Charlie was not amused at being kept waiting in the corridor outside the conference room for a long period of time. He was the owner of a large, successful and lucrative business and not used to being treated that way by anyone.

He was less than polite when he finally got into the room, and because he already had a solid history in the sport and knew most of the promoters personally, there was no way the Eastbourne application would be turned down. Possibly his presence helped our cause. It would have been very difficult to refuse Eastbourne a place in the league. Even more difficult to accept them but refuse us.

And so we were duly 'welcomed' aboard – provided we took on Howdy Byford as an experienced 'consultant'. We resented having this condition imposed upon us (although, in fairness, they did say that if we wanted to find our own man, provided he was acceptable to them, it would be OK) but really and truly it was a logical and sensible move on their part.

Looking back, I have to wonder how we had the nerve and the cheek to have taken on what was then a really tight closed shop. After all, we had almost no knowledge of the sport, no experience of promotions, no financial buffer and I think were both the grand old age of 23 at the time. We also discovered later, we were not the only ones who had been sniffing around Ipswich. Len Silver and Maurice Littlechild, on behalf of Allied Presentations Ltd, had also looked at it but had put it in the too hard basket.

As I recall, I think we kept our noses fairly clean in terms of upsetting the powers that be during our first season in 1969. Our only wrist slap was after a minor fracas at, would you believe, the other league newcomers, Eastbourne. Good, old Stan Mellish was in charge of his first ever meeting after passing his referee's test. He was just plain hopeless and, although a really nice bloke, never improved much over the years.

This, plus the tricks the Eastbourne promotion got up to, the less than calming influence of Bob Dugard, and the deliberately inflammatory behaviour and public address comments of their then manager, Dave Lanning, caused tempers to fray. It resulted in Lanning wearing the contents of a bottle of pop, courtesy of one of our riders, Ernie Baker.

The SCB took exception to us withdrawing our one remaining rider in the last heat of the match in protest, after yet another diabolical refereeing decision, and they subsequently fined Joe Thurley, as Ipswich team manager, £25, although both Joe and I were equally responsible for making the decision.

As the years progressed, Neither Bob Dugard's intra-meeting demeanour, nor the Ipswich management's refusal to be intimidated or take a backwards step, changed much, leading to several lively confrontations down at the pretty, little Sussex circuit, regardless of the many changing faces in both teams' line-ups.

Welcome Rowena

So why, at the end of Chapter One, did I say the 'sickly' Dave Stevens?

Well Dave was the manager when we became BSPA members. He was a slight, tidy man with a manicured grey beard. One of those characters you wouldn't like to try and put a date on. Was he a world-weary thirty-something, or was he a well preserved fifty- something?

All I knew was that he seemed a very pleasant bloke, an ex-press man but someone who was clearly not too comfortable in an abrasive atmosphere. Given that any sport is of a combative nature, and given that, in speedway at least, this attitude was as obvious between promotions away from the track as with riders on it, I felt Dave and his position were badly matched.

'Stress Leave' is a buzz phrase of the current era. In the late sixties it was not, but I suspect many of Dave's seemingly regular periods off for what appeared trivial matters could have been down to the pressures of the job.

I think it was at the end of our first year, in 1969, he made way for a female manager. Do I call her a manageress, or is that not acceptable terminology these days?

Rowena M Blackford was only in her early twenties and a mere slip of a thing. Had she been Dave Steven's secretary before taking over when he left? It matters not. What she lacked in stature though, she made up for in strength of character.

These were days when Tippex was King, when copies were typed on a waxed sheet and run off on a duplicator, and when only the biggest of companies could run to a Telex machine. Not even faxes were being used. Undaunted, Rowena and a single typist (who was eventually upgraded to 'assistant manager' when an office junior was introduced) were always on top of the job.

Remember, there were almost forty tracks to oversee by then and, unlike these days, everything (except the referee's appointments) was done in-house. Is it true that the current BSPA set-up employs 7 people, not counting the contracted out press and public relations, statistics, and International Affairs departments?

Perhaps, with Ipswich being in Division Two at that time it might have made me think things seemed to run so much easier then, as against the greater complexity of administration in Division One but each week the promoters would receive a report detailing all the events and decisions of the previous week, and a list of all the things they were required to do in the week to come. Time-wasting telephone calls to the office were not encouraged, but were not required either because the necessary information was supplied, complete and on time.

Of this list of things the promoters were required to do, woe betide anyone who failed! Like a really good schoolteacher, Rowena rarely had to issue punishments. Just the threat of being in her bad books was enough. No doubt most of the edicts originated from the respective Chairmen or Management Committees, but it was Rowena who put them into simple words and made them work.

I well recall her getting married and then some time later having a baby. I had occasion to telephone the BSPA office one day. She took my call whilst doing paperwork and feeding the baby, all at the same time!

Eventually we lost her to a less demanding lifestyle, and it was, indeed, a great loss. I don't think it is too much of a coincidence that from then onwards the running of the BSPA became more and more disjointed and less and less well regulated.

3 The Way We Were

Mem'ries light the corners of my mind,
Misty water-coloured mem'ries
Of the way we were.

Scattered pictures of the smiles we left behind,
Smiles we gave to one another
For the way we were.

Can it be that it was all so simple then?
Or has time rewritten every line?
If we had the chance to do it all again,
Tell me, would we, could we?

Our first end-of-season party in 1969.

Mem'ries may be beautiful and yet
What's too painful to remember,
We simply choose to forget.

So it's the laughter we will remember
Whenever we remember
The way we were.

So we had been given the go ahead to enter a team in the BL second division, always assuming we could put a good enough track and bunch of riders together, and on the understanding we 'employed' that old West Ham favourite, Howdy Byford.

I think several of the promoters liked Howdy, who had bounced back from many, many misfortunes life had thrown at him, and they just wanted to find him a job. We had yet to learn about the true facts of speedway life (or life in general) and the way things really worked.

Joe's uncle and dad worked to build the removable safety fence, which would have to be erected between the speedway and stock car tracks for each speedway meeting. After the basic track shape was cut out, Joe, myself, and some extra hands laid the concrete white line. We took advice on the actual track construction. We shouldn't have done.

We were told to lay down four inches of fly ash (the stuff left over from coal burning power stations), pack that down and apply another four inches of chalk to act as a smooth solid base, then add a three-inch layer of shale.

Meantime, we took more advice from a lighting consultant about how many and where to put the track lighting, using the then new fangled halogen lamps. We used scaffold poles as light posts and stuck the lamps on top, one on each post.

We then concreted sleeves in between the speedway and stock car tracks, so the lights poles could be taken up and down. The track electrician wired them all up using flexible cables. All of these cables were laid across the stock car track and plugged into the main underground electrical circuit at various places around the outside of the stock car track. Not sure how Health and Safety would cope with such a set up these days.

The various warning lights were hung on the safety fence around the track and were wired in the same way, with trailing cables. Thus, we had a track, a fence, lighting and warning lights.

We found the old starting gates and were able to rescue the electro-

Howdy Byford

Foxhall 1969. You can see the two tracks. The fence and lights have been taken down and the dark patches is water left from washing shale from the tarmac.

magnets, so a new set of gates was constructed, also connected to the referee's box by trailing leads.

The old pits were there, albeit in a fairly poor state, and one of the original little storage huts was cleaned out to act as a storage room, tea hut, speedway office and reception centre. The track telephone was a pay box in the Spedeworth race night cash office. Fortunately it had an outside bell!

Howdy managed to find a source for track rakes, track flags and starting gate tape, so we were on our way.

Getting hold of the tungsten halogen light fittings had proved to be a nightmare. The lights were not ready until the day of the meeting, so there was no time to test them.

I wish I could give you a minute-by-minute account of that first evening but, frankly, I can't. It was Ipswich versus Rochester (who failed in their efforts to gain approval for a new track in Kent and switched to Romford after four away matches) and took place on April 17, 1969. I can remember 'Rochester's' Barry Duke clocking 72.8 seconds, to become the first track record holder on the new track. I can also remember Howdy going off at the timekeeper, John Bennett, for 'allowing' a visiting rider to have been given the honour.

Most of all, though, I remember that, as it got dark, we realised that the advice we had been given about the track lighting had not been entirely good. Each little lighting head cast its own light but, unfortunately, those little pools of light didn't overlap. In fact, they never even got close to overlapping.

The riders zoomed in and out of view, as they sped in between light sources. Now you see them, now you don't...

That effect wasn't so noticeable on the track, because the riders were always focussing on the next patch of light ahead, so it wasn't dangerous as such, but it made for very difficult viewing from a spectator's point of view.

Worse, because the only stock car meetings run during the evenings were in mid-summer, they had not needed much public perimeter lighting, so all the spectators had by way of light was the odd 60 watt bulb on a stick to give the most basic of emergency lighting for the public. Other than that, they couldn't even see to fill in a programme.

Before the next meeting, we had doubled the number of track lights and put up some perimeter lighting for the people on the terraces who wanted to see to fill in their programmes. We were also told, fairly quickly, just how many speakers weren't working properly. It's fair to say, the track electrician was busy that week.

Of the 2,800 bodies who turned up for a look on opening night, about 1,800 came back the

Above: Joe and I get ready for tapes up.
Right: The Witches are back! Our 1969 team – left
to right: John Harrhy, Steve Chilman, Mike
Coomber, Joe Thurley, Neville Slee, Bernie
Aldridge, Pete Bailey. On bike: Ron Bagley.

next week to see the Witches lose to the Teesside Teessiders. Maurice Littlechild was the Northern team's manager on the night. He gently massaged our egos whilst stealing the points!

Mind you, the weather was lousy that second night. From then on, as we worked hard at getting both team and presentation to acceptable levels, the attendances rose slowly but steadily back towards the opening night figure.

We discovered fairly early on that putting the chalk down under the shale had been a big mistake. First of all, the shale wouldn't bind to the chalk. It was fine on the straights but not so on the bends, where the constant scrub of the tyres scoured the shale away. The riders got down to the chalk base every meeting. Worse, if it rained, the chalk became as greasy as hell and made it impossible to keep going.

In truth, to lay a shale speedway track, all you need is the shale and a device for rolling the shale it down hard. The elements will do the rest, provided they come in the right order.

We had also not taken enough care over drainage. In fact, we had done nothing at all. We had put a gentle natural fall on the track from outside to in, but the other thing we hadn't taken into account was that when it did rain, the water from both the stock car and speedway tracks ended up sitting on the inside of the speedway track, especially in the third/fourth turns – both tracks fall in that direction by about a foot over the length of the straight.

Still, that was what we had, and we just had to make the best of it. A further problem was the cost of shale, which is a by-product of coal mining. The stuff itself, at the time, wasn't that expensive. After all, slag heaps, which were really piles of unscreened shale, dotted the landscape all over the North of England and in Wales.

But there are very few coalmines in East Anglia and even fewer had the facilities to screen the shale to the required particle size. The nearest place that could was in the West Midlands, so we faced high costs in having the stuff transported across the country.

Howdy and Joe decided to try and source a substitute that might be found nearer to home and, therefore, be a good deal cheaper. They came across some stuff that looked like shale, I know not from whence it came but I suspect it was the ICI factory at Stowmarket, just up the road from Ipswich. They decided to try it, so a lorry load was put onto the track. To give you an idea, making the track from scratch would need about 50 of those sized lorry loads, so a lorry load was very much a top dressing.

The first problem was that when the stuff was watered, it became a bit gluggy. It was more of a powder than a mixture of granules and dust, which shale is. It meant we could not put down as much water as usual.

During the first race, red dust started coming up from the back wheels of the bikes. As the evening progressed, and the track dried out, more and more red dust appeared, until, by the end of the meeting, everything was covered by a thick red coating. What hadn't settled on everything, moving or still, was trapped in the cold night air and hung there, like a dense red fog. The 'stuff', it appeared, was pretty well pure red ochre!

It stained everything. We waited for the complaints, bills and abuse to get heaped on our shoulders. They never arrived. I think we had maybe a couple of letters and one phone call. We never used anything else but the best quality materials from then on but it took almost the rest of the season to get shot of the rest of the red ochre that had become mixed in with the shale on the track.

We also learned over time to use various cocktails of granite and limestone. These, when added to the shale, improved grip and the ability of the track to cope with wet weather. Good track preparation seems to have become a dying art these days.

On the face of it, the speedway was going well. In reality, though, there was tension in the Officer's Mess. Howdy was a great bloke and a super historical raconteur, or storyteller, depending on how much you felt was history and how much was his own colourful interpretation.

We heard all about his bad time as a prisoner of war in Japanese hands – and why he hated the whole of the Japanese race as a consequence. We heard of the lunatic things the olden day riders used to get up to. Even if a quarter of the stories were true, such actions these days would see them behind bars, let alone banned from speedway for life.

A couple of quick examples: like the night when the Haringay riders were a bit put out with their promoter, whom, they decided, had short-changed them. So after a meeting, when they were all suitably full of falling down water, they demolished the speedway office with the tractor to get to the safe.

And then there was the very well known rider who loved making bombs and letting them off in many and varied places.

It has to be said, whilst Howdy helped us to get things up and running, his involvement as the balancing force between Joe and myself just didn't work. If anything, he acted as an agent provocateur as the working relationship between Joe and I became strained.

In fairness, Joe had taken on the hard part of the promotion. He had moved from living comfortably at home with his parents and sister in Ware into digs on his own in Ipswich. A fair way from home, he had taken on the task of solving the day to day problems as they arose, and he had given up his previous social scene. As it happens, the social set he took up with in Ipswich was not the most ideal for the position he held, and his isolation and youth no doubt didn't help either.

On the other hand, I could work from home, and maintain the comfort zone of family and friends, giving up only a couple of days a week away from home at Ipswich. Therefore, when I turned up on a race day, it was all fresh and exciting, and I buzzed around full of good ideas and industry, not aware that I was stepping on Joe's toes.

Those things, plus the fact that I was responsible for all the paperwork, certainly would have made Joe feel that he was being treated like a second-class citizen, so our relationship suffered. What made it worse was that he is not the kind of person to stamp his foot and clear the air, which might have helped.

The team we had cobbled together for that year relied heavily on two Coventry juniors, John Harrhy and Pete Bailey. Apart from them and Ron Bagley, who enjoyed a renaissance in turning out for his local team, the rest was a bit of a case of liquorice allsorts.

We needed some of the 'elder statesmen' of the sport. Those who, for one reason or another (mostly to do with ability!), had drifted away before their sell-by dates. Other raw juniors, whom Joe and I had got to know during Joe's aborted attempt at becoming a speedway rider, were given a chance.

Most of the time the team was adequate. To be fair, that is all we, or the local public, could reasonably expect from such a pair of greenhorns like Joe and I, but we were on a fast learning curve.

Anyway, come the end of that first year of '69, we were aware of several things. First of all, that we were capable of running a speedway reasonably successfully. Secondly, we both, in our separate ways, enjoyed the challenge; and thirdly, we had distinctly different methods of going about things.

It was time to reassess.

4 **The Impossible Dream**

To dream the impossible dream,
to fight the unbeatable foe,
to bear with unbearable sorrow,
to run where the brave dare not go...

To right the unrightable wrong,
to love pure and chaste from afar,
to try when your arms are too weary
to reach the unreachable star!

This is my quest --
to follow that star
no matter how hopeless,
no matter how far --
To fight for the right
without question or pause,
to be willing to march into hell

The Tiger unleashed.

In 1970, Howdy Byford wrote a piece in his programme notes about John Louis. It said something like John Louis would be the first of many local riders to make the Ipswich team, and that one day Ipswich would win the league using all its own local lads.

Howdy was pretty good at hyperbole and this over-the-top comment slipped through to the keeper without causing too much of a ripple.

The basis for that dream had, however, already been put into place in my brain – and for that, I have to thank the legendary Belle Vue boss, Dent Oliver.

Dent was a man of few words – I suspect he would not have qualified for MENSA – but he understood speedway, he understood speedway riders and he understood what made people tick.

The Belle Vue Colts ruled supreme in the second division of both 1968 (its first year of operation) and '69. OK, so they had the might of the senior Belle Vue Aces to support them, they had the wonderful Belle Vue track on which to race, and the riders had the desire to make it into the first division Aces' line-up – the Manchester United of speedway at that time – to drive them on. But they also had Dent Oliver to guide them, and that was worth much by itself.

Ipswich was slaughtered for the second time in quick succession at the 'Zoo', or, more correctly, the Belle Vue Zoological Gardens, although even then the 'Zoological' part might have closed, leaving just the speedway, the funfair and the pavilions (halls).

I found myself once again seeking out Dent, shaking his hand and apologising for Ipswich not having put on a show. He put his arm around me before giving me one of his really long lectures. It must have lasted all of about 10 seconds. As I said, Dent was a man of very few words.

"Get rid of all the old boys," he said. "Speedway is a sport for young men. Get yourself some young kids and give them a go."

I brooded on his words all the way home. What he said made sense but it could not happen overnight. Ipswich Witches needed its senior citizens, like Ron Bagley, Ted Spittles and Ernie Baker to get themselves established, but there had to be a long-term plan.

Ted and Ernie – what a great pair of characters! Ernie was the smooth Londoner, straight out of an Eastenders set, and Ted, of the lilting Buckinghamshire accent and golden boots. These

Ron Bagley has his hands full trying to keep young guns John Louis and Tony Davey at bay, with Pete Bailey behind.

men were from the days when speedway riders were warriors, not jockeys. There was little hope of being able to order this pair around but they were great characters to have known, for all of that.

I wonder which came first? Was it John Louis, or the desire to take Ipswich right to the top? Buggered if I know really. I think I could best say, the desire was always there but John Louis turned it from a wish to a necessity.

The second year at Ipswich went much more smoothly than the first. In fact, it went rather well. Having been able to retain the use of John Harrhy and Pete Bailey for another season, and with John Louis starting his career like an express train and then moving on to jet liner proportions, the team was quite successful. Crowd figures were up to around 3,000 a meeting – all was going well

Sadly, though, our plan for solving the question of having too many chiefs at Ipswich had backfired badly. More on the debacle that was Doncaster later. All we need to record here is that we bought the Doncaster Speedway rights for £2,000, payable over two years. Joe moved up to Yorkshire in order to run that operation, which left me to take over full-time at Ipswich.

We did well to keep John at Ipswich for the 1971 season. Just a one year 'veteran', he was clearly ready for the top flight at that time, but I convinced him it would hurt his career none if he spent another season in the lower league, where he could enjoy the fruits of his first year of dedicated professionalism and where he could benefit from being a local personality.

He would also be able to take guest bookings at Division One tracks, which would supplement his income, give him plenty of senior league experience and provide him with the opportunity to put himself in the shop window for the following year.

He didn't take a lot of persuading. It was a good plan and should have worked well for him. It also worked well for Ipswich.

The Division One promoters, bless 'em, took a typically shortsighted view of this. In his first year, John had picked up a lot of Division One guest bookings and shown he was more than capable of holding his own in the top flight.

That 'Tiger' chose to stay in the lower league another year, and that he was contracted to a non-aligned second division club (i.e. a club with no first division connections), terrified the Division One promoters. What if all Division Two teams decided to hold on to their emerging stars? In a few years, the second division would be as strong as the first!

Of course, that would not have happened. Not in the short-term anyway. Ambitious riders like Louis were always going to want to reach the top, and to do so they would have to join the senior league.

John was not a young kid. He was a nigh on 30-year-old family man, who was entitled to have a second year cementing the first, basking in a bit more local glory and paying off a chunk of the mortgage, before continuing the climb up the rest of the mountain.

Nevertheless, the Division One promoters decided to 'punish' this upstart for not moving up and joining them. They thought they would make an example of him by banning him from taking any guest bookings in the top league during 1971.

Of course, they had to make this a blanket rule, and in doing so, what they did was to stop non-aligned Division Two riders from being able to test the water of Division One racing before progressing to the top league full-time. More of this decision later, but this crazy, thoughtless rule was to have a huge bearing on at least one rider down the line.

As for upsetting John or Ipswich, it didn't. The Ipswich promotion was more than happy not to have him wearing himself or his equipment out (and risking possible injury) with no return benefit to them at all (no loan fees at that stage). John also found he was as busy as he needed to be just keeping up with his Division Two bookings.

Meantime, another shooting star was emerging fast, in the shape of Tony Davey, and I was taking every opportunity to pension off those riders who had done us proud in our times of need but who were now clogging up the system. Not just Ted and Ernie, but such stalwarts as Neville Slee, Bernie Aldridge, Steve Chilman, Mike Coomber and many more. Luckily, I was able to do this more or less through natural attrition and with little bad feeling.

It was in the early season of '71, our third year of speedway promoting, that the dream of reaching the top of the tree became a plan – a plan based on two simple philosophies. These were: to put on a professional show, and to do it using young local riders.

First year crowds at Foxhall had been promising but barely covered our outlay. Our 'wages' were 10 quid a week each. The second year's attendances had increased but by then, as a company, Joe and I had branched out and bought Doncaster Speedway, which Joe had gone up to run.

Doncaster was a financial disaster from Day One and a testament to our conceit in thinking we only had to 'build it' and 'they' would come. 'They' did not come and any profits made by Ipswich were far more than swallowed up by losses at Doncaster. We would have been thankful for 10 quid a week that year.

The winter after the 1970 season was desperate for both of us. Joe and I owed money everywhere. We even sold our cars and put our wives out to work, whilst having no income at all ourselves.

I bought us a breathing space by managing to get a bank loan from an old-fashioned bank manager, who backed us with an overdraft facility of £3,000 (which had blown out to nearly four grand by the time of the first Ipswich meeting in 1971), despite the obvious risk.

In today's banking system it couldn't happen. Even in the system operating in 1970, that bank manager's job hung on our success (something he did not tell me at the time) but he was the only thing between us and bankruptcy.

As this is my book, I am allowed to indulge myself, and therefore I dedicate a small section here to Lindsey.

She had not that long left school when I first met her. I had my own fish and chip shop. There were a few years between us but a good deal more in life experience. Or at least, so we both imagined at the time.

Possibly even before Lindsey and I were introduced by a mutual friend at a party, Joe and I were making our early plans to take the speedway world by storm, and pretty

The 1970 Witches – left to right: Pete Bailey, Ted Spittles, Ron Bagley (on bike), Dave Whittaker, John Louis, John Harrhy, Bernie Aldridge.

soon she was roped in to type up letters for us at her place of work.

The small marketing company she worked for was also in need of someone with book-keeping ability, so Lindsey was despatched by them to day release classes. Even at this stage, I could see these newly acquired skills coming in handy for me. The accounting techniques needed to run a fish and chip shop were not exactly massive, whereas....

So now, as the time for our launch upon the speedway world moved ever nearer, Lindsey became more than just the honorary secretary, but also set up the company accounts for us, with all sorts of goodies like day books, ledgers and double entry accounting.

In 1969, our first year at Ipswich Speedway, Joe moved into 'digs' in Ipswich, whilst I stayed based at my parents' high rise council flat in Edmonton, north London. Joe was responsible

Veteran Gordon McGregor did his best for Doncaster.

for track and team, whilst I took care of the paperwork side. I would travel to Ipswich early on a Thursday, stay over Thursday night and travel back to London late on a Friday.

Lindsey's weekends would be taken up mainly with doing the company books and secretarial work. Sometimes, as a real treat, I would take her to a weekend away fixture! I should point out that Lindsey had never heard of speedway before meeting me.

Before the start of the 1970 season, we got married and moved to a new house in a development on the outskirts of Colchester. Why Colchester? Well, Ipswich just seemed so far away from our north London roots. We could get from 'home' to Colchester in an hour, whereas the further trek across the Deben Valley to Ipswich added a half-an -hour at least in those days.

To help get values in perspective, the new three-bedroomed, centrally heated house with cloakroom, large kitchen, meals area and very nice lounge cost £4,200.

Joe and I had decided by then that Ipswich Speedway had too many bosses and the best solution was to take on another speedway. We chose Doncaster, even though perhaps one of the most experienced promoters around at that time, Mike Parker, couldn't make it work. We thought we were bomb-proof.

The deal was that I would run Ipswich, Joe would rent a house up in Yorkshire, from where he could run the track and team from the Doncaster Stadium. Lindsey and I would look after all of the paperwork for the two tracks and help out on Doncaster's race days. Ipswich would retain Howdy's part-time services for one more year.

This meant that poor Lindsey was trapped with me on a 24/7 basis. I was not an easy taskmaster.

Pretty soon it was clear Doncaster was going to struggle. It was also obvious that even the £10 a week Joe and I were taking out of the company was 10 pounds a week too much. Lindsey got a job.

So she was working full-time, coming home, cooking, cleaning, running the house and doing all of the accounts and secretarial work, including the typing and preparing of two programmes a week.

On a Thursday evening she would come straight from work to the track at Ipswich and run the speedway office until 11pm. Then every Sunday we would leave our house in Colchester at around 7am and drive the three hours or so to Doncaster.

Lindsey would run the speedway office and turnstiles, whilst I helped run the meeting, and then we would leave around 7pm and drive back to Colchester in time to roll into bed exhausted.

These trips would not have been so bad if it wasn't so obvious just how much Doncaster was losing. It was seriously affecting my sense of fun – and Lindsey was in the direct firing line.

There was no reason why Doncaster should not have taken off like Ipswich had. We used the

KO Cup winners in only our second season. Left to right: John Harrhy, Pete Bailey, Tony Davey, John Louis, Ron Bagley, Ted Spittles, Stan Pepper.

same formula to build the team, relying on experienced old hands to do the bulk of the scoring and help out the young up and comers.

The stadium itself, although tucked away, was pretty enough and the track a good size and shape. The racing was always terrific, and the contests, at least the home ones, always tight and exciting. Some we lost and some we won but I thought it was always good entertainment.

Perhaps the good folk of Doncaster had other things to do on a Sunday afternoon, or perhaps they were only interested in instant team success. I was a long way away from Monday to Saturday but I have no reason to doubt Joe wasn't doing everything he could to make a go of it.

Certainly this was true until maybe the second half of the season, when I think we all lost enthusiasm, knowing we were losing big money on a week-to-week basis.

I finally decided we were never going to make it work when, for one meeting, only 420 bodies paid to come and watch. But we felt morally committed to at least see out the season.

Worst of all, for me, was that John Louis was taking speedway by storm and Ipswich was steadily moving forwards. We actually won the Division Two Knockout Cup in just our second year in existence, beating Berwick on aggregate, and I never had a moment to enjoy it.

The winter after the first season at Ipswich had been interesting. Somebody had got around to reading the small print in the Foxhall Stadium's planning permission terms, and it seemed that running speedway and stock car racing alongside each other breached these terms.

Foxhall Stadium stands some 100 yards or so outside of the Ipswich Borough boundaries. As such, the Borough of Ipswich gained all the benefits of having the speedway there. The speedway brought nationwide publicity to the town, it provided social amenity, it provided jobs, directly and indirectly, and any success it achieved helped with the 'feelgood factor' of the local people.

However, the Deben Rural District Council (to become Suffolk Coastal) had to cope with the downside. Mainly that consisted of complaints from the local housing estate about the noise.

Whilst the Borough of Ipswich is very much a working class community, Suffolk Coastal is blue rinse, and speedway doesn't really fit that image, so we had a battle to extend the planning enough to allow for the commercial running of the speedway and stock cars.

Our task wasn't helped by the very aggressive and adversarial stance towards the Council taken by Spedeworth, who seemed intent on bullying their way through. But with the assistance of a sympathetic and helpful local authority environmental officer, we were able to come to a sensible arrangement.

With that behind us, and John Louis' success encouraging other local lads to give speedway a try, Ipswich Speedway in 1970 should have returned enough profit to have paid off our start up costs and wages.

As it was, though, that next winter of 1970-71 was just so bad in every respect. Doncaster finally lost us £14,000. We had no money and were unable to even pay the mortgage. We had no car (sold to pay debts) and were always waiting for another knock on the door and another writ to be served.

The one we actually did receive was from Mike Parker. The original deal was that we would pay £2,000 for the Doncaster promotion, one thousand of which was payable up front and one thousand at the end of the season.

It goes without saying that the second instalment was beyond us at that stage, so I spoke to Parker and asked him to give us a little more time to pay. He simply said no.

I suppose I can accept him being hard-nosed about it now, but at the time it made things a nightmare for us. Without hesitation he served a writ on us.

Being as green as grass, we panicked and paid up within days, raising the money by selling the nice car I had bought from my fish shop days to pay for it. I am pleased to say, though, it cost him £500 for being so demanding.

There had been a clause in the agreement saying that if Doncaster didn't operate for a minimum two seasons, only £500 of the second payment would be payable. This was put into the agreement originally because the stadium owner was so unpredictable and the lease only annual, but we invoked it because of Parker's intransigence.

Most of the other debts were made up of routine bills from suppliers. During the season, the cash flow kept us going but come the end of the season the admissions monies stopped, but the bills kept on coming. Some suppliers were prepared to wait but others were not.

We did face the distinct possibility of having to bankrupt the company but we were desperate not to. The only two things that saved us was a very sympathetic bank manager and the chance to use the Doncaster licence and team to take a half share of the relaunched Birmingham Speedway.

All of this was going on whilst I was trying to plan and organise for a new season at Ipswich. You might presume the pressure meant I was at my snarling, self centred, aggressive best during this time. How Lindsey coped is beyond me.

Good Friday, 1971 saw the dawn of a new era. Suddenly, the sun started shining on us again and everything was on the up. OK, so it took a while to clear the backlog of debts but suddenly the road was clear. Possibly this was the best period together for Lindsey and myself. We began to socialise, we could afford to start going out and about.

Lindsey was able to restart her passion for horses and, on the surface, everything was going well. But in reality, we were now moving in slightly different directions. Lindsey's dream was a house in the country, with kids, dogs, horses and 'normal' friends – all the usual things in life. I was too busy chasing my own dream. The speedway dream.

I started trying to make up for my lack of attention to her by showering her with material things which could now be bought and paid for but after a couple of years the problem was becoming more acute. It really came down to my not wanting to commit to a family life. And even though it was not openly discussed, it was clear enough to me that Lindsey deserved better.

And so we parted. It was sad but I thought then, and I think now, it was for the best. We are still friends. She did eventually find her own niche and became a computer whiz, before settling down to her own family life with devoted husband, the kids and the house in the country.

It is easy to speak of contributions to the success of my time with Ipswich Speedway but Lindsey's role in those early, very difficult years should not be underestimated. She is a smashing person and I am proud to have known her.

That winter we managed to move Doncaster to Birmingham, using the rider assets and licence to gain us a half share of the Birmingham business. Joe moved on to Birmingham to run the show at Perry Barr.

This is, however, not a story about Birmingham, so all I need to say here was that this move took the financial pressure away from Ipswich, although for several more years we pooled our profits.

With John Louis and Tony Davey just demolishing all Division Two opposition before them from the off in 1971, I set about finding a way to get Ipswich into the top league.

'Tiger' Louis all crossed up but on his way to another victory. The Brummies had replaced Doncaster for the 1971 season.

Ted Howgego took on my trusty Wolseley.

Meanwhile, more local lads began emerging to claim team places. Clive Noy, a capable grass track rider who lived just around the corner from me in Colchester, and Ted Howgego, an Ipswich lad who started two wheeled life in moto cross, had graduated through the 1970 second half events into the team for '71.

This put five out of the seven team men as local lads (Pete Bailey and Ted Spittles being the others) and only two of the seven (Spittles and Ron Bagley) as old hands. By the end of the season both had been replaced in the team – Ted by Stan Pepper, who was another of our own 'products', and Ron by Rhodesian Peter Prinsloo, who had been struggling to break into the Wembley team.

Without a doubt, 1971 was the period of greatest fun in speedway for me. Gone was the flash Ford Corsair 2000E I had bought new when in the fish shop. It had been sold to pay bills during the winter and was replaced at the start of the season by an £100 old banger, a Wolseley 6/110.

This big, old bus was built like a tank, had the old freewheel overdrive and was good for 100-plus mph with all the comfort of hide leather and walnut trim. It put up with a season-and-a-half of pure abuse and never complained or let me down once.

Mind you, it was reassuring to have Clive Noy, a self-employed mechanic, and Ron Bagley, a more than capable spanner man, along on most of the long trips. In the end, I gave the car to Ted Howgego, replacing it with a brand new BMW.

Even those long trips were fun then. Clive was good company and Ron as sharp as a tack, in a laid back way, All three of us were also good drivers, so we shared the driving load. Those leather seats were just like armchairs.

This was a time when the relatively affordable-to-buy-and-run two-valve Jawas ruled the speedway scene and most riders had just the one bike, often having been bought second-hand. Engine failures were part and parcel of the game and added to the unpredictability of a match.

Of that team, John Louis was the only full-time rider. All the rest had some kind of day job. Despite this, and nearly all of us being domiciled on the far right edge of the country, I cannot remember an Ipswich rider not being ready to race at start time, with clean bike and leathers, at every meeting he was booked into that year.

Being only 26 myself, I was more or less the same generation as most of the lads. Owning that Wolseley and a three-bed semi on the outskirts of Colchester meant I was accepted as one of the boys. This was at a time when winning wasn't everything in sport and the standard of the riders was such that racing at home was a huge advantage.

Happiness was 40-38. The objective was to win as many home meetings as possible, whilst gaining the odd away victory. The racing was fun, the crowds were fun and the atmosphere was family and friendly. This was a time when war cries were OK and had no cringe factor, and the whole evening was based on having a good time.

We finished in third (equal second on points with Bradford and only four points adrift of champions Eastbourne) place in the league and again won the Knockout Cup, this time at the expense of Crewe. Not a bad show, but by then we were running out of things to do in the Second Division and faced the loss of John Louis if we stayed in the lower league. The idea of moving into Division One was fast progressing from a dream to a necessity. Without a move onwards and upwards, we would go backwards.

At that time, although the BL2 promoters had opened up their doors to outsiders, the senior league was still very much a closed shop. It had enjoyed perhaps the most successful period in UK speedway history following on from the formation in 1965 of the British League, from the amalgamation of the previous National and Provincial Leagues.

The inquiry by Lord Shawcross, and his subsequent report and recommendations, had brought the feuding bodies together. Although many of the various promoters still held deep personal grudges against each other, Shawcross had produced a working solution.

The first principle of that report had pointed out clearly, that speedway is a business first and a sport second. Sadly, over the years, too many enthusiasts entering the world of speedway promoting have overlooked this very important principle, to the detriment of the sport.

Using the Shawcross report, and the subsequent new BSPA constitution based upon it, the promotions accepted that, like it or not, their strength lay in keeping a tight knit operation where the strong did not feed upon the weak, but supported them. This was pure socialism at work, communism even. All for one and one for all.

Of course, it was very much Orwellian communism in that some promotions were always going to be more equal than others, but generally speaking the Association looked after its own. Pretty well all of the promoters had either a speedway riding background or a long association with the sport, so, effectively, they maintained a closed shop.

Sadly, communism, whilst wonderful in theory, has a huge downside, which will always, eventually, bring about its failure. Although the idea of the strong supporting the weak is great, one of two things must ultimately always happen.

Either the whole ship becomes lazy and complacent, because there is no incentive to push forward, and/or individuals begin to put personal ambition (greed if you like) before the common good and end up blowing the system.

Such was the cosiness of the Division One club in 1971 that the former situation was prominent. Those promotions who should have been pushing the barriers and developing the sport further had become fat, lazy and complacent.

They didn't see me coming!

Victory over Crewe in the final saw us retain the KO Cup in 1971. New team manager Ron Bagley shows off the trophy with (left to right): Ray Watkin, Clive Noy, Pete Bailey, John Louis, Peter Prinsloo, Tony Davey, Ted Howgego.

5 Climb Every Mountain

Climb every mountain, search high and low
Follow every byway, every path you know.
Climb every mountain, ford every stream,
Follow every rainbow, till you find your dream!

The three years of apprenticeship in the second division had not been wasted. I had learned who were the powerbrokers in the sport and who were merely foot soldiers. One of the biggest wheels of that time was Charles Ochiltree.

Charles had ridden up the ladder the hard way. He had progressed from speedway office boy to manager, to well respected promoter, but all as an employee and not as a principal. He must have been good at what he did, for in speedway that is a hard route.

Although Charles was, by 1971, the Coventry promoter, he was also a director and shareholder of Coventry's controlling company, Midland Sports Ltd, who had an interest in several other tracks, including West Ham.

The word leaked out that West Ham's famous Custom House track was being earmarked for development, so I gave Charles a ring. I had dealt with him before when he had loaned John Harrhy and Pete Bailey to Ipswich, so it was not difficult to reach his ear. I think it was also fair to say he had learned that I was a straight dealer and was honest and trustworthy.

Not that it was ever easy to meet the CO face to face, especially at Brandon, where he reigned supreme over his own little kingdom. Getting into Fortress Brandon, especially on a race night, and even more so on British Final night, was stuff of legend. You could have all of the passes, tickets and invitations in the world, but getting past the gate man was something else.

This man, who might well have suffered from a diabolical sex life, treated everyone with equal contempt. Not like my pit gate man at Ipswich, Paddy, who simply seemed to target individuals!

Paddy picked out Ole Olsen once. He demanded to see the Great Dane's SCB pass before he would let him through. I didn't know there was a problem until later but it seems Ole had actually started loading his equipment back into his van before thinking twice about it and producing his pass.

I had no alternative but to back up my man for doing his job – and, of course, Ole decided it had all been a ploy by me to unsettle him.

Mind you, when Ole became a promoter himself, a trip to his track at Vojens would always guarantee two things – rain and a set-to with his security staff.

Once past the stadium entrance at Brandon, the next task was to get into the pits. And if you were really brave, the final challenge was to go into the office to get a programme. Most times that would result in a long discussion with the lady behind the counter, who would then send for Mrs Ochiltree.

Of all the people within speedway at that time, Linda Ochiltree was the most feared. People reckoned they had seen stones bleed in that office! Only once ever, in the best part of 20 years, did I ever get the other side of that counter into the CO's inner sanctum, and, as I recall, that wasn't on a race night.

Anyway, over a few phone calls Charles admitted the rumour was true about West Ham Stadium being about to be sold for housing redevelopment. He, on behalf of the owners, agreed to transfer West Ham Speedway's Division One promoting rights to Ipswich for £4,000.

It doesn't sound a lot today but it was worth a good deal more in 1972. You could comfortably buy a reasonable house for that.

I must say I didn't realise then just how difficult it would be to steer the deal through the BSPA. Had it been anyone other than Charles, I don't think it would have been achieved. But I followed his instructions to the letter and eventually the Division One promoters allowed the transfer.

The most effective way to do the paperwork was for Ipswich to take over West Ham Speedway Ltd in its entirety, and I well remember having to meet Charles and the West Ham company secretary at the Custom House stadium for a ritual signing over. This meant I was given the company books, accounts, seal and articles of association as well as some sundry track equipment.

Olle Nygren offers advice to West Ham team-mate and fellow Swede, Christer Lofqvist, who didn't come as part of the package. Looks like another decent size Custom House crowd – but the figures still didn't add up. (AW)

It is not my place to comment on West Ham's demise being a classic case of complacent promoting. On glancing through the previous year's accounts, though, I did happen to notice that they actually sold more programmes per meeting than there were paying people coming through the gate.

Now given that the average percentage of people who bought programmes compared to those who attended speedway was around 70% at virtually all tracks, the fact that the West Ham percentage was greater than 100% might have caused me to raise my eyebrows had I been in charge.

As one of those who, when visiting the West Ham track prior to becoming a promoter myself, used to hop over the top of the turnstile and only pay half the admission fee to the attendant, I had a fair idea of why the figures looked so odd.

And so, thanks to £4,000 and Charles Ochiltree, Ipswich was now in the first division for the 1972 season.

Our first battle, once admitted, was in changing the race night from West Ham's Tuesday to Ipswich's traditional Thursday. You would think this would have been routine. I certainly had thought so but that was not how it panned out. Charles had removed his benevolent arm from around my shoulders as soon as the ink had dried on the cheque and I had to battle hard.

The BSPA objection was logical really. West Ham had been the only Tuesday night track, whereas Wimbledon, Sheffield and Oxford all operated on Thursdays. It wasn't that Ipswich would be liable to steal any of the Wimbledon, Oxford or Sheffield supporters (although Wimbledon argued that maybe we might!). The objection was that having four tracks racing on the same evening tied up a good number of riders and also made fixture planning far more difficult.

We won the day, but it was close, and I realised life in the fast lane was not going to be easy.

Now in those days, a 'licence', perhaps better described these days as a 'franchise to operate' in the first division, brought along with it the automatic provision of a ready-made team. Rider Control, also known as rider allocation, meant that during each winter the management committee played Robin Hood with the team strengths. It robbed from the strong and gave to the weak, so that, in theory anyway, the teams all began equal in strength at the start of each season.

It was a fairly blunt instrument and, quite apart from anything else, had one huge flaw. The management committee was made up of five of the promoters. It also doubled as the rider control committee.

With the best will in the world, it was impossible for those five people not to have half an eye on their own interests while supposedly playing Solomon when allocating riders to various tracks. Inevitably, it turned out that the strength of some teams was always going to be more equal than some others.

West Ham had not been particularly strong in 1971. Indeed, they finished rock bottom of 18 teams and failed to gain a single league point away from their East London base. Their team was a bit of a mish-mash of riders. Their only real current star was Swedish international Christer Lofqvist. The rest was made up of a very much past-his-best Olle Nygren, and a bunch of makeweights. One genuine heat leader/number one (Loftqvist), one number three/four (Nygren) and a few tail-enders. Hardly a winning team, and one you would expect to need to be considerably bolstered by rider control for the coming season.

Now given that it was known Ipswich had John Louis, who had managed a creditable seven point average when guesting in Div One in 1970, it was reasonable to look at a potential Ipswich line-up of, say:

1. Christer Lofqvist (ex-West Ham)
2. John Louis
3. A seven point man
4. Olle Nygren (ex-West Ham)
5. Alan Bellham (ex-West Ham)
6. Alan Sage (ex-West Ham)
7. Another rider from the Ipswich Div Two team. Say, Tony Davey.

A rare shot of Alan Bellham in Witches colours.

In other words, Ipswich needed all the left-overs from the previous year's West Ham team plus a third heat leader to add to its own riders.

It didn't quite work out that way! Poole promoter, Charles Foot, was a member of the management committee and he fancied Lofqvist for his Pirates team. Whoosh! In the blink of an eye, the only real current star in the West Ham line-up was whisked away to the south coast.

Well, OK, he would have to be replaced. Who with? The rider control (aka management) committee came up with another Swede, Hasse Holmqvist. Hasse was not a bad rider. Pushing to be called a number one, but not a bad rider. Except that Hasse hadn't ridden in England for a year following a serious injury, and in any case his Swedish team raced their home meetings on a Thursday, the same race night as Ipswich.

There was never a possibility that he would ever come and ride for the Witches. It would have required a particularly stupid, or a pretty cynical rider control committee, to expect the move might be even considered – and it wasn't. In fact, Hasse never rode in the British League again.

The 'seven point man' was Dave Hemus, erstwhile Belle Vue fill-in. I know he actually existed because I spoke to him on the phone. It would be fair to say he was not thrilled about being

moved from glamour side Belle Vue down to the wilds of Suffolk. He did actually agree to come down to the pre-season practice day but that was the last I ever heard of him. Well, he actually joined Exeter eventually. But as far as I was concerned, that was the last I heard of him.

So this is what rider control actually delivered to Ipswich Speedway as their contribution to the Witches' team of '72:

1. Blank
2. Blank
3. Blank
4. Nygren
5. Bellham
6. Sage
7. Blank

Like I said earlier, some teams were more equal than others!

The dream was alive, though. The dream of having a home-produced team of young kids win the league,

Olle and Alan Sage don't seem convinced.

that is. But for the time being, just survival would be nice.

We had already decided to include Tony Davey in the line-up. Everybody knew Tony was ready for it. Everybody except 'Shrimp' himself, I should say. Because of the ban on Division Two riders who rode for tracks with no Division One interests being allowed to guest ride in the top grade, the young Davey had never raced against top opposition, so had no yardstick with which to compare himself.

Realistically, I saw Shrimp as an immediate six point man, winning his share of races, but having a few blobs to go with them. Not many riders passed him when he got in front and he was an electric starter when he wanted to be. By the end of the first season he would be a match for anyone, I thought.

I had also followed up on a quiet word from Martin Rogers, then a full-time newspaperman, and part-time assistant at King's Lynn Speedway. He had pointed me to Australian scribe and speedway nut, Peter White, who was very keen on a barely 16-year-old Sydney-based rider named Billy Sanders. I chased that up and Billy was soon Ipswich bound. Clearly, though, the raw young kid would need to be nursed. We could expect nothing from him at the start.

So that left the team as:

1. Blank
2. Louis
3. Blank
4. Nygren
5. Bellham
6. Sage
7. Davey/Sanders

Alan Bellham never showed any interest or enthusiasm for riding at Ipswich. Although a nice enough bloke, he had never been much of a rider at West Ham – and looked dreadful at Ipswich. I don't know why.

Perhaps he really wanted to get back to King's Lynn, his local track? Perhaps he doubted his own desire to be a speedway racer, or maybe he just didn't feel comfortable at Ipswich. Neither myself nor Ron Bagley, who was the Ipswich team manager by now, could get near him and after very few meetings and very few points he was dropped and promptly retired to establish his successful speedway spares and tuning business.

So we were now down to just two riders (Nygren and Sage) who had been allocated by rider control. So much for equality.

We had a good break in managing to pick up Sandor Levai from Newport. A lovely man, Sandor had worked hard to become a nine-point rider at Somerton Park, principally because of his effort and enthusiasm on a track not many visitors tried too hard at. Already the wrong side of 40, Sandor had the strength and enthusiasm we would like to have seen in Alan Bellham.

A graceful, flowing style Sandor did not have – but he did have points on the board. With the best will in the world, I did not think we would be able to build a team around him but he would be a welcome addition. We would have to rely on John Louis to make the jump from Division Two star to first division star in one giant leap.

So now the team looked like this:

1. Louis
2. Levai
3. Blank
4. Nygren
5. Sage
6. Sanders
7. Davey

Getting better, but still short of a third heat leader ... and with a potentially weak tail.

Even as the season had started, we were still scavenging around the world, but the team we put out on the track for our first ever British League Division One match was:

1. Sandor Levai
2. Alan Sage
3. Olle Nygren
4. Alan Bellham
5. John Louis
6. Tony Davey
7. Billy Sanders.

They are the ones who prepared to do battle on . . .

THE LONGEST DAY

Friday, March 31, 1972. Good Friday.

The military operation had been devised half way through the 1971 season. For eight months Operation Division One had been meticulously planned.

In the early months, intelligence had isolated a target – West Ham Speedway. In the lead up to Christmas, the Diplomatic Corps had negotiated a bloodless coup and the take over of the Hammers had been completed.

From the New Year onwards, Ipswich Speedway was on war footing. On the home front there were massive fortifications and emplacements to be undertaken. With military precision the track was re-laid, new pits built and a new HQ created. New track lighting and reception areas were built, along with workshops and new changing facilities.

Time was of the essence but thanks to the devoted duty of The Few, these defences were put in place, even in time to have a full-scale war game (practice session) on the newly created battleground.

The only problem lay on the recruitment side.

We had been promised an army by the rider control committee. All we got were a few stragglers. We had to go searching for volunteers ourselves.

What we ended up with was more like the home guard, made up from raw recruits and old soldiers. Our only certainty for battle honours was John Louis.

The rest was in the lap of the gods.

But that day, Good Friday 1972, was not about winning the war. It was not even about winning the battle. It was about putting up a fight, putting on a show, and winning the hearts and minds of those whom we sought to serve. Always assuming they would turn up to witness the combat.

The day dawned cold and cloudy, but comparatively dry. The first major hurdle had been overcome. At least the battle could go ahead.

The scheduled start time was 2.30pm, so as to allow the troops time to finish at Foxhall after the first engagement and decamp to Hackney for the evening return fixture. I had arranged for the turnstiles to open at one o'clock, half an hour earlier than they would normally have done. The turnstile manager couldn't understand the panic, even though there were people beginning to queue by then.

John Louis swings a pick for a speedway publicity shot.

My normal procedure for such a big meeting would be to concentrate on making sure the pre-meeting entertainment went on at the right times, organise the troops, trouble-shoot in the pits and then co-ordinate the parade, before settling down to concentrate on the match.

This time, though, things were different.

As riders turned up, later than they had wanted, they told tales of queues of cars right back into the town centre and all around the Ipswich bypass.

**All roads leads to Foxhall . . . the massive Good Friday attendance caught out all of us. It was an incredible day.
Inset: For those who might have missed it, here's Tiger leading into the third bend of the first meeting of the senior
British League era at Ipswich from Hackney's Barry Thomas, with Alan Sage holding off Hawks' Dave Kennett.**

It was like the final scene from Field of Dreams. A line of cars stretched back forever. We had built it, and They had come!

I sent runners to report. I made telephone calls. I spoke to the local police. No question, we were under siege. Reports indicated this was truly a mass invasion of unimagined proportions.

You might have guessed I was beside myself with pleasure and excitement. You would have been wrong! The queues at the turnstiles got longer and longer, the cars continued to fill what had to be the biggest car park in the British League. With 30 minutes still to official start time, the police on traffic duty closed the Heath to vehicles. It was just full right up.

Riders were simply taking their, and everyone else's, lives in their hands by making a third lane all the way around the Ipswich bypass, which had been reduced to one long, thin parking facility.

I was one step from panic, running up to the turnstiles and seeing the queues of patient people, eight wide and now over 100 yards long and still building. I selected a person in the queue, ran back to make sure things were being organised in the pits, ran back up to the turnstiles, to see how far my selected person had moved, and calculated that at that rate, there would still be thousands marooned outside at start time.

And all the time the queues were growing.

Normally, we would have delayed the start until everyone was in but with the evening meeting at Hackney to think of, it would be difficult. Not only that but there was now a hint of rain in the air... Or was it snow?

I decided to hold the parade up for 15 minutes, which brought an immediate reaction from Len Silver, the Hackney promoter. He wanted nothing to affect his meeting due for an 8pm start at Hackney.

I explained to him that there was heaps and heaps of time but his attitude was simple. He knew there was plenty of time, and I knew there was plenty of time, but he reasoned the supporters, and particularly the Ipswich supporters, might decide to cancel going to the evening fixture if it got too late. I expect I would have been equally one-eyed had our positions been reversed.

I found half a dozen canvas bank cash bags and gave them to trusted family and friends. They part-opened the pass gates near the turnstiles and the exit gates up on the terracing, to allow those supporters who were still streaming across the Heath, provided they could come up with the correct money, through these entries.

This was not entirely fair on those who had been queuing patiently but it did ease the pressure on the main queues, which now, thankfully, started shortening.

My 15 minutes were soon up, though, with still thousands outside. People were telling stories about having had to abandon their vehicles up to three miles away and hike the remaining distance. They had set out in plenty of time and it wasn't their fault we couldn't get them into the stadium.

The parade started without me. I dashed back down and indicated to John Earrey, the announcer, to drag it out as long as possible. I explained what was happening to the referee but Len Silver, who was determined to get the thing underway, was harassing him.

The one ref I did not need on that day was L.D. Stripp. A ref with confidence and a bit of common sense, I could have done with. Even a weak-willed and malleable ref, I could have put pressure on. But Lew Stripp was neither one nor the other. He lacked the backbone to be a good ref and use common sense but he was as stubborn and intransigent as a spoiled child.

As soon as I turned my back and ran to the turnstiles again, Stripp put on the two-minute siren, so the first race started while I was at the top of the terracing. Sandor Levai broke the tapes, which meant a rerun was ordered. Then the same happened to Alan Sage. The people still queuing could hear the action going on, but could not see it.

Enough was enough. I told the stadium staff to open all of the exit gates wide and allow those not yet inside the stadium to walk straight in without paying. With that, I disappeared back to the pits.

Just to emphasise the point, I wasn't, at any stage, at all thrilled, elated, excited. If I had have been able to go and hide in a dark room, I would have. I was just drained.

I managed to snap myself back into gear, though, realising that now the crucial thing was to try and put on a show for these people who had turned up, and who would judge on what they saw, as to whether or not a return the following week was justified.

This was always what I was like. People didn't believe me but I was never bothered about how many people had turned up to watch a meeting. I never even used to look at the gate figures for any meeting until I got home. My only concern on race nights was to try to give those who had turned up enough value for money that they would want to come again the following week.

I never saw the third and successful attempt to run the first race, after both Levai and Sage had been excluded for tape breaking, leaving our reserves, Tony Davey and Billy Sanders, to take on Hackney number one and star man, Bengt Jansson, and Laurie Etheridge.

So I never saw Billy Sanders win his first race in England. What a thrill that must have been for the 16-year-old. I didn't see the second race either, but Billy won that as well. Tony Davey, on the other hand, had run two bad lasts (albeit one 'last' had earned him a point thanks to a Hackney faller) in the same two races.

I went to speak to Tony. Rarely have I seen anyone so beset with nerves. He was making his worst nightmares, about imagining he was not up to the big league, come true.

Given the state he was in, maybe I should have pulled him out of his scheduled heat four ride and stuck Billy in. After all, the Aussie kid was on a high and was clearly up for it, whereas Shrimp needed time to regroup.

But to do that would have meant showing a lack of faith in Shrimp, which was certainly not the case. To be honest, I was also struggling with my own nervous state, and maybe my own mind wasn't functioning entirely clearly.

No, I was right to leave Shrimp in. It was arm around the shoulder time and as I walked out with him to his bike, I insisted he was good enough to do the business.

Clearly, though, I could see he was nowhere near as confident as me.

He missed the start and tried to make up the ground. In front of him, riders were everywhere as they entered the first turn. There was going to be a fairly simple tumble. Somehow, though,

Above: Tony Davey's disastrous Good Friday crash with Roger Wright. Shrimp' never fully recovered physically or mentally from the damage, although he still became a world-class rider. Left: Ron Bagley attends to Tony whose seriously damaged hand can be seen more clearly from the close up (below).

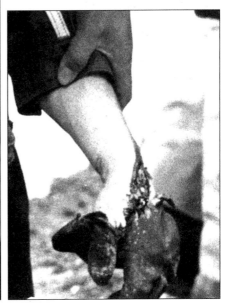

instead of thinking fast and taking avoiding action, Shrimp just trundled on into the mess.

Even then, it looked straightforward enough, but he had put his hand down to break his fall and it had gone straight between Roger Wright's chain and rear sprocket.

The damage to his hand was clearly extensive. Just how bad, it wasn't possible to judge, but it was very nasty.

Things really just happened around me from there. The chain was cut and Shrimp led away to the ambulance, with all involved doing their best not to let him see his hand and the great gash, black, not bleeding even, but full of chain lube. At a glance, you might have thought it was just a greasy stain.

The rest of the meeting was a typical first-event-of-the-year affair. John Louis and Billy Sanders equal top scored for Ipswich. It wouldn't be the last time over the years this was to happen. Sadly, though, this time it was with just eight points each, so clearly Ipswich was a heat leader short of being a competitive team. We lost by 10 points but by that time I was just numb.

I hate to imagine how long it took to extricate the cars from the car park. It must have been just about grid locked, which wouldn't have helped the riders who needed to get down to Hackney for the evening match. I just sat in my 'inner sanctum' trying to take it all in.

When almost everyone was gone, I emerged and went to Ipswich Hospital in Anglesea Road. The news was not good. A fair amount of Shrimp's hand would have to be sacrificed, along with at least one, and maybe two, fingers. This was almost a carbon copy of an injury to Ipswich junior Len Allum 18 months earlier. Len lost two fingers (left in his racing glove) and never rode again. One of the earliest safety changes after these accidents required front and rear chain guards to be fitted to all speedway bikes.

The Longest Day had claimed a casualty. Not just a casualty, but also one of the nicest blokes around. Also, with due respect to Louis, Sanders and all of the others, Tony Davey was potentially the biggest jewel in the Ipswich crown.

I had no interest in going to Hackney in the evening and had deliberately taken my time at the stadium and hospital in the hope that it would get to be too late. But there was still time to spare.

The roads were almost empty, the Hackney and Ipswich people had long since left, and after calling in at the bank to put the takings in the night safe, I arrived at Hackney Wick Stadium with plenty of time to spare.

The Witches didn't win at Waterden Road but they gave the Hawks a real scare. They showed so much resolve that, even in my shot-away mode, I was really, really proud of them all.

It wasn't until 10.30pm that I realised I hadn't eaten all day. It was only when we were sitting in a steak house in Stratford Broadway, I had time to draw breath and take in the events of that Longest Day.

Well over 13,000 people had paid to get in to the speedway at Foxhall. I reckon between another two and three thousand had not. I should have been over the moon. Every one of the chances I had taken, from the purchase of West Ham, to the expenditure on the capital works, and even the bringing over of the unknown and untried Billy Sanders, had paid off handsomely.

Every one except one.

I would cheerfully have given all the money back in return for a fit and well Tony Davey.

Tommy on duty

We needed a third heat leader desperately now and, finally, we found one. He was a Swedish soldier! Tommy Johansson had shown up well at the decidedly difficult in shape and surface Newport in 1971 but had been left out of their 1972 plans as he was doing his national service.

Left: A rare but well chosen Ipswich guest, Howard Cole, on his way to a maximum and track record.
Right: Louis leads an all out of shape Ivan Mauger on Belle Vue's first British League visit to Foxhall.

John and Pat Louis with their children, Chris and Joanne.

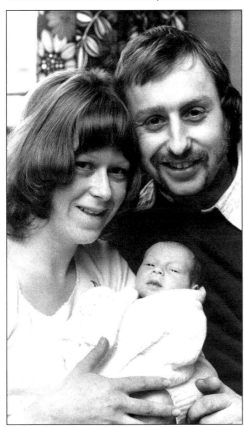

Audrey and Tony Davey with baby Claire.

Billy and Judy Sanders in happy times.

Welcome to the big-time!
The Ipswich Witches that started 1972 in the British League first division. Left to right: Alan Sage, Billy Sanders, Tommy Johansson, Sandor Levai, Tony Davey, John Louis (on bike), Olle Nygren and team manager Ron Bagley.

That service, though, could be completed, with some string-pulling, by May. It was worth the wait. Or put another way, we had no option.

The waiting period consisted mainly of the early season Spring Gold Cup competition and, bless 'em, the management committee generously allowed us the use of a guest to cover until he arrived.

We did use guests, and I can recall Kings Lynn's Howard Cole doing very well for us in one meeting, but even at this stage I decided the guest regulation was wholly unsatisfactory. In speedway it is difficult to cover for an unavailable top rider from a club's own resources. But, even so, the guest set up seemed to me to be a nonsense.

I decided that if possible I would not perpetuate the absurdity of using guest riders and added this resolve to my dream of producing a home-grown, winning team.

With plenty of local lads having tried speedway as a result of the success enjoyed by Louis and Davey, we had a reasonable pool of junior riders to cover for injuries, which was just as well because that serious injury to Tony in his first ever Division One meeting, the early form and retirement of Alan Bellham, and other injuries here and there, meant these kids got their chances.

Generally, they did better than not disgracing themselves, thus demonstrating to me that with enough encouragement, most people will respond positively to being given responsibility.

I had, on behalf of myself and Joe (still a 50% partner), stuck my neck out a long way with all the capital works we had completed at the stadium. Remember, as we were only the sub-lessees at Foxhall, there was just no asset value at all in these works should the venture fail. The new lights, pits, office, changing rooms, track, drainage system and many other stadium improvements we had invested in would be worthless to us. Once in place, all of these works could simply be written off in the accounts.

But it was clear from the bumper turn-out on the Good Friday that the decision to jump into the top league had been the correct one. Effectively, from then on, finance, or lack of it, was no longer a problem. What was important was giving value for money and putting on a good show for those who came to watch.

Despite the bad beginnings, this ragbag team did the supporters proud that year. And the Ipswich people did us proud in return, being by far the best travelled supporters in the league.

Olle Nygren engineered a victory for us at Sheffield, even though that track was to prove through the years to be our most difficult to win on. We stole a few points here and there at other places as well, and finished a very creditable sixth in the league.

For all of the contributions to the team of the senior riders, Levai, Nygren, Johansson, and of Alan Sage, the 1972 season was all about three riders. The trio of John Louis, Tony Davey and Billy Sanders was to become the backbone of the Ipswich set-up throughout the 70s and they deserve their own separate section, later in this book.

6 I Can See Clearly Now

I can see clearly now, the rain is gone,
I can see all obstacles in my way
Gone are the dark clouds that had me blind
It's gonna be a bright, bright, bright
Sun-Shiny day.

I think I can make it now, the pain is gone
All of the bad feelings have disappeared
Here is the rainbow I've been praying for
It's gonna be a bright, bright bright
Sun-Shiny day.

Look all around, there's nothing but blue skies
Look straight ahead, nothing but blue skies...

No wonder we're smiling – the 1976 Double celebrations begin here after victory over old rivals King's Lynn in the KO Cup final.

Clearly, on age alone, Olle Nygren and Sandor Levai were soon going to need to be replaced but it was in fact Tommy Johansson who was the first rider to move over and make way for a local youngster.

After his late start to the 1972 season, Tommy had done us proud in our opening year in the top league. He had a really sweet style, plenty of determination, lots of ability and was a really nice bloke and terrific team man. As he and Billy Sanders were the two in the team with no roots or family in the UK, they spent a good deal of time together, socially, which had worked very well.

But Tommy had a problem. Normally a whiter shade of pale, sometimes he looked just awful, as if about to flake out, and this lethargy certainly sometimes affected his racing. It seems he had a blood disorder and, as a consequence, tired very easily.

He could cope with riding speedway, he could cope with air travel. What he couldn't cope with was both in large doses. As a 'commuting Swede' required to ride on a weekly basis in Sweden, while trying to fit in a full BL season, he found the schedule just too exhausting.

His Swedish girlfriend had also recently given birth, so by the end of the season Tommy was drained. I have the feeling that had I twisted his arm right up his back, he might have been pushed into another season, but it would not have been fair on the lad, who deserved a chance to stay healthy. In 1973, riding solely in Sweden, he was just about unbeatable.

Locally based junior, Mick Hines, was the first of the new Ipswich brigade to be promoted into the team on a full time basis, joining John Louis and Tony Davey. Mick did not immediately replace Johansson's points contribution but several of the other riders improved to make up the difference. And to be honest, life was easier not having a commuting foreign rider in the side.

In our first season in the first division, we had scrambled to an unexpectedly high sixth place league finish, largely due to some 'off the wall' away performances, when different individuals had from time to time lifted themselves well above their normal standards and enabled us to pinch wins. This ability to find a random rider or pairing who could find that bit extra and rise to the event on any given night was to become the hallmark of the Witches' success over the years. In the main, though, 1972 would go down as a year of consolidation.

Off the track and on the terracing, 1972 had been an unforgettable and incredible success. Many times the attendance exceeded 10,000 and the average over the year was not too far short of that double figure mark. We took hordes and hordes of supporters away with us on our

Swedish international Tommy Johansson (left), our first 'foreigner', whose commuting took its toll.

Facing page (left to right):
Witches strong-man Sandor Levai in the pits and on the track.

Ted Howgego in the pits with his young son, Mark.

travels, although I do not think too many of my fellow promoters of the time were prepared to recognise this, nor certainly offer any reaction other than often poorly concealed jealousy.

Despite the two 'elder statesmen' of the team, Sandor and Olle, understandably going backwards in their scoring, 1973 actually saw us improve by a place in the league table due to improvement in the younger team members. There wasn't that much room for 'Tiger' Louis to improve. He was already in rarefied air but the others were all bounding ahead, including Davey, who was able to put that first nightmare season behind him but was never to fully recover, mentally, from the accident that robbed him of half a hand in the opening meeting of our first senior league campaign.

Sandor was the next to go. He was a real gentleman, a fiery individual who, when 'accused' of being Hungarian, would respond by pointing out he was more British than the rest, who were merely that way because of where they had been born, whereas he had chosen to be British! He had endured much sadness in his life, not least when the Russians invaded his birthplace and he had to flee home and family when, after first fighting, he knew there was no holding back the red army.

I never really got close to Sandor, because he didn't live locally and we only met up at speedway meetings, where we both had our game faces on. But this bear of a man was kind, thoughtful and considerate. He had a laugh that would rock buildings, often having the rest of the team rolling about in the dressing rooms before a meeting. It is important for all teams to have a joker, and Sandor was ours.

He reserved the other side of his emotions for referees. Never one to get left behind at the tapes, he sometimes counted to two when the ref was counting to two-and-a-half, which frustrated him no end. I don't know how much of his huffing and puffing, when excluded for tape breaking, was to cover his own disappointment and frustration with himself, but it is fair to say if I had been the referee, there were times I might have been nervous!

This big, strong man didn't fall often and when he did, the odds were that the ground would come off second best, but he did break a collarbone once. Can you imagine being a forty something year-old and riding a speedway bike one week after breaking your collarbone? Sandor gave it a go in an early world championship qualifying round. He never winced or complained once but he sweated gallons that night, even though it was cool. I cannot imagine how much pain he must have been in.

Never once in those two years did he and I have a cross word. Most riders you have to work on to get the best from. Some respond better to cajoling, while other improve with kid glove treatment. Sandor needed neither. What you got from him every time he threw his leg over a bike was his best effort. At that stage in his career, it did not always result in a race win, but you knew he had done his best. Few riders these days can say that.

Not that he wasn't averse to the odd fiery outburst – the relationship between Sandor and Olle was always good fun! There was many a 'full and frank discussion' between the pair of them in the pits, and on the occasions they were paired together on track, it was not a place for angels to tread.

Sandor Levai retired at the end of 1973. It was the correct decision for him to make. He was a

proud man and deserved to choose his own time and place. He made an error the following year, trying to help out an injury-hit Cradley Heath, but no doubt he simply could not refuse the request. He is that kind of person. The word is, he has returned to a Soviet-free Hungary. I wish him well. He did not play a major role in my dream but he did play a good one. I am proud to have known him.

In came Ted Howgego to replace Sandor for the 1974 season. This was a testament to how much we had moved forward in just two years. That we could replace the rider who had been signed originally to be the Ipswich number one with a junior from our own ranks, and for the second year running replacing a top rider with a kid, showed we had to be doing something right.

Edwin Russell Howgego was never a star. In fact, he was someone who was remembered more for his off beat surname than any huge riding ability. Ted remains a firm friend today, so I would not wish to embarrass or demean him, but even he recognised, both then and now, his speedway limits. He was never going to trouble the scorers on world final night.

But he was Ipswich born and bred, he was young, he was keen and he was honest with himself and with everyone else. Despite the fact that attendances were good, the local youngsters were never spoiled financially. I drove a hard bargain with them at the start of each

The Witches squad of 1973. Standing, left to right: Tony Davey, Mick Hines, Sandor Levai, Alan Sage, Olle Nygren, Billy Sanders, Ron Bagley. Kneeling: Trevor Jones, Ted Howgego, Clive Noy. On bike: John Louis.

year but that enabled me to be generous with bonuses and little extras as the season progressed. However, Ted, and many more similar riders to him, could not rely on earning their living solely from speedway. Despite this, he was always there when needed, always with his equipment bright, shiny and ready to race and he was as reliable as they come.

In American football you have the star players, then you have the foot soldiers, and then you have 'special teams' players. These are the unsung workers, who set things up for the star guys to knock 'em down. Ted was our Special Teams player. Nobody expected him to go out and beat Ivan Mauger. What we asked him to do was to go out and beat all those opposition riders who were of the same standard . . . and then one or two who were just above his own standard.

Sometimes the job would be even more direct. If we needed, for instance, a 3-3 in a race, and Ted was paired with John Louis, it was Ted's job to take the bad gate position, to get to the first turn in time and to make life as difficult for the opposition as possible so John could get clear. And then to look after himself and see what scraps he could pick up. It worked both ways, mind. In the event that John didn't get clear, it became his job to ensure he and Ted finished in second and third place. Speedway to me is a team sport.

As it happened, Ted had a terrible first year. He injured a wrist early on and got bad medical advice. Or maybe I should say, medical advice that turned out to be bad. The scaphoid bone in his wrist was broken. Three choices: the scaphoid is actually a piece of cartilage, more of a strengthener than anything, and could be removed, although it would weaken the wrist. Alternatively, the broken halves could be simply screwed together in a fairly straightforward operation. The third choice was to immobilise the wrist (plaster cast) and hope the two parts would knit back together.

The consultant opted for the easy option of immobilising the wrist but the thing did not mend. Eventually, after a long period and a visit to Galashiels General Hospital in Scotland, where speedway's supermedic, Carlo Biagi, ruled supreme, the screw was inserted – but not before the thick end of the season had gone.

So, in place of Ted Howgego, read Trevor Jones, or Mike Lanham, or Dave Gooderham. These were all Ipswich juniors, all on loan from the Witches to second division tracks and all wanting to show their talents while filling in Ted's vacant team position as he recovered.

Sanders, Davey and Hines all continued to improve while Louis remained a rock as number one and skipper.

Nygren was a world class rider for more years than he or I would care to remember. I do recall to this day, though, the first time I ever spoke to him. He was running one of his famous training schools, this one down at Eastbourne. It was midwinter and bitterly cold, and we were all rugged up. As we chatted, I noticed huge searing red crevices running all the way over the palms of his hands, making them look for all the world like a page from a city centre road atlas. He had recently undergone surgery to sort out a medical condition that, left untreated, would have seen his hands become claws. There is no doubt a long Latin name for the complaint but I only know it as 'claw hand'. No doubt, riding motorbikes all his life had not helped to combat the condition.

It was later that year, I think, when he was sent to Ipswich from the defunct West Ham. I never did ask him if his hands were OK! I can tell you cheerfully, I didn't want him to join the Ipswich team. He was well past being the legend of his and my youth and had a reputation for being

The unmistakable style of Ted Howgego, here seen inside Trevor Jones looking for a heat victory against Swindon.

difficult. He had had more clubs than Jack Nicklaus and was now living on former glories.

Beggars can't be choosers but it could be said that we both approached the tie-up between each other with more than a little trepidation. It is fair to say we tiptoed around each other for a while.

I had a huge respect for what Olle had achieved in the sport. After all, I used to go as a supporter and watch him at West Ham. What I admired best about him was his ability to win races seemingly at walking pace. I can remember once writing in my programme notes about just how much of the track he seemed to take up once in front. I suggested he seemed to ride around with his foot on the white line and his rear wheel up against the fence. That's certainly how it must have appeared to following riders, anyway.

Pretty quickly, we started to respect each other. Olle never tried to patronise me nor belittle my scant speedway knowledge or experience. Equally, I tried hard to converse with rather than talk to him.

He was a terrible example to the younger riders, though. His bike was, at best, 'lived in', where the youngsters' machines were burnished and bright, even after several nights of racing on the trot.

Olle's equipment always looked – well - scruffy. Often there was binding wire holding bits together here and there. If he'd had a couple of nights' racing in succession, you got the impression the nearest the bike had come to a wash was being left out in the rain.

As we became more comfortable with each other, I did gently point out that his machinery didn't set the best example. He did make an effort, while making the valid point to me that after the number of years he had been racing, polishing bikes did not figure high on his list of favourite tasks.

But what he lacked in presentation he made up for in valuable experience. He stole several away matches for us in those early couple of years, when we needed them most, and it was no bad thing having a rider in the team who you felt could just raise his game a fraction and get you out of trouble when the chips were down.

Olle had some wonderful one-liners and observations. When either he was put out, or the occasion demanded, he could be quite ruthless. But after he had hung yet another rider up on the fence one night, as I went to speak to him after the race, he rushed away. He came back a few minutes later, apologising, but making the point that he always went straight over to people he had stuffed to say sorry, explaining to them that it was an accident "So they don't hold a grudge and do it back to me sometime!" he reasoned.

I liked Olle very much. He was one of the old time riders. Away from the speedway, he was full of anecdotes about his amazing career. He never ever bragged, so it was difficult to relate this down to earth man as a superstar legend in his own land. To put things into perspective, he was certainly as equally loved as Ove Fundin and a rated ahead of so many Swedish stars.

Like many Swedish riders, he enjoyed a drink and it was perhaps at an end of season party at my house we finally let ourselves go and admitted we really quite liked each other. His long-suffering wife, Anne, finally managed to pour him into their car in the small hours of that night. The car was last seen being driven down Foxhall Road with Olle laid out on the back seat, a leg wearing a gorilla's foot on it, hanging out of the open rear window. I reckon I was at least two bottles of scotch lighter by then!

Olle and John celebrate the Dave Bickers Pairs victory in 1972 . . . and Olle shows the raw 'Kid' the way around Foxhall.

Olle, the team manager, with the 1978 KO Cup winners. Right: Loyal Mike Lanham, one of the real unsung heroes and perennial bonus points king, with wife Julie and their sons, Leigh and Nikki.

By our third year in the big league, Olle's importance in the team had diminished. And just as people respond positively to responsibility, so they respond negatively to a lack of it. Much as it was never actually said, or maybe even thought, the new kids on the block were now able to manage without him. Clearly, by the following year, his place would have been completely usurped.

That was not uppermost in my mind one August evening when Wimbledon were the visitors to Foxhall. The Dons hated any track with a bit of dirt on it and, it is fair to say, we never went out of our way to make life too easy for them. This day there was a fair sprinkling of dirt but to gain maximum use of the dirt, one requires to water well. It had been a nice, sunny day and under those conditions it was always difficult to get sufficient water onto the track, even though we were fully committed to it. Under the bright sun and brisk breeze, the moisture tends to burn off as soon as it goes on.

But while it had been a dry day, the wind dropped suddenly as the sun was getting low in the sky. Under those circumstances it is easy to overwater. One minute the track is drying out as fast as you can water it, the next, there is no drying at all. Too late we realised and the track was two races overwatered. Our normal watering regime tended to be heavier than at many tracks because I always believed in putting the paying public's comfort before that of the riders, so two races overwatered was bound to give the Wimbledon team plenty to grizzle about, which they duly did.

We knew we had slipped up and apologised to both sets of riders. The Wimbledon boys saw it as part of a dastardly plot. That it certainly was not. We could always beat the Dons at Ipswich without breaking sweat. They moaned while the Ipswich riders accepted the apology and made the best of it. All except Olle. Perhaps that was the week he had cleaned his bike, or perhaps he was just in a bad mood. Perhaps even, he had driven to Ipswich admiring the weather and looking forward to a good track surface on which to race.

Whatever, out of nowhere Olle just dug in his heels and decided not to ride. Thirteen riders

The Witches won the 1975 League title (left), but I had to attend Reading to be congratulated (right) by the managing director of Gulf Oil (UK). Facing page: I then enjoyed winding up the parochial Reading crowd.

I'd back JL against PC more times than not in domestic competition and I'm sure the records would bear me out.

had accepted that the first few races would be stickier than they should have been and got on with it. One did not. What would I have done if that one had been John Louis, or another key up and comer, and not a rider well into his veteran years and seeing out his time? Not a fair question, really, for it was because Olle was nearing the end of his career at that stage that he baulked.

I felt I had no alternative. I explained clearly to him that if he refused to ride, then there would no longer be a place for him in the team. We had a stand off. I could not back down, Olle would not lose face. We both stood our ground. Or rather, Olle went home and I dropped him from the team.

I still feel badly about it. This was not the way one of speedway's icons should have been treated but neither should he have walked out. Wires burned between Sweden and England. I am told, the Swedish authorities threatened to pull out all of their riders from the British League in protest.

I was pressured by the BSPA to back down. That was not in my nature but the situation was resolved when Coventry offered to find a place for Olle in their team. In the meantime, with Ted

Howgego returning from his wrist injury the following week, the Witches were not really weakened by the loss.

After some time, the word filtered back that Olle did not hold it against me. He started coming to watch the Witches ride and in the fullness of time, he even team managed the Ipswich team for a while after he had fully retired and Ron Bagley had left the fold. The team managing bit wasn't a complete success but at least Olle and I parted on the best of terms. Although we have not remained in touch, I am sure we will share a drink or three together the next time our paths cross.

So Ipswich finished the 1974 season with a team of youngsters, all of whom, except Billy Sanders and Alan Sage, were locals born and bred, and the results had continued to improve, seeing us finish in third place.

It was a sad day when we had to let Mick Hines (left) go as the dreaded Rider Control Committee finally got their way. Right: Team-riding wasn't a dying art in the days when John Louis guided Dave Gooderham round.

Given that we had now lost Johansson, Levai, Nygren and Alan Bellham from the team we had started with, and introduced four local junior riders to replace them, I thought it was a bit rich that the management committee, in the guise of the rider control committee, should come sniffing around with a view to taking Mick Hines away. I just used a couple of words in their direction, the second of which was 'off'.

It was now Lanham's turn to join the happy band of local likely lads in the Witches team proper and, just to rub it in, we released Alan Sage to the second division. Alan had gone into the top league too early at West Ham and although a really nice lad, never fully came to grips with either the Foxhall track or first division racing. He might also have felt just a touch out of place among all the Suffolk boys but always seemed to just lack that bit of confidence. The move down worked very well for him, though, and he remained a stalwart of the lower league for many years thereafter.

Phil Herne was supposed to have taken Alan's place. Billy had recommended the young Australian to us way back in 1972 He had come to Ipswich and settled there and we had nursed him along in the lower league at sister track, Birmingham. Although on a Birmingham contract, it was understood all through that he was an Ipswich 'asset' and was given all the benefits of any other Ipswich loaned out rider.

Now Phil was ready to move up into the First Division and we had made a place available for him at Ipswich. But Phil had an older brother, John. John was a mechanic who had worked for Qantas Airways, but was enjoying an extended sabbatical working as Phil's mechanic in England.

John had a very patriarchal attitude towards Phil, and to this day I don't know how much of that was brotherly love and how much was that John was enjoying his time in the UK and was happy to have his lifestyle financed by Phil's riding.

Having to deal with a rider's parents or wife was not uncommon, but John placed himself squarely between Phil and myself, which I was not comfortable about.

Several times during 1974 I tried to confirm with Phil that he would be riding for Ipswich in 1975 but could not get a straight answer. It was fairly clear that John was after a 'deal' that would allow him back the following year. I had factored this into my costings, but I was not prepared to have to 'negotiate' with John. Either Phil wanted to ride at Ipswich or he did not. Once he had given me a commitment I was prepared to help out, but it needed to be that way around.

It wasn't just John I was up against either. I have indicated here and there that the relationship between myself and Joe had become fairly competitive. As Philip's promoter at Birmingham he was in the position to bring pressure to bear, but I am not convinced Joe was too keen to see Phil being dropped into Ipswich as the final piece in the puzzle.

Call it arrogance on my part, call it selfishness on John's part, call it mistrust in me by Phil (mixed with perhaps a certain nervousness about having to live in Billy's shadow at Ipswich), but when Newport offered them a 'deal' involving John's fares and subsistence, they took the offer. My attitude was simple. I was not prepared to treat Phil any differently to the other lads in the team and it was for him to commit to Ipswich... Or not.

Much to my disappointment, Phil decided on the 'or not' leaving us looking for another team member and by bringing in Trevor Jones for Alan, we were really beginning to push our luck. I have to say I was disappointed in Phil's refusal to trust me. He was a very good rider and I think he would have done better at Ipswich than he did elsewhere.

However, after just three years in the world's top speedway league we had built a team of young, local riders. The dream was almost a reality. OK, the smart ones would notice that John Louis was by now in his thirties, albeit still a kid in speedway terms. Also they might spot that Billy Sanders was Australian but as he arrived as a 16-year-old novice, having lived all his UK life in Ipswich, he could be considered very much a local lad. More importantly, every one of these lads had started their speedway lives with Ipswich and were truly home grown riders.

I have to say, we were not entirely confident that the team would be strong enough with so many inexperienced riders. Nor were the Ipswich public and there was some muttering in the ranks. Worse, Ron Bagley and I indicated a doubt by looking at other options, concerned that we had set such high standards to live up to, the Ipswich public would not forgive a lapse.

In the event, and after a very nervy start to the season, the local lads covered for each other. While I think several of the lesser lights would have struggled in a different team, each pulled the other along. My dad, an avid supporter, even told me that the lads at the bottom end were not up to the mark but I pointed out it was neither possible nor reasonable to have a team of seven John Louis'. Each of the riders in a balanced team had his own job to do, and that year they did it well. Whenever one had a bad night, another would stand tall and cover.

Another factor that worked in our favour was that we pretty well escaped injury all year. Dave Gooderham, an up and coming junior rider, was called upon to fill in a few times and weakened the team not at all when drafted in here and there. And because we had no serious injuries, there was no loss of momentum or confidence.

From half way through the season the team just started on a roll, feeding on their own success. Such was their individual and collective confidence that they considered defeat to be impossible under any circumstances, just brushing the best of opposition aside in the last matches of the season.

One could argue that glamour team, Belle Vue, with twin warheads of Peter Collins and Chris Morton, were the strongest team in the league – but we robbed them. We snatched the title from under their noses in a major upset. Even our own supporters – even Ron and I – had shown doubt at the start of the year. But here we were, just four short years after having joined the big league with a make do and mend side, and we had taken them all on and won.

But the beauty of it was, we had done it our way. No favours, no handouts, no chasing top names with chequebooks. It was an incredible, unbelievable achievement which was not given anywhere near the accolades it deserved. Maybe it was because we had said no beg pardons to anyone on the way up. Maybe it was because the speedway press corps, which could be

Time to celebrate our first League championship.

The '76 double winners – one of the finest squads to grace the British League. From left to right: Kevin Jolly, Andy Hines, Colin Cook, Dave Gooderham, Trevor Jones, Ted Howgego, Mike Lanham, Tony Davey, Billy Sanders, John Louis.

measured in significant numbers at that time, was not on our side. Maybe there was jealousy within the ranks of the BSPA, because we had blown apart their cosy 'all mates together' attitude.

Certainly I know there was jealousy at our attendance figures, but I saw little disappointment when we took hordes of travelling supporters to swell other people's attendances. Bugger 'em!

Perhaps the only disappointment was in having won it by default, so to speak. We had finished our league fixtures and Belle Vue, with matches in hand, could have passed us. They didn't, because Ivan Mauger's Exeter beat them. I was grateful for that and for the fact that Ivan took the trouble to hike across to the Exeter office (no mobile phones then) to phone and let me know straight away after the match. It was the considerate act of a gentleman.

I phoned John Louis straight away and we met at the First Floor Club in Ipswich, one of the few places that wasn't locked and bolted by ten-thirty on a Monday night in Ipswich those days.

No great hollering and whooping, no back-slapping animated excitement, just a quiet celebratory drink and a reflection on what we had achieved together. Perhaps it was better that way. Certainly we, along with Ron Bagley, had been the central figures in The Dream.

Collecting the trophy was even more of a let down. Gulf Oil were the league sponsors and wished to make a formal presentation but were not prepared to come up to Ipswich. So I was instructed to make my way to Reading Speedway, where a presentation was made during the interval of a routine end of season meeting not involving Ipswich, nor any of our riders. No recognition for the team, no fanfares, and in front of a Reading public with whom Ipswich had always enjoyed a love/hate relationship.

Pretty piss poor really, but on par with the way speedway organises itself. In fairness, Gulf Oil did entertain the team to a lunch at the Playboy Club in London early the next year. Even now, I can see those homespun Suffolk lads admiring the bunnies, as a six-year old would admire the jars of sweets in an old fashioned sweet shop!

So that was it! The Dream had been achieved in just three years. Six years, if you count the three years' apprenticeship in the second division. There was still some unfinished business. Belle Vue, my original tormenter and the world's leading speedway, still had to be completely settled with, but by and large the next year, 1976, was really just one huge victory lap. The lap we had been robbed of at the end of '75.

The season long victory lap

If the dream became a reality in 1975, it was underlined in '76.

For those of you who don't recall, 1976 was the year when British weather went haywire. Despite a cold and late, but dry, winter, once summer started, rain simply didn't happen as one beautiful, hot day followed another. It was the year of the Minister for Drought, the year when it became socially acceptable to shower or bath with a friend, to have a dirty car and brown lawn. My kind of year!

At the speedway, we made arrangements to use river water, tankered in, to water the track. Shhhh! We didn't actually use that facility! But we did use much less water and started using a crop sprayer during meetings. This put down a fine, even water spray between races. Not enough to inconvenience the riders but enough so that the track need not have to be watered so heavily beforehand.

There was, before the season started though, a little matter of rider control to deal with. The year before, 'they' had tried to steal Mick Hines from us. This year, as league winners we could not avoid losing someone. They wanted a heat leader but no way was I going to lose Louis, Sanders or Davey from my side. These three were far too important to the team, we had invested far too much in them. From the riders' side, they were entitled to enjoy their success, especially Shrimp who had by now almost overcome his hand injury. So the spotlight shone straight onto Mick Hines again. He had proved to be the best of the rest of the lads, and a genuine heat leader in most company. He was also a very responsible, level-headed bloke, and was not necessarily a Foxhall track specialist.

Although I was realistic enough to understand that you cannot just keep building a stronger and stronger team, because in doing so you destroy the object of having a competitive league, it was still going to be desperately sad to see any of the team go.

This was really the first time there had been any downside to having achieved The Dream and possibly the hardest decision I had been required to make since starting in 1969. The job was made even worse by Mick's insistence that he wanted to stay.

In reality, though, my choice was simple. If I gave in with something approaching a good grace, I could, to some extent, sort something out which would be in Mick's best interests over the medium and long terms. If I fought the system all the way, one of two things would happen. Either I would lose, and in doing so, have no say at all on who would go, and where they would end up, or on what terms; or I would win the battle, but effectively destroy the fabric of the British League.

Mick felt he was being victimised. I think he felt that, if anyone should go, why should it have been him? Looking back, with many years in between, possibly the finger could have been pointed at Billy. But in all honesty, it would have left the team far too vulnerable, while anyone below Mick in the team would not have been acceptable to the powers that be.

Ron Bagley was a lot closer to Mick on a personal level than me but even he could see no alternative. The fickle finger of fate clearly pointed at Mick Hines.

I consoled myself with the knowledge that the move to Wimbledon would not work out badly for Mick but he took a long time to come to terms with what he considered my disloyalty and, I suspect, holds it against me to this day. Personally, I was delighted to see him become so successful over a long period with the Dons, and later at Mildenhall. He is a super bloke and was a credit to the sport.

Dave Gooderham was the next in line for a call to the team. It would be easy to dismiss him as a poseur and a wannabee but, despite being both, he put an awful lot of effort into getting as far as he did. Early on in his speedway life, he decided John Louis was his idol and that he would copy him. Why not? He could have done a lot worse for a role model! With lavish spending on equipment and accessories Dave certainly looked the part, developing quite a tidy, little style.

Direct replacement for Hines, Gooderham was not, but with each of the other team members shuffling up the list, the team only showed one small weakness. Trevor Jones was never going to be a master speedway rider and was running almost entirely on his effort and enthusiasm - and his wife's ambition! The team in 1976, though, was strong enough, to carry anyone.

I don't want this book to become a list of achievements. It was never meant to be full of facts and figures. Let's just say the team was awesome. We had what had become our trademark sloppy start to the season but we were still too good for most teams. We had a hiccup mid-season when Louis, our skipper and guiding light, suffered his first real speedway injury with a dislocated shoulder but the other lads, in particular Davey, picked up the slack.

There was also plenty more in the junior locker, with Andy Hines, Colin Cook and a young Kevin Jolly showing potential.

It was a season to savour. It was a season we ruled supreme, where our incredible production line was at its peak. Most satisfyingly, we even finally laid the Belle Vue bogey, beating the Aces in both the KO Cup and BL competitions, and even on their own incredible race track.

Those two meetings at 'The Zoo', in the KOC and then the league, both within a few weeks in October, deserve greater mention, because they were the absolute pinnacle of enjoyment and satisfaction for me in all my years in speedway.

Ipswich and Belle Vue were to finish the season at one and two in the league. They were clearly the best two sides in the world and the Aces' Hyde Road track was, for me, the best circuit in the world.

If ever there was a case for fiddling a cup draw, the 1976 Speedway Star Cup semi-finals was it. How the hell King's Lynn and Halifax had reached the semis is anyone's guess but the Witches should have despatched Lynn and the Aces taken care of northern rivals Halifax, setting up the dream final of Ipswich v Belle Vue.

No such luck. Sod's Law determined that Ipswich and Belle Vue were drawn together in the semi-finals. Clearly, the winner of this tie would go on to take the trophy, so this was effectively the final in all but name.

On a wet night (despite the drought) in late September, the Aces battled hard on a difficult Foxhall track to keep the Ipswich first leg lead to eight points. Believe me, an eight point lead is not much to take to Belle Vue against a fired up Aces team. They hadn't won at home by less than eight points since May and most of the Ipswich boys were not comfortable on the big, fast Manchester raceway. It was going to be a dogfight.

Newly-promoted into the team, Kevin Jolly won the reserves' race in heat two, inspiring the Witches' lesser lights to give everything. Mike Lanham had been having all sorts of bike troubles, so John Louis loaned Mike his second machine. That helped but even this, and the liberal use of tactical substitutes, had us six points down on the night and just two points up on aggregate going into the last heat.

Louis and Lanham were up against Peter Collins and Alan Wilkinson. It was time for a bit of reverse psychology, so before the race I pointed out to John that we just needed a shared heat. The easiest way for this to happen was for John to let PC go and concentrate on getting Mike home with him in second and third place.

As I spoke to him, I dwelled just a moment on the fact that John wasn't up to seeing off PC around his home track. Out came the jaw. Yes! The Tiger said he would take the responsibility upon himself to win the race. I remained apparently unconvinced and pointed out that in the event of Peter jumping clear, he was to go to plan B and make sure he and Mike finished second and third.

It was an epic race. I would have taken any odds on the faster starting Louis getting away first and so he did but Collins knew every inch of that track and had the faster equipment once they got up to top speed. He also knew how to make long straights in order to gain momentum and by the end of those straights was going significantly faster.

But going significantly faster and getting past were two different things. Every line he tried, PC seemed to run straight into JL's back wheel. It was as if there was a giant magnet drawing him there, and each time he had to back off and lose the momentum he had gained. Up against the fence, down tight on the white line, or mid-track, everywhere Peter tried, John had second-guessed him.

Meantime, some distance back, Lanham was hanging on in third place. This meant we had an insurance policy against Collins finding a way through - and enabled me to enjoy the race even more!

Ipswich scored a 4-2 heat win to lose the match by four points but to win the tie by the same margin. It had been a wonderful contest with never a beg pardon from anyone. At the end both teams all congratulated each other, sharing a lap of honour and the Belle Vue fans accepted the result with good grace. It really should have been the final.

As the number of matches each team had ridden in the league began to even out, the Ipswich dominance began to tell. By the time we returned to Belle Vue for our rearranged league encounter we were champions in all but name. Mathematically, we could have been caught but we could afford to lose at Belle Vue and still win the league comfortably enough. Even the then Aces team manager, Eric Boocock, had conceded the championship to us by that stage – but, then again, Eric was never really that good when it came to figures!

By now, though, the Witches were running on 100% premium grade confidence; some might even suggest a touch of arrogance. The magnificent Hyde Road track no longer held any terrors for them. Even though two of the Witches failed to score, with Tony Davey having a nightmare two lasts from two starts, and Dave Gooderham out of his depth, it was to be another classic encounter.

Although six points down at one stage, a John Louis tactical ride pulled us back into the match. With three races to go we were two points adrift but newly crowned world champion, Peter Collins, was in two of those last three heats.

Just as in the last heat of the Cup match, Louis lead Collins into the first turn of heat 11 and, just like the Cup match, JL managed to keep him at bay in a ferocious race.

Just as importantly, Ted Howgego beat Russ Hodgson for third to level the scores. Then Billy Sanders beat Chris Morton, while Kevin Jolly, having another night out following a good showing in the Cup match, beat Paul Tyrer for the third place, leaving Witches two points up.

There was no complication in the last heat. With Gooderham required to take at least two rides, we had to give him his last programmed outing, despite knowing his only chance of scoring was if one of the others didn't finish, Therefore, effectively, it was Louis versus Collins and Wilkinson – and 'Wilkie' had beaten John earlier in the meeting.

So the equation was simple: If John won the race, Ipswich won the match; if John came second, the match was drawn; and if John came third then the Aces won.

Now you have to remember, by this stage these riders were racing for nothing but pride. Forget the title, we had that anyway. Forget the money, one point either way would make no difference to these boys. This was just pure racing for fun and for pride.

Even as I type this, my chest is tightening and heartbeat increasing. I have never enjoyed a race so much in my life. As the tapes went up my chest had seized up and my knees were gone. I was trying to walk in thick, black treacle up to my waist. As I stood on the centre green, revolving on the spot to keep the riders in view, I found I was screaming out at the top of my voice! I wasn't saying anything but Oh! Oh! Oh...over and over for the whole length of the race. There was never daylight between the three riders. Should one of the Aces have dropped back and let the other use all of the track to attack? I don't think it would have made any difference. Louis had decided nobody was going to pass. Collins might even have nudged in front a couple of times but without the best position entering the next turn, had to give way again. The three of them went over the line together but with Tiger's nose in front and the Ipswich celebrations began...

I was just limp. I wandered into the pits but I was on the periphery of all the backslapping and hoopla. The team called for me to go on their victory parade but it was they who had earned it, and they who deserved it. I sat on a bench in what was now a deserted pits area. I don't think tears came out but I was so emotionally drained, I think had I not been on my own then they would have flowed. Fortunately, by the time the parade was over I had collected myself together and was able to join in the fun.

Perhaps the best part of the whole year was a civic reception in Ipswich at the end of the 1976 season. I have to tell you, when the Mayor's office first came up with the idea and their suggested plans I was more than uncertain. They wanted to rent an open-topped bus and parade us round the streets of Ipswich on a cold Tuesday November evening. All these types of function I had seen or heard of had taken place on a Saturday or Sunday during the day, not midweek at the dead of night. Still, the riders deserved a bit of showboating time, so I said yes.

The plan – published in the local press - was to get the riders together at the Post House Hotel on the A 12, right out of town, by seven o'clock, with our party ending up at the Cornhill and town hall, right in the town centre, where the Mayor would welcome us and we would go into the town hall for a civic reception.

As I remember, it was the week after the end of the season, three days before Guy Fawkes

Night, and it was a typically cold damp evening with mist and a threat of rain in the air. The kind of evening you look back on from a long time after and a long way away with deep nostalgia but, truth be told, at the time you had wished for the warmth and comfort of warmer climes.

I was in a worse state than ever I got before a speedway meeting. A few of the lads, as usual, cut things a bit fine, so I was at my snarling, bitching best. Far from going with the flow, I was playing my traditional role of stage manager, inspecting the cast, making sure they knew their lines and sticking them on the bus.

If I could have that time again, the first thing I would do would be to include riders' wives and girlfriends (one or the other, not both!) and their children. Being without kids myself at the time, I always played down the family aspect of the team, frowning on riders wanting to share their special moments with loved ones. I rationalised that most of the world didn't take their wives to work, so why should speedway riders?

It was the wrong attitude. I should have allowed the riders' families to share that moment (and many others). I am sure the public would have been at least as appreciative and not the slightest bit jealous. One thing about getting older is that we sometimes get wiser. Sadly, nine times out of ten, it is too late by then.

Anyway, off we went into the dark night, not knowing if we should freeze our nuts off up on top of the bus, or hide down below. Surprisingly, as we passed a huddle of half a dozen houses on the A12 right on the outskirts of town, a collection of maybe 20 or 30 folks had gathered to give us a cheer. I think that made everyone feel better. At least somebody had remembered!

As we moved along in the darkness between that small hamlet and the town proper, spirits were high. When the bus moved into the town proper we saw that hundreds of people had come out of their houses to wave. OK, so it wasn't exactly a Wall Street tickertape parade or a coronation, and I doubt that many had to queue through the day to gain a vantage spot, but there were people.

The nearer we got to the Cornhill, in the centre of town, the more crowded the pavements got. When we turned into the main shopping area, I can honestly say my heart skipped a beat. Wall to wall people, thousands of them, all wrapped up in anoraks and duffle coats and scarves and gloves, and all cheering and waving. The shiver down my spine that moment was nothing to do with the cold.

I always made a point at these things of keeping as far out of the limelight as possible. Two reasons really. First of all, since leaving school I had become less and less comfortable with people, especially crowds. I felt proud and excited, but also awkward but my main reason for keeping a low profile was because it was the riders who had achieved the results.

Nowadays it seems that team bosses receive more accolades than they used to. In my time it was the team players who took the glory and the boss who was responsible for the defeats. That is largely how I still think things should be. Stage managers don't receive knighthoods, only the actors. In recognition of this I shoved John Louis and Ron Bagley up the front to receive the Mayor's welcome, although, believe me, I felt prouder of the moment than anyone else present that night.

At the back of my mind lurked the question: 'where to from here', but nothing could spoil that night. It signalled the end of a magical year but I also recognised it was the beginning of having to try and hold onto ground hard won, rather than being able to conquer more territories.

Speedway for me was about to change. Climbing a mountain is easy – but where to from there?

Fan-tastic! The highlight of 1976 was the civic reception to mark our dominance of British League speedway . . .
Top: John Louis leads the team from the bus.
Left & below right: How many people can you recognise?
Below left: John Louis shows the BL trophy to the Mayor Cllr Hugh Davis.
Bottom: Tony Davey holds up the KO Cup, Billy Sanders has the BL Pairs trophy, and John Louis the BL trophy whilst Dave Gooderham and Ted Howgego look on.

7 It Takes Two

One can have a dream baby
Two can make a dream so real
One can talk about being in love
Two can say how they really feel
One can wish upon a star
Two can make a wish come true - Yeah
One can stand alone in the dark
Two can make a light shine through...

Ron Bagley played more than a passing role in my time at Ipswich Speedway.

I freely admit to not ever having heard of him before Joe and I began trying for the licence to join British League Division Two. It was the speedway follower, Joe Thurley, who knew of Ron, his being local to Ipswich and his speedway pedigree. I have to say, when we tracked the retired ex-Sheffield rider down through the local newspaper, I was suitably underwhelmed.

He was the wrong side of 30 and carried a few pounds more than his fighting weight. Indeed, he looked quite careworn and anything but a 'hunk'. On the positive side, Ron was quietly spoken, easy going and able to quickly disarm people, although there was an undertone that gave the impression what you saw was not all you got.

The word was that he was a bit of a ladies man - I could see he was something of a smoothie – but there was nothing apparent in the looks to back up the Casanova image.

On the track, he looked what he was: a thirty-something, slightly overweight ex-rider making a comeback on less than state of the art equipment, but in a division lower than the one he had left. His black leathers were sparkling clean and shiny, if perhaps a slightly tighter fit than when

they were new but the lack of flair and excitement was balanced by an obvious ability, an armchair style, and a quick mind.

More important, it suited Ron's ego to once again become a local celebrity and he was more than happy to play the part of good skipper and local face of Ipswich Speedway.

I didn't see much of him in that first year other than at speedway meetings, but I heard plenty about him. Most of what I heard involved ladies of all sorts of age, shape and size, and most of it is not really for family reading. He nominally had a wife but they were separated, except for when he popped back on a fairly regular basis. In between there were enough intrigues to make a soap opera plot seem positively tame by comparison.

The involvement between Ron and myself started properly at the start of 1970, our second year at the speedway and my first in sole control.

He would wander into the stadium during the week. Sometimes he would be hiding from creditors and/or the downside of his nocturnal dalliances but mostly he would be just happy to discuss team affairs (of the track kind). I had already picked up a fair bit of speedway knowledge myself by now but listening to Ron helped me understand more about what was going on in a rider's mind.

His manner was so disarming it is no surprise that, the previous year, he had led Joe into a less than perfect social circle. I think it would be fair to say he had 'cultivated' Joe. Ron didn't smoke, never swore and limited alcohol to the odd rare social half of lager. He only had the one vice – but enjoyed that one to the full!

The armchair style . . .

. . . And the bedroom eyes.

I don't know if it was openly discussed that Ron should take the novice John Louis under his wing. I expect it was, but I also expect it was a given that he would want to. Ron had an excellent philosophy on life. It was simply that Ron Bagley was his first consideration.

I don't mean that in an unkind way, especially when I tack on the other part, which is that he was able to think further ahead than today. He was able to follow the logic that a successful Ipswich Speedway would be good for Ron Bagley, so by helping the team he would be helping himself.

I do not base that philosophy, by the way, on guesswork. His attitude was simple and open. He admitted to having no real friends or really wanting any. On the other hand, his easy-going manner assured that, apart from creditors, and maybe the odd cuckold, he had very few natural enemies either.

Perhaps he also reasoned that any merit points he collected by involving himself helpfully at the speedway might offset the more than a few demerit points he managed to clock up with his less than conservative lifestyle.

In as much as it does not affect the story, this is the last time I will refer to Ron's social life away from the speedway. His private life would make its own book but we'll stick to the speedway side of things in an effort to avoid too much tacky stuff and to stay one step ahead of the civil courts! In any case, those activities rarely seemed to affect his speedway efforts – and might well have helped to swell the attendance figures!

Do you remember the Plymouth Valiant car? No reason why you should really. They were actually Australian-made but looked a bit like an American 50s gas guzzler gone wrong. Every one of them I ever saw was white and they looked just like a set of white Formica coffee tables surrounding a late model Humber Hawk. There were flat surfaces on all four corners. It was the perfect picnic car. No need to pack a table.

Several automatic cars of the period had electric gear sequencers operated by buttons on the dashboard, rather than a column or floor selector. Such automatics rejoiced in various splendid names and that of the Valiant was called Torqueflight.

At one stage Ron had two of these relics, one to keep on the road and one to rob parts from. The shocks on all were buggered and riding in the road-going version was like being on board a small cabin cruiser in the North Sea on a windy day.

Ron was still a rider then. Must have been 1971. He had his arm in a sling from a broken collarbone.

The road-worthy Valiant was playing up and Ron, along with Mick Pike, our stadium maintenance operative and good friend, set about sorting it out. They decided it was a fuel problem, so they stripped out and sorted the carburetor. They then put the basic bits back on to test the car but didn't bother with things like the air filter.

It didn't need too many tries of the starter before the battery tired of its efforts, even though the motor had coughed several times, showing a willingness to co-operate.

Now having an automatic gearbox makes push-starting a car something of an interesting procedure. You need to reach a speed of around 30mph before anything happens – and none of us could run that fast, even without pushing a huge white beast.

No problem. The pair of them recruited my car with me as driver to tow them across the bumpy Foxhall car park.

Reaching the required speed was hard enough. Quite soon we had run out of relatively flat area, and the cars were leaping and bucking over hillocks and potholes aplenty, with the gorse bushes in the distance looming a good deal closer.

Fifty yards like this maybe, with Mick and Ron, both in the Valiant, indicating to keep going. I had one eye on the gorse and the other on the rear view mirror. Surge, slack, surge, slack: the big old bus was trying its best to fire up.

Suddenly, the drag on the towrope disappeared, and at the same time the Valiant threw itself at the rear of my car. The back end of the monster sat down almost on the ground and the front reared up like a great white shark lunging at its prey. The bloody thing was after me!

I hit my accelerator, as suddenly I had gone from a sedate tower to a distinctly unhappy prey. I could see Ron's white face and normally bug eyes bulging out even more as he struggled, arm in sling, with the controls.

I expect it all took no more than five seconds but it was one of those never-to-be-forgotten moments. Doing upwards of 70mph by now, and still accelerating across a rapidly diminishing bumpy car park being chased by a Great White Valiant, is not the kind of thing one forgets.

Suddenly, the front of the Valiant dropped down, followed almost immediately by the jerk of the towrope going tight again. I was back in control. Ron, arm still in sling, had finally managed to hit the 'neutral' button on the dashboard with his one good hand while Mick steered from the passenger seat.

I was about to amble back across the car park with the now docile beast trotting along behind, when I saw Mick frantically waving me to stop. At the same time, I heard the sound of a Phantom jet taking off nearby.

Oops! Not a Phantom jet, but the Valiant, free of any air intake restrictions, howling at full revs. It seems that in their hurry to test out the car, they had overlooked the replacement of the throttle linkage, so the accelerator was wedged wide open.

The revs had now taken on their own life: just turning off the ignition wasn't enough to shut the motor down. Mick wrestled with the battery terminals as Ron tried to block the air inlet manifold. But it was some time before they managed to kill the beast and all the time I was waiting, at a suitable distance, for the whole engine to disappear in a volley of

Ron and John Louis with local motorcycle dealer and top scrambler Dave Bickers, who sponsored the pairs event.

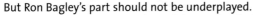
Ron leads from team-mate Stan Pepper, in front of Canterbury's Graham Banks. Below: Silver Helmet holder.

broken block bits, scattered con rods, and flesh-ripping shrapnel.

You can't destroy those old, tubs though, and when they had let it cool down and then finished putting back all the minor details, like throttle linkages, Ron reckoned the motor ran better than he had ever known before!

Unleashing the 'Tiger'

Joe Thurley and Howdy Byford have laid claim to 'discovering' John Louis. I have laid claim to maximizing his success by advising him on how to handle himself. No doubt John would claim, with justification, that his own efforts were by far and away the largest contributor.

But Ron Bagley's part should not be underplayed.

Ron got John onto a speedway bike in the first place. Then he gave the first, and most important, encouraging words, and he also pushed John into giving it a serious go. Because Ron was not part of the management, he could speak as a rider and equal. He could also speak as a fellow Suffolkite. Suffolk folk have a built in resistance to city slickers.

But Ron's most tangible help came on the track. Louis had always been a fast starter on the scrambles circuit and quickly adapted that ability to speedway. Pairing them together did two things. First, it meant that John had someone behind him to hold back the opposition and make a nuisance of himself in the critical first turn.

More importantly, he had a partner who did not object to the new boy taking the glory. Ron knew that if he finished behind John, he received the same payment as he would had he won the race. That isn't enough for many riders, especially those who are near the end of their riding life.

It would have been easy for Ron to have tried to keep the precocious, new talent in check in order to avoid being shown up. He made no effort at all to do that, instead assisting in every way possible to help the new boy.

Did he do it because he had a genuine desire to see John, and therefore the team, do well, or was he clever enough to realise that doing the 'team thing' would endear him far more to the home supporters? Did he also take into account that trying to match the rapidly improving Louis might become a problem very quickly? A bit of both, I suspect, but it matters not, nor diminishes anything from his efforts.

The two of them became a formidable pairing. The confidence John was able to build up because of Ron's early assistance was soon repaid, as they very quickly started looking for, and helping, each other. The dream of a locally based team had begun.

Next year, 1971, it was Tony Davey who was the precocious, new talent, and pretty soon there would be more. However, a mixture of time, plus a few knocks and a bad back, were wearing Bagley, the captain and senior pro, down fast. Performances were rapidly declining and he was running on empty.

Ron using all his experience to help rookie John Louis to a welcome 5-1 against King's Lynn.

The end of the year was clearly going to be the end of the line, riding-wise, and to be utterly frank, by halfway through the season, an embarrassment factor had crept in. It wasn't right to see the skipper riding at reserve, which is where he was heading.

So I floated the idea to him that he might like to join me on the management team. It solved many problems for him and took a lot of pressure off the team situation. It also made life much, much easier for me to have someone to bounce things off and with whom I could share ideas.

Also, clearly, Ron's experience would work in a double way with the team. Having been a rider himself, he was able to be closer to the riders' thoughts and emotions than I was. Secondly, any plans and ideas Ron and I hatched up together would be easier for the riders to accept if they appeared to come from him.

By this time, I had also decided that Division One was where our future lay, and along with the hoped for 'promotion' we would need to do a huge amount of work to the speedway track and surrounding areas. Ron was no mug when it came to using his hands, his brain, or his local knowledge and contacts.

Along with Mick Pike, we put in new, permanent track lighting. We had the posts made and erected them ourselves, sourced the light fittings ourselves, and using the track electrician to do the wiring work, we were thus able to avoid expensive contractors. We also moved the pits and rebuilt them, built new changing rooms and workshop and extended the speedway offices.

You will recall the track had been laid on a bed of chalk. It was time to rip this up, drop the inside of the bends by a couple of feet or so, to get some decent camber on and widen and reshape the whole thing. We also added an elaborate drainage system, which included drains between the stock car and speedway tracks.

It was a major task, but well worth it, because the opportunities for passing, and therefore, the standard of racing, was significantly improved. We tinkered with the shape of the track several more times over the years but I think this was the last time it was totally re-laid.

I was impressed with Ron's intelligence, speed of thought and his work ethic. His laid back approach also complemented my own semi-manic attitude. His soft voice and non-confrontational manner were also an ideal foil for my aggressive body language and sharp tongue.

Both of us were fairly casual about timekeeping (except when working to deadlines) but, at the other end of the day, we didn't clock-watch either. Many an hour was spent simply tossing ideas backwards and forwards between each other when the working day was done.

We both had a similarly healthy disrespect for just about everyone and everything, and would happily and ruthlessly strip everyone down to their basic parts and tear into any weaknesses we found. Nothing and nobody was safe from our private acid wit, and we were both comfortable that our mutual confidences would be respected.

We were not from the same mould but we became close confidantes.

And so, it was that we mapped out Ipswich Speedway's next course of action and our long-term plan.

The cards we had been dealt by the Division One promoters were laughable but in our three years at Second Division level, if I had learned nothing else, I had learned about the dog-eat-dog world of speedway. The promoters' creed was that everyone pulled in the same direction, so long as you never turned your back!

No doubt the Second Division was a mere millpond compared to the turbulent torrents that tried to hide the many and varied sharks of the big league. But at each kick in the guts, we shrugged our shoulders and resolved that we wouldn't get mad, we would just get even.

Babes in the wood we might have been, but we were not about to be pushed around, and the Fortress Foxhall mindset and attitude was formed in those first few months after Ipswich had been granted Division One status.

Life was never easy at that time and the whole of the first three years' work was on the line. The capital works had put Ipswich way over the top financially, with only the time gap between the receipt of invoices and their due date for payment (plus an extra week or three!) standing between the speedway, a decent return from the first few meetings and the abyss.

The shock of Tony Davey's terrible first meeting injury was only partly mitigated by the instant crowd appeal of the 16-year-old gamble, Billy Sanders, and the huge Good Friday crowd, that enabled me to wipe off all outstanding debts. Now it was clear the decision to promote ourselves into Division One had been the correct

At this stage, loose and largely casual divisions of labour between Ron and myself were drawn up. My strengths lay in planning and behind the scenes organisation. Ron's were generally of the more practical variety. It followed then that while I concentrated on the traditional role of 'promoter', Ron took on the responsibility for track and stadium. Our common ground, however, remained the team.

Everything from the macro decisions of who to sign and who not to sign, down to the tiniest details like how each rider's wife, girlfriend, or parent interacted with the others, was put under the microscope. Just about every decision was a joint one. I suspect, looking back, I might have pulled rank a few times, but certainly in those early years I don't recall a serious disagreement between us on team matters, or anything else.

It was much the same on race nights. I was good at the tactical side of things while Ron, with his riding experience, was good man on man But whatever moves either of us made, we consulted the other. Very little happened by chance, even to the point of deciding between us if a rider needed an arm around the shoulder and a word in the ear, which would be Ron's job, or a bollocking, which would be down to me.

The main thing was that we planned everything together. It would be a lie to say we were great friends. We were vastly different animals when it came to socialising, outlook and attitudes.

Perhaps this was part of our success. For although we might not really have been bosom pals, or indeed close confidantes on subjects away from speedway, I would like to think we trusted each other with all manner of thoughts and observations we would not wish to become common knowledge. When we were all in it, scratching a living together, there was a strong bond between Ron, Mick the maintenance man and myself. Although I was a bit younger than the others, and not from the area, we got on well together. If not totally 'all for one and one for all', then certainly we were close enough to share many a scrape or cover each other's backs when necessary.

As the speedway became more and more successful financially, Ron shared in the success to a point, but only to a point. Over several years, my own financial standing leapt considerably. Ron's also improved, especially compared with his situation previously, but not in the same quantum leaps.

As we moved forward, I have to say things became a lot less 'all mates together' and a bit more 'them and us'. This was not something I wanted, nor maybe even something we were both entirely aware of but, clearly, it was happening.

We had built the team from virtually nothing to the massive success of 1976, when we swept all before us. We had climbed the mountain the quick way: possibly too quickly. Where to from here?

Last minute advice for Mike Lanham and John Louis.

The chance for me to manage the England national team came along during 1976. It represented a new challenge, so I took it on, again with Ron sharing the load. We had been supporting John Louis in his World Championship endeavours, and this was simply an extension of that work, though I have to admit it was to be to the detriment of Ipswich Speedway. For us at the time, it was an opportunity to play on a bigger stage, but it also meant not giving full attention to the home front.

Attendances were beginning to tail off at Ipswich. We had achieved so much so soon, but now where to go? It was hardly surprising many supporters were of similar mind. We tried to keep moving forward but it was not easy.

Then two things happened. First, my domestic arrangements changed. I had become a 'bachelor' again, but not for long. It wasn't a state I enjoyed with any great relish. I rushed rather too quickly into a new domestic set up. Like most of these things, this proved to be a huge distraction, reducing the time and application I was giving to Ipswich Speedway.

This back peddling by me, though, was not entirely accidental. Ron had been pushing and pushing for more responsibility, so here was an opportunity to sit back a bit and give him his chance.

I think by now Ron had established a liaison with our secretary, Sue. The surprise there was not that it happened – I don't think too many of our secretaries over the years escaped from his charms unscathed – but that this affair seemed to be a lot less casual than the others. Sue was young, single and was swept off her equilibrium by Ron. Although neither the first, nor the last, she fell under his spell. For his part, Ron actually appeared to be enjoying something of a normal domestic relationship with Sue.

This left Ron and Sue 'minding the store' while I took a step back. I was still around but, by and large, I let things take their course.

On the surface, the speedway seemed to be going OK. I began, though, to notice the odd conversation ending mid-sentence when I walked in, the odd sideways glance between them when I made suggestions, but I decided to take the lazy way out and let things ride.

I know certain things happened during that time that I was never told about. I know I was becoming isolated from my own business. And I know I should have done something about it.

I could see there were things Ron and I used to be able to cover each other on which were now not being covered. I let them go instead of stepping in, partly because I was too lazy and partly because it would have been resented.

In short, the speedway suffered - not overtly, but quite badly. At best, it had become a holding operation and, more likely, the business, already struggling for a new purpose and direction, was in solid decline.

It was time for me to get involved again after my 'time out'. Ron, however, didn't see it the same way. He felt he had done a good job and quite clearly resented my reclaiming the executive spot. Our conspiratorial planning chats had long since dried up. When we did try to discuss policies, we seemed to disagree on everything.

Worse, Sue's loyalties were well and truly tested. Ahough she was a smashing girl, she was, by now, well under his spell. So, when Ron and I did disagree, it became two against one. Even more than before, I felt I was being excluded from my own organization and decisions I took were not being carried out with any enthusiasm, if at all, should Ron not agree with them.

Looking at things from Ron's point of view, he felt he had done a good job of being the Ipswich promoter and obviously felt he had been shoved backwards when I retook the reins. He had reached the stage in life where he wanted the authority to make his own decisions without fear of them being overridden.

It was not a comfortable time for any of us. Ron took solace in photography, which he had started as a hobby a little while previously and which had attracted him considerably.

From halfway through the 1977 season, I think all three of us knew the situation was untenable. Attendances were continuing to drop, the team was not doing particularly well and the business was pretty well in limbo. The only question really was how would it finish?

I got the ball rolling by warning Sue that, come the end of the season, the speedway would not be able to maintain her position through the winter. Finances just did not justify it. At the end of the season, Ron and I sat down, as we had done every other year, to review things. Very early in the piece, Ron announced he was calling it a day. Our whole arrangement had been based purely on trust and mutual understanding, and Ron had always been self-employed.

This had suited us, because in the early days he had been able to augment his speedway earnings with other work and, besides, had always felt more comfortable being an independent contractor rather than an employee. There had, however, always been a decent bonus at the end of each season.

Although there was no obligation or legal liability on either side, what followed was an ugly scene about severance terms. By now, we had both withdrawn into our separate corners. Neither could see any further back than the last few acrimonious months.

Ron took the stance that without him the speedway would never have succeeded and that his role had never been fully appreciated. I took the view that he had been very well recompensed for his efforts. Also, I pointed out the speedway had given him a direction and local respect, which he had previously lost, and that, of late, he had not pulled his weight.

The truth is, the deal had worked out very well for the two of us over the years but since the heights of 1976, things had never really been the same. Ron wanted to spread his wings further, while I had no doubt been my normal insensitive self.

In the event, I agreed to pay him what he thought he deserved - but on one condition. I had heard he had been getting very involved with things at Mildenhall Speedway, and I had a suspicion this is where he was headed. On the other hand, he insisted that he wanted to break entirely from speedway and was going to pursue a new career in photography.

Clearly, if Ron went to Mildenhall, who were very much a competitor and with whom I had a very poor relationship, he would take with him all of our collective ideas nutted out over the years. Mildenhall would benefit from that tremendous amount of insider knowledge, and the large amount of goodwill we, and not he, had generated over the years.

This could possibly affect supporters who lived between the two tracks and might decide to follow him. More importantly, junior riders, might well prefer to start their speedway at Mildenhall, with its training facilities and lower league status and with Ron as the coach.

I should have been above such small-minded reasoning. I should have adopted the attitude that if he did go to Mildenhall, those blind spots in him that I had been able to cover would become exposed. In any case, I should have relished such a challenge.

However, I did not, and I made his severance package conditional on him actually carrying out what he had told me he intended to do, which was to stay away from speedway. That was the deal and although I suspect we were beyond shaking hands by then, nevertheless, it was

...and so to Mildenhall. Ron dons his fedora to mark winning the 1979 National League championship with a Fen Tigers team that contained two riders with strong Witches connections. Back row, left to right: Mick Bates, Mike Spink, Ray Bales, Mel Taylor, Ron. Front: Richard Knight, Rob Henry, Mick Hines. (CC)

agreed on. Nothing in writing Just the same gentleman's agreement we had worked on since the day we had met. On that basis, I paid him out.

I'm not sure if it needed a stopwatch to time how long it took for him to become ensconced behind the promoter's desk at West Row, and also to time how much longer it took for that arrangement to fail.

Sadly though, that breach of trust between us is what has always stuck in my mind whenever I think of Ron, and has soured all of the positive and wonderful things he did in helping make my tenure at Ipswich so successful.

Indeed, after having spent the last, nearly 30 years living with that bitter taste of our split, and his broken gentleman's agreement, writing this chapter has enabled me to look at our complete relationship again.

It has given me the opportunity to recognise my part in our acrimonious split, and to be able to give Ron the benefit he fully deserves for the role he played in making Ipswich Speedway so successful in the 70s.

I understand he is now an excellent professional photographer, eventually found a partner who was able to domesticate him and enjoys a good and stable life in North Suffolk.

I wish him well...

8 The Silver Tongued Devil and I

I said Hey, don't you know he's the devil
He's everything that I ain't
Hiding intentions of evil under the smile of a saint
All he's good for is getting in trouble
And shifting his share of the blame
And some people swear he's my double
And some even say we're the same
But the silver-tongued devil's got nothing to lose
And I'll only live 'till I die
We take our own chances and pay our own dues
The silver tongued devil and I

I have referred to the palatial building at 31 Belgrave Square. No doubt many a fine meal was prepared down in the depths of the basement by a Mrs Bridges in the *Upstairs Downstairs* days, but in my time it was used for BSPA general council meetings. Also for Control Board tribunals, more commonly known as 'courts'.

I had my share of brushes with speedway officialdom and made a few trips to that place. John Cleese might have subtitled this chapter: "Who's a Naughty Boy, then!"

Workington joined the second division at the start of 1970, when the Witches' first ever visit to Derwent Park was also to be the cause of my first visit to the SCB's kangaroo court. It also set the scene for the ongoing relationship between Ian Thomas and myself.

For the uninitiated, Workington is a tad over 400 miles from Ipswich and, in 1970, the roads were nowhere near as good as they are today. In those days it was a good nine-hour trip on a Friday, the Comets' race day, and, coincidentally, the worst day to travel.

For that first ever trip to the new track at the other side of the Lake District, John Harrhy and Pete Bailey returned to their Coventry homes after the Thursday night meeting at Foxhall, and travelled up from there on the Friday. Buckinghamshire-based Ted Spittles and London-based Stan Pepper stayed overnight in Ipswich and arranged to travel with Ron Bagley.

The three of them were going to collect me and the body colours (which I had stayed up to clean in the early hours of the morning following the Thursday night meeting), from my home in Colchester on the way. John Louis and Tony Davey both travelled separately and independently.

Bagley, Spittles and Pepper were due to collect me at nine o'clock in the morning but there was no sign of them. At 10.15am I had a phone call from Ron Bagley to say there had been a coming together between Ted's car and a bus in the Ipswich town centre.

The cops were called, the bus company was called, every man and his dog were called, but the intrepid three riders were kept there at the scene, and then at the police station for nearly three hours, even though nobody was injured. I daresay Ted, who wasn't known for taking a backward step, didn't exactly assist the situation.

I got another call from Ron just after midday, saying they had finally been freed, were completing running repairs to the car and trailer, and would soon be on their way – but there would be no time for the detour to Colchester to collect me and the body colours.

Then more bad news. I received a call from Harrhy and Bailey to say they had broken down on their way north but expected to be able to find the problem, solve it, and get going again. They were both useful mechanics, after all – except that the car had holed a piston! They did actually repair the thing on the side of the motorway but by then it was too late to even think of trying to get up to Workington.

Ian Thomas (right) with his former Workington co-promoter Jeff Brownhutt and Comets rider Geoff Penniket. I don't ever remember Ian smiling when we were the visitors. Perhaps it was something I said? *(AW)*

Throughout this time I kept Ian Thomas informed of the situation as it was unfolding. He was not happy, as neither would I have been, but things were now well beyond my control.

In the event, Ron, Ted, and Stan arrived at the Workington track shortly after eight o'clock for a 7.30pm start. I would have thought they deserved the Victoria Cross for getting there at all but, of course, Thomas did not see things in quite the same way.

Knowing they would be late, he had run the second half individual part of the meeting first, so the Workington faithful were not massively inconvenienced. But Thomas still wanted his pound of flesh.

I was hauled in front of the SCB, down in the dungeons of 31 Belgrave Square, where I was accused of not having made enough effort to ensure our riders arrived on time. I explained all that had happened and was sure they would understand.

Hah! I was fined for not ensuring the whole team, team manager and body colours had arrived on time. I came out scratching my head and wondering just how I was supposed to be able to do that. I had ensured all the arrangements had been made. If I could have foreseen the accident and the breakdown, I wouldn't have been trying to scrape a living as a speedway promoter!

Thomas was without any compassion, put the boot in as hard as he could and gloated at the result. Actually, now I'm a bit older and wiser, I can accept that it was inevitable I should be fined. It would have been a bit easier to swallow, though, if they had said words to the effect of-

"Look, we know circumstances were beyond your control. You had been reasonable in your planning, but we have no alternative but to fine you, because otherwise we would be opening the door to all sorts of liberty taking by riders and promoters in the future. We also have to give the good burghers of Workington a bit of a sacrifice in the name of good public relations."

From that day onwards, Ian Thomas and I indulged in a running battle with each other. It never got violent, of course, and it never interfered with business. If anything, I think we were ultra polite in our dealings in-between times. But when it came to match days, anything went.

I would like to think that, over the years, I gave as good as I got. Certainly Ipswich won at Workington a few times. The real fireworks, though, were saved for some years later, when Ian had left Workington and taken over promoting at Hull.

I detested what was, before the dualling of the road from Ipswich to the A1 and the building of the M62 from the A1 to Hull, a nightmare of a drive from the one place to the other. I also hated the long, skinny Hull track, which was never kept in particularly good nick. I also resented the attempts by the home promotion to detune the visiting team.

One thing in particular used to enrage me, and that was the way the home side of the riders' pit area was (fairly) spacious, well lit and clean, whilst the visitors' side was cramped, badly covered, always filthy dirty and – when we were the visitors at any rate – virtually unlit.

But worst of all was the quality of the local referees. Possibly things have changed these days, but back then referees were always drawn from the area local to the home team - and we always seemed to get the worst of them on our visits.

All in all, I used to take our trips to Hull personally.

The Ipswich riders were a loyal bunch of lads. Yes, they rode for the money, but they also rode for the fun of it. They all got on well with each other, and with me. I had learned how to press a few buttons with most of them, and I pressed them all repeatedly on our trips to the Boulevard.

Some tracks you arrive at and feel it's just another meeting. At others, the aggression meets you at the front gate, so you have to be ready to respond. Actually, once having arrived in the

city of Hull, the trip from the main road to the stadium, down some of the seediest back streets you could wish to see, helped get us into the right mood.

Steve Waugh, bless him, justified the Australian cricket team's constantly aggressive behaviour, sledging and generally bad attitude on a cricket pitch as part of the game. He called it tactics to promote mental disintegration in the opposition (enemy would be a better description). So it was with Ipswich at Hull, where they tried everything to detune us.

Immediately upon arrival, Ron Bagley and I would hunt around for something to get the Ipswich team's back up. The state of the pits was always a good start, as was the general attitude of the home promotion, the track staff and the crowd.

There was always plenty of feeling to feed on and an early diabolical refereeing decision (almost a guarantee) would really help things along. We got ourselves into the mood, our team into the mood, and no doubt provided great entertainment for the crowd, who loved to join in the spirit of things.

Under these circumstances, we stole more than our share of results and had a great deal of fun into the bargain. As match results go, I would reckon I well and truly won the points decision over Ian Thomas by a street and would normally think I had come out in front. All except for his Golden Moment, which I was never able to top.

The Hull track barely fitted around the rugby league pitch. Well, to be entirely truthful, it was nowhere near fitting. The corners of the pitch had to be taken up in order to race. Even then, the track did not conform to the minimum SCB requirements.

In particular, it was a good couple of feet skinny on the back straight. I can only presume that, once the track had been inspected and granted a licence, the inner edge had been moved. Over the years I have even heard stories of a certain promoter offering to hold one end of the tape measure for the track inspector, and maybe not holding the tape right at the end, although I cannot say for certain this happened at Hull!

As a wind up, I always used to note on my team manager's report sheet to the referee that the track seemed too narrow. In theory, that sheet should have been forwarded to the SCB, and something should have been done about it, but somewhere along the line it never seemed to happen.

So, on one trip up there, we took a tape measure with us. The referee that night was, as usual, the one we always had the most trouble with. His name was Vic Harris. I don't know if he was frightened or in awe of Thomas, or just disliked me, but the man was a new level of bad when it came to referees. He was not afraid to let his personal attitudes show either.

The match was its normal 'interesting' self and, as usual, we wound up the crowd who enjoyed venting their feelings. During the course of the match we had been banned from the centre green in another childish display of petulance by the home promotion, so Ron and I thought a bit of theatre was in order.

During the interval (13 heat matches then, followed by a second half) we wandered out across the rugby pitch to the back straight, tape in hands, and commenced to measure the width of the track.

I suppose it is fair to say, the crowd took exception to this. I think we learned some new words, but we reckoned we were just giving them full value for their entrance money. We had made our theatrical point and were wandering back to the pits, when the home clerk of the course hustled out with a couple of local bobbies. They must have been used to football crowds because they started muttering about behaviour likely to cause a breach of the peace!

Then the referee phoned down to say that, on a complaint from Thomas, he was reporting me (just me, not Ron!) to the SCB for ungentlemanly conduct.

Now I have to admit, our actions had been designed to be provocative, but I can hardly see where use of a tape measure can be considered an offence, so I was happy to have my day in court. Except it occurred to me that, as I was then the England team manager, any kind of sanction against me by the Board, be it even only a reprimand, would demand that I resign my England post. I doubt I would have seen sacked as such, but I would have chosen to resign.

The local Ipswich Member of Parliament was a barrister and Queen's Council by the name of Ernle Money. His chambers were in London. Ernle read about the charges against me in the East Anglian Daily Times and telephoned, asking if he could help. Ernle never missed the opportunity for a bit of self-promotion.

Now normally, I would have been happy to take on the duffers at the SCB on such a spurious charge by myself and would have enjoyed the joust. The only thing was, the way such 'courts' were run ensured no certainty of natural justice at all.

Again, in the normal course of things, it would have been worth the risk of a slap on the wrist for the fun of crucifying the inept referee and dragging Ian Thomas down to London from his lair on Ilkley Moor.

But, as I say, there was a bit more riding on this. Even a reprimand would require my conscience to make me resign the England job. In hindsight, that would have been no bad thing but at the time it was important to me, as was my reputation for being aggressive, but scrupulous.

So I accepted Ernle's offer of help.

I met most of the local Ipswich MPs in my time with the speedway but Ernle was the best of them. I say that in a non-partisan way, because I never have had much time for politics, nor never will. My natural cynicism won't allow it.

Ernle though, was everybody's caricature of a Tory MP. He was big, loud, outgoing and with no inbuilt inhibitions of any nature. He had public school stamped all over him and as a successful Queen's Council, was clearly no mug. In amateur dramatics, he would have made a great Mr McAwber.

The Borough of Ipswich is, by and large, made up of working class types and Ernle grabbed the seat, against the odds, from long time local man Dingle Foot by a mere handful or two of votes. It was never a natural Conservative seat, though, and he did brilliantly well to hold it for a second term.

The man was an excellent constituency MP. He worked hard for the town and although he wasn't averse to a bit of self-promotion, he also did a fair bit of behind the scenes work.

I was invited to lunch at his house one Saturday. He lived in a remote place near Bentwaters air force base, but he didn't actually drive a car himself. I'm sure it would have interfered with his liking for fine reds. So it was arranged for me to collect him from his Saturday morning constituency surgery in Town.

When I arrived at his Ipswich rooms, one of the appointments had not turned up. All he knew was that it was a young mum having a serious domestic problem. We hung around but it was clear she was not going to show. He could have shrugged his shoulders. The address she had given was clearly one where Tory party voters would be as rare as hen's teeth, so there was certainly no political mileage to be gained. He was genuinely concerned, though, and prevailed on me, like King Wensleslace's servant, to conduct him to the address.

I won't tell you where it was. All I will say is that, even on a Saturday lunchtime, I was nervous about being there! I certainly wasn't going to get out of the car - for two reasons. First, I would sooner be sitting there with the engine running, just in case; and second, because I reckoned the car, or at least significantly large parts of it, would have gone missing within seconds should I not be in it. A large Mercedes rather stood out parked in that street.

Given this was a domestic dispute, given it was a fair bet the big, hairy, problem part of the complaint could have been at home, and given that this was the kind of area police would only go to mob handed, I have to say it was approaching foolhardy to go bouncing up to the front door, but I don't think Ernle even gave that side of things a thought. He disappeared inside the tatty council house, emerging the best part of an hour later. At barrister's rates, I hate to think what such an interview would have normally cost!

Although quite correctly reluctant to discuss with me what the problems were, he was clearly concerned, and I have no doubt he would have spent more time at a later date trying to sort things out for the unfortunate lady.

Ernle's wife was obviously used to him not adopting routine schedules. When we arrived at his home, she had not even started preparing food. It mattered not, because by the time the food did appear we had enjoyed a couple of bottles of rather nice claret, surrounded by lurchers and the kind of disarray only eccentric 'upper class' families can get away with.

Inevitably, the seat of Ipswich would revert back to Labour. By that time Ernle was eyeing off a seat in the European Parliament, although I don't know if he actually made it. A truly wonderful character, though, and a pleasure to have known.

Judge and jury

Just to set the picture regarding these kinds of speedway tribunal, the procedure for these events was for the SCB manager – in this instance, the particularly unpleasant Dick Bracher – to act as master of ceremonies and chief inquisitor. A sort of court usher, prosecutor, court clerk, minute taker and secretary. A couple of bods from the RAC/ACU acted as the judge and jury. That was it.

Except that, in the event of a defendant wishing to avail himself of legal representation, they also dragged out from his office in Pall Mall, a very junior RAC solicitor to balance things up.

And so I had informed the SCB manager I intended having legal representation. I had no need to divulge more information than that. They would have expected a dusty, old family solicitor.

When Ron and I turned up at the appointed time, we found Ernle had done me proud and had arrived mob handed. Apart from himself, he had gathered up several available juniors from his London chambers. When we flounced into the 'courtroom', I introduced, with a flourish, Mr Ernle Money QC, MP. He, in turn, introduced his three 'junior councils' and our own stenographer. We had them outnumbered!

The look on the poor RAC duty solicitor's face was a picture. As Ernle took control of proceedings, Bracher almost vanished through the back of his chair, whilst the jurists seemed to jump to attention.

My witness was Ron Bagley, 'theirs' were Ian Thomas and Vic Harris, the referee. Richard Head would be a much more suitable moniker for him, as he sat there looking extremely nervous and uncomfortable.

Thomas had not yet arrived, so we waited – us on one side of the room, and them on the other. Pure Perry Mason.

And we waited, and we waited...

An hour after the allotted start time, and still no Ian Thomas, Ernle again rose to his feet and demanded the 'trial' begin. The inquisitors huddled before emerging to announce that in the absence of their chief witness, there was insufficient evidence on which to base a case. The charge was dismissed.

Initially I was elated. We celebrated by my treating the party to coffee and cake in the cafe around the corner (my sole cost for Ernle and his team's involvement in the proceedings!) before they wandered back to their offices, whilst Ron and I caught the train back to Ipswich.

It wasn't really until I sat down on that train before I realised Ian had done us like a dinner.

He must have realised the case against me was desperately weak. He must also have known I intended to have a field day about the Hull track, its condition and the general surrounds (including safety fence height, pits and all sorts of other things). The SCB, faced with these things being officially brought to their notice, would have had to take action, involving Thomas in a tremendous amount of aggravation and expense.

He would also have had to spend a day of his life, never mind the cost, travelling down to London and back from his Yorkshire home for the case.

By simply not turning up, he had assured putting me to the maximum amount of inconvenience, whilst minimising his own. He had also not risked either the face-losing possibility of my winning the case, or the possibility of any subsequent Control Board investigation into the conditions at Hull.

Brilliant! Pure genius!

Had he thought the whole thing through that far? Could he simply not be bothered to turn up, or had he just forgotten? I don't know, but I just had to sit back, smile and admire him.

Fuel for thought

My own best chance to play Perry Mason at Belgrave Square was not on my own behalf.

The word had come back to John Louis that the fuel he had used in a World Championship qualifying round in 1973 was not pure methanol. The testing lab had found a small percentage of hydrogen peroxide in the routine sample taken during the meeting.

Ladies will immediately recognise hydrogen peroxide as hair bleach. Those who have more interest in space travel might recognise it as rocket fuel! Going back to my schoolboy chemistry lessons, I understand it to be a chemical used for oxygenation, or increasing oxygen in a mixture – ie, improving the burn properties.

John Louis and Tony Davey on the World Championship trail in 1973. Tiger was ruled out of the title race that year after a fuel problem.

The SCB notified the FIM about the results of the test, and the FIM in turn asked the Board to investigate and act upon the situation.

And so it was that I accompanied John Louis to that dreaded basement at 31 Belgrave Square.

It seems John regularly bought his fuel from an independent supplier, even though racing fuel was always available from every track on race nights. Now on the surface of it, the buying of his own fuel could be viewed with suspicion. But for one meeting at Cradley Heath, all of the Ipswich team who had bought fuel at that track on that night had engine problems, whilst those who were using other fuel didn't have any problems at all.

Even stranger was that when those Ipswich riders who had experienced trouble emptied out the locally bought fuel, and replaced it with fuel borrowed from other riders, their bike troubles seemed to vanish. Weirder than that even, none of the home team had any bike problems at all.

From then on, Ipswich riders never bought fuel from places other than their home track. It seems JL went one better – he decided to use his own.

John's fuel supplier not only supplied racing fuel to speedway riders but also to other motorsport competitors. Not all motorsports ban the use of additives and, indeed, fuel destined for use on drag machines contained a small percentage of peroxide as an easy-start agent. John had been supplied with one of these drums in error and he was armed with a letter from the supplier to that effect.

I didn't quite have the wig and gown, nor did I use the words 'my client' or m'lud', but I put on a brilliant display of advocacy, explaining how a mistake had been made, and how the additive had in fact reduced the efficiency of the fuel rather than improved it. Therefore John, who was a completely innocent victim, had only managed to qualify for the next round of the World Championships by being such a brilliant rider.

By the time I had finished, I had even convinced myself this was the case, and it came as no surprise when the highly intelligent and well-qualified members of the tribunal agreed with me! Not guilty was the verdict, with a friendly warning issued to John to be careful where he bought his fuel in future.

The hearing was only a few days before the next round of the World Championship trail, the European Final in Abensberg, Germany, where John was accompanied by Ron Bagley (I think

Ipswich might have had a meeting that weekend, so I stayed home).

The word leaked back that the FIM had overruled the SCB decision, and had decided John could not race in the meeting. I went off like a hand grenade as usual and was about to sue everyone in the world. It seems, though, what really happened was that someone in the FIM, who knew a little bit about chemistry, mentioned that far from being a nuisance, the additive in John's fuel might just have given him an advantage. They put this to the SCB representative before the meeting and 'invited' him to withdraw JL's nomination to the event.

Subsequently, the Control Board reviewed John's case and he was banned from FIM events until the start of the following year. Given that all the FIM events by then were finished for the season, it was hardly a huge punishment. Personally, on careful reflection, I thought John got away lightly even though it was a huge blow to him at the time.

Shark-infested waters

Up until buying into Division One in 1972, and in the relative backwaters of the second division, I had been learning the ropes involved in speedway promoting and, in general, keeping my nose clean. The shark-infested waters of Division One, though, were a hugely different proposition, and we had been thrown (or rather, had jumped) into the deep end with no life jacket.

It was sink or swim, there were no beg pardons for rookies, as I learned straight away, so I decided to strike out. No more Mr Nice Guy. It was a case of every man for himself, and I was happy to let anyone who wanted to listen know that I felt we had been short changed and put upon in the way we had been treated by the laughable 'Rider Control'. I stood on my hind legs and hollered that we were prepared to fight back against those who chose to do us injustice.

Guess what? Everyone in and around Ipswich seemed to rally around the cause. Riders, staff, the local paper, and especially the Suffolk public seemed to warm to this backs-to-the-wall, us against the world stuff, and so the die was cast. There would be no backward steps, and no kowtowing to authority. We would do our own thing.

The further out on a limb I went, the more those involved in Ipswich Speedway approved, and the more the rest of the speedway world did not. I quickly learned that with riders like John Louis, the more you backed them up, the better they responded.

Everyone seemed to rally around the flag, so Ron Bagley and myself in particular started getting cheekier and cheekier with our programme comments. And the more I heard that those notes were getting up the noses of people in high places, the more outrageous we got.

At almost every promoters' meeting the question of comments in the Ipswich programme was raised, and more than once those comments were passed on to the SCB, with an invitation for them to take action. But it is truly amazing how much you can get away with saying, provided you say it carefully enough. I only once felt I overstepped the mark, and wished I had not printed a comment. This concerned Len Silver's private life.

There was no question of any official action being taken even then, as the comments were all entirely accurate, but they were also far too personal, and it was wholly reasonable that Len demand a public apology. Even then I was less than genuine and generous with the apology. But I now fully realise I was well out of order.

The only time I was actually pinged for adverse comment, it wasn't my fault. Normally, I edited the weekly programme myself, including sometimes having to tidy up other contributors' comments, but one weekend I was away with the England team, leaving Ron and my secretary to 'put the programme to bed'.

It wasn't until the programmes arrived on the following Thursday afternoon that I read Ron's column. The previous week we had been at home to Leicester, and by coincidence, the referee that night had been a fully paid up Leicester supporter. I think he even did honorary work for them.

It would have been fair to say we had not felt we had been given unbiased treatment by the ref that night. Then again, I think we felt that way most nights, and it is not impossible our aggressive stance against officialdom did sometimes work against us.

But Ron had suggested in his notes that the referee had sat in his box wearing a Leicester supporters' club scarf and rosette! I don't think it is unreasonable to suggest a referee has had a poor meeting, nor even to say our opinion differed from his here and there, but what you can never do is to accuse a referee of bias.

Needless to say, as promoter and being ultimately responsible for what appeared in the programme, I was dragged back to the dungeons of Belgrave Square. Here I confessed to the heinous crime of being away looking after the England team's interests on an honorary basis, and therefore had not made sure the programme carried no naughty stuff.

Even allowing for the fact that I held my hands up to the 'crime', and had printed an apology the following week off my own back, I suspect my fine was marginally greater than had I been a model speedway citizen instead of a thorn in the side of authority.

They got me in the end, though. They put a stop to my being tongue in cheek and forever ridiculing the speedway authorities. They drafted me onto the management committee! Talk about poacher turned gamekeeper.

But I like to think I managed to retain a certain amount of impish cynicism.

From then on, the only columns in the Ipswich programme that carried a heavy sting were still written by me – but under pen names.

9 19th Nervous Breakdown

You're the kind of person you meet at certain
Dismal, dull affairs
Centre of the crowd, talkin' much too loud
Runnin' up and down the stairs
Well it seems to me that you have seen
Too much in too few years
And though you try you just can't hide
Your eyes are edged with tears

You better stop and look around
Here it comes, here it comes
Here it comes, here it comes
Here comes your 19th nervous breakdown

The easiest way to shut up a troublemaker is to promote him.

Having proved to be more than a small thorn in the side of speedway's establishment, they did the sensible thing and elected me to the Management Committee. Please note, this will be the last time this august body gets capital letters in this book.

I suppose I should explain how the hierarchy of the BSPA was supposed to work, and then how it really did work – and I don't think too much has changed since my time.

The Association should have been made up of one delegate from each track with that delegate being required to hold a promoter's licence and have the authority to represent and make decisions for his track. Generally the delegate was the principal or owner of the particular 'franchise' (a word not really used at all in the mid-70s, but one that describes very well what a place in the British League represented for a promotion).

Sometimes, though, where the owner of the franchise, such as Belle Vue (which was then owned by the Trust House Forte group) was a part of a large company, then it was the speedway manager who represented the promotion.

Written into the BSPA constitution was that a General Council of the BSPA should be made up of one such licensed representative from each track. Originally, this was taken literally, and a council meeting would involve around 18 people plus the BSPA manager and maybe a minute taker.

This group was responsible for the operation of all speedway racing in the UK other than FIM-controlled international events. Much has been made for many years of these general council meetings, and in particular the Annual General Meeting (or conference), where decisions affecting the general running of the sport during the following season were made. However, the day to day responsibility for running the sport was ceded to a management committee consisting of a chairman and four other council members, all elected from and by the general council.

In the BSPA, the chairman was therefore the man with the most power, but because the continental countries recognised the position of president as the highest post, the BSPA eventually decided to establish such a position within its own structure. This was so that Charles Foot, the BSPA foreign representative and ambassador, could negotiate at what appeared to be on an equal level to his continental counterparts. The post was otherwise designed to be largely ceremonial.

The role of the BSPA manager was purely administrative. He (or she) had no decision-making authority at all.

Now what actually happened was that several tracks started turning up for council meetings with more than one representative. General opinion had it that some partners in tracks didn't trust each other to make decisions on each other's behalf, and I suspect there was a modicum of truth in that. Other theories were that if a track only had a single delegate, and he happened to pop out for a call of nature, he would find his pet project had been torpedoed whilst his back was turned. There was more than a shred of truth in that as well!

Consequently, general council meeting numbers swelled into the thirties, and often beyond. As each person wished to stick in his own two pennyworth, meetings dragged on for ever. It was not uncommon for one representative from a track to speak for a motion and then another from the same track to speak against the same motion. Often, we had a situation where one representative would even vote for a motion, and then another from the same track would vote (or try to vote) against it!

So intra-season general council meetings became merely talkfests. Each one of the management committee's decisions since the previous meeting would be carefully examined, argued about, with the benefit of hindsight, and often criticised. But rarely, if ever, changed.

The reason for not changing decisions was simple. To reverse a management committee decision would have been, to all intent and purpose, a vote of no confidence in that management committee. The committee knew this, and often, when the going got particularly sticky, the members would make theatrical threats to resign, until the dissenters settled down.

In theory these general council meetings were supposed to start at 10.30am and finish before five o'clock but I have known them go on until well into the evening. And after a full day cooped up in a smoke-filled room tempers sometimes – make that often – became frayed. Also, with so many different personalities on collision course and many of the promoters having a 'history' with each other, the odd personal war broke out.

At one time the Peterborough and Oxford promoter, Danny Dunton, with his wonderful lilting Buckinghamshire accent, was having a loud and heated slanging match across the table with the very Norfolk Cyril Crane, who was in charge at King's Lynn and Boston. These flare-ups were very much like schoolyard fights. Although there were plenty of onlookers, everybody sat back and enjoyed the moment rather than put an end to it.

And so these two promoters, on their feet, arms flailing like windmills, hurled abuse at each other for several minutes, much to the amusement of the rest. Dave Lanning, representing Reading, finally put an end to it. During a brief respite when both protagonists were drawing breath, he suggested it was just like listening to an episode of The Archers.

Sometimes these various spats got very personal indeed, often prompting the chairman to call a short break, but, generally speaking, things settled back down and normality, whatever that was, would be restored. Only very occasionally did one or other party storm out of the meeting. They were all too frightened of missing something.

Time after time, though, the real issues affecting the sport were presented to the general council already set in stone, having been decided and acted upon by the management committee. Often the reasoning for these decisions was never explained and sometimes decisions were not even reported. As mere promoters, the general council members were expected to simply accept things.

For the non-smokers these meetings were a nightmare. They would emerge having been subjected to more smoke than a kipper, with runny eyes and sore throats, and having inhaled enough carcinogens to last a (short) lifetime.

Of course, when I was just one of the great unwashed, a mere drone, I never realised what was going on. I would stand up in those meetings like a cross between Perry Mason and Mark Anthony and sound off at great length about everything under the sun. Little did I realise it was all so much piss and wind. The real substance was being passed in private.

What I didn't know then is that the chairman would often make decisions without even referring to the committee, who were then expected to endorse these without query. Sometimes, such decision-making was necessary. It is not always possible in every given situation to stop in the middle of delicate negotiations and say: "I'd like to phone a friend... or four."

But successive chairmen knew this and often deliberately indulged in keeping quiet about contentious issues until decisions were taken and were effectively irreversible.

Dear Charles Foot was the king of this tactic – and yet he was never actually chairman. He was the treasurer, foreign negotiator, godfather and wheeler and dealer in chief.

He was also the first president. The position was created with him in mind.

Charles scoffed openly at general council meetings – and even at their decisions. He would go his own sweet way, making his own decisions without reference to anyone, and expected to be backed up every time by the management committee. He regarded the council meetings as simply a place where the proletariat went to let off steam, the Roman senate in the time of the emperors.

I was some time as a management committee member until I again realised I was little more than a rubber-stamp there also. OK, so there were times when we actually got around a table and debated things, but there were very few occasions when an agenda item was actually voted on.

With only five people looking into each other's eyes, it was not easy to stick with a dissenting position, especially if it was the chairman or president you were dissenting to. It was even more difficult to actually challenge a decision that had already been taken by, or was being pushed hard by, the chairman. Anyway, the odds were he would have lobbied like-minded committee members beforehand and been confident of his position before the meeting took place.

So what was the benefit for a promoter in being a rank and file management committee member then? Simple really, and the answer is in the previous paragraph. It is much harder to get shafted when you are looking the potential shafters in the eye! Membership on the committee conferred a preferred status on your track. Nothing spoken, of course, just a quiet sort of repayment for giving up so much time and trouble to the cause and for toeing the 'company' line.

Of course, that was a real problem for me. With my supposedly being one of the 'chosen few', I found myself having to defend all management committee decisions – even those which I didn't like. I was also unable to make public comment on the more bizarre procedures in the sport.

I got around the second of those two problems by introducing a couple of *nom de plume* features in the Ipswich programme, where I could indulge in giving my real thoughts and opinions, although I did have to tone down my more strident comments.

More and more, managers rather than owners began to represent tracks at general council meetings. These managers were always considered as second-class citizens. Whilst we all used the same toilets, a clear apartheid operated, and one would hear several times throughout each meeting, those well worn words: "What right do you have to make such a comment/suggestion/proposal/vote when you have no money in the sport?"

I mean, perish the thought that most of these people had more of their lives on the line than the soft bellied businessmen who employed them. And perish the thought that these people were in place through their speedway merit and nous, rather than because they had enough money to buy a speedway to play with.

It grieved me to sit there and listen to so many promoters coming up with so many objections to suggestions on ways of improving the sport. I won't say 'without exception' and I won't say 'with malice aforethought' but it seemed to me that just about every vote at general council meetings was cast on the precept of 'is this good for my track and my promotion?' rather than 'is this good for speedway?'

I was the exception. Every decision I took, every vote I made, every suggestion I put forward, was based on nothing other than that which was good of the sport... as I saw it. And there's the rub.

I rationalised this system to myself by saying, if every promoter voted for what was best for his club, logic then followed that what was best for the majority of tracks must have also been best for the sport. Of course, it doesn't work that way. The choices we were giving ourselves were between choice A and choice B. Choice C never got a look in, whilst we should have been thinking and planning towards choices X, Y, and Z.

Worst of all, there was no pre-planning. Anyone who had a bright idea just used to blurt it out at a council meeting. No careful thought, no circulation of the idea beforehand – and no chance to go away and brood on all of the ramifications. Idea- short debate-vote.

Indeed, some promoters were so good at this they would wait until the meeting was almost breaking up, and several delegates had left to catch trains or attend speedway meetings, before dropping a contentious issue on the table, hoping to minimise debate and slide it through quickly. It was even said that delegates dare not go for a pee during meetings, for fear of what might get voted on whilst their back was turned.

Share issue

One of the primary duties of the administration at that time was to organise the running of 'Shared Events'. I think it is worth explaining the procedures for these events and my own thoughts on them.

A shared event' was a meeting staged by a track on behalf of the BSPA. The staging promoter would take a percentage of the gate receipts (it used to be 20%) to cover his fixed overheads like rent, rates, office, and the like, and then he would deduct direct meeting costs (riders' payments, advertising, etc) from the takings. The balance of the monies would go to a central pool.

That pool of money would be used to pay for the running of the BSPA offices, with any surplus (less a small reserve) shared among the promoters at the end of the season.

Those meetings qualifying as shared events were international Test matches, the British League Riders' Championships (first and second division), the Internationale, the Daily Express Spring Classic, the British Final (and semi-finals) and various other meetings from time to time.

You will note, the list does not include what were referred to as FIM Championship (or Trophy) events. These were the international rounds (those rounds after the British Final) of the individual World Championship, and all rounds of the World Team Cup and World Pairs.

These Trophy meetings, when held in the UK, became the responsibility of the Control Board, which was charged with staging the events on behalf of the FIM, but which retained all of the profits (or covered all of the losses) incurred from those meetings.

The SCB would use any surplus monies to pay for its own running costs and then pass on any surplus to the BSPA, which then distributed it back to the promotions.

Disregarding the FIM Championship events for the moment, there were two reasons for staging the 'domestic' BSPA shared events. The first was, of course, to give the supporters a varied selection of meetings and to give an opportunity for international competition. The second, like any professional sport, was to make a profit.

As far as finances were concerned, whilst many supporters seemed to think this payout was simply to line the promoters' pockets, in fact the payout was often the difference between profit and loss for many tracks. The events would be placed at the better attended tracks in order to maximise returns, so the 'poorer' tracks would benefit from the revenue raised.

I don't doubt that for the better off promotions, their share was something of a 'bonus'. But what it allowed me to do at Ipswich, for instance, was to provide perks for the Witches riders' extras over and above their standard rates, to spend money on the stadium and riders facilities, to provide things like track spares, and the like, and to pay for enough staff to make Ipswich Speedway the best organised and operated in the country.

So that explains the What and Why of shared events. Now for the 'How'.

It was the task of the management committee to allocate the various events to the tracks each year. In terms of the Internationale and the Spring Classic (Wimbledon), and the British League Riders' Championship (Belle Vue), these dates and venues were maintained from year to year, as were the British Championship (Coventry) and semis (Leicester and Sheffield), so most of those decisions were easy. It was the Test match series that needed positioning.

For these the committee would take into account such things as which tracks would draw the best crowds, how much disruption would be caused to other tracks operating on the same day, a sensible geographical spread to give supporters in all areas a chance of having a match in their area, and what tracks put on the best show.

Particularly with a genuine touring team made up from non-British League riders (unlike, for example, an Australian team), there was also the practical situation of fitting in the series over a short space of time in order to minimise that team's need to be away from their home (and the cost of maintaining them whilst on tour).

As I said earlier, the committee would, by and large, try to maximise return by using those

Anders Michanek, winner of the 1973 Daily Express Spring Classic at Wimbledon, from Bengt Jansson (left) and Terry Betts. The big, televised early season meeting at Plough Lane was one of the BSPA's shared events. *(AW)*

tracks which made most money from such events. But they also needed to take into account that the staging of big meetings was something of an honour, and that the lesser attended places also deserved an opportunity.

In the early days of Rowena Blackford, she would send each probable staging track a questionnaire in which they needed to list their usual outgoings for things like advertising, medical expenses, event staff costs, and the like. Also the normal admission charges, transfers to more expensive areas, programme sales and prices . . .

When the management committee had confirmed the staging venues, a list of instructions fixing special meeting prices, maximum budgets for outgoings such as advertising and promotion, provision of for accommodation and entertainment facilities for the visiting tourists and/or guests, and so on would be sent from the BSPA office.

After the event, the staging promoter was required to complete a standard analysis sheet documenting all income and expenses, complete with receipts and detail. As a new boy, I was punctilious in being scrupulously fair to the association. I would list out the meeting costs down to the last penny, with accompanying proof, and was proud to have made substantial contributions to the shared event pool.

When I saw the returns from other tracks, I didn't believe many of the figures presented but the BSPA manager did not have the status to demand proof of the accuracy of the claims. And because the management committee was made up of promoters, it was not easy to effectively challenge the honesty of their fellow BSPA members. Even Charles Foot, the treasurer, was a promoter and rarely queried returns. With the leaving of Rowena, things were also done on a far more casual basis and staging promotions tended not to have their responsibilities spelled out to them in detail.

I'll not say the staging tracks "cheated" on the other promoters, but as the system became more and more lax, and as new promoters replaced the 'old school' people, the returns to the Association got smaller and smaller, mainly because the promoters did not have the correct procedures spelled out to them, and because there was not a strong enough management role by the BSPA.

Eventually, such were the poor returns coming from these events that they were failing to provide much at all for the 'pool' and, finally, the BSPA decided to 'sell' the events, effectively to the highest bidders, taking a pittance in return. Nowadays I think it is the TV money that makes up the majority of the pool – but that is not a road I wish to go down just here.

The answer

I know the answer to how the BSPA should be run now. Now it is too late, and now that I can examine the situation from the outside looking in, rather than the inside looking out. Speedway is no different to any other professional sport. The participants are colleagues and combatants both at the same time, and they stand too close to the game to be able to make sensible and unbiased decisions on its day to day, or even long term operation.

I cheerfully accept that the stakeholders within the sport (the promoters) have a right to have their say, in the same way as the shareholders in a company have the same right. Yet you would not expect each shareholder in an organisation to sit around making decisions on the running of that company. They elect directors to do that for them. Some of those directors might be shareholders, but some definitely are not, and that normally includes the chairman.

Why should speedway be any different? They should elect a 'board' or 'commission' made up of a minority of promoters and a majority of independent people with an intimate knowledge of the sport, no current ties with or interest in any promotion, and with a well known history of fairness and integrity. Like company directors, they would be voted in by the stakeholders (promoters) and subject to re-election on a periodic basis.

That commission would then set up its own independent administration with a decision-making chief executive officer to look after the running of the sport overall, leaving the promoters to look after their own individual businesses.

Hardly rocket science, this. So simple, in fact, you wonder why it has not been done long ago – until you fully understand the distrust inherent within the promoting fraternity, and the wild notion that only the promoters themselves know what is best. Absolute tosh, but I have no doubt the promoters will fight to the death before giving an inch of ground to such plain common sense.

10 Land of Hope and Glory

Land of Hope and Glory,
Mother of the Free,
How shall we extol thee,
Who are born of thee?
Wider still and wider
Shall thy bounds be set;
God, who made thee mighty,
Make thee mightier yet.

I did some pretty silly things in my speedway time but one stands out head and shoulders above the others. When I was asked if I would be the England manager, I said yes. Three times! What do they say? To make a mistake is forgivable, but to make the same mistake twice is plain stupid. So what do you call me, when I did it three times!

It wasn't until 1975 that the idea of UK speedway having a designated England speedway manager was considered. I can well remember the general council meeting at which the idea arose. It occurred to someone sitting there that having a position of England manager might give speedway a little more kudos with the press. Really! That was the reason a regular manager was appointed.

As I recall, did Dent Oliver get offered the job? I think so, but either Dent's employers, Belle Vue, decided he couldn't take it on, or he did he accept the position, but sadly suffered a fatal heart attack shortly afterwards?

Len Silver was asked if he would assume the role, and he accepted. The terms were these: reimbursement of travel and telephone expenses and £5 per meeting, meal money! The management committee would continue to make the team selections (with the help of the manager).

For all Test matches in Britain, the England team would be selected taking into account on which circuits the matches were staged (so as to use local favourites) and without disrupting league matches taking place on the same nights.

Up until then, England selections had always been made exclusively by the management committee, and for matches in the UK, normally the promoter of the staging track acted as manager on the night. For FIM events, the management committee chose one of their own to act as England's representative.

I use the term 'England' although, for FIM events, it should be Great Britain, which included not just the home countries but Australia and New Zealand as well, until Australia decided to represent itself and New Zealand followed suit.

Technically, I suppose the name should then have been changed to 'The British Isles', but as 'Great Britain' appears to have given back just about all of what used to constitute GREAT Britain, Great Britain effectively now does just mean the British Isles (and the Falklands!)

For UK-based internationals, the term 'England' was used most of the time, although I recall a Division Two series in 1971 referring to 'Young Britain', because one of the matches took place at a Scottish track. Certainly, in my time, whilst possibly not politically correct, the term England did the job, because I cannot recall any of the other home countries providing a representative. For the rest of this chapter (or book), please consider 'England' or 'Great Britain' as interchangeable according to your own preference.

In 1969 I don't think Ipswich was entrusted with an international match but in 1970 we had two, in midsummer, just two weeks apart. The first match, against a true Young Sweden, was hardly memorable as England cruised to a 71-37 win but it did give us the opportunity to get a

Miroslav Verner and John Louis on the Czechs' first visit to Ipswich.

look at young Christer Lofqvist, who was drafted in despite being already a British League Division One rider with West Ham, and a very young Tommy Johansson. Without those two, the Swedes would have been fairly ordinary.

The second was against a 'Young Czechoslovakia' side which looked remarkably like that country's best possible senior international team and included many riders who were, or went on to become, world stars – Miroslav Verner, Vaclav Verner, Jiri Stancl, Milan Spinka. That was an excellent fourth Test match.

It was a very close affair that England was in danger of losing before they ran out 56-51 winners No permanent England manager then so, as the home promoter, the job fell to me.

In the proper 18-heat Test match race formula used for the event, the reserves were just that. They were substitutes with no programmed rides. Pete Bailey was a reserve.

Things were looking difficult so I called Pete off the bench and put him into heat 16. He won it, so I put him into heat 17. He won that as well.

Now two rides on the trot well and truly takes it out of a rider. This was even more the case in the 'good old days' when bikes were harder to ride, riders only part time pros, and 'training' consisted of smoking and drinking.

So it was not on to ask Pete, slumped in a heap and wheezing in a corner of the pits, to go again.

The scores were level going into the last heat. Rayleigh's Geoff Maloney and John Louis were up against Miroslav Verner and Jan Klokocka. Maloney managed to fall halfway along the back straight on the first lap. Did he fall, or was he pushed? The Czechs were a fairly physical bunch. Verner was excluded, so we presume Geoff was pushed. After a few seconds to collect himself, Maloney picked himself up and started heading off to prepare for the rerun of the race.

I arrived on the scene just at that time, and commanded him to have a relapse. Somewhat surprised, he let his legs collapse under him. The St John's and I fussed over him. I think even the track doctor, who was very young and keen at the time, joined us in the huddle.

Meantime I had sent a runner to the pits to resuscitate Pete and get him ready for the rerun.

I reckon our little group was there on the back straight for about five minutes chatting, telling jokes and, for all the world, doing everything but giving Geoff the kiss of life. Finally, and theatrically, we hauled him off on a stretcher, after having had word from the pits that Pete was ready to go.

Like most of the Czechs, Klokocka never knew when to accept defeat, ending up on the deck in the re-run, leaving John and Pete to win the heat and the match.

Maloney found he had been paid for an extra race win when he received his pay cheque.

So my first taste of international management was actually in the Division Two days. But discounting these (and repeats in 1971), I began my England managing career right at the top.

I thought it was a huge, huge honour when, in September 1975, Reg Fearman asked me if I would like to be in charge of the England riders' interests in the World Final at Wembley. A great honour.

What I had failed to realise was that all those who would normally have done the job would be in their best bibs and tuckers with their families and friends, swanking in the Twin Towers. They would be having cocktails and nibbles before the meeting, waving regally to the proletariat from the Royal Box during the event and enjoying a slap-up silver service meal afterwards. I was just the mug who was daft enough not to realise why it was me who was 'selected' to be on duty in the pits.

Actually, I did realise, But, believe me, I reckon I enjoyed myself far more than any of the other promoters that day, strutting around all of the nooks and crannies behind the public places of that wonderful old stadium, being waved through any door with my 'all areas' pass.

I rubbed shoulders with the crème de la crème of speedway talent that day and, above all, was able to watch the racing from the hallowed turf. I don't expect the world would have ground

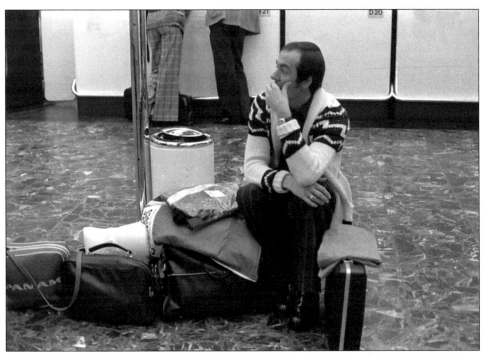

Should have stayed home . . . I didn't exactly look enthusiastic even before leaving for the Lions tour. *(AW)*

to a halt if I had not been on duty but that didn't stop me from feeling pretty special.

My presence there also had the benefit of allowing Ron Bagley to get into the pits as part of John Louis' entourage, so both Ron and myself were available to help him. If we did nothing else that day, we insisted which gate position the uncertain Louis should select if he won the toss for the third place run-off with Ivan Mauger. John called correctly when the coin was tossed and claimed a rostrum place.

That winter (1975-76), I was invited by the BSPA to take the British Lions on a tour of Australia and New Zealand. Up until the year previous, there had been an annual 'unofficial' tour organised by Nigel Boocock. Unofficial as far as the BSPA was concerned, but from the moment those lads arrived in Australia they had been the 'British Lions', were called the British Lions and billed as the British Lions. The matches they took part in were billed as 'Test matches'.

Reasonably, the UK promoters adopted the attitude that if the team was to be called a representative one and the matches given representative status, then the tour should come under their auspices. The riders should be selected and endorsed by them, and be accompanied by a manager of their choice.

The first such tour was managed by Reg Fearman in 1974-75, the second by myself. Reg, a promoter and former BSPA chairman I have always admired, was a hard act to follow.

We were billed officially as the English Lions and I received from BSPA manager, Ron Bott, a list of those riders selected to tour, an itinerary (subject to change) and a copy of the agreed tour conditions, which were, to say the least, short, vague, and cheap. I had no input into any of these things.

As I recall, the tour organisers agreed to supply transport to and around Australia, hotel accommodation for team and manager and the most basic of start and points monies. The pay was just about enough to cover the cost to the riders of a 'working holiday'.

The party 'selected' was Chris Pusey (captain), Peter Collins, Doug Wyer, Dave and Chris Morton, John Davis and Gordon Kennett. All of these riders eventually became top-liners but, at that time, only Pusey, Collins and Wyer were established first division heat leaders. The others were youngsters still finding their feet. It was a good line-up, in keeping with the image of the Lions, being a mix of youth and experience, but not in any way representative of the strongest team the UK could field.

I should have stayed at home.

The tour was jinxed from the start. My first direct involvement with the riders was when we met at Heathrow. Typically, Ron Bott had come to the airport to see us off. This was not part of his brief but he was a genuinely nice guy. He had also found up 10 matching blue windcheater jackets for the riders and myself to wear.

Ron and I had assumed the riders would have armed themselves with the necessary visas for the trip. Some had not, though, and there we stood at the check-in desk with at least two riders minus their visas. We were due to fly with Qantas, whose check-in supervisor was really helpful.

He told us the plane was a little delayed, which might just give us time to dash into central London to the Australian Embassy and back. He telephoned the Embassy, whilst Ron and I grabbed the offending passports and hopped into a cab.

The Australian High Commission visa department in London, not normally known for being courteous and helpful, were stars, turning the passports around in record time.

But even allowing for their assistance, a trip into central London and back from Heathrow in a black cab is not a five-minute job. It took a good couple of hours. No mobile phones then to keep a check on things, so we had no idea if we had missed the plane or not, but we dashed to the check-in desk where the whole group was still (im)patiently waiting.

From there the supervisor whisked us through the back corridors of Heathrow to the aircraft. Everyone except our party were sitting on board and as we took our seats, the plane started taxiing. I think you can presume our check-in supervisor had stood with his foot in the door to stop it from being closed. In recognition for his help, I presented him with a spare windcheater.

Was it plain sailing from there? I should coco! We were met at Perth airport and taken to an old-fashioned 'hotel' or pub with basic accommodation. 'Our Dougie' and PC rejected it out of hand. I have to say I saw their point. It was a rough place in a rough area. It was to be 'home' for nearly three weeks, so needed at least some basic comforts.

So my first duty, on stepping down from the plane, was to pick a fight with the home promoter. We won the day and were placed in a much newer motel, still convenient to the city centre, but with reasonable rooms and amenities. Next, we were told that the crate with all bikes and spares was still on the wharf at Fremantle. There was an almost permanent dock strike on in WA those days. Just to fill in the picture, there was also a petrol tanker drivers' strike, so no petrol anywhere.

The 1974-75 touring England Lions – back row, left to right: Peter Collins, Gordon Kennett, myself, Doug Wyer, Chris Morton. Front: Dave Morton, John Davis, Chris Pusey. *(AW)*

Con Migro, the home promoter, used his influence to get the bikes released at the eleventh hour but we were then informed that the Claremont Speedway in Perth had a noise problem and all riders were required to use silencers (this was before silencers began to be used in the UK) Not just any old silencers mind. These were called suitcase silencers, on account of their size and shape.

Now the Lions riders had all brought the then new fangled four-valve Weslake engines with them, which were not yet readily available in Australia. Mutterings were afoot within the home community that the Lions' use of these things almost amounted to cheating.

One thing was for sure. The fitting of these huge silencers was going to result in a massive back pressure in the bikes' exhaust systems, destroying the more temperamental power of the four-valvers, as against the grunty but decidedly unsophisticated by comparison two-valve Jawa machines.

Also, the locals had been using these silencers for a while, had been given the opportunity to tune their engines to them, or to weld a straight piece of tube through the middle, which was the standard 'illegal' option.

Captain Chris Pusey was tbe biggest casualty of a sorry night at Sydney. *(AW)*

So, after just two days in the country, we had yet another stand-off. A compromise was reached. The home promotion had a supply of curved exhaust tail end pieces manufactured. Instead of the silencers, these 'swan necks' were to be bolted onto the end of the exhausts, so as to deflect the exhaust emissions, and therefore the noise, downwards.

To this day, I'm not sure how effective this would have been in reducing noise but it mattered little. Come race night, one of the Australian team tossed his away after his first race, so the Lions followed suit. Still, I suppose the local council and residents would have read of the determination of the local speedway promoter to abide by the new noise abatement rulings, and would have been suitably impressed.

The next problem was in dealing with the home referee. In theory, the ref, or 'steward' as they are called in Australia, is independent and licensed by the Australian governing body. In practice, he was hired and paid for by the home promotion and had been doing the job his (and their) way for quite a few years.

'His way', though, had little to do with accepted international practice and nothing to do with the rulebook, especially the bit governing the most important part, at the start of each race.

I don't know what the books say these days, but then, it said words to the effect of: "The starting line marshal shall call all the riders up to the tapes. When they are all stationary and ready, the referee will put on the green light. He will then allow the riders enough time to spin their engines, before releasing the tapes".

At that time, tape-touching was not forbidden, provided the tapes didn't break. Not that they were ever likely to at Claremont. The tapes were stretchy enough for a rider to ride right over the top of them without them breaking.

Now this is where it got tricky. All riders considered it their job to beat the referee, and so get a flying start. They still do now, but the rules and penalties are enough to dissuade them from trying too much.

But at that time, the Claremont promoter was more interested in keeping the show moving than being picky about giving all the riders a fair chance. The steward would wait just long enough for the last rider to come up to the start line before putting on the green light and then letting the tapes go in one movement.

In theory, it then became very difficult for the riders to try to anticipate when the tapes would go up once the green light went on. In theory, it meant that when the green light came on, you dropped your clutch. In theory, this sped up the running of the meeting.

In practice, the riders no longer tried to anticipate the tapes going up, but tried to anticipate the green light coming on. The rider last up to the tapes and last into position effectively controlled the start, as, once all riders were at the line, it was green light on and tapes up!

I tried to explain the proper technique to the steward, and why it was necessary. Mixed in with the more colourful expletives, his reply was littered with phrases like 'whinging Poms', 'this way for 20 years' and '... back where you came from'.

From this, I deduced my lessons to him on starting technique were neither appreciated nor would be acted upon. There was no higher authority with whom I could confer, so I got the lads together and we adopted an 'if you can't beat 'em, join 'em' attitude.

Towards the end of the first meeting, we had things sorted out in our minds. The races actually started at the pit gate. It was possible, if you were the last one up to the tapes, to actually still be moving when the tapes went up. But to counteract that, it was also possible to be first up to the tapes, check in, so to speak, and then, as the last man was making his slow run to the line, pull back and turn around at the last second, thereby now taking over as the 'active starter'.

In this way, we had bikes going round and round in circles, like so many wheeling and diving seagulls over the top of a fishing boat as the nets are being hauled aboard.

The object was achieved, though. The 'local knowledge' starting procedure was totally disrupted and, given any kind of fair(ish) starts, I fancied our boys over the locals. In fact, come the second and third meetings, we had become far more adept at this technique than the home riders – our last victory there was embarrassingly easy. We didn't win too many brownie points with the home promotion, though, because the meetings were delayed whilst all this nonsense took place.

As an aside, I found on the way around Australia, each ref had his own particular version of how races should be started, so generally we just figured it out and got on with beating it. One particular steward was proud of the fact that he had found a way of stopping the riders dropping their clutches as the green light came on. He didn't put the green light on until the riders had reached the first turn!

Another, whose starts I dared to query, was even more to the point. He said he would punch my lights out if I spoke to him again! Mind you, I've had the same response from a particular Scottish referee in Edinburgh in answer to my tactful approaches questioning his knowledge of the regulations. Perhaps it's the way I tell 'em!

With all this rancour and aggro, you might be surprised to learn that in just three weeks in Perth I made lots of lifetime friends, including the long time Claremont promoter, Con Migro, and it was at the end of this short time in 'God's Country' that I decided this is where I wanted to see out my days.

It was around this time I began to realise how lucky I was with the Ipswich team. We had all 'grown up' together in speedway. They knew that, whilst I had not ridden a bike, I had a rough idea what I was talking about. They also knew that although I often had my 'game face' on, I would back them to the hilt and make sure nobody did them down. If I had been touring with the Ipswich team, this trip would have been a breeze and we would all have had a ball.

But I wasn't, so I just had to make the best of it. I spent a lot of time on that trip isolated and on my own. Three of the riders were more experienced than me about and around Australia, and they only used me when they wanted some dirty work to be done.

Of the others, the Morton brothers naturally gravitated to the more senior northern trio, John Davis enjoyed the lighter side of life (whilst being dedicated to his speedway) but Gordon Kennett was also isolated and plainly homesick and, in the role of travelling reserve, did not have enough speedway to occupy him.

Typical of the trip was when we flew up for a meeting at Ayr in North Queensland. We were there a week, stuck in a grotty motel in a hick town. Almost just a stone's throw away were the pristine North Queensland beaches, leading straight to the Great Barrier Reef – the same beaches that are part of legend, and the same Barrier Reef that is one of the natural wonders of the world.

We never even got as far as seeing the sea, which was a spit into the wind away. We spent the entire week just mooching around the motel. Perhaps I should have organised something but, to be frank, there was no incentive. So we just hung around.

The Ayr promoter, a nice man named Brian Hodder, was the local tycoon. He appeared to own half the town. The local area was dominated by sugar cane growing, a hard life but very well paid in those days. When Hodder picked us up from Townsville airport on the Monday, he said the meeting scheduled for the following Saturday would be rained off.

Bit of a strong statement coming the best part of a week before the event and with solid blue skies and ninety-degree temperatures. Brian was a typical promoter. Each day I saw him, he said the same thing, as the sun continued to burn down from the traditional azure blue, cloudless sky. Saturday, the day of the meeting, was another glorious day but Brian remained adamant.

Just as we left for the evening meeting, around six, the few wispy white clouds that had appeared in the afternoon started to get bigger. By the time it had got dark, the clouds were beginning to join together.

The bikes had been warmed up ready, and the track staff were beginning to line up for the parade, when I was hit on the head by a missile. Except that it wasn't a missile, but a single drop of water, about the size of a half crown.

I looked around and in the dry and dusty pit area, ricochets, like you see in movies when the gunfight starts, seemed to be going off. Puffs of dust just leapt into the air. I looked up to the floodlights illuminating the pits area, where just 10 minutes earlier swarms of flying insects, some the size of birds, had been trying to blot out the light.

Huge beautiful, white pearls were sparkling down and exploding. Soon there were more and more. It was anything but cold, but the drops actually stung and by comparison to the ambient temperature, they were freezing, so it was time to duck for whatever cover there was available.

Within a minute, the beautiful single droplets had become a solid, wet curtain. The noise of the waterfall bouncing off everything was awesome. Those who had ducked for cover, were now running the other way trying to rescue everything that was open to the elements. This was one of those times when it was better to be a manager, with only a ballpoint pen to rescue! Through all of this mayhem, I could hear Brian Hodder saying: "I told you so!"

It rained all night and into the next day. There was no point in waiting for it to stop. The monsoon season had started. It was still raining when we got back onto the plane.

It was not possible to rearrange the meeting but what we did was organise with Brian to fly up a couple of riders with their bikes so they could put on a show a few weeks later. Peter Collins, our star man, was an obvious choice. The other opportunity I gave to Gordon Kennett, who had, as non-programmed meeting reserve, been given almost no riding opportunities at all on the trip.

Typical of Doug Wyer's attitude throughout the tour was that he complained bitterly because I had selected Gordon instead of him. The best I can say about 'Our Dougie' was that his wife, who was on part of the trip with him, was a really smashing person! Some people are easier to pigeonhole than others. Dougie was born to be an HGV driver.

I had decided the BSPA annual conference in Mallorca during December was too important for me to miss, so I flew back from Australia for the three-day meeting. I flew into Heathrow, transferred to Gatwick, joined the charter flight to Mallorca, did the conference and then flew back to Sydney. The return trip was complicated by fog at Heathrow, causing a 48-hour camp-down with a million other stranded travellers in Terminal 3.

Thanks to British Airways cancelling a Jumbo full of people a week before Christmas, it looked as if I would be unable to get a flight until the New Year, but I spotted that same helpful Qantas check-in supervisor who had helped us first time, across the crowded check-in hall, and he managed to squeeze me onto one of their flights.

That flight actually broke the record for the fastest commercial flight from London to Sydney and might well still hold the record today. The 747 plane got awfully close to breaking the sound barrier on the way.

The crowning glory, speedway-wise, on this tour was yet to come. The Lions were winning everything at a canter. They were just too good for the Australian team. The Aussies blamed this on the Lions being mounted on four-valve engines. That certainly helped. But the fact that

SPEEDWAY STAR January 3,

SPEEDWAY STA___ s to England manager John Berry in Sydney THRE__

'I COULDN'T HAVE A DEATH ON MY CONSCIENCE'

ENGLAND STAGED a dramatic walk-out after skipper Chris Pusey had been injured in a Heat 4 crash during last Saturday's sixth test against Australia in Sydney. It was the climax to a night of angry protests by England manager John Berry and the Lions riders over the state of the Showground track.

After a considerable delay the England riders unloaded their equipment and agreed to continue. Manager John Berry explained: "I felt we had a duty to the Australian public, to hold the England team that they must ___ks and attempt any passing from

___ to have a death on my ___ Mr Berry. "There are ___way but the conditions ___rmal danger limit."
___ent on to win the match 62-45 ___ first success in the seven match ___usey's other injuries were uncertain ___en we spoke to Mr Berry on Monday.
"He has not broken a leg as we feared," reported the England boss. "He has chipped a bone in his right knee but the full extent of the ligament damage will not be clear until the ___ere swelling goes down. He has also ___sed his left wrist and foot and has several ___nd bruises. It is too early to say whether ___be fit to ride in the final test in Brisbane ___ry 10 or undertake the short trip to

pretty shaken up by the incident. He jarred his arm and only completed three rides."
The referee was called to inspect the track

Chris Pusey pictured in action in Australia.

Australia 47 England 61
(Fifth Test)
Australia: P. Crump 17, B. Sanders 11, 0

The Page 3 lead of Speedway Star said it all about the Sydney shambles.

the Australian 'selectors' had relied heavily on local riders throughout the series was significant. Had they gone to the expense of flying all, instead of just a few, of their best riders from place to place, the results would have been closer.

It is also always easier for a touring party, because they have few distractions and tend to concentrate on the job in hand, whereas local riders simply go about their day-to-day lives until 10 minutes before start time. In all honesty, though, this group of Lions were just too good for the opposition.

But, as I have come to discover over the years, Australians are bad winners and even worse losers. The media and the public, maybe even the government, rely, almost entirely it seems, on sporting achievements to give Australia some kind of international and national identity. Be it tiddlywinks, Scrabble, cricket or rugby, losing heavily, especially to the 'Poms', is not acceptable to them.

We heard there was a plan afoot to produce a really deep, heavy track at the infamous Sydney Showgrounds for the fifth Test, along with pretty much a 'full' Australian team. The theory was that the Lions' four valvers wouldn't cope with the heavy conditions. But The Lions were up for it though and a bit of extra dirt wasn't going to stop them.

But odd things happened. As well as adding tons and tons of extra dressing to the track, which didn't alarm us, the Showground centre green automated grass watering system had watered more than just the grass. It had also watered, or rather, soaked, the insides of the four distinct corners of the Showground track.

Then, a water cart had gone around the track, watering the rest of the racing surface, but sinking deep into the soaked and softened corners, leaving deep tyre ruts on each of the critical parts of the racing line. These had been filled in and camouflaged with more loose shale.

The Showground track was never a favourite of solo riders. It was a bad shape, with particularly the third and fourth bends requiring riders to get dangerously close to the fence mid-turn. With a high, solid concrete wall for a 'safety' fence, and the high speeds riders reached around the place, there was potential for really serious injury – even on a good day.

I'll try to keep the events of that evening down to the basic facts.

I doubt the inside of the corners being soaked or the deep ruts were part of the home promoter's cunning plan but, it has to be said, it suited their cause, making the track dangerous beyond reasonable limits.

The attitude of the organisers and local steward when I approached them, after Peter Collins hit a rut and all but fell in heat three, asking for some remedial work to be done on the track, was, shall we say, less than polite. They clearly enjoyed the Lions' discomfort.

Several of the home riders were also apprehensive. But Billy Sanders was always a superb rabble-rouser and their other star, Phil Crump, was as strong as an ox. These two riders pointed out to their team-mates how easy points would be to come by against a detuned opposition.

I was caught between a rock and a hard place. On the one hand, I was responsible for the safety of the riders in my control. But on the other, I was also responsible for ensuring those riders fulfilled their commitments. It didn't help that the attitude and comments on the entire Australian side of the fence were designed to be mischievous.

They challenged us to walk out – and nothing would have given me greater pleasure. There were 30,000 or so people in the stadium and the home promotion deserved all the unrest of an irate crowd should there have been no meeting.

On the other hand, the man in charge, the steward, such as he was, had ruled the track was OK – without even looking at my complaints. But like it or not, he was the man in charge. So in the event of the meeting not going ahead they had a built-in fall guy. Me!

To this day, what happened next still rankles. When bluff failed to bring about any remedial track work, my only avenue was to lean on Chris Pusey, a good and genuine leader despite his scatterbrained image, to help me get the troops up and running. The youngsters were OK but PC and Wyer less so.

Then the worst possible thing happened. Chris, out in the first race after the delay, our most experienced rider, second best in the team and brilliant motorcyclist, got caught in one of those ruts in the first turn and crashed heavily. We all thought, as the ambulance took him away, he had broken his thigh.

Peter Collins and Doug Wyer downed tools in a loud and determined way. The younger lads were uncertain but dominated by their more experienced team-mates. Without 'Puse', I was on my own. And all the time the home promoter, supporters and media were goading us.

After what must have been a full half hour of stalemate, with my begging the lads to at least go through the motions, I reached a breakthrough. Collins told me quietly that he just hated the Showground anyway and was not prepared to ride under any circumstances, although he agreed that if I excused him, he would stop trying to influence the rest of the team.

With him in the background, I was able to get the other five to accept that they would at least go up to the start line. To be honest, I would not have been disappointed had they all decided to make a start and then pull onto the centre green. We would have been fulfilling our contract and, besides, the home promotion deserved nothing better.

One or two took that course whilst some of the others gave it a go. By the time the second half came around, the track had become rideable and the lads actually outscored the opposition. We could even have won the meeting but we ran out of riders, being down to just the five.

Collins watched all of this from the pits. Even had he just ridden in the second half of the match, when the track had become acceptable, we could still have won. But he ignored my pleas.

I had decided I would be on my way back home to England the next morning. There was no point in my staying on as manager if I could not manage. John Davis realised what I planned to do and tried to talk me out of it. When that failed, he then called the other riders together to give me a vote of confidence. Wyer's was clearly with a pinch of salt, as was the vote of Collins. I cannot really recall if I have ever spoken to Wyer since the trip. Anyway, I'm sure neither of us has lost any sleep about that.

For Peter Collins and myself it was the start of a very long history of constant personality clashes, even though, as England manager, I always went out of my way to do my level best for him. Most people love him. I love his riding. As for the rest, I accept that I am in the minority, so no doubt the problem lies with me and not him.

I should add that a week later, on admittedly a much better prepared surface, PC won an international individual meeting at the Sydney Showground – the track he 'hated' – at a canter.

Do you think that tour could have got any worse? The answer is 'yes'. We had moved on to Brisbane when I received a telephone call from the UK. It was my brother-in-law, Ian, to say my mum had been taken into hospital. My mum had been in and out of hospital more times than a consultant surgeon over the previous 20 years, so another visit didn't seem a big deal.

I telephoned the next day. No change. I phoned Ian again the following day, and he was in the process of saying the same "no change" when my sister Pam grabbed the phone from him and said: "GET YOUR ARSE OVER HERE. SHE'S DYING!"

Old mate, Joe Thurley, who was in Australia on a break, agreed to take over the job for the New Zealand leg of the tour, which was all that was left. I jumped straight onto a plane. At a refuelling stop in Perth, I telephoned home. Mum had died. She had been asking for me just beforehand.

Apart from the aggro and heartache on that trip, with the cost of the extra return home for the conference, having to put my hand in my pocket to treat the riders here and there, and to

England recovery ensures 6-1 win

ENGLAND STAGED a great fightback to win the seventh and final Test match in Brisbane last Saturday and so ended the series with a magnificent 6-1 Ashes victory.

England manager John Berry told us from there: "There had been quite a bit of rain in the day and it had left the track quite greasy. Gating was vital otherwise it got filled up on the first turn and for the first half of the meeting it was all a bit processional.

"All the Australian team were mounted on Neil Street four-valve conversions and they were very quick from the gate and by Heat 11 they were six points ahead. But as the track dried out our boys came back into it and were eventually quite comfortable winners.

Doug Wyer, stand-in skipper in the absence of Chris Pusey, did a fine job for the Lions. His victory over Phil Crump in Heat 13 was decisive and in Heat 14 England scored a match-winning 5-0. John Titman fell on the last turn, the referee ordered a rerun and Mike Farrell packed up to leave the English riders on their own.

"From then it was out match," said Mr Berry, "but a switch to new Dunlop tyres after the interval also helped do the trick."

Pusey had a tough practice session on Friday in an effort to take his place in the Test side. "He came through it pretty well," added Mr Berry. "But he decided for the sake of the team that it might be better if he didn't ride."

Malcolm Simmons came in at number one and was down on power on two pointless opening rides. He missed his 10 outing, during which time he change magneto and ran a third in the first race after the interval. Then, using Doug Wyer's abandoned Peter Collins' machines, Simmo came out to score two race wins as England powered to victory.

AUSTRALIA 50, ENGLAND 57
(Seventh Test)

Australia: P. Crump 17, B. Sanders 8, J. Titman 7, P. Herne 7, R. Henderson 6, M. Farrell 4, N. Coddington 1.

England: P. Collins 15, D. Wyer 13, J. Davis 10, M. Simmons 7, D. Morton 7, C. Morton 5, G. Kennett 0.

The Lions are competing in an Inter-Nations Cup in Brisbane this weekend before heading for New Zealand, and a thirty-match Test series.

An easy series win – but it was at a price.

socialise with the locals, I reckon the tour cost me around £3,000-£4,000 in 1976 currency. It was of little consolation to me that the England Lions won the series 6-1.

Ron Bott, as I said at the start, was a real gentleman and bought me, on behalf of the BSPA, a Parker pen for my troubles. That was a hard-earned pen – not just in financial terms but also in blood, sweat and tears.

If at first you succeed...

You would think after that Australian trip, I would have kept well away from anything that started with the word 'honorary', wouldn't you? Some people, though, are just slow, slow learners. What made me do it? Pride? Vanity? Boredom? National pride? (Sheesh!)? Altruism? Conceit? Now we're getting closer!

Maybe it was a desire to do better than Len Silver. Len had blown the England job big time when his untouchables had been embarrassingly beaten by Australia in a World Team Cup qualifier at Ipswich in 1976.

That loss had caused a huge dent in revenue for UK speedway, because there had been no England as home team in the final at White City. I would be a liar if I said I hadn't had a quiet smirk at his discomfort. Well, none of us are perfect! But I was to discover later just how easy it was to lose under the World Team Cup format, especially when you have two strong teams and two makeweights.

The upside to being the national team manager is that you got to do a lot of travelling and heard several national anthems – the British one, more often than not, given that we had such a strong side at the time. I was apparently self-effacing enough to describe my job as having to "carry the race jackets". In honesty, it was nice to be a proud Englishman (sorry to the other Brits) and stand up straight watching the Union Jack being raised.

The downsides were plenty, but not immediately clear. The first of these was that Ipswich moved to second place on my list of priorities. The number of phone calls and the amount of organisation required doing the England job was fearsome. So was the amount of brain and worry power. And whilst these were being devoted to the England cause, they were not being used to look after my own business.

Then, every press man I didn't kow-tow to, every rider I didn't select, every promoter I could not accommodate, every referee I had to take on... all made it that much more difficult for Ipswich.

Likewise, every Ipswich rider had to be twice as good as anyone else to gain an international place in case I was accused of favouritism. Every decision I made was scrutinised intently, particularly by some sections of the media.

It was good to have 'Puse' back when the Lions faced England's 1975 WTC champs at Ray Wilson's Leicester. *(AW)*

Len Silver's England that suffered a shock WTC qualifying defeat at Foxhall in 1976. It spelt the end for Len.

Jack Fearnley manages to gatecrash the biggest moment in Peter Collins' career at Katowice in '76.

The Leyland girls left no room for Jack after victory in the WTC qualifier at Reading in '77. Eyes front, JD! *(AW)*

I found out just how easy it had been to sit on the sidelines hurling criticism (a position I had revelled in myself) compared to being in the centre of things fending it off.

I was left to eat sleep, travel with and act as nursemaid and valet to the riders whilst the Fearmans, Foots and Fearnleys collected the trophies, stayed at the best hotels, were at the banquets doing the 'networking' and keeping their hands nice and clean in all respects.

That famous photo of Jack Fearnley hogging Peter Collins' moment of glory after Peter had won the world crown at Katowice in 1976 is a case in point. Jack had spent the entire weekend being wined and dined, had watched the meeting from the VIP box, and had disappeared again as soon as the photographers had gone. I had spent three days living with the riders and being their gopher.

I will admit that some of the job was indeed fun. I didn't mind the travelling, either in the UK or abroad, and there is a certain satisfaction in seeing things you have put together turn out right. When John Louis was the England skipper I was at my happiest. Not that John and I were that close. Simply that we respected and understood each other, we thought along similar lines.

Those early teams, featuring Louis, Collins, Malcolm Simmons, Terry Betts, Dave Jessup and co. just had to be good. All of these riders were knowledgeable enough and independent enough not to need nursemaiding, either in travelling to tracks or once there. I, literally, was their representative rather than some kind of boss or coach.

I was happy to sort out logistics, to keep riders informed of their situation and maybe to pass on observations I might have noticed during meetings. But it was not for me to tell them how to ride their bikes.

And it wasn't all work. After meetings, particularly abroad, we were able to let our hair down a bit. I got the worst for wear I have ever been in my life after a victory in Poland.

I have to say, I never actually got up to extra-curricular activities myself on any of these trips. But many of the lads did – and good luck to them. I was the team manager, not chaperone or padre.

Then came the 1978 World Team Cup final at Landshut in Bavaria, southern Germany. As usual, we were red-hot

Deep in thought as PC and Simmo prepare for a race against Rest of the World at Ole Olsen's Vojens in '76. *(AW)*

There was nothing for England to smile about once the parade at the '78 WTC final at Landshut ended. *(AW)*

favourites to retain the trophy. The night before the meeting, the teams were invited to a traditional dinner in a beer cellar in town. The local club who were promoting the speedway event had put a great deal of effort into the whole weekend, and the beer cellar evening was a great example. It was not full of stuffy old speeches but a genuinely relaxing evening.

The Czechs and Poles, still under Soviet Communist rule at the time, looked a bit stunned at the informality and as soon as the meal was over, they were led away by their minders, leaving the Brits and the Danes to have a couple of beers and chat up the more than friendly waitresses, all dressed in traditional outfits and clearly revelling in the fun.

Several of the riders, who were not exactly shy, thought their luck was in – until I suddenly twigged what was going on. The 'waitresses' were, in fact, wives of the local club officials, who were also joining in the fun and enjoying the situation!

To the meeting, and the track, although big and wide, was flat and slick, with a surface of what looked like crushed limestone. Clearly, there would be very little passing around the outside. Indeed, it would not be until well into the meeting, if at all, that any other part of the track but the inside yard would get used.

Whilst Len Silver's England graveyard was Ipswich, so my first nightmare was to be there in Landshut in '78. It was one of those meetings where you see it, but you just do not believe it.

First, it has to be said, the four-team format used then in the World Team Cup is a bad one. All riders meet each other once in the 16 heats but in order to achieve that, the gate positions are totally wrong. Admittedly, all teams end up with the same number of each gate position but one team is favoured by enjoying a lot of inside gates early on. The format also gives them outside gates later on, when what little 'dirt' there was has moved out. Another team is penalised by having the reverse draw.

The other huge disadvantage with the four-team format is that if you have two strong teams, and two weak teams, then if one of the two strong teams gets behind, say by a tape exclusion or engine failure, it is very difficult to recover the deficit. That one slip loses three points to the other, strong side and with the other two teams not likely to act as spoilers, it's very difficult to make that ground back up.

I offer those above observations, not as an excuse for why England lost to Denmark that day, although it didn't help. England lost because Ole Olsen had the Danes really up for it, and our riders were of the attitude that they merely needed to turn up to win.

From the practice session, it was clear that the inside line was the only line and that there would be no passing, certainly in the first half of the meeting, anyway. This was even more obvious from heat one onwards, as was the fact that the distance from the outside gate positions of this very wide track to the inside of the first turn was considerably further than from the inside.

I can't remember the details of the first three heats, except to say I think an England rider had either an engine failure or tape exclusion. Gifting points to the third and fourth placed teams meant making up the leeway on the Danes was, from then on, going to be difficult. Just to get back level, you had to win three straight races.

Peter Collins' World Team Cup record was second to none. On the big Polish tracks he had always been an inspiration, able to pull higher gears and ride a wider line than anyone else.

But this was not Poland, and with Peter out in heat four, and the team already under pressure, I begged him to ride a tight line. He did not. He tried to ride the three-quarter track line he would have ridden in Poland – and he was made to look silly. The race formula was such that he was out again in heat five. Again, I begged him to ride the line. Again, he sailed out to three-quarter track. From then on we were playing desperate catch up. And the more the team tried, the harder it got.

We were never able to make up the difference, and the Danes had produced a massive upset win to collect their first-ever World Team Championship. Full marks to them for the way they rode. They did not have a formidable line-up. They had a true world-beater in Olsen but Hans Nielsen was very young at the time, Finn Thomsen was never anything but a makeweight in international terms, whilst Mike Lohmann was just an aggressive trapper who should only have been there to complete the numbers.

On the other hand, we had a team full of solid, tried and tested, international standard riders.

For Ole, it was a brilliant victory, and the first of many which saw Denmark leap onto the international stage and dominate for long periods throughout the 80s. For me, it was a nightmare of the highest proportions.

At that time, the Speedway Writers' and Photographers' Association (SWAPA) had started to run junkets to these events. Most national newspapers sent a reporter and then there were all the lads representing the provincial papers and the speedway trade magazines. There was a busload of UK reporters at Landshut, where, as it happened, SWAPA held its first gathering of journos and snappers.

Now I knew I wasn't the most popular promoter/England manager there had ever been with the press boys. I am not an outgoing person and tended to keep my thoughts and ideas to myself in terms of team planning and the like.

I was always polite(ish!) when dealing with enquiries from the media men but perhaps I rocked back on the defensive a bit too quickly, tending to become aggressive if I thought my riders had been unfairly criticised. I had no reason, though, to think any of these reporters bore any personal grudge.

Was I wrong! This was the chance they had been waiting for. They got to me just outside the riders' changing rooms. Fortunately, I had my back against the wall! When I think back to that moment, there is only one way to describe it. They were a pack of wolves.

I looked from face to face, searching for just the tiniest hint of some kind of sympathy but there was none. All I saw was wide, glaring eyes, snarling teeth and sharpened claws. It was not a pleasant sight. Questions – nay, accusations – were being flung from many different directions all at once.

"Was it true the team had been out drinking till all hours the night before?"

"Was it true that the other teams retired to bed early, but England partied on into the night?"

"Was it true that the riders weren't trying?"

"Was it true that I had totally underestimated the opposition?"

"Did I feel I should resign?"

"Had the riders and I let England down?"

This went on for what seemed like forever. There was not one friendly face, nor even an understanding or sympathetic nod. Many of these people had been in speedway far longer than me. They had just seen what had happened. We had been beaten by circumstances, a better-prepared team on the day, and yes, a large dose of complacency, which was why I had to go. I didn't need to be told.

You would think that kick in the slabs would have taught me a lesson. Some people, though, just never learn.

By the way, you might think these comments are the overreaction of a frustrated and bitter beaten manager. But such respected speedway scribes as the late Graham Baker, of the *Daily Mirror*, and also Andrew Edwards, of *Motor Cycle News*, subsequently went into print confirming they felt I was badly treated by the UK pressmen that night.

I handed in my resignation. Not because of the press boys' reaction, but because I felt the

England effort had not been good enough.

Here's the sad part. It wasn't accepted! The person who was first to my defence was . . . Len Silver.

On a brighter note, I made some good friends at Landshut on that trip. Twice I was invited to take the Ipswich team there for challenge matches over the next couple of years. The AC Landshut club and their organisers were, and no doubt still are, a great bunch of speedway enthusiasts and people.

Surreal saga

The record books tell me England managed to lose what was termed the Overseas Final of the World Team Cup at Reading the following year, 1979. I recall a diabolically wet, Sunday afternoon, where the meeting should not have started, and everyone expected it to be called off at any second during the whole sad saga.

It was surreal. The riders from all teams were more concerned with staying upright rather than racing, and it was one of those meetings where team managers were too busy sorting out minor crises and battling with the referee rather than plotting a result.

It was almost as an afterthought the scores were tallied up at the end. Was it England? Australia? USA?

Abracadabra! Out from the hat popped the rabbit, in the shape of . . . New Zealand. Worse, USA was second, with those two teams qualifying to the next round.

For the sake of losing a bit of money restaging the Reading round, when England would have been walk-up favourites, the 'powers that be' preferred to run the meeting as a lottery, and once again England failed to have a team in the final at White City.

I felt no guilt at this result. It was a fluke, and the fact that New Zealand then went on to win the final didn't make that Reading meeting anything less of a joke. I had made all the correct selections, carrying out my part of the deal properly. It was difficult to even point the finger at the England riders. With all due respect to Ivan and his motivational skills in the Kiwi camp, the conditions were solely responsible for this farce of a meeting and nonsense of a result.

The World Pairs final that year was not a lottery. It was a robbery. Michael Lee and Malcolm Simmons were the England pair. The meeting was at Olsen's track, Vojens, in Denmark. As I recall, it was another one of those wet weekends we had come to expect there. If I am right, the original staging was rained off. On the first attempt at putting the event on, Ole was strutting around in full race gear, organising all kinds of work on the track, in the rain.

Everyone in the place knew it wasn't on, but Ole was just like another Dane before him, King Canute. Nothing would persuade him to call it off. A very young Hans Nielsen was his partner. Every other rider there, including Hans, quite rightly refused to get changed. Despite an impassioned speech by Ole, backed up by the DMU officials and the referee, this was a non-meeting. Poor Hans was put through the wringer by Ole and the DMU. I think it was the beginning of the Olsen/Nielsen feud.

Anyway, when the meeting finally went ahead the next day, Simmons was not at his best. He struggled but put in a hard, professional effort in support of Lee. In fact, Simmo and Michael defeated Olsen to record a 4-2 in what was, on paper, our toughest race.

Olsen did well, as did Nielsen, and the local favourites were in the box seat. With Steve Gresham absent, Bruce Penhall was the only US representative and put on a really classy show. I'm sure that had he been supported with a partner, he would have been scored more than he did. But with no incentive, he didn't push himself much as the meeting progressed.

Through hard graft, we kept ourselves in with a shout, but come the last race, heat 21, the Danes needed a 5-1 against the Poles to pip England by a point. Olsen got away but Eddie Jancarz was not going to make it easy for Hans. I could see a tight finish coming, so, being on the centre green, I positioned myself level with the start/finish line.

Sure enough, Eddie slipped alongside Hans on the run in to the flag, heading him by certainly a full wheel on the line.

I filled in my programme and rushed to the pits in order to sort out the race-off for the title. It was some little time before I realised the result had been announced as Eddie coming third. Tore Kittilsen was the referee. Kittilsen's claim to fame was that he was Norwegian! As such, he was almost always considered a 'neutral' referee and seemed to be allocated all the top events.

I don't expect it hurt his career that he was always very keen not to rock the boat, and he had an even longer term career as a high ranking FIM official set firmly in his sights. I cannot ever remember Kittilsen making a hard decision. In fact, I have a job to recall any decision at all he ever made that was other than the easiest.

When I gently pointed out to him that Eddie had finished half a bike in front of Hans, he told me that he had left the decision as to the way the riders crossed the line to the timekeeper – the DANISH timekeeper. The Danish timekeeper, who knew a second place for Nielsen would hand the title to Denmark for the first time in their history.

There was a TV monitor in the referee's box. I begged Kittilsen to check the finish himself on the replay. He told me he was not allowed. Olsen was already a powerful figure in FIM circles and I am sure this was not lost on the referee.

The UK press corps always camped on the fourth bend near the pits at Vojens. They were clearly not in a good position to make up their minds about the finishing order of that race. I was in the best position in the stadium – but they dismissed my protestations as the sour grapes of an even sourer manager.

I should tell you that Bob Radford, well-respected announcer and journalist, was in the ref's box that night working as the English language announcer. He confirms that between them, the timekeeper and the referee got the finishing order wrong.

I would like to say the Danish timekeeper simply made a mistake. I'd like to, but I can't.

The official results have it as Denmark, England and Poland. It might well have finished that way had Olsen beaten Lee in the run off for the championship there should have been. But I can tell you now, we was robbed.

I wonder what was going through Nielsen's brain at the time? He would have known a mistake had been made. Not that I hold it against Hans in any way. It wasn't his decision to make, and I have yet to find a rider who would have admitted a mistake having been made in his favour.

This had not been a happy year for me, not in my private domestic life, my business at Ipswich, nor my England duties. It was a year I should really have spent in bed.

I recall the 1979 season finishing on yet another sour note. There was an England/Australia 'Test' series. Australia, at that time, couldn't really put together a seven-man team to compete with the best side England could put out, so under 'suggestions' from the management committee, I selected a mix of top boys and up and comers, so as to keep the series interesting.

Now I would be lying if I said I remembered all of the details, but such a policy puts one on a hiding to nothing. You end up pleasing nobody, which is pretty well what happened. I finally decided I was fed up with being everybody's Aunt Sally and took my bat and ball home.

Technically, because it was the end of the season, I didn't resign. I just did not nominate for the position the following year. Not surprisingly, given the previous season, there was not a queue of promoters pushing me forward anyway.

Ian Thomas changed the ground rules for the job when he took over in 1980. First of all, he had an assistant. In theory, Eric Boocock and Ian Thomas were joint managers. In practice, I have no doubt that one was the back-room legman and the other the front-office smoothie. You don't need to be a genius to work out which way round they were.

They demanded that they be given total control over all decisions. In truth, although I had been answerable to the management committee, in

England's 1980 World Cup winners – Dave Jessup, John Davis, Peter Collins, Michael Lee and Chris Morton. *(AW)*

practice, I had also been able to do more or less what I wished anyway.

A bit like the rest of the BSPA (and most other similarly run associations), I expected the support of the other management committee members for any decisions I made. Had they attempted to overrule me, I would have been on my bike pretty quick, so Thomas' 'condition for accepting the job' was so much self-promotion really.

I have to (grudgingly) admit, Thomas and Boocock did a really good job. They made a good team, and were able to 'work' the media far better than I had with my over-abrasive approach. It would be churlish of me to criticise them in any way and they came away at the end of the year with England holding all three World Championship trophies – team, pairs and, thanks to Michael Lee, the individual crown, too.

They couldn't better that, so Ian had the sense to get out whilst in front. Maybe he was just smart enough to realise also, glory doesn't pay the rent. Good luck to him. A sensible career move.

A couple of years later, and once again the BSPA were searching for a manager. Boocock was again showing interest, but clearly lacked the necessary organisational skills to cope on his own – and 'had no money in the sport'.

I was approached to help out again. Somebody suggested what a good idea it would be to have Eric and myself together. North and South covered, racing and mechanical experience covered on the one hand; promotorial and administrative on the other. The Dream Team.

Except for one minor problem. Eric and I did not hit it off together. Perhaps it was the old North/South thing again, or was it that I was more of a control freak than the far more down to earth Yorkshireman? Maybe Booey resented my air of superiority and I had difficulty with his 'man of the people' blue-collar approach. Whatever it was, I suspect we both knew it was not going to work.

We were always terribly polite to each other. In fact, neither was prepared to fart without the other's permission, but it was no way to work together. One of us had to go – and I decided it would be me. I had been there, done that and didn't really need the aggro any more.

I needed to be spending more time at Ipswich. I wished Eric well, sincerely. I was now too experienced and grown up to hold any grudges. Maybe I was a bit disappointed that my relationship with Peter Collins had never really got off the ground, but that was it.

I'm a bit hazy as to what went on after that but suddenly, for 1985, I found myself with the baton yet again. I really cannot say I wanted it this time. I was three quarters of the way through passing Ipswich Speedway over to Chris Shears and the man I had appointed to succeed me at Foxhall, John Louis.

The lads I had grown up with in speedway had gone. In Kenny Carter, England now had only the one genuine international star. After that, it thinned out very quickly. Chris Morton was very experienced and John Davis was still trying his best. Then there were several good club men like Simon Cross and Phil Collins at Cradley, maybe Neil Collins and Neil Evitts, the Grahame boys, Andy Smith... and no doubt countless others who don't come readily to mind. But there was no depth of true and experienced talent.

The time to rebuild had come and gone and England was no longer a serious international force. It was time to accept the situation and start again with youngsters. To their credit, the BSPA members also knew the score and it was on this basis, and being aware that I was on a hiding to nothing, I took the task on when nobody else would.

Sadly, the private war between the Belle Vue boys and Halifax No.1 Kenny Carter was also harming the England team's unity. The Danes were now clearly ruling the roost, and the Americans were still a very strong outfit, so silverware was likely to be in short supply. It was to be a year for British speedway to go back to the drawing board and the majority of the promoters recognised this.

Peter Collins and Chris Morton were the holders of the World Pairs title. However, PC had never fully recovered from an injured shoulder, and had also changed his equipment because he had been offered a works sponsorship from Jawa, even though, by then the Czech motor was not the engine of majority choice.

The new bikes didn't suit him and, along with the shoulder injury, this had caused his form to collapse. He was having difficulty just holding down a heat leader spot, even allowing for the fact that half his matches were at his beloved Belle Vue. But the speedway press, as always, sympathetic to the Collins cause, were pushing for the pair to have a chance to defend 'their' title.

What the press did not know was that Collins had telephoned me at the start of the season to say he did not want to be considered for any representative duties. Most riders lost money when representing their country, and it was fair to say Peter had done his bit in flying the flag.

I respected his request – and the fact that he had asked me not to broadcast it. It fitted into my own team rebuilding plans anyway. Peter had told me he was prepared to make an exception regarding the Pairs final, but this just would not have been fair to everyone else, even if his form had warranted it.

It would have been the easiest thing in the world for Peter to have let it be known in the press that he didn't think his form was up to it, or whatever, but he didn't. Instead, he made it clear he wanted to go to Poland for the Pairs final. He

Kenny Carter always wore the England racejacket with pride. *(KC)*

was being unfair and unreasonable in my opinion.

Going on British League form, the obvious pairing to take was Carter and Morton. By that time they simply hated each other, though. Some pairing that would have been. Perhaps I should have just selected the pair of them, banged their heads together and told them to get on with it.

That would have been the easy option but I did think England had a chance to win the event. It is my opinion that at the very highest level you can't give the other riders a head start at the gate, as Chris had a habit of doing. It is one thing if you have your mate, PC, making space for you in the first turn, but would Carter be prepared to do the same for Mort?

I decided it was not a risk worth taking, because out of the blue had appeared Kelvin Tatum at Wimbledon. Kelvin was wet behind the ears but one thing he could do well was hop out of the start. It was a long shot asking him to take on, in particular, the Danes, but it was the only chance we had to win something that year.

The selection also fitted in with my rebuilding brief. I spoke to Chris on the telephone, explaining my thinking and decision in detail. He didn't say much to me – but he had plenty to say to the press.

I can remember that Pairs final at Rybnik in every detail. Before the meeting it rained and it rained. The track was so bad nobody would have considered starting had it been just another match. World finals involve so much organising though, if it is humanly possible, the meeting goes on.

It did stop raining, but not before the track had become a quagmire. Trying to just walk on it meant leaving two inch deep footprints and having the equivalent of diver's boots attached to your feet after just a couple of steps.

The seven-team, 21-heat, pairs format is a beautiful one. Every pair meets all the others once, and each pairing has gates one and three, three times, and two and four, three times.

Normal procedure in these events is for the riders in a pairing to alternate their choice between the available gate positions – but Kenny was in for a shock. I pulled him to one side

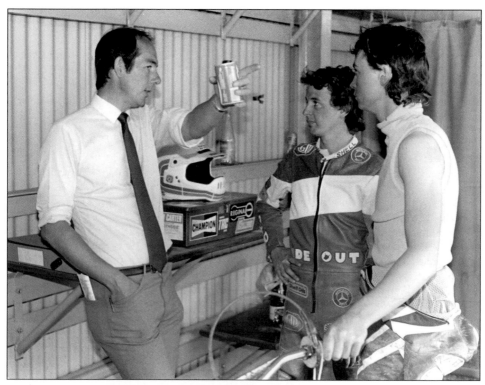

Planning our World Pairs strategy with Kenny Carter and Kelvin Tatum in 1985. *(RA)*

and explained to him that the only chance we had of winning the event was if the fast-starting but inexperienced Tatum took all six inside gate positions, leaving Kenny to make the best of the outside slots.

Kenny gave me a very old fashioned look. You could hear his mind whirring. It was a big ask in those conditions. Then he shrugged his shoulders and got on with it. I always found him easy to handle and never had one moment's problem with him.

I love pairs events, always have. They are the purest form of the sport. The format is fair, the requirement for the riders to help each other out is always prominent and with six rides each there is the opportunity for them to strut their stuff.

These two kids were up against it. Terrible track conditions and a really classy international field including Shawn Moran and Bobby Schwartz; Ivan Mauger and Mitch Shirra; Jan Andersson and Per Jonsson; Phil Crump and Steve Regeling; and the outstanding pairing of Erik Gundersen and Tommy Knudsen. The only possibly weak pairing in the field was that of the home nation, who did at least have local knowledge and support on their side.

Given the amount of bad comment I had suffered at the hands of the speedway press and others, and given that even I realised I had stuck my neck out by putting in Tatum, I was as pumped up for this meeting as I had ever been for any. Never mind the two riders, *I* had a point to prove!

It went like a dream even though the track was dreadful. There was no question of grading it. A tractor would just have bogged down. As the meeting went on, the sticky, grey bog that the track surface had become was thrown out by the back wheels of the bikes, leaving a racing line about 15 feet wide. Kelvin was gating like a train, whilst Kenny's first turn work was just out of this world. They were never headed after the first turn in their first three rides.

Neither, though, were the Danes. Managed by Ole Olsen, they also had their own point to prove. Hans Nielsen had been overlooked for selection when clearly he was the man who, on form, should have partnered Gundersen. But there was a well-publicised rift between Olsen and Nielsen, so the Danes were also under media scrutiny.

The crunch heat was just after the interval. We had gates one and three, which was a slight advantage. As I watched on the centre, the tapes went up and Kelvin flew from them with

Kenny on his shoulder. Kenny waited long enough to make sure Erik could not double back under from gate four, and then put his back wheel on the edge of the morass that was effectively the outside of the racetrack.

We had done it! Knudsen had a look to come back under Kelvin as they emerged from the turn. Talking to Kenny after, he said he saw Knudsen making his move and, content in his mind that Erik had been hung up, leaned back on Kelvin to push him tighter onto the line.

What Kenny, nor me or anyone else in the stadium had taken into account was Erik's bravery, desperation and pure riding ability. Up until that time, I admit I was one of those who thought Erik was 'just a gater'. But at that very moment he won me over forever.

He should have been in a fearful muddle but he held his throttle wide, hung on and ploughed fully 12 feet wider into the heavy wet clag than anyone had been or would go for the rest of that night. You had to be close up to the track and see its condition to fully appreciate what he did.

Had Kenny stayed out wide, he would still have blocked Erik's run, but he wasn't even looking because Gundersen had no right to be there. Whilst Kenny, Kelvin and Tommy were having their own little sort out, Erik bolted right around them and was gone. Kenny was caught in no man's land. Did he try to help Kelvin or go after Erik? He tried to go after Erik, leaving Tommy to slip past the unprotected Kelvin.

It was not the best race I have ever witnessed, but it was the best single move I have ever seen a rider carry off, simply because it contained every ingredient. It was a desperate situation in a critical heat in a World Final. It was bravery beyond compare, and its execution required the maximum degree of skill.

I was less generous at the time, though. I was so worked up that I ranted uncontrolled at my pair. They had the win in the palms of their hands and, as I told them, had given it away. It wasn't true. It had been snatched from them by a bit of genius, and that is not a word I use often.

There was still the possibility the Danes might slip up, so the England pair soldiered on and finished the meeting without dropping another point. Sadly for us, so did the Danes, who had pipped us by the smallest possible margin.

At the time, I was devastated and my humour was not improved when the first question I was asked at the post-meeting press conference was if I thought I had made a mistake with my selections, and that Collins and Morton would have done better.

The speedway press, I don't think, quite reported it so crudely in the UK, but certainly the English pair on that night were not given anywhere near the amount of praise they deserved.

As I say, at the time, and for a good while after, I allowed my disappointment to dominate. But now I can look back and enjoy in my mind, the great efforts made by the young English pair against top opposition in diabolical conditions. And then admire the sheer brilliance of Erik Gundersen's riding on the day.

This really was a madcap year on the international calendar. The individual World final was to be at Bradford, and Kenny virtually had his name on the trophy. The disappointment of the previous year at the LA Coliseum in California was gone, along with Penhall, his nemesis, and the way was clear for the local hero.

But fate was always dealing Kenny bad blows. On the way home from the Pairs final, his van crashed, his mechanics inside were injured, and the van and gear totally destroyed. Kelvin's as well. To compound a very bad

Erik Gundersen and Kelvin Tatum battling on a dry track. *(JHa)*

Phil Collins, Chris Morton and Kenny Carter. Pity Kenny didn't insure his van for our trip to Poland. *(KC)*

situation, Kenny hadn't bothered to organise the van's overseas insurance cover.

Just seven days later, the World Team Cup squad had a qualifier in Vojens. The FIM were in full madness mode by then, with the WTC consisting of, for England, the Overseas Final at Bradford, where the top two teams from England (42), Australia (21), New Zealand (17) and Finland (16) moved on to Vojens for the Inter-continental final, simply to drop one team from Denmark (37, straight to final), England (27), Sweden (19) and Australia (13, and eliminated).

Then yet another round (no wonder PC didn't want to bother!), in Germany, called the Continental final, where the top two from Sweden (40), England (31), Czechoslovakia (17) and Poland (7) joined the USA (seeded) and Denmark for the final in Long Beach.

Now I made a blunder here. Not that I thought so at the time. At the start of the year, both Kenny and Mort were both desperately keen to be the England skipper. Whichever rider I chose, given their attitude to each other, the other would take as a slap in the face, so I had chosen to select neither. Both had genuine credentials but these qualities were entirely different.

In the event, given that Chris had been overlooked for the Pairs, and because he was the most experienced rider and the best ambassador, I should have appointed him skipper for the World Team Cup. Kenny would have accepted the role of top star and kingpin (I think!), whilst Chris was really the best choice overall as skipper.

Perhaps there was just too much buzzing around in my brain to think clearly. More likely, I was still uptight about the way the press were handling things.

If failing to make Chris skipper was an error, I compounded it in Germany for the Continental final of the WTC. The riders had made their way overland, whereas I had to be in Ipswich for a Thursday meeting, so flew over on the Friday. I found the hotel the team had been booked into but there were no riders there, and no message. A couple of hours of hunting down later, I

Jeremy Doncaster takes off as Simon Wigg steers clear of trouble around the inside against Denmark pair Bo Petersen and Preben Eriksen in our 58-50 second Test win at Oxford in '85. Alas, the Danes won at Coventry and Cradley. *(JH)*

found Chris Morton had decided he knew a better hotel in the area, so had taken the team there

It was a better hotel, I do not argue, but after having spent the last two hours chasing my tail, I had a go at Chris in front of the others for changing my arrangements without asking me. It was wrong of me. Even if my annoyance was justified, I should have spoken to Mort on his own, and not shown him up in front of the others.

Chris Morton shows his leadership qualities with advice for Phil Collins. I made a mistake in not making Mort captain. *(JH)*

He did his bit for the team at the speedway meeting, but then let it be known he was making himself unavailable for England in future - whilst I was around, anyway. I knew he would not have long to wait!

At the time I was nonplussed, but far from prepared to back down. Youth and pride have a habit of going together, and we were none of us that old, although when I look back, I was 40 by then and should have known better.

So now add Mort to the list of missing English riders. In the previous few years England had lost Peter Collins, John Louis, Malcolm Simmons, Michael Lee, Dave Jessup, Simon Wigg (suspended), Gordon Kennett and more. Not a bad array of talent.

Never mind, we had Kenny Carter, Kelvin Tatum, Phil Collins, Jeremy Doncaster and the now vastly experienced, but perennial bridesmaid (in speedway terms) John Davis.

But there was more fun to come.

I did say this was a mad, mad season for FIM events, and the Inter-continental final of the individual World Championship was scheduled for Vetlanda, in one of the most remote places in Sweden, just seven days before the World Team Cup final in the USA.

Kenny's luck continued to go from worse to diabolical. Through no fault of his own, he finished with a broken leg during the rain-affected Inter-continental final of the individual event in Sweden.

By the time I had sorted him out and got myself back to England, it was effectively Tuesday. The party travelling to California for the WTC final had been pre-booked on a special deal for a Wednesday night or Thursday morning flight, I can't remember which. There were no such things as mobile phones then, remember, and it wasn't until the Tuesday that I effectively got my hands onto a phone.

Not only had we lost our only true world-beater, but finding a replacement – any replacement – at that notice was going to be desperately difficult. I ate humble pie and spoke to Chris Morton. He wasn't budging. I tried Andy Smith. Bless him, he tried and tried to get himself organised but just didn't have the time he needed.

I tried Dave Jessup, who was then happily taking sweets off kids at National League Mildenhall. He was very sympathetic but explained his equipment was now second division standard, and not up to international requirements. DJ felt he did not wish to show himself or England up. The time I had given Andy Smith to try and sort himself out was now time I didn't have to spare, so in desperation I asked Ipswich rider, Richard Knight, to fill the gap.

It wasn't that silly, given the circumstances. He could hop out of the gate when he put his mind to it, was quite happy on big tracks, had more than useful equipment and was a super bloke who I could rely on to give his all. If only he could hop out of the box and have a good first ride . . .

I had previously spoken to John Davis, explaining that with Doncaster, Tatum and Phil Collins in the team, we had very little experience, so I was putting John at reserve. That way I could utilise him to plug gaps. This wasn't just a line. I meant it, and considered John sensible enough to understand.

Danes Preben Eriksen, Tommy Knudsen, Hans Nielsen and Bo Petersen walk the Long Beach track before the '85 World Team Cup final. *(SD)*

All aboard for the trip to Hell and back . . .

Almost as soon as I took on the role of England manager that year, I had made enquiries of people, ending with the FIM (through the proper channels) about the financial and travel arrangements for this event.

You see, whilst there was a laid down scale of prize money, and travel and subsistence monies for these FIM events when they were held in Europe, it did not apply to transatlantic meetings. True, taken literally, we could have requested travel payment at the going rate per kilometre but that was hardly practical.

The answer I received was that the various teams should make arrangements direct with the organisers. So I contacted the Long Beach promoter, Harry Oxley. Harry was a gentleman. We had been dealing with each other for years and had a good respect and understanding for each other. As I expected, we were soon able to arrive at a suitable deal.

This was all done and finished and confirmed in writing by May for an August meeting. I don't know what arrangements the other teams made. That was between them and Oxley. Even allowing for the deal I had done with Harry, the BSPA would be subsidising the trip by over £2,000.

I have been to places where we have been made really welcome. I have been to places where the welcome has not been so warm, but Long Beach was the first time I have been to an event where the atmosphere from start to finish was pure hostility.

I see it all the time on the TV these days. Any sporting trip to the States seems to become a war, as the Americans appear to go to any lengths to detune the visitors. But I hadn't expected it at Long Beach in 1985.

I hadn't expected the aggressive and officious 'security men' who dictated our every move within the stadium. I hadn't expected the way we were given no assistance whatsoever, that our 'pits' area was to be a tiny, dusty open corner reachable by the public, whilst the American team got star treatment.

I had not expected the bitchiness and all the attempts to make our practice session so disrupted and stop-watch timed as to make it just about useless. And I hadn't expected the American riders, all so amenable and good natured in the UK, to be so rude and provocative.

Worse, I had not expected Bruce Penhall, USA team manager, to be as petty and small-minded as he was. The little, childish pranks, such as locking the door from the changing rooms to the pits area, thereby forcing us to have to walk the entire length of the straight and back to get the few paces it should have been from changing room to pits. This kind of thing went on the whole time.

The young Swedish team knew they were only there to look, learn and make up the numbers, but the English riders clearly allowed this treatment from the host nation to get to them. The Danes, however, just became more and more determined at every new needle that was thrown at them. How I admired Olsen and his tight knit group on that trip.

With such a makeshift team, our only hope was to try to get something going early on in the meeting. We needed a flying start, something to get the lads' tails up and give me something on which to build confidence.

Phil Collins was in the first heat off gate four. He steamed out and was gone. Nobody was going to catch him. Once Phil got in front, he was virtually unbeatable. Except that somebody behind him fell. Can't remember who it was. The race was stopped.

I was on the centre, by the starting gates, for the restart. The rider in gate three tried to jump the start and shoved the tapes. Phil, on seeing the tapes move, dropped his clutch, but the tapes had stuck on the other rider's front wheel, so Phil went through them. By 1985, tape-touching, even in FIM events, meant exclusion with no replacement allowed, so I was quite happy. That was until I had got back to the pits, when I found it was Phil who had been excluded.

I had to fight to get use of a phone and when I did, Gunther Sorber, the German referee, said that from what he could see, Phil had gone through the tapes. I asked him about the rider on three who had pushed them. Gunther told me he could not see that. Not that he hadn't seen that, but that he couldn't see that.

I looked down the track from the pits, which were on the first turn. The solid wall between the track and the grandstand was about seven feet high! I looked up at the referee's box, which was at the back of the very gently banked stand.

From where he was seated, I doubt the referee could see any of the outside rider at all, and possibly only the helmet of the rider in gate three. I told Gunther I could see what he could not, and that he had made a wrong decision. He told me that if he had, then he would apologise after the meeting.

He did apologise to me the next day, when he had see a video, but, of course, by then it was too late.

From a likely win in heat one, we had slumped to no points at all, which had a desperate effect on team morale. One by one, Jeremy, Kelvin and Richard made their starts but were way out of their depth. Time to stick in super sub, John Davis. John made a really good start but just went back and back, finishing a poor last. At least he had made the gate, so I put him out again.

Again, he made the gate and again finished a bad last. He came up to me and asked not to be called upon a third time because his motor was no good. Then he said he had known it was no good in the practice. We had lugged two spare engines over there with us, and I asked him why the hell he hadn't changed his for one of them. His answer was that, as he was only down as reserve, he didn't think it was worth it!

Poor Phil never recovered from the disappointment of that first heat, whilst Kelvin and Richard struggled all night. Jeremy finally got angry and scored a few points, which is just as well, because otherwise we would have lost out to a desperately raw Swedish side who really were only there for the experience, and finished stone motherless last.

Towards the end of the meeting Kelvin managed to beat an American, Sam Ermolenko, which coincidentally got the Danes over the line in the end.

With a long history of intense rivalry between the Danes and ourselves, it was weird being delighted they had won. But they really deserved it, battling against all the odds. I have seen it written that they regard it as their best ever win. I wouldn't dispute that for one minute.

There was more to come. The morning after the event, co-promoter Barry Briggs came to the motel room I was sharing with Colin Pratt (oh yes, a seedy motel in a not so plush area and booked by the home promotion, of course). He said he wanted to settle up the finances for the team.

I got out my copy of the agreement with Oxley. Briggs laughed, swore a lot, told me the team was getting what he thought he would pay, which was just an insulting pittance, and when I refused to accept it, he just threw the dollar bills onto the bed and walked out with more obscenities. Prattie just stood there dumbstruck. Having had dealings with Briggs before, I was not that

Colin Pratt looks as if he could be explaining to Bruce Penhall what he thought of the American behaviour the visiting teams had to cope with. *(JB)*

surprised.

I raised Harry Oxley on the phone. He was most apologetic, but said Briggs had been delegated to look after the financial side of things and he didn't feel he could intervene.

It was not my money nor was it my fight. I was merely the UK rep. I gave the BSPA and SCB a full report, along with all the costings and my recommendations as to how to go about retrieving the shortfall via the FIM. Of course, the BSPA, as far as I know, did nothing, and Briggs got away with it.

Briggs and my paths crossed again soon afterwards. I was at Bradford for the World Final there, looking after the England riders in the pits. Kelvin Tatum had been doing quite well on the day but was out off the hopeless gate four against clear meeting favourite Hans Nielsen.

Nielsen never took prisoners in the first turn, so I was advising Kelvin that if he failed to beat Hans out of the gate, he must not allow himself to be outside the Dane in the first turn, because Hans would be ruthless and run him so wide, he would be effectively out of the race. I suggested to him that if he didn't gate clear, he should make an early decision to double back under and hopefully be able to nip past Hans on the inside of the turn.

Now Kelvin is no mug, and although still on the up at that stage, I didn't think the advice I gave him was beyond his comprehension. But Briggs, who had been lurking and listening, immediately rounded on me, pushed me out of the way and with an intensity that was almost physical, demanded that Kelvin forget everything I had said, and go concentrate on just one thing.

This one thing was to get to the turn in front of Hans. Kelvin's eyes got even bigger than usual, and he wandered out onto the track, Dalek style, almost saying "exterminate, exterminate", whilst Briggs continued to give me a mouthful about putting negative thoughts into riders' minds.

For the record, as I recall, I think it was the guy off three who did the damage to Kelvin in the first turn. He was never, even if he had afterburners attached, going to be the first away from that diabolical gate four.

I have Briggs down as a brash overbearing bully. And he no doubt has me down as a negative wimp.

My love affair, not just with the England job, but with speedway generally and all the backbiting and politics, was fading fast.

As I read through the above it leaves an impression that doing the England job was just one long, grinding, grumpy hassle. That wasn't the case at all, and most of the job, though time consuming, was really enjoyable.

Looking back, there is little doubt that I took everything too seriously and too personally, and that I expected too much of myself and others. But even allowing for my over-abrasive nature and manic desire for England to be the best at everything, we had plenty of laughs and I would like to think I made more friends than enemies.

Some of the antics of the riders and teams I dare not go into detail about, but in general they were harmless and simply due to high spirits and youthful enthusiasm. And in many cases, an over-supply of testosterone.

My relationship with the speedway press wasn't really all that bad either in general terms. Speedway tended to be a bit of a happy family, where more often than not, press, riders and often supporters shared the same travel arrangements and all swapped stories on long, boring trips or in hotel lounges.

Dave Lanning, I recall, was always a brilliant raconteur. Given the limelight, he could have a group entranced with so many stories of ITV's *World of Sport* team on their many travels. Gary Newbon was also very good – his description of his encounter with the alcoholic genius, Tommy Cooper ,will never be forgotten.

I was never one for being up the front leading the charge. My forte was in planning the battle, not leading the troops over the top, and as such, I spent most of these trips enjoying the exploits and company of more outgoing people rather than supplying much of the action myself.

We skipped the light fandango
Turned cartwheels cross the floor.
I was feeling kind of sea sick,
The crowd called out for more.
The room was humming harder
As the ceiling flew away.
When we called out for another drink
The waiter brought a tray.

And so it was that later
As the miller told his tale
That her face at first just ghostly
Turned a whiter shade of pale.

It was something of a standing joke that I was a bit starchy, although, as I mentioned earlier, I caught myself out once. At one of the regular and boring Polish after-meeting banquets (all beetroot and speeches), I found myself sitting next to a friend and travelling companion of Norwegian referee Tore Kittilsen. Sven was this man's name. Eight feet high, four feet wide he was, and had a big, black bushy beard. He just had to have been a lumberjack!

Whilst waiting for the interminable and diabolical speeches to be translated from Polish to French (the official language of the FIM) and English, and then back again, we two amused ourselves with inter-toast vodka tastings. The waiters were always on hand to top up glasses, and so a little three-way contest developed between Sven, myself and the waiters, to see how quickly we could empty our glasses – and how quickly the waiters could refill them.

Pretty soon, the shot glasses were pushed to one side, and the soft drink tumblers brought into play instead! I seem to recall they were half-filled with the Polish fire water and downed several times, but by then things were getting hazy. Indeed, I vaguely recall making something of an impromptu speech myself, clearly indicating that Dutch courage (or Polish vodka) had kicked in.

It had become a matter of national honour that I could keep up with Sven, but I have to say I was not too disappointed when the banquet ended. The next thing I remember was being back at our hotel.

There was a nightclub in the basement, so we wandered down there to have a 'nightcap' in the form of Russian champagne – very cheap and very good. Sven ordered a couple of bottles. I got halfway through my second glass before I finally admitted to myself that I was way out of my depth.

I excused myself 'for a pee' and decided a long walk was in order. By this time there was no feeling of connection between head and legs, although asking the legs to move seemed to work, up to a point.

I knew now I was in real trouble. I was fairly OK whilst I kept moving, but I knew that even stopping and sitting were out of the question. Lying down was a complete no-no. I reckon I walked around for an hour or so. I even traversed the nightclub again, to find Sven entertaining a couple of young ladies of the night, the table strewn with dead champagne bottles.

I realised there was to be only one ending, and resigned myself to it. I found my way to my room and carefully lowered myself onto the bed. I don't think I actually got into a supine position. The walls and ceiling turned into a mad kaleidoscope and that old, familiar feeling started around the back of the throat and in the cheeks.

I made it to the bathroom but not to the porcelain privy. The first, and only, time I have ever been caught short. After due time making Clinton-style love to the throne, I dragged myself back to the bed and passed out.

Next thing I knew, there was a hammering on the door. It was John Bloomfield, John Louis' mechanic. It was 5.30 am, and the coach to the airport to catch our charter flight was due to leave at six.

John packed my gear whilst I lay by the side of the bath with cold water from the hand shower playing on my head. Standing was a problem. I was OK bent over, but I couldn't straighten. John got me downstairs. Now don't laugh, but I was in charge of the whole chartered planeload of riders, mechanics and pressmen! I stood by the coach steps trying to count them as they climbed on board. That is difficult when all you can see are feet!

I had a sip of water at the airport. That lasted no more than 10 seconds before making the reverse trip. I was collected at Gatwick and lay on the back seat of the car for the journey to Ipswich. I begged Mick, the driver, and Ron Bagley, not to stop on the way, but they left me on the back seat covered with coats whilst they went and had breakfast, offering to bring me back a bacon sandwich. On arrival at my house, they opened the front door for me and I crawled, still bent double, up the stairs and onto my bed. I didn't come down for two days.

I understand that these days the position of England (or GB) team manager has changed from being honorary to being a paid position. That's interesting, given the parlous position British speedway is in these days compared to how it was then. Still, good luck to those who take it on.

The matter of money was never a consideration when I did the job. Perhaps it should have been. But if anything suffered during my spells as England boss, it was Ipswich rather than England, although I suspect some might well wish to dispute that.

I consider myself lucky to have had an opportunity to hold the position and it gave me many more memories to lock away. I find it strange when people say of the past that they wouldn't change a thing. There would be plenty I would change if I could have my time back. At the end of the day it was a labour of love, and I am proud to have done it.

I suppose also, to have been asked to take it on three different times would indicate I must have got some parts of the job right, even though the speedway media of the time would have you believe otherwise.

11 Love is All Around

I feel it in my fingers
I feel it in my toes
The love that's all around me
And so the feeling grows
It's written on the wind
It's everywhere I go
So if you really love me
Come on and let it show
You know I love you, I always will
My mind's made up by the way that I feel
There's no beginning, there'll be no end
'Cause on my love you can depend
I see your face before me
As I lay on my bed
I cannot get to thinking
Of all the things you said

I mentioned in the previous chapter that my relationship with the press was not all it might have been. Maybe we ought to look at that side of things a bit closer.

When I first started promoting, there were three levels of press coverage. These were the local press, the national press and the weekly *Speedway Star*, complemented by its sister monthly, *Speedway Post*. Generally speaking, there was little or no speedway mention on radio or TV before the early 70s.

Speedway Star was – still is – speedway's trade magazine. Compulsory reading for promoters, riders and dedicated supporters, it was the way you kept in touch with what was happening around the speedway country. It was a newsletter, forum and opinion-giver, along with being a fanzine specialising in excellent picture coverage and background pieces on riders.

In my early days the magazine was based in central London, just off Fleet Street. But the spiritual home of *Speedway Star* was, and no doubt will always remain, in Plough Lane, Wimbledon. Or, more particularly, on the viewing steps outside the pits area under the main stand at Wimbledon Stadium.

Eric Linden was long term editor of this publication and a more prolific writer and lover of the sport you would not find. He could make speedway come alive off the pages, whether writing about events in the wilds of Scotland or the depths of Devon.

The only thing was, Eric Linden resided in south London and virtually all his superbly descriptive prose from far away places was pulled from the back of his brilliant mind.

Needless to say, he could be seen supporting a pillar at Plough Lane most Thursday evenings, but he never ventured far from there. Not in my time anyway. I vaguely remember him making the 100-mile expedition to Ipswich once, I think, and maybe I spotted him at Brandon, in the hospitality lounge during a British Final another time. But to all intent and purpose, Plough Lane, SW17 was his one and only speedway base.

Although he remained a regular contributor to the *Star*, the baton had been passed to the urbane Paul Parish by the time I had become involved. Paul was a lovely man and just the kind of person you would expect as an editor. Slightly aloof, well manicured, self assured.

I, on the other hand, was brash, bombastic and quick to take offence or to spot partisan reporting, even when maybe it wasn't there. Paul and I had some lively discussions – I think I managed to get under his skin more than once, which is not a sensible thing to do with a man

No anorak for Paul Parish on the night he found his way to Ipswich to present the Speedway Star Knockout Cup to JL in 1978.

Bet Ivan Mauger had an easier time at the hands of SWAPA than I did! Some of the journos I recognise from this gathering are Philip Rising (far left), Richard Frost, Pat Foley, Dick Bott, John Huxley and Keith Fisher. *(AL)*

in his position.

Despite all his 'cool', I often saw Paul at unfashionable Hackney. He might have looked and acted like a smooth Plough Lane punter but I wonder if Paul had north-of-the-Thames blood in him?

I learned an adage many years later. Had I not been so full of my own importance for most of my promoting life, I would have worked it out for myself, but I never did. The adage is: never pick a fight with a man holding a pen or a microphone. You might win the odd skirmish, but they hold all the aces – and he will get you in the end.

I have no reason to believe Paul allowed my overzealous and less than neutral grizzles to influence the *Speedway Star's* attitude towards its treatment of Ipswich, and hopefully he will have been able to see through my lack of grace to the passion beneath.

Paul had always steered a pretty neutral line in his time with the *Star*. Nothing too radical, no great controversies or tub-thumping. To be fair, most of the promoters were quite capable of providing plenty of lively banter anyway, and the magazine was always full of feuds between rival teams and promotions. Some, of course, were artificially manufactured, but others were genuine enough. Although Paul no doubt enjoyed speedway, I don't think he was an 'anorak'.

The same could not be said for his successor, Philip Rising. Speedway was awash at that time with so many quality journalists who had become caught up in the sport. Sensible and well respected wordsmiths, who had got the smell of methanol and Castrol 'R' in their nostrils and fallen under its influence.

Names like Peter Oakes, Martin Rogers, Keir Radnedge, Dick Bott, Graham Baker, Andrew Edwards, Dave Lanning, Richard Frost . . . the list seemed endless and Philip, who contributed regularly to the *Daily Express*, was up there with the best of them.

But Philip was more than a speedway nut. He was a Wimbledon nut and, worse, an anything-remotely-to-do-with-Wimbledon nut. It was great to have an editor of *Speedway Star* so full of passion for the sport and I don't doubt that Philip treated all promotions with equal respect. Maybe it was just as well for the other tracks that throughout my era in promoting, the Dons seemed never to graduate from the ugly duckling stage, making it difficult for the *Star* to overplay its natural bias. As it was, the worst that happened was that *Speedway Star* has long suffered from a chronic and long running condition called Tatumitis. This is a more modern variant on the Mooritis and Briggitis viruses that superceded it by a generation.

In Philip's hands the *Star* suddenly gained teeth. No tiptoeing a mid-course for him. The magazine was always running one crusade or another. Let's face it, finding fault with the way speedway was run at that time was not entirely difficult. And whilst I was a regular sufferer at his hands, it was good to see the paper having a position on things. Generally speaking, the sport was viable enough to cope with public scrutiny and it did little harm to bring some things to public attention. My only objection at the time was that all tracks and personalities were not necessarily treated with the same even handed objectivity. I've no doubt personal feelings clouded judgements.

I cannot put a finger on the date. I think it was after I had finished promoting at Ipswich, and/or maybe when I turned down the position of BSPA manager, when Philip printed something of a eulogy about me and my involvement in the sport. I think it was meant to be generally positive and complimentary. In essence, it was an excellent summing up of my strengths and weaknesses. I think I was as unsettled with the accuracy of the piece as I was disappointed to have been damned by faint praise!

Just after my time, IPC, the then publishers of the magazine, decided it was no longer worth the bother, so Philip and the rest of the *Speedway Star* team were offered a management buyout, and thus, along with some carefully hand-picked financial backers, became the new owners of a title that has served the sport well since 1952.

Richard Clark, a long time employee, another (Wimbledon) speedway nut, and something of an anti-establishment figure, became editor of the *Star*, with Philip moving into a more overseeing role as managing editor.

Richard is a superb journalist with a keen eye for detail and a lively understanding of the sport. It was a shame that his time was – still is – often to be taken up editing the work of others less talented than himself, but he is more than up to the job.

But suddenly, though, as owners and not just employees, I think priorities changed within the set up. It could, of course, have been that during the 10 years or so of Philip's reign, speedway itself, or should that be British speedway, could no longer afford to look at itself objectively and critically. Certainly, the new *Speedway Star* toned down its comments considerably. Did the new owners work on the basis that 'you don't kick a man when he's down' or was it that they needed to be a lot more careful about offending people? Perhaps it was simply that the Aunt Sally's like me were no longer around!

To their credit, the staff at their Surbiton office recognised and understood the dangers the proposed Speedway Grand Prix represented to UK speedway right from the outset. They got as near as they possibly could to mounting a full scale campaign against it, because they saw the dangers that the British promoters of the time either couldn't see or preferred to ignore.

Once the thing was up and running, though, Rising and co. clearly took the view that it deserved full support – and I agree with their logic. As reporters of the sport worldwide, they needed to be on board. Also, from their point of view, something needed to replace the column inches previously reserved for the various rounds of the individual World Championships.

Some might suggest that, these days, it must be very difficult for the 'SS' to be completely objective towards the current GP series and its organisers, given that their managing editor holds a position of some authority within that set up, and I wouldn't dispute that line of thinking. Still, the *Star* is now truly an international publication devoting significant space, not just to the Grand Prix series, but to the whole world of speedway. The publication merely mirrors the swing in the sport away from its UK roots.

I don't suppose that if I had my time again, I would be much different the second time around. After all, you are what you are, and generally I got by with my actions and attitudes. Perhaps, though, I would try to treat the *Speedway Star* and the national press boys with a little more humility. Perhaps I could have seen them a bit more for what they were; a good bunch of blokes who sometimes needed to step on corns as part of their job.

The Ipswich media

Before the advent of local radio, the local newspaper was *the* most important outlet through which to get the speedway message across. Possibly it still is. National media coverage was important to keep the speedway message in front of the non-supporters. *Speedway Star* and, latterly, *Speedway Mail*, provided the real enthusiasts with detailed information, pics and news

Barry Rackham, then managing director of the East Anglian Daily Times, talks speedway with Ole Olsen.

on a weekly basis. However, it was the local newspapers that kept the casual supporter up to speed on who this week's visitors were, what time the match started, how the team was performing away from home, how injured riders were fairing.

One should also take into account, the provincial newspaper editor/proprietor also relies on speedway supporters (amongst others) to buy his newspapers. Whilst the journalists have a duty to 'tell it like it is', they also have to take into account goodwill on both sides is always desirable. At the same time, the promoter should understand the newspaper is not simply doing the sport a favour by covering events.

At Ipswich in the early days, there was an air of paternalism about the way the local newspapers, the morning daily *East Anglian Daily Times* and its sister evening paper, the *Ipswich Evening Star*, handled speedway. (If I refer to the EADT, I mean the East Anglian Daily Times Company, publishers of both papers.)

Generally speaking, a provincial newspaper's bread and butter reporting is based around the local football team, especially if that team is in the top league.

It is no surprise then that if you read a report of a football game in the home team's local paper, and then read a report of the same game in the away team's local newspaper, there will be no comparison. The reports need to reflect the needs and prejudices of the people they are aimed at.

I don't know too much about provincial newspaper sports departments up and down the country but I suspect they are much the same as at Ipswich. There was a huge pecking order. The 'senior reporters' were the ones who got to travel to the away football matches, whilst the new boys got allocated the sports that nobody else wanted to cover.

So it was at Ipswich when the speedway came along again in 1969, and for a short time the job was shared around the EADT sports department. I reckon it must have been something like

a pass the parcel contest, or, perhaps nearer the mark, a don't fall foul of the sports editor contest. These press men, or should I say, pressed men, quite obviously looked down their noses at the speedway and paid it the lip service they felt it warranted.

But they say one volunteer is worth ten pressed men, so when new boy, Mike Horne, took on the job of speedway correspondent without a fight, things improved considerably for us at Foxhall.

Mike (like me) knew little or

We stole some of the attention away from Bobby Robson and his players the day we paraded the British League trophy around the pitch at Portman Road.

nothing about speedway racing at first but he did know what it was like to be the new boy in the sports room. I don't know to this day really whether or not he was happy to take on the role because he enjoyed the sport, or because he saw it as a chance to establish his own little niche in a sport's department full of egos and blinkers.

Whatever the reason, he learned to cope with my aggressive manner, and learned quickly the various intricacies of the sport. Once he got past my bark, he found my bite to be much less savage, and he also discovered that being the local speedway correspondent earned him a little extra on the side, doing reports and write-ups for *Speedway Star* and other press outlets.

Photographer Dave Kindred has covered the Witches since the reopening in 1969.

I don't think Mike ever became sycophantic, although I know he was accused of such by some of the elements within the EADT sports department. Bit of a joke considering how those elements used to suck up to Bobby Robson and co. at Ipswich Town FC.

However, Mike and I struck up a good professional relationship. I was prepared to give him the tip on possible happenings, and because of this, he could put together his own background stuff so as to be ready when the news was released. Such arrangements work well and are not uncommon, where the promoter can trust his local press man not to betray a confidence and the reporter gets at least equality, if not a head start, on breaking news. This is very different to the national boys, who were far more interested in 'scoops', sensationalism, and eyebrow-raising one-liners.

The national press coverage was important to speedway, but only in a general sense. Really and truly, the stories in themselves were unimportant. The benefit to speedway was in having the general public be aware that speedway racing was a big enough sport to warrant the attentions of the national press. Indeed, even the 'exposes' I don't think did much harm. As far as the national papers were concerned, any publicity is good publicity, although I have to say I was less charitable at the times, when it was often myself who was their target!

More often than not, Mike also often benefited from a lift to away matches from me, no doubt enabling him to make a bob or two on expenses! In return, I got good company and a sounding board.

It has to be said, though, when Mike was away, sick or on holiday, I had to take pot luck with whoever covered him. Some of the guys deployed to cover the Witches were very good but one in particular was a nasty piece of work. He and I fell out very early on in the piece. When he was delegated to do reports, we would be sure of a hard time, purely out of spite. It was he, and my reaction to his decidedly negative attitude, that caused relations between the speedway and the paper to become strained more than once.

When Mike eventually moved on, Elvin King took his place. Like Mike, Elvin knew little of speedway when he first became involved, and was wary about being labelled as an easy touch, as Horney had been, by the senior members of the sports desk. Because of this, it took a good while for us to trust each other but we got there in the end.

Elvin and I still don't see eye to eye on everything even now but this is healthy and never stopped us from having a good working relationship. I wouldn't be me without the odd bit of umbrage here and there, and Elvin is not famous for taking backward steps, so the odd stoush was to be expected. At the end of the day, though, I hope we like and respect each other.

It has been the close relationship – first with Mike Horne, then with Elvin King – that has

Mike Bacon interviewing Hans Andersen.

maintained such good coverage for Ipswich Speedway in the local papers over the years. Things have changed substantially since the days of the old parochial attitudes, and I am sure the EADT respects the fact that the speedway has brought kudos to the town, and also helps to sell newspapers, whilst for their part, Ipswich Speedway relies heavily on the local morning and evening papers for their publicity.

I understand the morning paper in the EADT stable, the *East Anglian Daily Times*, now has its own speedway correspondent in the shape of Mike Bacon. This can only be good for the sport in Ipswich and I congratulate the two sister newspapers for their coverage over the years.

I suspect Ipswich Speedway has enjoyed the best local newspaper coverage in the sport over three-and-a-half decades.

It should also be pointed out that the EADT has also been an avid supporter of the speedway over the years, both by way of sponsorship, and also by supporting the current promoters through some difficult times.

On the airwaves

![257 Radio Orwell]

Around 1973, I went to a public meeting where a consortium was canvassing support for Ipswich to have its own local radio station. It was the usual mayhem at the meeting, with each little interest group clamouring for the opportunity to lobby for special airtime. The God botherers were out in full force, I recall.

David Cox, on behalf of the consortium, promised each interested party in turn that their own particular fetish would be suitably covered. He also smoothed the brows of those seemingly professional doomsayers who were there to make sure the radio signals wouldn't stop their hens from laying nor interfere with their own particular scenic view.

As it happens, Orwell and Ipswich Speedway were to become very close neighbours. Well, at least, the stadium and the transmitter were. In fact the transmitter ended up no more than 20 paces from the stadium fence! Rumour has it the company that owns Foxhall Heath earn as much in rent from the 20 square yards or so occupied by the mast and building housing the transmitter as from the stadium itself, but I have no knowledge of that!

The station, by then named Radio Orwell, in recognition of the river that links Ipswich with the sea, finally burst onto the airwaves in November 1975. It was certainly a novelty to have a radio station based in the town.

The locals were all very much used to commercial radio, though, as most had followed the fortunes of the various pirate stations based off the local east coast in the 60s.

By now the bulk of those teenage kids who had enjoyed the rough and ready pop music coming from the North Sea, were now the mums and dads of the mid-70s and were largely Orwell's target audience. In fact, the radio station target audience profile pretty well mirrored that of the speedway, as did its catchment area.

In the early days, the station was just superb. It could best be described as BBC Radio 2 with local interest Radio 4-type inserts. Every day someone heard their own name or the name of a friend mentioned on air, and even listened to the boring bits because they were local and recognisable. There was a real feeling of community both from and towards the station.

This was backed up by a great bunch of presenters. As one of the earliest of the small local stations, there was a huge pool of talent from which the managers could choose - and they chose wisely. The 'disc jockeys' were excellent, having either the professionalism to learn the

Andy Archer, a great character and good friend who invented the 'anorak'.

local pronunciations or were local enough to know them already. The news and sports departments gave opportunities to a couple of young stars in the making in Tim Ewart, as head of news, and Pete Barraclough, head of sport.

Both of these lads were dedicated professionals and although I won neither of them over as close friends, nor indeed, speedway devotees, they were sensible enough to recognise the natural affinity between the speedway and the radio station, to realise and understand a relationship was in everyone's interests.

Whereas I had never believed adverts in the local newspaper encouraged one person through the turnstiles, and I only spent money with the paper in order to show some kind of quid pro quo, it was different with the local radio station.

Given that we were having a very successful run of results, given the novelty of having a local radio for the bulk of the people in the area, given that the catchment area of the speedway was almost identical to that of the radio station, given that the station and ourselves were both aiming for the same socio-economic group, and given that you can scan through a newspaper and not see an advert, but a TV or radio advert is 'in your face', this was the place on which to concentrate our advertising.

I cannot say if those adverts actually produced bodies through the turnstiles. Maybe, if they only reminded people about the upcoming match, they had done their job. I have to say, though, in my own cynical way, I was concerned about the dangers of running adverts for a while and then ceasing. There was always the danger of people, on not hearing an ad, assuming there would be no speedway event that week.

Anyway, I digress. I also encouraged the radio presenters from the station to come and give us a visit, and one in particular developed a natural liking for the sport. As luck would have it, he was also head and shoulders their best man and most locals tuned into presenter Andy Archer's show.

Andy and I hit it off well on a social basis, too. Although hailing from Terrington St Clement in Norfolk, and dangerously close to King's Lynn (!), he was/is as sharp as a tack and very much anti-establishment. His spells on pirate radio had either sharpened or pandered to his lack of respect for authority, I don't quite know which.

Although he was a free spirit, he was very much a well-educated and well-read free spirit. He could hold a conversation on pop music or Proust and was far more than a monosyllabic disc jockey.

Andy was a nightmare for the station managers, though. Once the microphone switch was thrown, he was the consummate professional. But as soon as the mike was off, he was a handful.

He enjoyed a drink or three and was absolutely hopeless at keeping appointments. He just loved cricket and was a very good player in the Orwell Allstars team, which I was lucky enough to play in, but many is the time we would have to go and round him up before a match.

Andy is credited with being the person who first coined the use of the word 'anorak' to mean a very committed fan. The story goes that when broadcasting on the offshore Radio Caroline, some three miles or so off the Suffolk coast, a boatload of pirate radio devotees chartered a small boat one day, sailing out to the pirate ship.

Andy commented that all he could see on the chartered boat was 'anoraks' and, thenceforward, referred to any pirate radio enthusiasts who made the boat trip out as 'anoraks'. The term soon came into general usage to represent anyone who was so much of a supporter as to go to extraordinary lengths to show that support.

As with the speedway, the novelty value of Radio Orwell eventually started dropping off. The original group of excellent professionals from both front and back offices began moving away to better jobs and bigger stations, being replaced by cheap alternatives.

The old downward spiral set in. Advertising revenue fell, so budget cuts were made. The budget cuts affected the presentation adversely, so the advertising revenue fell further...

Anyway, the station owners sold out to a Norwich-based outfit and the whole point of having a truly local radio station was lost.

Orwell, in a very short space of time, had become the heart of Ipswich and East Suffolk and it was sad for the town that it could not be maintained as such.

12 All in the Game

Many tear has to fall
But it's all in the game...

At the time of my becoming involved in speedway, there was a perception in many of the general public's eyes that the sport was little better than wrestling, and was all rigged. Indeed, one of the reporters on the sports desk of our local newspaper would have nothing to do with speedway because he was convinced this was the case. The joke was that he was a big horse racing man!

Some time later, in the early 80s, the *Sunday People* carried out a covert operation to find out if the sport was crooked. They came up with enough to splash it over their front pages, carefully picking out the most lurid parts, but missing the point completely in their desire to be sensational. They dwelt on the odd untoward happening but failed to point out these things were very much the exception rather ran the rule. Why let the facts ruin a good story?

I'll tell you what I know, as much as I can within the laws of libel. Before I do, though, I'll tell you this: I don't think there is a professional sport around where cheating does not exist to some degree. I know of many instances of skulduggery in lesser sports, which are not public knowledge, and therefore legally not open for discussion.

I also know that in soccer, every now and then this issue raises its ugly head but nobody claims that 'soccer is fixed'. In recent years cricket has had its own share of unwanted 'cheat' headlines. I'll bet my boots malpractice in most pro sports is, if not common, then certainly routine.

I was still a wet behind the ears promoter when the Witches were invited to ride in a challenge match away from home. It looked as if we might win but the home promoter was desperate that his side should succeed. Too many details here would identify the occasion, so I cannot be more explicit. The home promoter begged me, as it was a meaningless challenge, not to beat his team.

Pete Bailey crashed trying NOT to win!

I was reluctant but agreed. I told the late Pete Bailey, if it looked like Ipswich would win in the last heat, he was to slow down. He would be paid for the win regardless. Pete gated in front and in his efforts to avoid winning, he fell off! I vowed then and there, never again to try to 'pull' a race or meeting, regardless of circumstances.

In the 1976 World Final in Poland, Malcolm Simmons had a chance to finish on the rostrum. In those days, the riders who had just failed to qualify for the final were expected to turn up in case any of the field was unable to take their place on the day.

Worse, when these riders were no longer needed as 'meeting reserves' with a genuine chance to participate fully in the event, they were expected to become 'replacement riders', if a programmed rider failed to take his place in an individual race. This particular year, Anders Michanek just failed to qualify from the Inter-continental final at Wembley, so he became a meeting reserve at the final in Katowice. Then he became a 'replacement rider', even though he was certainly among the best handful of riders in the world.

One of the many east European also-rans, who littered world final fields then, was unable to take his place in a later heat involving Simmons, so 'Mitch' was summoned to take his place. Hardly fair on Malcolm, who would have been assured of beating the rider Anders was replacing.

As manager in charge of the England riders, I wandered over to Anders to explain the situation. I never had a chance to open my mouth. "Don't worry, Yon, I understand," was all he said, and he dutifully kept out of Simmo's way.

Fortunately, after that year, meeting reserves were allowed to pack up their things if not required by heat four (when all 16 contestants had taken their first ride and therefore the reserves could no longer have the full five rides). I neither see nor saw anything underhand or wrong in what Anders did; just the opposite. To have had him come from nowhere and take points from those in with a chance of winning the meeting would have been wrong.

Not to say plain skulduggery did not take place. A very young Billy Sanders was doing very well in an early World Championship qualifier (the Anzacs followed the British route through the World Championship rounds then). A huge household name was not doing as well and became in danger of being eliminated from the title race at a very early stage.

Just prior to a race involving Billy and the household name, I saw another equally big household name take Billy to one side. I enquired what the 'chat' had been about, and it seemed he had asked Billy, who had already scored enough points to go through to the next round, to let his friend win the race.

I pointed out to Bill that he would be throwing away a rostrum place and the chance to eliminate a huge rival early on in the competition, and he agreed with me. Mysteriously, though, he had engine failure on the last bend of that race whilst leading!

You would have to be a complete mug not to believe some horse trading went on at all levels of the World Championships. Friend to friend, colleague to colleague, countryman to countryman, and all points in between. At what level does this become 'fixing' or 'cheating' and at what level is it no more than tactics? I mean, look at modern day middle distance running? Pace makers, team plans and even blockers sent out in races.

I don't know where you draw the line – but I do know Ole Olsen hated this old pals network. Much as I dislike the Grand Prix system and also its race formula, you may be sure Ole had it firmly in his mind that he wanted a meeting format where collusion was not able to influence results. In this, if gossip is to be believed, he has not entirely succeeded as yet.

By and large, though, speedway racing is 'clean'. There really is not enough money involved in the sport to encourage wholesale fixing and I do not think it exists in any measurable form in the day-to-day running of team events.

I have to say, though, I get very nervous when I see huge bonuses being offered for teams winning competitions. Also, I cannot see how allowing betting in speedway can be considered a good thing. Such steps represent a very shortsighted way to go and merely invite suspicion.

Beware of Indian bookmakers asking advice on track conditions . . .

Ole Olsen hated the old pals network.

13 Take it to the Limit

...So put me on a speedway
Show me a sign
And take it to the limit one more time...

When I was in Sydney around 1976-77, Billy Sanders (or, more correctly, his mum) showed me a video featuring Bill that had been put together by a Sydney sports journalist.

The video itself was eminently forgettable but for one piece at the opening, which has forever stuck in my mind. The journalist was interviewing supporters before a meeting at the notoriously fast and scary Sydney Royale (Sydney Showgrounds) track. He buttonholed a little old lady, the kind of whom you see at speedways all over the world.

"Do you think speedway racing is dangerous?" he asked her.

She thought about the question for a second, then gave him the best answer she could.

" Not if you sit in the right place dear," she said, "and I'm always very careful!"

I have to say, that particular phrase has always been my own mantra. I did once push-start a speedway bike and bring it back to the rider concerned, and I often helped out with the warming of engines in the pits whilst riders and/or mechanics busied themselves with other things, but I have never actually ridden one.

I did my share of motorbike riding as a youth, though. At 16, like any self-respecting kid of that age, I grew tired of pedal pushing and resorted to 50cc assistance. Then, without the finance necessary for four-wheeled mobility, I moved on to a Lambrettor scooter (cursed thing, and I was anything but a 'mod') and then to a 'proper' motorbike.

Provisional drivers were limited to 250cc engines for solos, which meant second hand bikes of under 250ccs carried a premium whereas the bigger engined models did not. Of course, the law being the ass it was, decreed that it was OK to ride a bike on a provisional licence if it had three wheels! Let me tell you, three wheels are undoubtedly more dangerous than two when it comes to motorbikes, but that was the law.

So in 1962, I was able to lay my hands on a 1949 BSA B31. A 350cc single barrelled, solid rear end model (with six inch thick foam rubber seat to compensate!) for next to nothing; thence to the breaker's yard for the bare bones of a sidecar chassis and wheel. As I recall the bike was £25 and the sidecar chassis £9.

Bananas in those days were shipped in sturdy, long wooden boxes and one of these, broken down and cut to size, provided wooden running boards where the passenger cockpit would normally go. I was in business. My headgear for the time was a Robin Hood hat (complete with small feather) purchased from a souvenir shop at Southend-on-Sea. Crash helmets were not made compulsory until my biking days were over, and I never ever wore one.

I only had one crash on that bike, and none on the 1954 BSA B34 (forerunner to the Gold Star) complete with Garrard sidecar that eventually replaced the B31. After that one crash, though, I should have changed my name to 'Lucky'.

Several friends and I were celebrating the start of the school summer holidays by having a bike ride around the country lanes of Epping Forest. The others were all on solos, with me on my trusty B31 combination.

We came to a road junction. Well, more a fork in the road really. I was bringing up the rear and knew we needed to take the left fork, which was more or less straight on. At the last second, the leader decided to take the sharper right fork, with the others following suit.

I sat there, grumbling to myself that they had gone the wrong way, not taking into account that, at around 50mph, all they had needed to do was to lean their bikes over in order to adjust to the late decision. Life was not so simple on a 'combination' but I was so busy thinking about the fact that they had gone the wrong way, that I just absent-mindedly followed them.

The bike obeyed my wishes until halfway around the turn. Then it decided the whole exercise was way beyond it – and straightened up. I hit the two-feet high grassy bank straight on. The bike launched up and over the bank, but I went further. I flew through the air, cleared the 10-feet wide grassy verge and ditch, and finished neatly half way up a high hedge. We've all seen it a million times in cartoons. All the picture was short of was fingernail marks as I slid down the hedge into the (dry) ditch.

You can see I am a natural risk taker.

By the time the others had returned, I had worked out that apart from a few scratches and bruises and a hugely sore shin where I had taken out the bike's windscreen, all was where it should be. They started recovering the bike whilst I sat there laughing, nervously.

As they began to pull the bike out (which, by the way, apart from the screen, was fine), it became clear there was a telegraph pole on the bank. Not just any old telegraph pole, but one which was held upright by a straining wire, set at 45 degrees to the ground.

I had gone between the pole and the straining wire. There was virtually no tolerance through that gap - six inches either way and I would have been dead. I immediately stopped laughing and it was a minute or two before my knees could support the rest of me.

I was no bike freak, and as soon as I reasonably could, I progressed to four-wheeled transport. Not like Joe Thurley, who considered two wheels and an engine the nearest thing to heaven he could find. Then again, he's also a huge country and western fan!

When people ask me if I have ridden a speedway bike, the answer is always the same. In order to be a speedway rider, one has to be 'blessed' with a certain disregard for one's own safety. Such a blessing, I am pleased to say, I did not receive.

In my more honest moments, I have been known to be a bit more forthright, and to have suggested that anyone who wished to risk life and limb riding speedway must have a certain chemical imbalance in the brain. That doesn't imply they should all be certified, but runs it close!

What shall we call it? Bravery? Stupidity? Insanity? Possibly a bit of all of these things if we are being entirely honest. I mean, I can understand F1 drivers, and boxers, taking those kinds of risks because of the potentially huge returns. Why the hell, though, should anyone want to be a speedway rider, when being a golfer, tennis player, footballer, cricketer, or a million other sporting heroes must give you a considerably better risk/ reward potential?

Perhaps that is why so many kids want to be a David Beckham rather than a Tony Rickardsson. Perhaps this also explains why the majority of riders these days come from the less mainstream countries. Possibly they feel they have less to lose!

If I needed proof of my thoughts on the subject of riders and loose screws, a situation at Foxhall only a few weeks after we had reopened the place tended to provide it.

Mike Coomber, whom we had dug out of an early retirement to help fill the original Ipswich team, managed to crash into the starting gate. His bike finished in two pieces, joined only by the clutch cable. Mike came up, holding his arm.

The referee had excluded one of the opposition riders and not Mike, who we needed in the rerun of the race, even if just to score a point by finishing. Howdy Byford, the ex-rider who had been wished upon us as a condition of being granted a licence, marched over to Mike, who announced:

"'Owdy, I fink I broke me arm!"

Mike Coomber

Alf Busk finds flying is easy . . .

. . . The trouble is the landing.

Alan Sage tries being a bird . . .

. . . and ends with a sore undercarriage.

Howdy got hold of Mike's arm, gave the wrist a vigorous pull, and said:

"Ace, it's not broken. There's nothing wrong with it. Now, get in the pits whilst I borrow you a bike, because you are in the rerun."

Mike duly completed the four laps on a borrowed bike to score the point, and was then allowed to go to hospital to get his broken wrist put in a cast.

He and Steve Chilman were a pair of full-blown cockneys and were it not for their well-blessed heads of hair, could have done a passable impression of the notorious *Eastenders'* brothers, Phil and Grant Mitchell. Neither lasted too long in their comebacks but Steve still potters with the vintage bikes even today.

Soon I was able to be as ruthless as Howdy. I rationalised it this way: if the riders were daft enough to ride speedway bikes in the first place, then they might just as well earn as much money and glory as possible by doing it well.

So I learned during the second division days how to weigh riders up and how to press the right buttons. Some respond best to an arm around the shoulder, some to a kick up the bum, and some to both or either at different times. For some, money is the best carrot, although others just love to win. And more just do it for the thrill. The job of a manager is to decide which approach works best with each individual rider at any given time.

But the trick is, to get a rider to perform at 99% of his ability. Anything above this sees him sitting on the track watching the others disappear into the distance. That's no good to anybody. I love the old cliché, 'he gave 110%'! How could 'he' do that, for God's sake?

However, often getting a rider to perform at 99% of his actual ability means getting him to ride at 110% (or more) of what he thinks is the best of his ability.

Of course, a big responsibility goes with winding up a rider. Push him into trying harder than he is capable of coping with and disaster looms. If that rider hurts himself as a consequence, who takes the blame?

I plead guilty to having sometimes deliberately asked a rider to do more than he was capable of. Fortunately, I never had to carry a really serious injury, or worse, on my conscience as a consequence. Indeed, more often than not, it is the silly little falls that result in the more serious injuries.

Nevertheless, the longer I did the job, the more reluctant I became to push riders to their limits. Likewise, you can always tell when a rider reaches a point in his career after which he will not improve. It's when he starts wanting to return to his own bed every night, instead of risking a trip to the hospital. At that moment, he has reached his maximum potential. It's all downhill from there.

Some speedway tracks are potentially more dangerous than others. That is pretty obvious really, but picking which is which is not always easy. Exeter is a place most riders dislike, because of the sheer speeds involved. Any fall there is more likely to cause serious injury, simply because the riders are going that much quicker. But it is my bet, the injury record at Exeter would stand up against that of most other tracks.

The County Ground circuit is a natural racing shape and the solid fence is more likely to save bad smashes than to cause them, because riders are more likely to strike it a glancing blow than hit it head on.

Wolverhampton, however, in my time anyway (I think they have since adjusted the shape), although seeming to be a fairly innocuous place, where the riders almost stopped mid-turn, was always a worry to me. The straights were too long compared to the tightness of the turns.

As you know, speedway bikes don't have gearboxes. Riders adjust their front and rear sprockets, and therefore the gearing, according to the track they are racing on. Using an analogy, the gearing they would use at Exeter would be like your car's top gear, whilst the gearing at, say, Arena Essex, would be like your car's second gear.

It doesn't follow, though, that the smaller the track, the lower the gear needed. It is the tightness of the corners, rather than the size of the track, that is important. At Wolverhampton, you needed a low gear for the bends, but then that gear would be too low for the straights. The bikes would run out of top end speed too early. So it was necessary to use a gear that would make the bikes fast enough down the straights but also able to give control around the bends.

Often, riders would go for speed, which sometimes resulted in the engines labouring coming out of the turns, encouraging the rear wheel to grip too much. The bikes would then tend to

Above: Wolverhampton, where I was always concerned for the safety of four riders, never mind eight!
Below: Alan Mogridge will have felt this one in the morning after a close inspection of Exeter's steel fence.

Hans Wasserman – worst injury.

John Simmons – a valued guest.

rear out of control. I saw it time after time there, and with the closeness of the fence posts and lamp standards, a bad accident was always on the cards.

Wolverhampton would have benefited hugely from a modern-day air fence. Exeter, generally speaking, would not.

Ipswich was a bit like Wolverhampton. The straights were too long for the tightness of the bends. We altered the track shape and camber many times to improve things, but our saving grace in terms of safety was our collapsible fence and stock car track which provided a 'no man's land', or run off area.

Initially, we made the mistake of using metal fence posts but soon changed them to timber. The only bad injury at Ipswich involving the fence in the 35 years since then has been to Reading's German, Hans Wasserman, who was unlucky enough to catch a fence post with his back after another rider had taken out a fence panel. The spinal damage was enough to finish his career and leave him with a permanent bad limp.

Hans' injury has been the worst to happen at Ipswich on the new track inside the old one, although several Witches carry permanent physical damage from track crashes elsewhere. Mike Lanham lost the use of an arm in a crash at Leicester that nearly cost him his life. Jeremy Doncaster's elder brother, Nick, lost the use of a hand in a far less serious looking fall at Mildenhall. But the worst damage to an Ipswich rider was what happened to promising junior rider, John Simmons.

John was having a try out at the East of England Showground with a view to going on loan to Peterborough. He hit Peterborough's solid fence, breaking his neck and becoming a quadriplegic.

John was only 17 at the time. That was in 1973. His mum gave up her job as a nursing sister to look after him. After more than 30 years, and now well into her 80s, she remains his full time carer. The only connection they now have with the speedway is a regular Christmas card from John Davis, who was a junior rider at Peterborough at the time of the injury.

In my time as Ipswich promoter, the wheelchair-bound John Simmons was always a valued guest on a Thursday night, where he was able to at least enjoy the opportunity of soaking up the atmosphere from a corner of the pits. Sadly - cruelly in my opinion – a subsequent promotion at Ipswich withdrew his access to the pits on the basis that it might be disconcerting to the riders to have someone wheelchair-bound in there, as a ready reminder of the dangers of the sport.

John is more bitter about that than about the injury.

When I was a young, fit, and naive promoter, I always made a point of being first to a fallen rider. I don't know why really, because I have no special medical skills. And whilst having happily played with fluffy, white rabbits at school, before gassing them and cutting them up in the name of learning, I am rather squeamish. I think it must have either been my desire to show the riders I cared, or perhaps, more likely, it was my early lack of ability to delegate.

Medical assistance varies massively from track to track. St John Ambulance personnel are not always the most competent, although we were very lucky at Ipswich, and in any case, knowing the character and the pain threshold of each individual rider is often important.

Some riders want to bounce up as soon as they hit the deck, so they have to be encouraged to check that things are all functioning more or less properly first. Others take longer to re-orientate themselves and might need a bit of encouraging to discover which way is up.

As experience began to take over from enthusiasm, I discovered that most times, a brisk walk to a fallen rider, rather than a panic-stricken dash, gave him a chance to regain a bit of equilibrium, making diagnosis of potential injuries that much easier. Often, also, it was possible to diagnose likely injuries just from the nature of the fall.

Long time track doctor Chris Clarke.

I understand meeting doctors are now required to remain on the centre green or in the pits during a meeting. That beats the hell out of having to drag them out of the bar, which was the procedure at many tracks in my day. But Chris Clarke, our track doctor for many years, had a good understanding of what was required.

He always watched the racing but did not overreact in the event of a spill. He would wait for a signal from the clerk of the course or myself to see if he was required. Chris also learned fast and if the crash looked bad enough, he would move at the trot without being summoned.

In all my years at speedway, only twice did I chicken out from helping with an injured rider. The first was when Berwick's Andy Meldrum, in the time before full-face helmets, crashed face-

The result of giving more than 100% effort.

Kevin Jolly cleared for take off...

...Flaps up...

...Take off aborted!

first into a fence post at Ipswich. Andy suffered a broken jaw and some nasty, but not permanent, facial damage. Doctor Chris admitted to me afterwards, he too was a bit squeamish when it came to faces!

The other time was at Poole. Eric Broadbelt's throttle jammed open when he and another rider tangled at the start. Eric was going flat out when he hit the fence in the first turn, was thrown high into the air and hit a light pole so hard with his torso, the post finished up bent almost to the ground. Showers of sparks from the overhead light cables added to the drama.

I was sure that was the end for Eric but, apart from a few broken ribs and internal injuries, he was fine. I think he was out for some time but he courageously came back to ride for many seasons after that.

Without doubt, though, one of the worst moments for me in speedway was in having to sort out a young Aussie boy called Brett Alderton, who was trying to make his mark with Milton Keynes. It was at King's Lynn on April 17, 1982, and I was on the centre green when the lad piled into the third bend fence headfirst.

From the time he hit the fence, this was clearly very serious. As it happens, I had wandered over to the third bend to watch the race, so I got there pretty quickly. He was unconscious and struggling to breathe. It seemed as if his helmet strap was restricting his breathing.

The St John members all stood around wringing their hands. This was all too much for them, and they were not game to take any responsibility at all. I looked around, expecting to see the doctor legging it across the grass. He was not. Preben Eriksen was there. He had been in the race I think and had stopped to help.

I have always had a massive respect for Preben, the man. He was one of many who you would think would have had more sense than to be a speedway rider. He was intelligent, resourceful and brave; the sort of bloke you would want to be the Best Man at your wedding. Dennis Sigalos was also quickly onto the scene. He was another one who I reckon you would be happy to have on the other end of your rope when mountain-climbing.

Clearly, we needed to get the lad's helmet off. Preben was more familiar than me on the mechanics of such a task and between us we managed to remove it. We both looked at each other. Although Brett was fighting for breath, and therefore still alive, we both knew the score there and then. Never mind any other injuries, there was only one thing to do and that was to get him onto a ventilator. And with the hospital only a couple of minutes away by ambulance, it needed to be done quickly.

By this time, our collective shouting at the St John's people had galvanised some kind of reaction, and when the ambulance arrived at the scene there were enough bodies to get the lad on board. I well recall one of those tragi/comic moments when the lad's forearm got caught in the ambulance door – and Siggy instinctively apologised to him.

I had met 18-year-old Brett's dad, Dennis, in Australia many years before, when he himself had tried his hand at the sport. Nice bloke. Can you imagine getting a phone call back home in Australia, being told your son is in hospital on life support? That plane journey must have been a nightmare for him, always hoping by the time he got there that his son would be sitting up in bed nursing nothing more serious than a sore head.

Sadly, it was not to be. The best the hospital staff could offer was for Dennis to make the decision about turning the machines off. Oh, and by the way, please could they have his son's various bits and pieces?

I'm not sure I could have coped with that. I think I would have tried to kill whoever had the temerity to ask me. How brave then, that Dennis said 'yes' to both questions. At least he knows Brett helped other people.

Although it was just another incident in the life of a speedway promoter, the moments just after the accident have never left me. I had no kids of my own then, and so I couldn't fully understand that bond between parents and their children, but even so I was never able to be as ruthless a team manager again.

14 The Kid, The Shrimp and The Tiger

I spent my entire speedway promoting life playing down the individual aspects of speedway and playing up the team side of the sport.

These days, it seems the world has adopted the American way of placing star performers on pedestals for commercial reasons, even in team sports. It also has to be said, speedway racing in the 'good old days' used to give maximum opportunity (choice of gate positions, stars meeting only once in a match, etc) for 'superstars' to maintain positions of dominance so that they might be draw cards.

Maybe I was out of step with this thinking in wanting to concentrate on the team aspects of the sport but I reasoned that if that is how I saw things, maybe others saw them the same way.

In the event, my method seemed to work quite well from both the commercial and also sporting angles. Ipswich, in my time, did fairly well at both.

But that does not mean I underestimate the contributions of individuals. With due respect to the many others who helped make Ipswich Speedway so successful, three riders were at the core of the Witches success story of my time there. These three totally different characters were the heart, the soul and the backbone of the set-up and their contributions should be given full appreciation...

I may not always love you
But long as there are stars above you
You never need to doubt it
I'll make you so sure about it
God only knows what I'd be without you

Above: JL and a young Billy on course for another 5-1.

Right: John holds the inside line this time as Billy moves out to block the opposition in the BL Pairs Championship which they won together at Foxhall in 1976.

Below: The late 70s and John (left) and Tony Davey try different lines at pre-season practice.

Billy 'The Kid' Sanders

Faded photographs, covered now with lines and creases
Tickets torn in half, memories in bits and pieces
Traces of love, in the night, that didn't work out right
I've got traces of love tonight

You remember that little girl, who had a little curl, right in the middle of her forehead? Well Billy had no curls, although just like the girl, when he was good he was very, very, good; and when he was bad, he was . . . hard work.

I think I would be correct if I said that Billy Sanders caused me more emotional turmoil than any other rider – and that includes John Cook.

To briefly set the scene, Billy started riding in Australia when he was 15, having lied about his age. Needing to pull a rabbit out of a hat, I played a long shot in 1972 and offered him a team place in British League Division One. He was 16-years-old and agreed terms with me on the telephone without even telling his parents. Because of his age, the distance between England and his Sydney home, and my promise to his mother, I had to keep a fatherly eye on him until he reached 18.

He arrived in Ipswich to become an overnight sensation. Then reality kicked in, as he struggled, not just to find his speedway feet, but also come to terms with the reality of having to make his own decisions and live so far away from the safety and security of home.

In those first few weeks, though, with the team under-strength and the bad injury to Tony Davey, it was Billy who grabbed the headlines and the imagination of the public. He played a very important role until a series of tumbles slowed his on-track progression.

I put him 'in digs' with very sensible people for the first few years but, shall we just say, he matured quickly, both as a rider and as an individual. If you wanted to be humorous, you could say he had undergone a crash course.

Staying with people who had 'old fashioned values' in a comparatively quiet backwater town, was possibly no bad thing at that stage. But even this early on he showed those traits that were to become typical.

There was the determination, the sense of fun, the ambition, the horseplay and the ability to ride a speedway bike and to understand what was going on underneath him. There was also a big bottom lip when all was not well.

It says volumes for 'The Kid's' ability to bounce when he hit the track, and for his strength and fitness levels, that despite so many tumbles, he never missed a fixture in that first year. But an overall return of only four-and-a-half points a meeting showed the learning period was hard. Most of those points were scored at Foxhall. The away tracks were very much a learning exercise.

In the main, he saved his letting down of hair for his off-season time in New South Wales, Australia. I went to see him and meet his parents over there in our winter of 1974, and again in 1975. In '74 he had bought his mum an air conditioner that took up half the tiny sitting room.

By '75, he had bought her the biggest colour TV he could find (that was the first year of colour broadcasts in Australia), which took up the other half! He had also bought himself the biggest, baddest, fastest, production car he could find. This 150mph Ford Falcon GT was not designed to be driven by teenagers. It was a rocket ship on wheels and it gave me a fright just to sit alongside him, but he and the car emerged unscathed by the time it was sold.

Whereas Billy had launched himself onto the British scene in the first few weeks of his first year, only to settle back, his second season started much quieter, but soon raced along. This year saw him start the season as number seven and finish as number three. Quite a leap considering this campaign was again not without its bumps and bruises. In fact, an arm injury in September saw him disappear back to Australia well before the first English autumn breezes.

When Sandor Levai left the team before the 1974 season, Billy took over as the team joker. He was the one who clowned around and did the silly things that helped the team relax before and after meetings. On the minus side, he also started showing signs of having a very quick temper. He had done a bit of amateur schoolboy boxing and, although scrawny when he first arrived, was filling out to be very fit and strong for his size. He could look after himself on and

Ron Bagley with The Kid fresh from the airport.

off the track.

Once again this fit, strong boy was able to bounce back from the odd tumble and complete a full quota of official fixtures. The 1974 season was really his breakthrough year and saw him finish with close to a 10-point average - mighty good going for an 18-year-old.

I think he would have been only 19 when he brought over his Australian girlfriend, soon to become wife, Judy, for the 1975 season and with her arrival came a sea change in attitude. They set up house and Billy was now totally independent of outside influences. Until then, I had kept him on a fairly tight leash. He was expected to be a good team man and role model but now he started seeking further horizons.

By the time of Billy and Judy's sudden, and secret, marriage in the UK, before the lump, which was to become their son Dean, showed too much, the pseudo father/son relationship between us was long gone. I think he respected me in as much as my advice was generally sound and sensible. I also think, though, he began to resent slightly my attitude of always putting the team interest first.

That attitude had helped him very much as a raw youngster, feeling his way forwards and having others help him out, but now it was his turn to shoulder some of the responsibility associated with being one of the better riders there was always a bit of underlying resentment.

One thing you could be sure about with Billy was his unpredictable attitude. With his really neat, tidy riding style, his strength and his mechanical and riding knowledge, he was as good a wet weather and bad track rider as you would ever meet. It wasn't long past his move from trainee to senior team man, though, that he decided to develop a phobia about wet weather.

The one thing about real champions is that they relish difficult conditions, because the more difficult those conditions are, the easier it is to sort the pretenders from the real class acts. As a promoter, Ole Olsen would demand riders race under the most diabolical of conditions. But give him his due, as a rider, he never ever refused to race whatever the state of a track. In fact, as a rider, I have seen him (and Ivan Mauger) get really annoyed when refs have called meetings off.

Billy would bitch and moan, trying to detune everyone in sight, but if and when he lost the battle to get a meeting called off, he would get on and race – and make a mockery of the most difficult of conditions. Often, he would score a maximum and yet be grizzling before, during and after the meeting.

Other times, he would be as chirpy as a cricket, running around pumping up his team-mates and getting the place buzzing. At those times he was a real joy to have in the side. Unfortunately, you were never really sure which Billy was going to turn up. Most times it was the bouncy, enthusiastic joker, but sometimes it was the other one.

Most captains worth their salt have a difficult time because one of their jobs is to balance their loyalty to their team-mates with their

Billy on his first ever ride in England.

responsibility to the management and promotion. Often, the two loyalties run along the same course but there are times when they do not.

There are times when the team, or members of it, have a grouse. Most times this hinges around home track conditions but it could be any amount of other things, like team pairings, riders having been pulled out of rides, and riders being asked to take rides they don't want.

In these circumstances, it is the captain's job to take any team complaints to the management, and then to relay any reply. As such, the skipper is often considered to have a foot in both camps. Billy would never have been accused of that. Whilst a brilliant motivator, he was more of a natural shop steward than captain. One thing such a reputation did, though, was assure you that in tight situations, the riders often looked at (rather than to) him. And if he gave it the nod, then so did they.

Despite being referred to constantly as an adopted son of Suffolk, he patently was not. He was jealous of John Louis and the position John held in the team and in the community. Even when he could equal John in points scoring, he could not equal him in the hearts of the supporters. I think Billy put that down to his being Australian. I would put it the other way around and say that because Billy publicly put his Australian nationality before everything else, supporters became wary.

To be frank, on the question of self, club, country, I don't think there was that much between John and Billy's approach but John was able (under constant lobbying from me) to consistently say and do the right things, and of course, it was far easier to represent the country your fans supported.

I suspect that if you had asked Billy about his greatest moments in the sport, his international exploits would come before his many great club efforts. To my mind, the way he led Australia to their shock victory over England in the World Team Cup qualifier at Ipswich in 1976 would have to be one of those golden moments. He really was awesome that day.

Not that I am suggesting he didn't give his best to the Ipswich cause. I clearly recall three typical Sanders situations. In 1975 we had our first two home meetings snowed off. The third, against Oxford, was run in less than ideal conditions. Tony Davey made light of the difficult track, as he always did, but the rest of the team, including a still young Billy, struggled.

We needed a 5-1 in the last heat to win the match. 'Shrimp' was always going to win the race but the team riding Richard Hellsen and Dag Lovaas kept Billy firmly at the back. On the last bend, our young Aussie chose to go where none other had dared all night. He dived under the Oxford pair desperately tight to the inside line. I suspect he might well have had his eyes closed!

But instead of falling or careering into the pair in front, he passed them as clean as a whistle to snatch two points and the match. It might have only been our first match of the season, but in the wash up, it was the difference between winning the league and not that year.

In 1976, whilst Ipswich seemed to be winning everything

Top: Sometimes a big bottom lip.
Above: The fun Billy with Ted Howgego.
Below: In awesome form for his country.
Bottom: 1974 was a good year.

No longer a Kid.

else, we contrived to put ourselves out of the Inter-League Cup by losing 40-38 at Workington. Billy was one of those Ipswich riders that night who put in far less effort than he should have. He had a very poor meeting. Not only that, but he overindulged in the hotel bar afterwards and made a real nuisance of himself.

We were riding at Halifax the next night and I was so angry with him, I didn't speak to him all that day. He knew he was in the doghouse and he knew that, when I gave the team a dressing down over the previous night's showing, most of my comments were aimed squarely at him. He rode like a real champion at Halifax, scoring a maximum and we won the meeting.

The third important incident that stands out in my mind was much later, in 1984. We had a showdown meeting at Belle Vue. It was October and there had been heavy frosts. The home promoter, the late Stuart Bamforth, had made the mistake of adding lots of fresh shale and packing it down. When there is frost in the ground, doing this turns the track into a mattress! It becomes the consistency of something between Dunlopillo and Plastecine. It makes turning a bike very, very difficult indeed, because the back wheel refuses to slide.

Bamforth was aware the track was not good and in fairness to him, put no pressure on us to ensure the meeting took place. He said he would leave the decision up to the riders. Now I have to tell you, having Billy around at that time of the year was most unusual. His scoring always dropped off from the individual World final in September onwards, when his thoughts moved to his home in the sun. The first frosts of the English winter were normally enough to see him up and away, just like a migratory bird.

When all the Ipswich riders had arrived, the team walked, as a group, from the pits on the fourth turn, along the home straight and into the first turn. I pointed out a couple of things. First, that a difficult track always affects the home team more than the away team. The away team ride it how they see it, whereas the home riders tend to want to ride it the way they did every other week.

I also pointed out that if the Witches jointly chose to ride, then there would be no going through the motions. We were there to win. During the walk along that straight, I also pulled Billy to one side and pointed out that a postponement would almost certainly see the season last another week and I would require him to see it out.

Billy was a great wet weather rider.

There was much umming and erring among the team and things looked, if you will pardon the pun, very sticky. Then Billy, no doubt thinking of the beckoning blue waters of Bondi, declared we would do it! On the way around the rest of the track and back to the pits, he took charge; he told the riders how to set up their equipment and how to ride on that surface. We blitzed 'em to effectively tie up the League and Cup double again.

In 1975 and '76 Billy didn't really increase his League average, but what he did was to become able to win the important races. They were great years for the club and he was very much in the middle of things. I would think, looking over his time in England, these are the years he most enjoyed, scoring freely, enjoying the life of a star rider and having a young wife and son.

Riding for Australia always brought out the best in Bill.

Not counting the sweet, lovable John Cook, though, I had more problems sorting out Billy's 'deal' each year than that of any of the other team members. I suspect the biggest reason for this was that he lived in Australia during the time each year when deals were done. There he was, surrounded by adoring family and friends, enjoying the Aussie lifestyle and not wishing to dash back to the cold, north winds of late March.

It was easy under those circumstances to listen to and believe all the advice being thrown at him by well meaning admirers and hangers-on.

The game would be this: He would get his sister to write, saying he had decided to stay in Australia that year, unless I paid him XYZ amount. I would write back, or telephone offering a figure of about half of that, and a cat and mouse game would be played for the next few weeks.

Finally the deal would get done at the level I had intended to pay in the first place. It was never referred to again until the next year, and I don't believe Billy thought any more about it. For me, though, this bluff and the bad feeling it caused used to leave a lingering sour taste in my mouth.

Part of the difficulty was that he had only ridden for Ipswich, so he believed all the nonsense the other Aussies would spout when trying to bignote themselves. In the end, I tired of the game and he went to Birmingham for 1979.

In 1977 he had overtaken John Louis as the top Ipswich rider with a massive 10-and-a-half point average, reaching his first World final. I think he felt he was not getting the full respect he deserved and wanted to take on more challenges.

The move to Birmingham didn't last a full season. Billy found that the grass was decidedly less green elsewhere and, it is fair to say, Brummies' promoter and old mate Joe Thurley found the forthright Aussie such a pain in the rear, he was glad to see the back of him.

I'd like to say Billy had learned a lesson from his time away, had matured and was prepared to settle down and enjoy his second time with the Witches. But, of course, he was the same old Billy

Not having a Hull of a good time.

and jumped straight back into his old ways.

By that time, he had taken to showing his displeasure with people by wanting to fight them rather than just sulking and, given a few beers, the whole world seemed to displease him. One of these times was when the team was down riding in Landshut, deepest southern Germany, and he had been on the beer. I made the mistake of telling him to behave himself and stop acting like a child.

The intervention of our commercial manager and flag marshall extraordinaire, Paul Johnson, only partly slowed Billy's beeline toward me. In those few seconds, I was quite happy to take on the physical onslaught and defend myself as capably as possible. But I was also acutely aware that as soon as the coming together happened, he would no longer be able to stay an Ipswich rider.

For all of that, I was pretty cross about Paul having to fight my battles for me, and told him to let Billy go. I quickly decided that what will be, will be. But just at that second, the proprietor of the hotel where we were staying appeared. You could see why the majority of German stormtroopers came from Bavaria!

This man simply took Billy in a bear hug, lifted him, walked him backwards into a wall and pinned him there whilst telling him not to be a silly boy in his guesthouse. I've never seen such a display of controlled strength and power in my life. Billy just deflated like a balloon and went to his room to sleep it off. The incident was never referred to again.

So, as I explain in a later chapter, when the time came, it really was not difficult to trade him on. It wasn't that I disliked him. In fact, I loved the little sod in many ways. It was that he was just too much hard work. The decision to transfer him to Hull for 1981 is covered elsewhere.

When he returned to Ipswich for the second time, in 1983, he had grown up a lot. I think he finally realised I was really on his side, and that Ipswich was a good place to ride at. The experience of riding for three different promoters had led him to believe life at Ipswich wasn't that bad after all.

Things should have gone well. In fact they did. Bill got on very well with Dennis Sigalos and between them they made a formidable pair. It was just that Billy had become totally fixated, obsessed, with the idea of becoming world champion. The notion had taken him over completely.

He had started messing with 'social' drugs. I well remember a time, years before, when Billy came back from one of his winters in sunny Oz, telling me what an idiot Michael Lee was. He

Billy, Belinda, Dean and Judy in happier times.

said how they had all gone water skiing one day, and that everyone had a whale of an afternoon whilst Michael sat on the river bank off his face.

I tried to remind Billy of that occasion when he became enmeshed himself but if ever you've tried to tell a 10-year-old what is good for him, you know that he might be listening, but hearing nothing. You know damn well you are talking to yourself.

By and large, I have tried to avoid discussing riders' domestic circumstances except where they impinged onto their speedway. The way Billy's life finished means it is inevitable that these things have to be discussed here.

Billy and Judy were very young when they married and young to start a family. Billy's chosen profession made a normal family life unlikely; his attitude to life made it absolutely impossible.

For most people, life is a series of compromises. We know what our dreams and ambitions are but somewhere along the line, we realise that compromises have to be made. Real life is something a bit less than our ultimate desires would demand.

Not so with Billy, who lived his life in three colours: black, white . . . and seeing red. He had to be the best at riding. He had to be the best at drinking and in winning popularity shows. He had to be the best at everything, and he put his every effort into all of the things he took on.

I often wondered how Judy coped. Most riders' wives resent their husband's bosses, and she was no exception. Sometimes, when Billy was having a prolonged black mood, I might get a call from her. But generally, I was the big, bad guy who made her husband do things he didn't want to.

I tried to keep out of their domestic life as much as possible. When I first started as a promoter, there wasn't that much difference between my age and that of the riders, but by now the team and I were a generation apart. Even had I wanted to be part of their social scene, it would not have been welcomed.

I was fairly sure, though, Judy had more than her hands full with her husband's mood swings, his partying and his self-centeredness. Having said that, she was a pretty fiery character herself. I doubt there were too many dull moments around that house when they were there together.

As the years clicked on, Billy became more and more obsessed with wanting to become world champion. It began to take him over completely, except when he was in party mode. I think relaxing became more and more of a struggle for him. Just how much of a state he used to get in became apparent at Norden when we were there for the World final in 1983.

He wanted his family around him in Germany, and they all shared the same small hotel as me, but the night before the final, he simply threw them all out of his room. The hotel was, of course, packed to the rafters and in the middle of the night, Judy and the kids were left standing in the corridor, evicted by Billy's temper.

He came second to Egon Müller the next day. Billy had proved himself the best speedway rider in the world on that afternoon, only to be beaten by a long track rider on whom all the speedway gods in the world shined for one magical moment.

I don't think Billy ever got over that.

Judy knew Billy had always put himself about with the easy female pickings that surround speedway stars. I don't know if she led the life of a nun in between. I don't really want to. It's not my business. But it did come as a shock, when I got the word back from Australia in our winter of 1984-85 that she was having an affair with another Aussie international rider, Coventry's Gary Guglielmi, and that it was breaking Billy into pieces.

I did hear various tales of the things Bill got up to trying to win her back - and the other things he got up to when his efforts failed. Remember, he did nothing by halves. There is one story of him going into a notorious biker-gang pub, getting drunk, deliberately pouring beer over a pool table and then taking off his jeans to wipe the table with. He had been simply spoiling for a fight.

The worm had clearly turned, though, and whilst it might be wrong of me to suspect Judy was quite enjoying suddenly being in the driving seat, and whilst I wouldn't go so far as to suggest she might have taken the opportunity to kick a few goals herself, there is no doubting he took it more than badly.

Billy arrived in England for the 1985 season with his son Dean. They expected Judy to follow. What had been said or not said by Judy to back this up, I do not know. I suspect it was easier for her to say things she didn't mean than to stand her ground.

From friends and partners (here in the 1983 World Pairs), Billy and Guglielmi became sworn enemies. *(AW)*

Anyway, Billy clearly felt that having Dean with him swung the odds of a family reunion in his favour. Perhaps Judy and Guglielmi were of the opinion they would be happier having Dean 12,000 miles away. I don't know.

Whatever was said before Billy left Australia, it became clear Judy had no intention of joining him. Billy was riding (like a champion) and trying to look after his son, the house, himself and his equipment. He just could not cope. Eventually, he ended up in my speedway office, saying he was going back to Australia to sort things out.

Billy had finally realised that Guglielmi, a person who had been a very close friend as well as international team-mate, had simply taken over his place in Judy's life. This 'friend' hadn't just taken his wife, but had taken over his home, his daughter, and everything he had in Australia. For all Billy knew, Gary was even wearing his underpants.

Put yourself in that situation. Then try to imagine how you would feel if you were someone who lived life only in black and white.

I was way past worrying about Billy's speedway career by then. In talking him out of catching a plane back to Sydney there and then, I had it in mind I was saving Judy and Gary from a violent confrontation, and Billy from spending a long time in jail. I hadn't even considered a worse possibility.

What Billy needed first and foremost was some stability in his life. I told him we needed to come up with a 'housekeeper' to look after the house and Dean. This would ease a lot of the strain on him. He telephoned a girl in Australia and asked her if she would like to take on the role. A bit much, expecting her to drop everything and jump on a plane, but Australians are far more relaxed about these things.

In the event, she said no, so he and I spent quite some time in my office considering alternatives. Suddenly, he perked up. He looked much brighter and said he had come to terms with it. He said he had some other names he would try. I said that if he was unsuccessful, he would get straight back to me and we would sort something out. I won't say he was whistling a happy tune when he drove away, but he looked much, much, better.

To say I was gobsmacked when I got the call from the police that late afternoon would be to put it mildly. Never, at any time, had I considered suicide as a possibility.

I should have done.

That was Billy's life. No series of ups and downs for him, but UPS and DOWNS. It was a desperately sad way for anybody's life to end. All I can say is that he packed more into his short life than most people would do if they lived to be a hundred.

There is more good and bad news on the ongoing story. Judy and Gary Guglielmi are, as far as I know, still together. I broke off relations with her because of her attitude over Billy's death. She seemed unprepared to accept that any of her own actions had anything to do with it, which fitted in with many of the private things Billy had told me about the break up and the way she treated him.

The fact that she didn't come over for the funeral or to pick up Dean, leaving that to Billy's mother, also concerned me. But worse was the positively financially grasping attitude she took which included demanding the balance of Billy's contract payments for that season.

I could see how things were and simply put her in touch with my own solicitor, who handled all things financial for her. I didn't want to deal with her. After arranging and laying on everything for Billy's funeral, the only cost I passed on to his estate was the costs of the funeral directors. I didn't find out until at least a year afterwards, she refused to release the money, so the Speedway Riders' Benevolent Fund had paid it.

With so much water under the bridge since then, I bear no grudge. Sadly, though, the bad news is that Dean never really got over it. He was never an easy kid to deal with and Judy couldn't really cope with him. After a troubled short life, he decided to end it himself.

In the final analysis, with Billy, you just have to look at the whole package. Despite the problems, the fights, the stand offs, Billy Sanders was a wonderful speedway rider and a good person. I am glad I knew him and that we shared some of our lives together.

If it seems that my comments about 'The Kid' are a bit severe, it was not intended. I suspect the truth of the matter is, I was too close to him and still remain so. I suspect a part of me still feels some responsibility for what happened and I suspect all of this prevents me from being as positive as I might have been.

For those who want to know more about Billy's Australian background, and for a really good history of his speedway life, I can refer you Ross Garrigan's excellent work on the website http://www.ausm.info – and navigate through 'aussie O/S' then 'riders from another era'.

Tony 'Shrimp' Davey

This time we almost made the pieces fit, didn't we?
This time we almost some sense of it, didn't we?
This time I have the answer right here in my hand,
Then I touched it, and it has turned to sand.

This time we almost sang the song in tune, didn't we?
This time we almost made it to the moon, didn't we?
This time, we almost made a poem rhyme
And this time we almost made that long hard climb.
Didn't we almost make it this time . . . this time.

I always manage to get raised eyebrows when I describe Tony Davey as simply the best natural speedway rider I ever saw.

Most people remember him as a fast-gating Ipswich heat leader who was difficult to pass. He certainly wouldn't feature in many people's lists of all-time greats.

I can support my claims with hard facts, though. Tony began riding second half races towards the end of 1970. As an absolute raw novice, and after just four junior races spread over two weeks, he caught the eye enough to find himself making his team debut by riding in the Division Two Knockout Cup final against Berwick that year.

A winter Olle Nygren training school, a few practice sessions and a new bike later, and he started 1971 as a fully paid up member of the Witches team, albeit in the reserve position to begin with. He established track records to go with 15-point maxima in his first two matches (both away) and dropped just one point to the opposition in his first five team outings.

That represented an average of 11.83. I should also point out, many of those points were gained from the back and on tracks he had never seen before. Nobody had told him speedway racing was difficult!

He went from reserve to the number one position in the team in one leap. How many riders can boast a start to their career like that? John Louis? Peter Collins? Michael Lee? I think not.

Tony Davey was just a phenomenon. His natural riding ability was boundless. On the surface at least, he was the complete, ready-made package. For anyone who doubts my opinion or is too young to remember, I list the facts from the first six meetings:

- 21-3-71 – Boston away. Five rides, 15 points.
- 25-3-71 – Romford away. Five rides, 15 points. Track record.
- 1-4-71 – Canterbury home. Four rides, 12 points. Track record.
- 3-4-71 – Canterbury away. Five rides, paid 14 points.
- 9-4-71 – Romford home. Five rides, 15 points. Fastest time of the night.
- 15-4-71 – Rayleigh home. Four rides, 9 points, one fall.

That fall, and another at Rayleigh, both involved the 'willing' Geoff Maloney, starting a long and bitter rivalry between the two. In fact, Maloney seemed to have feuds with pretty well all of the Witches at one time or another.

In all of the time he rode a speedway bike I never can remember Tony falling as a result of simply getting out of control. I can recall him being knocked off, and I can remember him being involved in crashes with other riders, but I cannot remember him falling by himself.

I should add that Shrimp, named obviously because of his diminutive stature by the scrambling fraternity before he reached speedway, was not at all worldly wise.

He was only 19 then, and had been brought up in a tied cottage on a farm not far from a village near a Town close to Ipswich. I think we can safely say he was a 'country boy' through and through. Relaxed among family and friends, he was confident, funny and self-assured, but decidedly less so outside of that comfort zone.

The supporters loved him, though, for his down to earth manner and wicked sense of humour. Being tiny somehow added to the effect. His broadest of broad Suffolk accents, delivered at machine gun speed and earthy frankness, was a real delight. He was a true man of the people. It was a real problem getting him to speak on the microphone but whenever he did, he brought the house down.

His lightning reactions at the starting gate always brought forth accusations of cheating and

there were times when he was moving as the tapes rose. But he was rarely excluded for starting gate infringements and the new, tougher regulations, whereby merely touching the tapes resulted in exclusion, had no effect on his starting abilities.

So I put his great starts down to fast reactions and an ability to get maximum drive from the starting area to the first turn. I will go as far as to say I don't think he ever missed a start he wanted to make when racing with riders he trusted.

That same ability to adjust throttle and balance to gain maximum traction also applied on the bends, and in particular the exits from them.

If there was a weakness, it was a reluctance to 'mix it' in the first turn. In that first full year, 1971, as his reputation began to spread, Tony got bundled off a few times in tight first bends and although he was happy to pass riders on either side, he became happier to pick them off cleanly rather than to become involved in a melee.

Shrimp had realised early that very few riders had the same motorcycling ability as him. Some of those lads tried to make up for this by riding beyond their means, placing both themselves

All balance and drive from Day One.

and their opponents in danger. Others were just plain aggressive and these unpredictable riders he never trusted nor did well against.

Not surprisingly, the exploits of his first few matches in '71 could not be fully maintained as he took a few knocks. Also, the continued meteoric rise to stardom of John Louis tended to overshadow Tony's achievements but finishing your novice year with an average only a smidge under 10 points was no mean feat.

I don't think anyone actually passed him in that year. All it needed was for Shrimp to believe he was as good a rider as he was, and he would have been a world-beater.

If Ipswich had stayed in the second division for 1972, Tony Davey would have done so also. Unfortunately, those rules that prevented Louis from taking any first division bookings in 1971 also affected Shrimp. Not once in his first whole year did Tony have the opportunity to race against top flight riders or on first division tracks. Not like Peter Collins, who doubled up between Rochdale and Belle Vue.

Shrimp had seen Louis have an extra year in the lower league, and I think he fancied the chance to clean up as John had done, but also I think he was genuinely concerned that he would not be able to cope with the big boys. This was patently not true. In fact, generally speaking, Division One riders were more in control and less erratic than those in Division Two.

I admit that if Ipswich had not moved up in 1972, I would have wanted to keep Shrimp down in the second division. But we had moved up and, in any case, it would have been a purely selfish move on my part to have held him back. He was clearly ready for the challenge of top line racing, of that I had no doubt.

Even with the benefit of hindsight, I would still have talked him into the move up with the Witches. Another year with the minnows would have been a waste for a rider of his ability.

The best laid plans ...

A pair of cheeky Chappies.

The circumstances and injury to Tony's left hand in his first ever meeting in the senior league is detailed earlier in the book.

It only took three months for the hand to heal. Well, what was left of it, anyway. The little finger couldn't be saved, and was removed down to the wrist, along with a fair chunk of palm. The ring finger remained, but pretty much as a useless ornament. What was left of the palm of the hand was also a less than perfect shape.

Such physical problems were always going to be a challenge, especially when you realise Tony's greatest attribute was his fast gating – the injury was to his clutch hand. However, a specially modified handlebar, with half inch tubing replacing the normal handgrip, solved the physical handicap.

Nothing, but nothing could heal the mental scar, though. The first time I visited this young homespun country lad in the hospital after he had fully woken up from the operation, told me all I needed to know. There was just the two of us there and he was plain distraught.

Nobody enjoys being in hospital, I think that's plain to say. Having to stay in hospital when you are not sick, and merely injured, is even worse.

But for the home-loving Shrimp, being away from his family, stuck in the nineteenth century and utterly depressing Anglesea Road Hospital, caused him major trauma. He vowed to me, he would never, ever spend another night in a hospital bed.

Now for a speedway rider to say such a thing makes it become an oxymoron. Being a speedway rider has an inbuilt possibility – nay, probability – that you will see the inside of a casualty department at some stage, and be happy to escape with just that.

Tony, though, meant his vow sincerely. From then on throughout the rest of his magnificent career, he never stuck his neck out or took an uncalculated risk on the track again.

His initial reaction not to ride at all any more after the injury was soon dismissed but there was to be no fairytale recovery. When he did get back onto his bike, more than three months later, he was painfully nervous and slow.

Riding around on his own, Shrimp showed that he was capable of overcoming the physical damage to the hand. But as soon as he was expected to mix it with three other riders, the old magic was gone, replaced by a defensive determination not to put himself into a dangerous position.

It was a painfully slow rehabilitation, and not without a good deal of soul-searching on all sides. I tried everything to get him going again but nothing worked. I recall one particular meeting at Hampden Park in Scotland, where I started by reasoning with him, then tried

A modified handlebar enabled Tony to maintain his slick starting technique.

begging and finished up cursing him, all in an effort to light a spark. I have no doubt that during that prolonged period of time he must have seriously wondered if it was all worth the effort.

The beginning of the 1973 season still saw Tony lacking in confidence but at least now, if he could get clear from the start of a race, he was fast enough to keep out of trouble. Bad track surfaces, either through weather or poor preparation, never ever bothered him. He was such a good motorcyclist, he made a mockery of tracks many others considered unrideable.

He also became a real giant killer, regularly beating top stars, whilst dropping points to ordinary riders. The reason for this was simple. He could trust the stars not to do anything rash, whereas the lesser lights were not so predictable.

By the end of the season he was scoring the odd maximum, finishing with an average of just over seven-and-a-half points, which put him as second heat leader, slightly in front of Billy Sanders. This is the bare minimum I would have expected from him in the '72 season had it not been for the injury.

Two points are worthy of comment. By then, Shrimp virtually refused to start from the inside gate positions, even though these were nearly always more favourable than the outside draw. Therefore, he was a great man to have in the number three position, because that meant he was more often than not paired with a reserve, who then was able to have the benefit of the inside gates.

First away again.

Secondly, his heat wins were nearly always in slow times, because once in front, he would enter turns slowly, powering out fast, which was the opposite to how most riders approached things. Consequently, chasing riders would find themselves getting into a muddle as they caught up with Shrimp in mid turn, only to see him power away from them.

I do not think Tony ever rode to within 80% of his maximum capability after the 1972 crash, and most times nowhere near that. With most riders, such a waste of talent and ability would see me tearing my hair out. But with Shrimp, things were different.

This was never a case of 'cheating' on his team-mates or the public. Just the opposite really: every time Shrimp got onto a bike, he had to race against his own demons as well as the opposition and it was a constant battle.

Yes, I do think he had dreams of being world champion, but they were just that – dreams. Friends, family, quality of life and, most important of all, being able to wake up in his own bed

Shrimp – the Character and Country Boy.

Left: Shrimp with his dad and brother (and mechanic), Jim. Right: A rare shot of Tony going from the inside gate.

every morning, were far more important. Anyway, it was impossible to be angry with this plain, honest, open hearted country boy whose conversation was always delivered with a twinkle in the eye and a splash of sharp humour.

Far from being a liability to the team, as the matches, and then seasons, ticked by, he became its heart and soul. John Louis was the team leader, Billy Sanders the enforcer, but Shrimp was its heart. He was the one who made the whole team gel. Tony Davey represented everything Ipswich Speedway stood for.

Here's a little story.

No self-respecting crow would bother to fly from Ipswich to Hull but if it had to, the distance would not be that great.

But there is a good deal of water and (in the 70s), not many decent roads in between the two places, so us poor sods who had to do it the hard way, on the ground, would have to slog all the way over to the A1, then up to the M62, and back across to the east coast again.

So that is how it was when the Witches rode at Hull in 1974. I had a sparkling new Mercedes then, and Tony Davey had a mark 4 Ford Zephyr. Being the professional he was, he had taken a full entourage and a trailer load of bikes with him.

Normally I didn't hang about after an away meeting and especially a Wednesday night jaunt with a looming home event to run the next day, but somehow Shrimp and company had managed to get away from the Boulevard in front of us (Tony never spent longer than the bare minimum necessary away from his beloved backwoods of Suffolk).

Just after turning off the M62 onto the A1, we cantered past a stopped Zephyr by the side of the road. Back tracking, we found Shrimp and co. with a dead Ford. Out came the towrope to make up a kind of three carriage train: Mercedes, Zephyr and bike trailer full of bikes. I'm not sure how Mr Plod would have taken to this arrangement, but needs must...

The first couple of hours weren't too bad. Not in the Merc, where it was cosy and warm anyway. A bit different in the Zephyr, though. No motor, so no heater, no power steering and no brake servo. Denied the latter two benefits, it was not wise to thunder through the night at normal speeds. We were reduced to 40mph. Well, 40 for the first half-hour, gradually moving to 50 as boredom set in, and then maybe a little more.

Just our luck. At the Norman Cross roundabout, a lorry travelling north was turning right and we had to almost stop. The rope went slack, then tightened quickly as we went to pull away. Ping: two halves of rope!

This left an uncomfortable distance, or lack of it, between the rear of the Merc and the front of the Ford when adjustments had been made, but we reached the A45 without further incident.

Only the A45 then was not a dual carriageway through-road by-passing everything. It meandered through Huntingdon, Cambridge, Newmarket, Bury St Edmunds and Needham Market, before requiring us to cut across country to the metropolis of Framsden.

Now I'll be kind and put the blame on the fact that the tow-rope was not designed to take a convoy. I'll also point to the lack of turning and stopping ability of the dead Zephyr, but when you are towing it is imperative to keep the rope tight. This means the front car should do all the going forwards, whilst the rear car should do all the braking.

Left: So often a match-winner. Here with Billy in front of Shirra and Guglielmi of Coventry.
Right: Less than perfect conditions were never a problem.

This was not happening in our case, and every time the rope was allowed to go slack, we heard that same 'ping' as we tried to pull away and the rope was halved again.

By the time we had turned off the A45, the only thing left of the rope was a series of knots. Why had we, in such a cavalier manner, abandoned pieces of tow-rope of two feet or less on our earlier travels, or should that be travailes?

We were now headed for the farm where Shrimp lived with his parents, but by now the rear bumper on the Mercedes and the front one on the Zephyr were almost rubbing together. Some mile or so from home, the tow-rope would no longer allow daylight (and, oh yes, it was daylight!) between the two vehicles. We were reduced to using a couple of leather belts normally reserved for holding the bikes onto the trailer. We managed to snap them, too.

The convoy was now on single-track byways but as luck would have it, just as we finally ran out of every conceivable means of joining the two (three!) vehicles, the Davey farm cottage hove into sight. We had made it back without accident, without a ticket and without sleep. It was nine o'clock in the morning when we said goodnight ... and then all went straight to work!

Stopped in his tracks

Tony was always there, always reliable, always friendly, always a thorn in the other team's side. But mainly, and most importantly, he became the team's 'go to' man. Most of the time, we could allow him the luxury of doing his own thing, and if that meant operating on not much more than half throttle, then so be it. Half throttle for Tony was still good enough to win his share of races.

But when the chips were down, and we needed something extra, he would nearly always respond to the situation with something a bit special. He had so much in hand (excuse the pun), it was just frightening.

And so, from 1973 Shrimp played a vital part in the Witches successes of the 70s, even attaining a 10-and-a-half point average in 1978, topping the Witches' scorechart and becoming a regular England international rider, although he never made it to a world final.

Right through this period, I can only ever remember him missing two matches in a seven-year run, and they were for good reason. He was drawn to ride British Championship semi-finals at Sheffield on a Thursday night when Ipswich had a home meeting - not just once, but two years in succession.

In all of that time the only limiting factor to his riding was just how fast his built-in self-preservation factor would let him go.

The big, fast Leicester track

Half throttle enough to see off PC in the Golden Helmet.

was one of his favourites. On April 24, 1979 we were there for a league match. By that time, Shrimp was at the top of his form. If not forgotten, the ghost of that 1972 crash was at last beginning to fade. Finally the old flair and dash, not seen for eight years, was beginning to show through.

Full of confidence, in his first ride he took the high, wide and handsome line around the outside, to draw alongside partner Mike Lanham, who may or may not have known he was there, and into the lead. Anyway,

Always happy to race Ivan Mauger.

there wasn't a whole heap of room, tight up against the back straight fence as The Framsden Flier drew alongside.

Suddenly, Tony's bike stopped. Shrimp did not and he sailed over his handlebars, finishing a good deal further along the track. We checked afterwards, and what should have been a continuous kickboard at the bottom of the fence had a board sticking out.

With no video available, I cannot say for sure, but I am willing to bet, his footrest caught the jutting out kickboard and it was this that dragged the bike into the fence. I would guess Shrimp's thigh broke on the handlebars on his way over the top.

You could count the number of times Tony Davey hit the track over the preceding seven years on one hand – even on Tony's own left hand – and yet here he was with a second major injury and not his fault. To all intent and purpose, Shrimp's speedway career was finished that night.

Even sadder, it wasn't the injury that did it, although breaking a femur is bad enough. From the moment he arrived in Leicester Royal Infirmary, he wanted to get out and home. So insistent was he, and so unhappy, that the people there decided to ship him off to Ipswich rather than start treatment in Leicester. He was transferred to the Ipswich Hospital within days.

There are two ways to mend a broken bone. The first is to 'set' the bone in the correct position and allow the body to heal itself. With most broken bones, this means a plaster cast, but with femurs it generally means the leg being put in traction, which involves a three-month hospital stay to allow the broken bones to knit together.

Doctors favoured this method. if the break was relatively simple. It avoided surgery and produced a result whereby the bone ended up stronger than it had been originally and, because of the slow healing time, could be carefully monitored and controlled.

The other method was to set some kind of metal plate or pin into position and screw the broken bones to it. This method was usually reserved for complex breaks where 'normal' healing was unlikely to be successful. The one advantage of the surgical method was that the hospital stay was reduced from about three months to three weeks, although the actual healing period remained much the same.

Once back in Ipswich, Tony made such a fuss and demanded so loudly about not wanting to spend three months in hospital, his surgeon agreed to insert a plate. Shrimp was out and about inside the month, a much relieved family man who hated not being able to sleep in his own bed.

It took a full five months for Shrimp to get back on a bike. We were happy to write the season off as far as he was concerned, so it was no great worry to see him take things easy on his return to the saddle. In fact, if anything, I was pleased he was able to go out and win races at all. He had been riding so well before the injury, there was no reason why he shouldn't bounce back to form next season.

In his first match of the 1980 season, his 10th and testimonial year, we were overjoyed to see Shrimp record a maximum against an admittedly very weak Halifax side.

He flattered to deceive, though. There were odd flashes of the old style but he was clearly a

It looked fairly innocuous when Belle Vue's Peter Carr clattered into Tony's left leg going into the turn (above) . . . but, as you can see (below), Tony's leg just folded on impact and a once richly promising career was finally over.

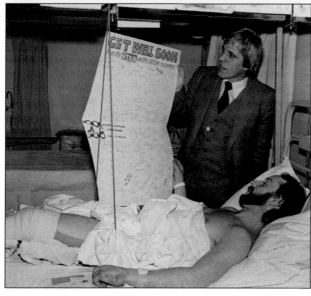

EADT public relations manager and speedway fan Terry Sheppard brings a huge get-well-soon card signed by hundreds of supporters.

shadow of the rider who had been on top of his form before the thigh injury. I knew it would be a long way back for him and when he complained of soreness in the thigh after each meeting, I first put it down to a mixture of lack of use in the muscles, along with a certain amount of reluctance to push himself.

Slowly, though, it became clear there was more to it than that. Eventually, we came to realise the plate the surgeon had fitted was entirely wrong. You could push on his thigh muscle and feel the sharp edge of the plate underneath. It was in absolutely the wrong place for a speedway rider — the sharp edge was cutting into the muscle every time he pressed the leg against the bike, which was every time he rode a race.

After each meeting, and especially on the tighter or bumpier tracks, his knee would blow up like a balloon where the muscle tissue was being constantly damaged by the metal plate and 'bled' into the knee joint.

I have never seen the X-rays but people who have, and are more qualified than me to say, were in no doubt that the surgery had been bungled. No doubt at all, in this day and age, a malpractice suit would almost certainly have followed. But in 1979, people believed the medical profession could do no wrong.

What to do? I certainly wasn't brave enough to tell Shrimp he needed to go back into hospital and have the job redone. The alternative was clear: The leg would probably be strong enough for him to lead a normal life but no good for a professional speedway rider.

By now, we were months into

Sadly, Shrimp was in hospital on the day of his testimonial meeting, but a good turn out of riders and supporters showed their respect for the rider who epitomised everything that Ipswich Speedway was about in the early days.

the season, with Tony's testimonial meeting looming. To be brutally honest, his form was such by then, given a different scenario or a different rider, his place in the team would have been under serious threat. A decision, one way or the other, would need to be taken as soon as the testimonial meeting was over.

I have the feeling Tony hated hospitals so much, he would have made the wrong choice and settled for having a gammy leg for the rest of his life. In the end, the decision was taken out of his hands.

Belle Vue were at Ipswich, three days before his testimonial meeting, when Peter Carr ran into Tony's leg mid-turn. It was nothing malicious. To be fair on Peter, Shrimp was going into turns so slowly by then that the Aces rider would have been wrong not to try and pass.

The whole thing seemed to happen in slow motion. Nobody, even now, knows if it was the light blow from the other rider, or if the leg just gave way by itself. But by the time Tony hit the ground, the leg had folded neatly into half.

The Shrimp's speedway career was over. He must be the only rider ever not to attend his own testimonial. He was still in hospital on the day it was staged.

I gave Shrimp the courtesy of asking if he was going to ride again but the answer was clear. I believe more than one lower league team chased him but he was wise to turn them down.

There was a whisper of him having another go a couple of years later but he satisfied his racing urges by having the odd grass track run out and, at 50, still does.

Becoming a world champion and speedway legend requires more than natural riding skill. Without that original damage to the hand and mind, would the decidedly worldly unwise country boy have been able to cope with the pressures required in reaching the very top?

We'll never know the answer, but one thing is sure. On pure riding ability alone, the tiny Shrimp was head and shoulders above all the rest.

John 'Tiger' Louis

Memories light the corners of my mind,
Misty water-coloured memories
of the way we were.
Scattered pictures of the smiles we left behind,
Smiles we gave to one another for the way we were.

Can it be that it was all so simple then?
Or has time rewritten every line?
If we had the chance to do it all again,
Tell me, would we, could we?

Memories may be beautiful and yet
What's too painful to remember,
We simply choose to forget.
So it's the laughter we will remember
Whenever we remember
The way we were,

In 1969, when I was the 'absentee co-promoter', turning up like the Lord of the Manor on a race day and responsible for the office side of things at Ipswich, Joe Thurley, Ron Bagley and Howdy Byford issued a general invitation to all local moto-cross and grass track riders to come and have a try at speedway. I don't know who made the first suggestion but it was a great idea and laid the foundation for the next 20 years or so.

Several lads turned up, but not John Louis. He needed persuading. And Ron Bagley did that. Actually, he persuaded John to go straight out into a second half junior race, wearing decidedly tatty brown two-piece leathers covered by a rugby jersey, and mounted on Ron's bike. It has to be said, he didn't look too much like a superstar at that stage. What he demonstrated on the track, though, was a good starting technique, great determination . . . and a very good moto-cross style!

Just from that ride, however, it was clear the potential was there and Howdy Byford bestowed the 'Tiger' tag by virtue of John's aggressive, all action style. He was that little bit of local talent we had been searching for and he had some character about him to boot. Within a few weeks Tiger had made it to a team place but, almost immediately, the end of the season arrived.

Now the question is, did the near 30-year-old motorcycle shop stores assistant really have

Before Tiger earned his stripes . . . John with (left to right) Stan Pepper, Bob Jennings, Joe Thurley, Brian Osborne and Howdy Byford. Right: Stripes now fully earned in his first Division One season.

doubts about taking the plunge at his age and with a wife, kids and mortgage?

I recall us having several conversations early on in the winter of 1969-70, where John made the point that if he decided to become a professional speedway rider, he would give it 100% effort. Finally, when he committed himself, that's just what he did. Possibly the coyness was a negotiating ploy.

A brand new bike — a rarity those days even among established team men – and several winter training schools and practice sessions showed he was serious. Not only that, but he went along to watch just about every early season meeting he could, studying carefully the riding style and technique of as many top stars as he could.

I tried to get him to have his new leathers made in a tiger skin design but the furthest he would go was to have black and orange stripes on the sleeves.

He listened to Bagley, Byford and everyone who was prepared to offer advice on riding speedway. But here was the clever bit. He was able to filter out the good advice from the bad by being able to

either realise immediately its benefit or otherwise, or by trying it out and making up his own mind.

My own part, at that stage and pretty well throughout his career, was to offer advice — not on riding a speedway bike, but on all the other things important to becoming a star. Things like presenting himself well, always appreciating that speedway is (was!) primarily a team sport, being helpful and polite to supporters and media people, and generally being aware of his image. If anything, as far as the actual technique of speedway racing is concerned, I learned more from John than he ever learned from me.

Always willing to help. This was a local children's home.

He always understood the importance of public relations. This was the advantage of dealing with a mature person and not a starry eyed teenager. John knew he had to get where he was going fast. Time was not on his side and he was happy to play his full role in promoting himself and Ipswich Speedway. It was a good partnership.

Realising just how much potential he had, and aware that he was a mature, sensible grown up, over the first two or three months I used to make more and more outrageous claims about him in both the local and speedway media. The more I stuck my neck out, the more he responded to the challenge. It was as if he simply believed everything he read about himself.

Help in the workshop from father Jack.

I have also touched before on the role Ron Bagley played in helping the inexperienced Louis in his early and short learning period, and this should not go unrecognised. However much, though, we all like to claim a part of his success, John Louis and his family were the overall driving force in his success and achievements. All anyone else did was to smooth the path.

More good work in the local community.

By the end of his first full season (1970), the Tiger had shown he was clearly the best rider in the second division and had also demonstrated, through a succession of guest bookings in Division One, that he could easily adjust to the big time.

Bob Radford, at that time tied up with the Newport promotion, also recognised this star quality, but from many other directions came the back-stabbing put downs that he was an 'old man, just a flash in the pan'.

From a selfish point of view, I wanted John to stay at Ipswich another year, and he was not

A kiss from actress Millicent Martin after winning the Division Two Riders' Championship at Hackney in 1971.

Peter and John in opposition . . . and then on the same side.

averse to the idea. Not that he didn't think he was ready for the top league but because he saw an opportunity to establish himself firmly as a local celebrity, put a few bob in the bank and enjoy the opportunity to make a bit of a name for himself.

Riding for your hometown team is a double-edged sword, especially when things go badly, but Tiger was on the up and the benefits of local adoration at that time far outweighed any downside.

I spoke to Charles Ochiltree. He had been kind enough to loan Coventry juniors to us in our hour of need, and in return, I offered him John Louis for nothing, with the proviso he stayed on loan to Ipswich for the extra year. He haughtily rejected the idea, telling me 'thanks but no thanks'. Coventry Speedway relied entirely on its own devices for their team needs, he told me. Just as well he didn't say yes!

Whilst John was tearing all opposition apart in the second division in 1971, another local discovery was being unearthed in far off Manchester.

It would have been much fairer to compare Peter Collins with Tony Davey. They both started speedway at the same time, late in the 1970 season, both were from junior motorcycle racing and were both much the same age. They were also both phenomenal finds, and if John Louis had moved up to Division One in 1971, Peter and Tony would have shared domination of the lower league.

Peter's official team debut was in April 1971. Apart from the two cup matches in 1970, effectively, Shrimp started in March of the same year. Collins finished that season with an average of 9.83; Shrimp's was 9.86.

There was one huge difference between Collins and Davey, though – and that was Belle Vue. Not just that the old Hyde Road track was such a wonderful track to ride. After all, technically, Collins also rode for Rochdale, again on a big, fast circuit.

No, the difference was that because Collins was 'attached' to Belle Vue, he was able to have regular additional first division racing with them, and was used extensively in their senior team during '71. Davey, on the other hand, by virtue of Ipswich not being aligned to a first division track, was denied any Division One experience whatsoever.

So when Collins made the full time leap from one league to the other, the step was, for him, a minor one. For Davey, having never faced a Division One rider in his life before, the gap was psychologically so huge that he stumbled and literally fell at that very first hurdle,

Left to right: Tony Davey, Brian Goodchild and another mechanic, Clive Noy, John Louis and Ray Chinnery at a John Louis Fan Club 'do'.

lost half a hand and his nerve and was never the same force again.

So instead of the constant comparison between Collins and Davey, in which it is my humble opinion Shrimp would have more than held his own given equal opportunity and without the hand injury, the comparison was always between PC and Louis.

Peter Collins has a World Championship win to his name and was also a spectacular and wonderful rider to watch, especially on the expansive Hyde Road circuit.

Collins caught the eye. Young, cheeky and also able to enjoy the freedom of not

John takes son Chris for his first ride around Foxhall.

having to carry a team, he was given licence to simply go and have fun racing. No wife and family to support at that stage, and without a care in the world. Also, he was a Big City boy.

John Louis, on the other hand, was a mature family man. Whereas 'The Zoo' encouraged flair and style, Ipswich required technical correctness, a compact style and, like most tracks, a good starting technique and first turn strategy.

At Ipswich, John did his 'fun thing' in 1971. From 1972 onwards, he was required to be the lynchpin of an unfashionable provincial rag, tag and bobtail team. Instead of giving him free licence, I required him to be the rock on which the team was built.

In short, John put Ipswich Speedway first, and his own personal ambitions on the individual front were always a secondary concern. For all of Peter's wonderful skill and flair, for all of my full appreciation of his ability, and for all the fact that he was as skilful and committed a team rider as I have ever seen, I do not think he could have done the job that John did at Ipswich.

Further, even given Peter's advantages of a brilliant home track, big city team and big company backing, I am happy to compare the Ipswich team's history over the period John was head of the Witches against Belle Vue's record during the time Peter was the captain of Belle Vue.

People say I underestimate just how good Peter Collins was. I don't think I do. I was the England manager when he lifted the world title in Poland in 1976, and a more comprehensive victory you would have a job to find. I was also in his corner the following year when he almost won it on one leg. That performance was just so good, it was scary.

It's just that if I needed a man to guide a team of kids through a wet meeting away from home, against a strong team at Exeter or Eastbourne, Wimbledon or Wolverhampton, I know which one I would pick between Peter and John.

During the time from 1972 until '76, I doubt many days passed when John and I did not speak on the phone. Often, it might have been simply to pass on a booking, or something similar, but most calls ended up in a conversation about speedway. Just like Ron and myself, the relationship with John was that of two people who might well have slightly differing goals, but who needed each other's help in achieving them and respected the other's ability to assist. Symbiotic is the posh word for the arrangement.

Not that John and I were that close on a personal level. I don't think, apart from speedway, we had too many things in common. As I have mentioned, I tried not to get too involved socially with any of the riders.

I never missed any of John's (or anyone else's) fan club social events as long as I was available, and often backed up John and others when they were opening fetes or the like. Likewise, we had several get togethers as a team, either at my place or, more often, at a steak house or pub. But I could count on one hand the number of times I got past the Louis' garage/workshop and into the house. To my mind, though, that lack of familiarity helped the relationship between us rather than hindered it.

Sadly, though, the Louis family was always highly suspicious of me. It is true that I encouraged John to be a team player rather than concentrate on himself but to my mind it helped his own standing, inside and outside of speedway, as well as helping the team effort.

Once well established, John came to me with a few ideas for business ventures he was considering becoming involved in. They were all bad choices - and I told him so. The obvious direction for him to go in was a motorcycle shop or similar venture, but here he would run straight up against Dave Bickers Motorcycles, for whom he had worked and which was the leading sporting orientated motorcycle business in the area.

In the event, John invested heavily in the formation of a company to make small motorbikes for young kids. The deal was all signed and sealed before I knew about it. I asked John why he hadn't spoken to me first. He told me it was because I would have tried to talk him out of it. I certainly would have! He lost a lot of money, friends and a whole lot of blood, sweat and tears over the next couple of years before the thing collapsed.

With what he had earned – his local reputation, excellent manner with the local people and with the advantage of the local radio, on which he was very good and could have given him a great opportunity for self-promotion – he should have been investing in a local retail, recreation, or social outlet. He could have employed managers or partners to do the work and would have just been a figurehead. Sadly, the break up of his marriage to Pat prevented him from cashing in.

One thing I have not done so far is to pick out many of Tiger's speedway highlights. Not because there weren't many, but because there were so many and it is difficult to isolate a few incidents from the mass.

Certainly, his trips to Wembley for his World final appearances stand out in the mind. I can only think of visits to Ipswich by The Queen, and the lifting of the FA Cup by Ipswich Town in 1978, as being bigger local events. I reckon there was a minimum of 10,000 bodies from East Suffolk at Wembley for his 1972 effort, and many more from around the country giving him their support. He might not have finished on the rostrum, but he was the darling of the crowd that night.

Just out of interest, let's have a look at the British final field, in finishing order that year, and compare it with the World final field.

1. Ivan Mauger 14
2. Nigel Boocock 12
3. Barry Briggs 11
4. John Louis 11
5. Eric Boocoock 10
6. Jim McMillan 10
7. Terry Betts 9
8. Ray Wilson 7
9. Dave Jessup 7
10. John Boulger 7
11. Martin Ashby 6
12. Arnold Haley 5
13. Garry Middleton 4
14. Peter Collins 3
15. Trevor Hedge 2
16. Ronnie Moore 2

A rare sight . . . John hits the deck at Ipswich along with Reading's Swedish star Anders Michanek.

Not a bad line up for a 'domestic' round, and a bit more difficult than today's Grand Prix fields. The top five, by the way, went straight to the final at Wembley, making that British final a real cut-throat event.

At Wembley, those five met a motley group of Nordic and eastern European riders, and here are the results:

1. Ivan Mauger 13
2. Bernt Persson 13

3. Ole Olsen 12
4. Christer Lofqvist 11
5. John Louis 11
6. Alexander Pavlov 8
7. Anders Michanek 8
8. Pawel Waloszek 6
9. Viktor Trofimov 6
10. Nigel Boocock 6
11. Viktor Kalmykov 6
12. Anatoli Kuzmin 4
13. Gregori Khlynovski 4
14. Barry Briggs 3 (inj)
15. Eric Boocock 2
16. Valeri Gordeev 2

Ipswich virtually closed for the night when JL was riding at Wembley. The others joining me alongside Tiger after his third place in the 1975 world final are Ron Bagley and mechanics John Bloomfield and Mick.

With the best will in the world, I think you have to say the British final was considerably harder than the World final that year, and to finish equal third on points at Coventry and equal fourth on points at Wembley were no mean feats, especially taking into account this was John's first year in the senior league.

Perhaps 1975 was his best year individually. He followed up the winning of the British Final at Coventry with a rostrum finish in the World Final at Wembley. Just as Olsen was the undisputed winner at Wembley that year, so John had dominated the field at Coventry.

Both times, the Ipswich support was huge and, again, I would suggest John had the most support of any of the riders from the packed Wembley crowd. Ron and I were quietly disappointed that night. We really thought John would win, although we were delighted to join in with the celebrations for the third place.

There's nothing like taking the top spot, though, and the British Final celebrations were great. The Ipswich fans invaded the Coventry track and we all had a ball.

One of the incidents most talked about by the Ipswich supporters from the early days was when Rochdale came to Ipswich for a KO Cup match way back in 1970. The tie hinged on a race between John and Eric Broadbelt, who was just about top dog of Division Two at the time.

Belle Vue always raced the same way. No beg pardons, just good, hard racing and maximum determination. Eric typified that spirit and had something of a reputation for being hard as well as fast. He and 'The Tiger' had already established a history when it came to the pair of them racing against each other that night.

Ipswich needed to avoid a 5-1 against them in heat 13.

Eric 'stuffed' John in the first turn, effectively putting him out of the race and the Hornets pair on the 5-1 they needed. Tiger hadn't picked up the nickname for nothing, though, and set off after the Rochdale duo. It looked as if they would get the result but Louis just would not give in, refusing to shut off at all going into the third turn of the last lap.

He had passed the second placed Alan Wilkinson and then, just for good measure, drove under a shocked Broadbelt, who had no alternative but to move over. Who knows whether there was contact? I was watching from the pits, with roughly the same view as the ref, and from that position you have to make your decision on gut feeling rather than vision.

John was past before Eric slid from his bike. It could be that Eric got a slight bump, or it could be that he was just inconvenienced, or it might have been that he decided his best chance was, by then, to go down and put the verdict in the hands of the ref. For my money, he just did not expect John to go through and was not prepared for it.

Hard-man Eric Broadbelt reached for the rake.

I've always been a staunch supporter of the collapsible wooden fence at Foxhall – and here's another good example why.
A nasty tangle between John Louis and Sheffield's Reg Wilson would have left both riders nursing serious injuries at many other tracks but the only damage this time was to pride.

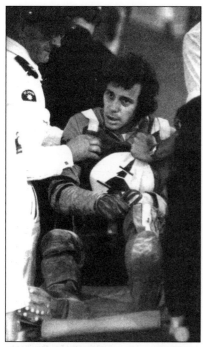

Clearly in pain with a dislocated shoulder. That's my hand with the watch on.

I started running as Eric hit the ground. I imagined how he would be feeling. I was right. As soon as he realised no exclusion lights were going to come on, he jumped up ready to fight the world. All eyes were on Tiger as he passed the winning line but Ron Bagley, the other Ipswich rider in the race, had also summed things up.

Now I was fairly young then, fairly fit and fairly quick on my pins. With track staff close to him, but cheering JL on his victory lap and not paying attention, Eric picked up one of the rakes used to pull the shale back to the inside of the track. Eric, rake in hand, went hunting for John as he continued on his lap of honour, oblivious to what was happening.

Bagley had spotted the potential problem and was trying to get between John and Eric, who was brandishing the rake and looking for all the world like an extra from Gladiator by this time.

With me coming from one direction, and Louis and a rapidly catching up Bagley, on their slow down lap, coming from another direction, we were only a few yards away when Eric hesitated. The red mist, I suspect, had cleared enough for him to realise the potential consequences of his next move. Or was it that with Ron now in the mix, he had no clear shot at John?

I have to say, I don't think Eric would have gone through with whatever he had in mind, but now was not the time to find out. There was no time for niceties, so I just launched myself and hit him around the waist in a classic rugby tackle.

Louis and Bagley had passed by the time I had got up. I found it somehow comforting that John, our track carpenter and bear of a man, was cuddling me - not in friendship, but in case I should wish to go on with it. There was no chance of that but, more importantly, there were several people around Eric also.

Sadly, Eric had a trip to the Control Board and a couple of weeks off for his troubles. He had brought a bit of theatre along, given the locals something to talk about, added to the folklore, and got punished into the bargain.

I think the visits of Ole Olsen to Foxhall were what I looked forward to most, though. Very few could match John Louis around Ipswich but Ole, from the day he first saw the place, had taken a liking to it. Those two riders were as evenly matched around that track as you could get and always put on a grand show.

The Olsen/Louis rivalry was not confined to Ipswich either. When Olsen was at Wolverhampton their races were always X-certificate affairs and I well recall Ole driving so hard under John into the first turn in a key race at Wolves, some part of his bike put a gash right through the top of John's left boot and also the foot underneath, cracking a bone or two on the way.

That was just before a World Championship qualifier and the trip to the Wolverhampton hospital was an eye opener. John arrived around the time of a shift change. The registrar who was going off duty wanted to plaster the foot, whilst the incoming man wanted to operate, although neither seemed to know which way up to hold the X-rays!

We took our own option of a couple of Aspirin and a bandage and got out of there fast, with John getting proper medical attention in Ipswich the next day. He did ride at Ipswich the following Thursday wearing a special boot and scored enough points in the qualifier to ensure getting through to the next round, before retiring hurt.

Other than Ole, I think Reg Wilson was, surprisingly, the one John had most trouble with. Reg was anything but an ideal small track rider but he was fiery and made up for in effort what he lacked in technique. The problem was, he needed every inch of track to do so. His harum-scarum efforts were not always fully appreciated by the home riders but he was a good trier.

Unfortunately, not once, but several times over the years, John, in order to pass him, was forced into having to take up space Reg wanted, or needed, and so more than once the former Sheffield star found himself with no room left on the track and nothing to do but test the Foxhall safety fence.

Poor Reg must have wondered if this was all part of a conspiracy to see how many times he could be used as a crash dummy, and he decided to try and take the law into his own hands more than once.

Lots of huffing and puffing, and even a few punches thrown, but I always wondered about the logic of trying to punch someone who was dressed so as to prevent injury when falling off a bike at 60mph, full face helmet and all.

Those spectators who go to speedway races to enjoy the crashes (and there are many who do so, whether or not they care to admit it, even to themselves) would have been disappointed with Tiger. I expect he slid off a few times but I can only recall three injuries, other than the damaged foot, during his time in speedway.

The first was a bang on the head. I cannot remember the actual event but it was fairly early on in his career. In terms of bangs on the head, it was only a two or three on the Richter scale (although it's two or three more than I would want) but it shook John up and it was several weeks before he got back to his best.

Then, in the middle of the Witches' best ever season, 1976, he fell at Foxhall and dislocated his shoulder. It was not my normal procedure but seeing the state he was in, I went to the hospital in the ambulance with him. It would be fair to say he was, as the medical profession likes to say, in a 'certain degree of discomfort'.

Fortunately, the joint went back in without too much obvious damage. However, the muscles and ligaments had clearly been stretched further than they should have been and some treatment and recuperation was required.

This had come at a difficult time given that, after our customary slow start, the team was putting together its mid-season charge. The other riders filled the gap remarkably well but both myself and physio Brian Simpson were a little surprised at how long it took John to get back onto a bike.

The third, and most serious, injury was when he hurt his wrist whilst riding for Halifax but, in truth, I know little of the detail of that injury or the recovery period.

The greatest rides of John's I recall were those when he team-rode team-mates home. Mike Lanham, who just about every season finished as the league's highest bonus point earner, did so by virtue of his own determination – and being paired many times with John. Dave Gooderham gained tremendously from John Louis' team riding abilities. Dave was, in truth, a very average rider who relied on good equipment and being paired with JL to help earn his

John closes the door on King's Lynn's Terry Betts to unselfishly create space on the outside for partner Mike Lanham.

Lifting the KO Cup in 1978.

points.

The early Billy Sanders was only one year less experienced than John in speedway terms but was nursed around by him in the early days, before forming a formidable last heat pairing that won us many a match in the glory years. Ted Howgego was the most awkward looking rider you would wish to see on a bike but John was still able to fill in the gaps whenever the opportunity arose. Tiger and the Shrimp made a natural pair.

The list of riders John helped goes on and it wasn't just on the track where the help came. Lending bikes, helping team-mates who had machine troubles and carrying the banner up at the front when a captain's innings was needed, were all attributes that made him a great skipper.

Of all the riders I saw during my time, I suspect Olsen was the greatest captain and motivator at the track. But because John did so much for the Ipswich promotion both at and away from the track, he has to have been the best all round skipper of his time.

John and I used to do a spot on the local radio mid-morning show with the very popular and keen on speedway Andy Archer. I would be all stiff necked and factual whilst JL was able to just be himself, turning the thing into good broadcasting as well as giving the speedway a plug.

Finally, my part on the show was made redundant and I am sure even the non-speedway fans enjoyed the 10-minute spot (which sometimes overran by half an hour!) even more as a result.

And who will forget the party we had on air during the Saturday morning after winning the league and cup double in 1976? Andy Archer invited a couple of the team onto his show to do a short spot - and they all turned up. Bottles of champers were opened but my lot were not daft enough to use them as fire extinguishers!

No breakfast and a couple of glasses of champagne were a good mix on a mid-Saturday morning and instead of being part of a 10-minute segment, they took over the show and things came close to getting out of hand. But I know the speedway fans loved it and I suspect it made for good radio even among the non-speedway listeners, especially those from the rural areas

Two great skippers. Pat and John Louis with their children, Joanne and Chris, with Ipswich Town's Mick Mills and his son.

Thanks Tiger! I and Ipswich Speedway owes you so much more than these words can really say . . .

who would have been able to follow the accents as they got broader and broader Suffolk.

I've covered the problems in the latter years of John's reign at Foxhall elsewhere. You have to appreciate that this book is about things as I saw them. I am sure John would have a different point of view in many areas, and I am equally sure that somewhere between things as I recall them and as he recalls them, lies the objective truth.

As I read back through this piece on John, I feel it does not do him enough credit. The individual lines refer to his achievements and his efforts on behalf of the team and the promotion. What I have failed to capture is just how important his role in the club was. Whichever way you look at it, without him things would just not have happened as they did.

Ipswich, Ipswich Speedway and John Berry all owe a huge debt of gratitude to 'Tiger' Louis. He is truly Mr Ipswich Speedway.

It was sad that John didn't see his days out as an Ipswich rider. It would have been fitting. This was very much in my mind when I got him back there in a managerial role in the Shears years. I am doubly delighted that he has been able to continue his long history with the club even up until now. I have great concern about even the eventual viability of UK domestic speedway but by final crunch time, hopefully John will have settled for pipe and slippers and a few bob in the bank. Perhaps then he too will have the time to sit down and write his own memoirs.

15 Alone Again (naturally)

To think that only yesterday
I was cheerful
bright and gay
looking forward to, well who wouldn't do
the role I was about to play
but as if to knock me down
reality came around
and without so much
as a mere touch
cut me into little pieces
leaving me to doubt talk about
god in his mercy who if
he really does exist
why did he desert me in my hour of need
I truly am indeed
alone again naturally.

For all of the on track success of the mid and late 70s, the attendance figures had drifted since the early Division One days. Not only that, but the running costs had ballooned. One of the main reasons for this was that I had taken my eye off the ball.

At the end of the 1974 season, my wife, Lindsey, and I split up. I didn't enjoy the subsequent bachelor life and rushed into a domestic relationship that was not ideal and which took up a lot of my time. It would not be fair on the other party to go into great detail but it is essential to explain how it affected the speedway

After Lindsey and I had split I was living on my own. Had I been a gregarious type, who enjoyed the nightclub scene and mixing with people, things would have been different, but I had discovered that Jack the Lad from my schooldays had gone walkabout, taking all his bravado with him.

I hated being something of a minor celebrity. At the stadium I was a brilliant manager and was putting together a formidable team, both on the track and off, but I had avoided as much direct contact with the fans as possible.

This was just as well, because on race days I put on my 'game face' and was just about unapproachable. In fact, so uncomfortable was I in dealing with people that I had a private signal that only Ray Chinnery, long-time start marshal and then clerk of the course, and Mick Pike, head of security and trouble-shooter, knew about.

If they saw me tugging at my right ear lobe, it was a clear sign I had been trapped into a conversation or situation I did not want to be in. One or the other of them would come and rescue me with a report of urgent business elsewhere I was needed for.

I have to admit, even now, when in a situation I would rather not be in, I find myself tugging at my ear!

I rarely, if ever, made mistakes. And rarely allowed others to make them either. Not more than once, anyway.

Unfortunately, I also very rarely smiled or praised others. My focus and attitude were simple: I gave everything of myself and I expected similar from others. If they produced the goods, they were paid well so to do. If they did not, then they were told or replaced.

I had gained a tremendous amount of respect whilst establishing the speedway but precious few friends.

So instead of putting myself about and enjoying my new found bachelor life, I stayed at home with my dogs. Quite regularly, I would find myself doing the vacuuming or the ironing after 10 o'clock in the evening. Running a business, two dogs, and a four-bedroom house with fair sized grounds was getting too much for me - but I was too proud to admit it.

A circle was formed. My business was other people's leisure, I had no time to go out and mix with non-speedway types, so therefore life had become a constant round of work and run the house. There was no play. I had become a very boring person.

I spent Christmas in Australia and whilst there I had a holiday fling. Like many before me and many since, I tried to turn that fling into a long-term relationship by inviting the young lady, Denise, and her toddler daughter to come back and live with me.

It was a mistake. It took about three months for me to realise the set up was wrong and I resolved to sort it out at the end of the 1975 season but things got complicated because Denise broke a thigh and was in hospital for three months. Instead of leading a bachelor existence I now had to fit in constant hospital visiting, along with looking after and potty training a toddler, in addition to all the previous duties.

The injury to Denise and the difficulties involved in her being able to return to her previous Australian life meant the inevitable parting of the ways between us drifted on for a while. About 10 years, to be precise!

Actually, this initial distraction from the speedway coincided with a deliberate decision on my part to give Ron Bagley more responsibility. I had in mind the hope that Ron would be able to take over running the speedway himself, leaving me to search for new challenges. This was a good opportunity to see how things would go.

Unfortunately, as I explained earlier in the book, I don't think the experiment was completely successful and I felt committed to going back to a more active role.

Needless to say, this was not entirely to Ron's satisfaction. He no doubt felt resentful and from the beginning of 1977 onwards, speedway promoting for me went from being an adventure to being a hard-nosed business.

I had been partially responsible for managing to get the old fashioned rider control or rider allocation policy changed. A team's make up from 1977 onwards was determined by statistics based on rider averages, rather than by a committee. This had enabled us to keep the previous year's all-conquering team together.

Other teams had improved, though, and possibly the motivation at Ipswich was not all it had been. Possibly I had also been paying too much attention to the international duties I had taken on. Anyway, although we finished with some silverware in the Inter-League Cup, the league hat trick just escaped us. We finished in fourth place, only four points behind champions White City.

Ron moved on at the end of the season, along with his girlfriend, Sue Bugg, who had been my secretary for the last few years, but the team stayed pretty much the same again in 1978. This time the KO Cup finished up back with us, after victory over Belle Vue in the final, but we slipped from fourth to sixth in the league. Hardly a catastrophe but certainly not what the local supporters were used to. It has to be said, the team was getting stale. It was also getting top heavy.

The lesser lights had struggled with form and injury and in order to liven things up and also to have a look at him, Georg Hack was brought in as an experiment towards the end of the

Georg Hack (left) combines with John Louis in our KO Cup final victory against Belle Vue in 1978.

season.

Georg was a fantastic long track rider and something of a legend in his Bavarian homeland. He was to southern Germany what Egon Müller was to the north of the country. He expected to be able to adapt to the tiny British tracks easily, and to be able to take on and beat the world's best at speedway, as he did regularly on the continental long tracks. I had an eye on winning the KO Cup and Georg made a big impact in both legs of the final against Belle Vue.

Tony Davey had a tremendous season, finishing higher up than both John Louis and Billy Sanders in the averages. Billy was keen to move on to another club where he could take on the kudos of being a skipper and number one, whilst Kevin Jolly had made very good progress from the junior ranks to be pushing for the number three spot.

Georg Hack receives a warm welcome . . . but Billy Sanders was soon on his way to Birmingham.

It was logical to allow Billy to move to Birmingham for 1979, where he could strengthen a weak Brummies team. Birmingham had followed Ipswich into the top league and, like ourselves, had never been given a fair go rider-wise.

Hack had made a big impression in his short stay at the end of 1978 and was a natural to be included the following year. But, as I said, he was already a star in his own homeland, where he had huge commitments to his time and effort. He did want to make it in the world's top speedway league, though, and agreed to give things a try.

He was so close to doing it but spoke no English, felt uncomfortable with the constant commuting and was very homesick. Georg wasn't a teenage kid, he was married with a family and found he just could not combine British speedway with his German commitments, so we lost him after a couple of months.

This Bavarian was really a German version of Tony Davey. He was far more comfortable among family and close friends than with strangers and must have found it difficult to cope in another country, despite being under the combined wings of John Louis and myself. When Georg was either riding or playing with bikes (he was a brilliant mechanic), he was comfortable, but the rest of if was hard work for him.

I always had time for Preben Eriksen.

He stayed at my house a few times – and seemed to communicate with my two Alsatians better than anyone else. Except one night, when he turned up very late after a meeting and everyone had gone to bed. I found him sleeping in his car when I got up next morning. It seems the dogs wouldn't let him into the house!

I recall another evening I decided to treat myself to some fresh picked buttered sweet corn as a supper snack. What can beat that lovely salty buttery taste! I offered some to Georg but he looked decidedly put out. It took about 10 minutes of hard work and some good charades-style miming to work out what he wanted to say, but eventually it translated as: "Where I come from, we only feed that stuff to the pigs!"

The other foreign rider we brought in was Dane, Preben Eriksen. Preben's all out effort, attitude, enthusiasm and determination to succeed were simply first class and encouraged me to persevere with him despite his having a suspect style and being very much a learner.

The Danes at the start of their dominance in the 80s. Team managers Oluf Pedersen and Jorgen Jensen with (left to right) Tommy Knudsen, Ole Olsen, Hans Nielsen, Preben Eriksen and Erik Gundersen.

Maybe Preben is an odd choice of rider to pick out of a bunch to talk about, but there's plenty to say. There were not many riders at that, or any other time, who were prepared to take on Ole Olsen. The only ones I know of were Preben, Bo Petersen and Hans Nielsen.

Hans paid dearly for opposing Ole early in his career, when only his brilliant riding and strength of character got him through. I suppose in the end, Hans would say that the feud actually helped to firm his resolve, and it no doubt did not harm his long-term aspirations, but it was doing things the hard way. Bo also found life in Ole's bad books was not easy.

Ole, then, as now, a control freak, considered himself to be the Godfather to all Danish riders, and so dictated all their UK career moves. Preben was earmarked for Wolverhampton, and duly rode once for them, but the paperwork was never completed because the strong-minded youngster wanted to keep his options open.

This actually resulted in Preben having to serve a period of suspension issued by the Danish speedway authorities, although I wonder if Ole maybe had a hand in this.

For some reason I am not aware of, Preben decided he did not want to continue with Wolves, so when he had finished his suspension he considered himself a free agent, having signed for nobody.

I suspect this defection from Ole's chosen route had much to do with his full season suspension but from the time I saw him practice at Mildenhall during the following winter, I was happy to give him a try. What impressed me far more than his riding was his massive enthusiasm and his intelligence.

Preben was not an overnight sensation. In fact, I would go so far as to say his natural speedway talent was limited. They tell me he is a brilliant snow skier, and perhaps that is where his best talents lay, but he was hooked on speedway.

If you want something badly enough, and are prepared to

A tough competitor, Preben Eriksen shows fellow Dane Hans Nielsen, then of Birmingham, the fastest way round Ipswich.

Former World Champion Anders Michanek came for a brief though expensive spell in 1979.

dedicate yourself to making it work, then look no further than Preben for inspiration.

The Foxhall track is one of the most demanding in speedway. It is a place where naturally talented riders dominate and pretenders get found out. This is not the place for 'triers'. That said, so many of the Witches middle order men who learned their speedway at Foxhall were also able to score points away from home. If you could ride Ipswich, you could ride anywhere.

With courage, determination, intelligence and sheer racing effort, Preben made his mark. Many times he rode beyond his ability. He knew what he wanted to do but it didn't always go exactly according to plan. As a result, he gained himself something of a reputation for being a wild man.

He wasn't that; he was just someone who always tried desperately hard and sometimes paid the penalty. Being very intelligent, I suspect he also began to realise that having a bit of a reputation was no really bad thing.

Opposition riders became well aware that he was rarely bluffing and, as such, the less committed were often prepared to wave him through. Because he was so gregarious and likeable off the track, he even managed, by and large, not to get involved in too many silly feuds.

Perhaps because he was always prepared to accept the hard riding of others with good grace, people just accepted him for what he was. He was somebody who often allowed his enthusiasm and determination to get ahead of his on track ability.

More importantly for Preben, Olsen eventually forgave him his 'indiscretion' in abandoning Wolverhampton for Ipswich and allowed him into the Danish national set up. Here, Preben's outstanding qualities of intelligence, mechanical expertise, resourcefulness and bravery stood him in good stead.

Because the majority of continental speedway tracks are a good deal easier to ride than Foxhall, he was able to cope well, within the limits of his natural ability. He had a good international record, well above that which you would expect.

But it wasn't Preben the speedway rider I recall best, but Preben the person. He is the only speedway rider who actually stayed at my house (apart from the odd sleepover) and was a thoughtful and helpful guest. In fact, you would go a long way to find a nicer bloke than him.

All Danes tend to have an air of superiority about them and he certainly was no exception. Also he had a rather 'modern' approach to the sanctity of marriage, when viewed from a bachelor's angle, but within those parameters he was as nice a bloke as you would wish, and certainly you'd pick him to be on your side in a crisis.

How ironic that in the end he finished up back at Wolverhampton. That saga is revisited elsewhere. It's enough to say here, he proved to be a formidable rival on his return to Ipswich wearing the Wolves race jacket!

Nevertheless, Preben's points contribution in his first year at Ipswich was not great, and the weaknesses at the back end of the team put tremendous pressure onto Louis, Davey and Kevin Jolly, but I have always worked on the

Injuries to Kevin Jolly and Tony Davey brought more pressure to use guests.

basis that riders will respond to a challenge.

Knowing we had riders who needed time to settle, I had also arranged the Ipswich fixtures in 1979 so that most of our league matches were to be later in the season rather than earlier.

What the team did not need was for Davey, riding better than ever before in his life, to go and break a thigh before April was out. My refusal to use guest riders really caught up with me now, with Hack having gone home, Eriksen really struggling after a series of knocks and the Witches second strings simply being asked to do too much.

The decision not to use guest riders in the Ipswich team had been made in 1972. In theory, the use of guest riders was brought into speedway because it was felt by promoters that supporters would not come to watch a team that was short of a star rider.

Now my attitude was that the rider replacement facility, which allowed other members of the team to take an extra ride to cover for a missing rider, was a much better option.

First of all, the fans and the riders in the team felt far more of a tight unit relying on themselves rather than outsiders, and there is nothing like adversity to bring out the best in people. Second, the other riders in the team, being paid on performance, shared the missing rider's races and therefore increased their earning potential. Third, most guest riders considered these bookings as merely an extra run out.

Guests would occasionally use these bookings to try out different bike set ups, sometimes merely going through the motions and sometimes even accepting bribes from the opposing team. The only way to ensure a guest would give his best efforts was to spoil him with high pay rates and win bonus incentives.

Of course, this was not always the case and some riders were in constant demand for guest bookings because they had a reputation for giving maximum effort. Judicious selection of guest riders could often actually strengthen a team.

I never actually said I would not use guest riders on principle because it was a pathetic regulation that made a mockery of the sport. I did say I thought the regulation was wrong and that generally we were better to do our own thing.

However, the longer we went without using guests, the more the pressure not to cave in increased. I have to say, there was also a deal of stubbornness in my not backing down.

The very expensive exercise of bringing in 1974 World Champion, Anders Michanek, for a short spell to cover for the injury to Shrimp didn't really provide the answer, although he was a pleasure to work with, a real gentleman. I would have enjoyed having 'Mitch' in a team of mine when he was in his prime.

Then, just to rub it in, Kevin Jolly broke his arm riding at Eastbourne.

You can say that 1979 was a bad hair year. Finally, Billy Sanders, who had discovered the grass

was not greener elsewhere, and who Birmingham promoter Joe Thurley was quietly pleased to unload as more trouble than he was worth, returned to the fold. With Davey and Jolly having returned from their respective injuries, things had finally improved and we finished the year with a flourish.

Actually, the return of the prodigal Sanders really wasn't the long-term answer at that time. It simply moved the team backwards instead of forwards.

One thing did happen worthy of mention that year though. It was the arrival of Paul Johnson as commercial manager.

I had met Paul when in Australia three years earlier. He was a sensational and spectacular flag-waver and commercial manager at Claremont Speedway in Perth at the time. He had lived in Australia for more years than in his backwoods Lancashire birthplace but the accent had never changed.

Encouraged by my enthusiasm, he had brought his spectacular flag-waving skills to Britain for a whistle-stop

Extrovert Paul Johnson brought colour and character to the Ipswich Speedway set-up.

Barbie added glamour to the start line.

tour a couple of years earlier, but it was for his 'can do' enthusiasm and fresh approach that I invited him back to become part of the Ipswich set up.

The one thing you have to say about Paul was that life was never dull when he was around! Not everyone in Suffolk took to his bluff and bluster but he was a good sounding board for me and paid his way by bringing in extra sponsorship and advertising revenue.

This side of the business had always been my weak spot but as attendance figures eased it was important to find other sources of revenue. Paul was ideal, a one-man publicity machine as he ran around town banging on doors.

It was Paul who brought in a female starting marshal, Barbie. She learned quickly and became a very good starting marshal as well as adding some glamour to the scene.

He also got Radio Orwell to use all of their contacts in the music business to bring a collection of pop stars to a Good Friday meeting. Perhaps Suzie Quattro was the best known but as she refused to mix with anyone without a phalanx of security men around her, it was the PG Tips chimps who stole the show.

Paul also got the *Evening Star* promotions department onside, leading to the introduction of the highly successful and top-line annual event, The Star Of Anglia individual meeting, featuring the best available riders in the world.

His greatest claim to fame, though, is the 16-Lapper event that has been held every year at Ipswich since its inception in 1980. The concept derived from a 20-lap marathon grass track race in Bendigo, Victoria. Paul and I spent many hours together working on the idea and eventually came up with an eight-rider, 16-lap speedway race.

There are few things in speedway that leave me breathless but this was one of those. All of the planning, the fighting with authority, the worrying and the waiting were all made worthwhile at the sight of those eight riders thundering into the tiny first turn at Foxhall. I have never known a spectacle like it in speedway.

That first attempt to complete the race lasted about four laps in the drizzly rain before Kevin Jolly slid off his bike. Clearly uninjured, Kevin decided to make no attempt to clear the track, and the memory of Paul trying to drag him off sticks clearly in my mind.

Rarely has the race run all 16 laps without a restart, but it doesn't matter. The spectacle remains the same, which is why the event is still on the calendar. It is the only event in speedway, now the traditional world final is lost, that draws viewers for the race itself and not because of the riders taking part.

For the life of me, I do not understand why promoters today do not try to dream up and present more of these 'novelty' type events in an effort to keep things fresh.

Whilst the 16-Lapper became a fixture, Paul did not. With my thanks and blessing, after two years he moved to Swindon in order to better his chances of fulfilling his dream of being the starting marshal in a World Final. He was to achieve that at Wembley in 1981, adding to the

Dennis Sigalos hits the front in the breathtaking 16-Lapper, which we originated at Ipswich thanks to Paul Johnson.

John Louis slides off under pressure from Billy Sanders. Team-mates but also rivals.

background colour of Bruce Penhall's memorable first crown. Paul also did the job again at the ill-fated World Final double header in Amsterdam in 1987.

Paul and I now both live in Perth and remain the firmest of friends.

So come 1980, things had almost returned to 'the good old days'. The team was again made up of local lads who had learned their trade at Ipswich, even if one spent his winters in Australia and another was Danish.

So much had things returned to 'normal' that Billy Sanders decided he wouldn't bother to return to the UK until May had arrived. Fortunately, Eriksen began the season on a mission, putting into practice all he had learned the previous year. Jolly had, by then, recovered from the previous year's injury and he blossomed into a true heat leader.

Then, once more, everything started piling up again. Shrimp had returned from his broken thigh towards the end of the previous season but was never the same rider and was forced into retirement when his leg broke again. Jolly, after looking really good, broke his leg guesting at Hackney and was out for the season.

Worst of all, Louis and Sanders, instead of responding to the situation, seemed to save their best efforts for individual events, or whenever they were lined up against each other.

The lesser lights all did their bit but at the end of the day, a mid-table finish and a general lack of enthusiasm around the place, coupled with the top guns not earning their inflated payments, could not go unaddressed.

For the first time in many years neither of the dynamic duo could boast an average anywhere near nine points, so Kevin Jolly, albeit from a very truncated season before he broke his leg, finished as the top rider in the team with a league average of 9.18.

Really and truly, what was needed at that stage was a change right at the top. It needed new ideas and new directions. Once again, it was time to get out of the hot seat and let someone else have a go. Just about the most difficult thing in the world to do, though, is to sack yourself, so it was time to have a good, hard look at the rest of the speedway world...

Kevin Jolly leads against Birmingham.

16 Three Great Riders – *Three Different People*

Ivan

When the night has been too lonely
and the road ahead too long,
and you think that love is only
for the lucky and the strong,
just remember in the winter,
far beneath the bitter snows,
lies the seed that with the sun`s love
in the spring becomes the rose.

You know when you have joined the legends in a sport when you end up being recognised from just a Christian name. OK, so there's 'Magic' (Johnson) and 'Tiger' (Woods), but they are both nicknames. However much they have replaced the original Christian name, they don't count. Those that do count are names like Wayne (Gretzky) or Michael (Jordan). Commonplace names that you would think would not identify a particular person, but they do. Likewise, 'Ivan' in speedway, can only refer to one person.

I was a supporter (spectator would be a better word) when Ivan was carving out his reputation at Newcastle. I only saw him ride once or twice then and, to be honest, didn't know what all the fuss was about. I recall the girlfriend of a friend wearing an Ivan Mauger rosette to a meeting at Wembley. Can't remember what the meeting was, but I did know that even in those days, you either loved Ivan or hated him. There was no middle ground.

The Lovers enjoyed his professional approach, his superb gating skills and his smooth style. The Haters, considerably in the majority, called him a starting gate cheat, because he would use various tactics and techniques to put the other riders off, and also try to put one over on the referee.

These people perhaps failed to appreciate that beating the opposition didn't start at the first bend, or even at the tapes. It didn't even start in the workshops. It started with meticulous and careful planning and in the plain determination to be the best.

They also complained that he was 'just a gater'. In truth, that was invariably a guess on their part, because it was so rare to see him anywhere but in front.

In my second division learning days, it was also fashionable among promoters in the top league to hate the bloke. The success of the British League had been built on the way the promoters backed each other up. They might well have had their ups and downs within the 'family' but they maintained a good discipline in dealing with outsiders.

Riders came under the heading of 'outsiders' and the promoters, by and large, were able to keep them under control. Ivan, though, was a maverick. He didn't jump when the promoters said boo and his move to Belle Vue gave him the kind of backing he needed.

They were prepared to indulge him in his many whims, especially in terms of fitting around his non UK fixtures, and in return he provided the leadership and professionalism a club of their status required. The same was the case when he moved on to Exeter, and then Hull.

Now I wouldn't say I agreed with everything that Ivan did but I do believe he has huge personal integrity. I think there were many times when he put himself before the common good but I also think that the promoters collectively were perhaps a bit nineteenth century in some of their human resources procedures.

I think the arrangement among the promoters at that time was to keep the main body of riders very much under control. This allowed individual promotions to make 'private' arrangements with those they felt 'deserved' it.

I suppose it comes down to the law of the jungle really. Those riders highest in the pecking order got the lion's share of the meal and this attitude, in life as well as speedway, seems to have become more and more prevalent as the world becomes more Americanised. It's dog eat dog, and to hell with those who cannot keep up.

So did that make him Ivan the Great or Ivan the Terrible?

There might well have been others before him, but it seems to me that what Ivan did was to simply work on the concept that even though speedway is a team sport, he was a star who could put extra bums on seats. Although he

signed a Speedway Control Board contract each season, I am equally certain he made his own arrangement with his various promotions that effectively over-rode several of the clauses.

I think he saw himself very much in terms of being 'an entertainer' in the same way as pop singers or movie stars, and as speedway promoters do not 'employ' their riders, but merely contract them, his attitude seemed to be that he could make whatever arrangements he liked with whoever he liked, provided he honoured the commitment.

He put a high price on his talents. It used to be that only the current World Champion could request a booking fee for his services and all the others riders were expected to ride for the 'official' rates.

Actually, when I first started promoting, that was almost the case. Because there were so many riders to choose from, it was possible to work around any who held their hands out.

But Ivan was an exception. He said simply, either a deal needed to be done or he would not ride. Of course, a lot of the time he was the World Champion anyway but it made no difference either way. One time, when asked to ride in an individual meeting at Ipswich, he discovered it was being sponsored by a carpet and bedding store.

I had a sum in mind I was prepared to pay as a booking fee but Ivan wanted more. In the end, we did a deal involving Ivan, the sponsor, a flash new double bed and myself.

He was never anything but fair, though, and always tried to put on a good show. He always gave value for money and never simply went through the motions. The one time he had a very bad meeting at Ipswich, he still took all his booking fee and earnings, but offered to come back and do another meeting with no booking fee involved.

What infuriated the BSPA about Ivan was that he put his individual ambitions well in front of his team commitments and, in particular, took time off from his regular UK fixtures to simply prepare for big meetings. In this, I thought he was wrong. In riding for a league team he took on certain responsibilities and should have seen them through.

Generally speaking, his various promoters could accommodate most of his home fixture wishes but the determination to appear at all his teams' away matches did not always appear to be so strong, suggesting the absences may have been 'sanctioned' by his promoter, very much against both the regulations and the spirit of the British League.

Wherever Ivan parked his bikes they would draw a crowd. Every other rider was convinced Ivan's machines contained 'stuff' not available to them. I suspect it is true that in the early days he simply paid far greater attention to detail with his equipment than did the vast majority of riders.

Possibly once he had established his reputation, equipment suppliers were keen to let him try their latest products before they were generally available, but I am not sure that his bikes were so different to everyone else's. I am sure, for instance, the chequered design on his helmet

Kiwi legends Ivan Mauger, Barry Briggs and Ronnie Moore discuss the state of the Ipswich track in 1976 after they had arrived too late to influence the decision to postpone the WTC qualifier.

didn't improve his speed but a remarkable number of riders decided to copy the idea just in case!

Although an undoubted superstar and always prepared to back his speedway aims and ambitions against those of others, on a personal level, he was never full of his own importance like some. I cannot remember an unpleasant confrontation with the man ever.

I don't doubt that he had plenty of influence, particularly at Exeter where he joined what was a particularly ordinary outfit and a not hugely ambitious promotion and turned them into attractive visitors and league champions, albeit only the once.

Likewise, on race nights you wouldn't see him racing around his side of the pits cajoling or berating riders but he would lead by example and team-ride his partners home whenever he could.

He was decidedly put out when the UK promoters, fed up with being held to ransom by himself and Barry Briggs in particular, decided in 1973 they could provide enough talent from England riders to fill the Great Britain (and Commonwealth) international team without resorting to riders from Australia or New Zealand.

The consequence of this BSPA decision was that Australia and then New Zealand decided to seek direct affiliation with the FIM instead of having the ACU handle their international affairs for them.

In 1974 an 'Overseas' round of the World Team Cup competition was run at King's Lynn between England, Scotland, Australia and New Zealand to decide who would represent 'Great Britain' in the final. It was held on a weekend, when Ivan and Briggo decided they had better things to do.

The first time Ivan (and Briggo) decided to represent New Zealand in the World Team Cup was the following year, 1975, when the Overseas final was held at Reading (on a Monday!). Ivan scored 11 and Briggs three, ensuring New Zealand beat Scotland.

In 1976, the Dream Team of Ronnie Moore, Barry Briggs and Ivan Mauger (albeit, not all in the first flush of youth) were due to line up with Larry Ross and Bruce Cribb to form a potent New Zealand outfit.

This meeting was scheduled for a Thursday evening at Ipswich but the weather was bad and the track wet. I have seen meetings take place on far worse surfaces but after much wringing of hands, and without any input from me, the FIM-appointed officials, rightly or wrongly, decided to postpone until the Sunday, which was the official restage date.

Ivan (and Briggo) did not appear until 7.15pm, after the decision had been made. Boy, did they make a fuss. It is not often you hear of riders being upset with a decision to postpone because of a wet track, but these two, had they been inside the stadium before the decision was made, would undoubtedly have talked the riders and the officials into letting the meeting go ahead.

They wanted the meeting on that night – not because they loved racing on wet tracks, but for purely personal reasons. Both had bookings to race on the Continent that Sunday, so the rain-off left them double booked.

Their attitude was that they had contracted to race in their respective meetings abroad, that the promoters of those meetings had advertised their presence, and therefore they had a duty to be there. The fact that they would no doubt be earning the equivalent of shed loads of beds, as against a miserly pittance from the World Team Cup round, might well have also had a bearing.

In the end, supported by their team manager, Trevor Redmond, who himself didn't bother to show for the restaged event, they decided to miss the restaging of the Ipswich meeting, laying the blame on the fact that the event should not have been rained off. They left their makeshift team of countrymen to score a total of six points from 16 heats.

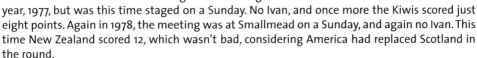

This represented the last opportunity for the legendary three riders to represent their country in an FIM event. It was a shame it never happened.

The following year neither Briggs nor Mauger even nominated for the meeting, this time back at Ipswich and scheduled for a Sunday, leaving their countrymen to score a massive eight points this time. Never on Sundays, it seems. Or, at least, never in the UK on a Sunday.

The round went back to Reading the following year, 1977, but was this time staged on a Sunday. No Ivan, and once more the Kiwis scored just eight points. Again in 1978, the meeting was at Smallmead on a Sunday, and again no Ivan. This time New Zealand scored 12, which wasn't bad, considering America had replaced Scotland in the round.

I really don't know what happened to make Ivan turn out in 1979 but, as England team manager at the time, I wished he hadn't! Perhaps it was because New Zealand now had a remotely competitive team with the Aussie-born Mitch Shirra deciding he was a Kiwi, and with Ross and Cribb making up the four. Ironically, in weather conditions far worse than when the meeting at Ipswich in 1976 was rained off, New Zealand won the event.

This put the Kiwis through to another qualifying round in Sweden, where they showed the previous victory was no fluke by beating Denmark, USA and the Swedes in their own back yard.

And then, just for the hell of it, they won the final at London White City from Denmark, with Czechoslovakia and Poland making up the numbers.

The new dawn for New Zealand speedway did not last too long, though. The Kiwis finished last in the first round qualifier again the following year, with Ivan turning up, but only managing three points. Ivan had ended his earlier self-imposed exile, but New Zealand never looked like getting past the qualifying round again. Although he never missed a meeting from then onwards, I think it would be fair to say the great champion was no longer the force he had been on the world stage.

Remarkably, and in complete contrast, Ivan appears to have ridden in every World Pairs event barring only one in the period from its inception in 1969 until 1985. A statistic made even more remarkable for the fact that most events, both finals and semi-finals, were held on the continent and on Sundays.

Perhaps it is surprising also that despite Ivan having any number of partners, New Zealand's only two successes were in the first two finals, in 1969 with Bob Andrews and 1970 with Ronnie Moore. Later in this chapter is the story of how Ivan just missed out in 1978 and the second place in Poland that season had several more to go with it over the years.

Most people remember Ivan for his incredible individual World Final performances. I am afraid I do not have a great personal leaning towards the theory that riders should be judged on that particular competition alone.

Indeed, being partisan, I prefer to judge riders on their results spread over many different performances, under a host of different conditions, on a variety of different tracks in what was undisputedly the strongest competition in the world, the British League.

In this particular arena, Ivan's consistency was just as breathtaking. At that time there were not just one or two superstars. Every team had at least one potential World Champion and even though top riders only tended to meet each other once in a meeting, you still have to marvel at how few points Ivan dropped over the thick end of two decades. OK, perhaps the last few years were not quite as convincing as the earlier ones, but from the inception of – nay, from before the inception of the British League in 1965 – the man was a giant.

You would consider such a colossus in the sport would be a bit of an egotist. Well, it has to be said, he was very confident of himself and his riding ability, but it was a quiet, assured confidence and not at all bombastic.

Above: Ivan sets a new record of World Championship wins after grabbing his sixth individual titrle at Poland in 1979. *(AW)*
Below: He has always been able to count on the rock solid support of Raye, seen here congratulating Ivan after his first world title success in 1970. *(AW)*

Perhaps a lot of that was due to the strong bond between himself and his wife Raye, one of the sport's fabulous leading ladies. Ivan and Raye had coped with the bad times together and were not to have their heads turned by success and achievement.

Ivan was a dedicated speedway fanatic but so was Raye and they stood side by side. They and their kids were a true family. You might imagine spending an evening with Ivan to be all about the titles he has won and the people he has beaten, but he is far happier pulling out snaps of his kids and their kids, and it was like that also when he was riding.

To sum things up, it has to be said that he and I often had differences of opinion, but rarely, if ever, had words. He is not a man to be taken lightly and remains, for me, the most complete speedway rider of my time. I have called him names many times, both publicly and privately, but only on a business level. We are not great mates, we do not know each other well enough to be, but I have a huge respect for him and would have liked to have known him better.

A great rider, a great man and a great family.

Ole Olsen

Oh Lord, It's hard to be humble
When you're perfect in every way
I can't wait to look in the mirror
Cos I get better looking each day

To know me is to love me
I must be a hell of a man
Oh Lord it's hard to be humble
But I'm doing the best that I can...

Of all the star riders during my period of promoting I think Ole was the most interesting. I don't think I have ever disagreed more with a person in speedway, be it when he was a rider, promoter, Danish team manager and general dictator to the Danish Motor Union, or, latterly, as one of the original creators of and general factotum to the Speedway Grand Prix. And yet, scarcely can I think of a rider, team manager, or carer about speedway who I have more respect for than Ole Olsen.

I think this dichotomy comes about mainly because we are from different countries, and also because we invariably found ourselves on opposite sides in just about all things.

Olsen, the rider

Whilst I reserve the title of greatest rider of my time for Ivan, Ole is only fractionally behind in my reckoning, and I have no hesitation in saying he was the best visiting rider at Ipswich. The Foxhall track is not a 'trick track'. The shape simply demands all the requirements of a good speedway rider to master it: technical understanding, natural ability, aggression and full confidence in one's own ability. Olsen had plenty of all these qualities.

So Ole was the first name pencilled in for big individual meetings at Ipswich, like the 1973 Golden Sovereign. The finishing order of the top three in this meeting, by coincidence, was the same as in the 1975 Wembley World Final.

In fact, the two meeting fields bear comparison:

Golden Sovereign, Ipswich, 1973
1. Ole Olsen 15
2. Anders Michanek 14
3. John Louis 10 (after run-off)
4. Tony Davey 10
5. Soren Sjosten 8
6. Ivan Mauger 8
7. Arnold Haley 8
8. Bengt Jansson 8
9. Garry Middleton 7
10. Martin Ashby 7
11. Pete Smith 6
12. Reidar Eide 5
13. Reg Wilson 4
14. Howard Cole DNR
15. Peter Collins DNR
16. Malcolm Simmons DNR

Golden Wonder! Ole Olsen flanked by Anders Michanek and John Louis after the prestigious 1973 Golden Sovereign classic.

183

World final, Wembley, 1975
1. Ole Olsen 15
2. Anders Michanek 13
3. John Louis 12 (after run-off)
4. Ivan Mauger 12
5. Peter Collins 10
6. Phil Crump 10
7. Malcolm Simmons 10
8. Viktor Trofimov 8
9. Tommy Jansson 7
10. Bernt Persson 5
11. Ray Wilson 5
12. Edward Jancarz 4
13. Valeri Gordeev 4
14. Zenon Plech 4
15. Marek Cieslak 1
16. Henryk Glucklick 0

Ole's on top again, with Anders and JL again taking the runners-up places at the 1975 Wembley World final.

Had Messrs Cole, Collins and Simmons bothered to turn up to the 'Sovereign', I think the Ipswich meeting would have been a much stronger field than the World final, albeit without the romantic sounding names of Wembley's Iron Curtain competitors.

It can be said that we never made it easy for visiting riders at Ipswich. We didn't resort to petty things like dirty, unlit pits, or badly prepared track surfaces, but we did present something of a competitive atmosphere, which many visiting riders and teams found daunting.

Not so Olsen. He relished a challenge, enjoying the extra competitive edge. And one thing Ole never suffered from was a lack of belief in his own ability. There can be no doubting that when Olsen came to Foxhall there was always an extra bit of excitement in the air.

In 1980, he triumphed over another World class field (Sanders, Carter, Schwartz, Olsen, Louis, Lee, Crump, Petersen, Autrey, Lanham, Jessup, Sigalos, Andersson, Nielsen, K Moran, Penhall) to take the Star of Anglia event.

I suppose being ultra-strong willed, to the point of egotism, goes with being a superstar. It is difficult to have one without the other. Ole was no shrinking violet. For instance, he felt that it was wrong of the BSPA to restrict the kind of silencer allowed for use in domestic speedway to those designs that had been tested and approved.

The alternative for the promoters would have been for each bike to have been individually noise tested before every meeting in order to make sure it conformed, which was patently impractical. Therefore, the simple and straightforward alternative was for the BSPA to test out any new silencers on the market and have them 'homologated'.

Olsen, a Jawa works rider at the time, held an almost paranoid view that everything the BSPA did of a technical nature was designed to inconvenience Jawa and encourage the British Weslake. This was not so. However, when the Jawa factory in Czechoslovakia designed a silencer to suit their engine and gave a prototype to Ole, he couldn't be bothered to wait until it was tested and homologated. He simply bolted it onto his bike and defied anyone to challenge him.

Now the Ipswich machine examiner, Fred Cotton, was very good at his job. Very little got by him. Many visiting riders thought he was deliberately picking on them and giving the home riders an easy time. This wasn't true.

Ole, riding for Wolverhampton in 1971, leads his great rival Ivan Mauger of Belle Vue at Monmore Green. (AW)

As far as Fred was concerned, all riders were treated the same. The difference was, the Ipswich boys were aware of what was required, and that their equipment would be examined in detail, so they never tried it on.

I well remember Fred finding that Joe Owen's crash helmet was cracked. Once a crash helmet is cracked, it loses all of its strength and is effectively useless. Joe was furious that he should have been prevented from using his cracked helmet and we had a real scene over it, but there is no question Fred was in the right. Joe's complaints, that other machine examiners had not stopped him from using the helmet, were a pretty poor argument.

Anyway, Olsen arrived at Ipswich with the non-homologated Jawa silencer, Fred correctly refused to pass it, and we had a stand off. The referee agreed with Fred. Well, it was a clear-cut case of Olsen trying to break the rules. But Ole just dug his toes in, decided he was going to make a stand (some might say, act like a spoiled child) and refused to take part in the meeting.

As if that was not bad enough, he then got the rest of the Coventry team to back him up and refuse to race if he did not. That left me with a clear decision to make. I could either scrap the meeting, or bow to the blackmail.

I bowed to the blackmail, happy in my mind that Ole would pay a very heavy price at the Control Board for defying both the referee and the regulations. Needless to say, he got away with it. The silencer was presented for testing shortly afterwards and, because it passed, nothing more was done.

This was not the only time Ole's sometimes slightly skewed reasoning of what was fair and unfair allowed him to get away with things mere mortals would not have and, of course, each success strengthened his resolve for the next time.

The one battle he was to lose was when the BSPA decided to limit the size of carburettor intake manifolds. It was the Jawa engine design that could make best use of ever increasing amounts of fuel, so it is fair to say the new rule affected the Czech-made motor more than any others, but it was a sensible rule.

Despite all of Olsen's huffing and puffing and threats of legal action, this was a battle he was to lose, and it pretty well signalled the end of those Jawa four-valve overhead cam rocket machines in British speedway.

Another one of Olsen's pet hates as a rider was the collusion that went on between riders during World Championship events. Being the only Danish rider of consequence at that time, and having pretty well isolated himself from the other star riders, it is fair to say he had little opportunity to utilise the 'old boys rule' himself, although I like to think his objections were on principle.

The scene was the World Pairs final at Chorzow, Poland, in 1978, when Malcolm Simmons and Gordon Kennett were representing England. Simmo was at the top of his form whilst Gordon was struggling. It wasn't a great field. Olsen had a very weak Finn Thomsen as his partner; Jan Andersson had the eminently forgettable Borge Klingberg; Eddie Jancarz, the less than mercurial Boleslaw Proch; and then there were the Germans and Czechs, with Ivan Mauger and Larry Ross representing New Zealand.

As the afternoon panned out, New Zealand needed at least four points from their last race against Poland to sneak ahead of England and win the meeting. Normally Eddie Jancarz would give them a run on Polish tracks but before the race I noticed Ivan in deep conversation with Eddie. Perhaps they were discussing the weather but remember it was Ivan who had 'discovered' Eddie, had taken him around the world with his troupe in the early 70s and who had also been instrumental in getting him into the British League at Wimbledon.

I pointed out the two of them to Ole and shrugged my shoulders, resigned to the situation. By this time

In Coventry colours for 1976, Ole winning this battle with Cradley Heath's Aussie John Boulger. *(AW)*

185

the Danish pairing could not win the event but Ole got really angry and disappeared. He came back just as the race was starting, looking very self-satisfied.

Ivan and Larry Ross made good starts and were putting on quite a show of team riding, with Eddie apparently chasing hard. Then suddenly, on the third lap, Eddie bolted between the two New Zealanders and disappeared into the distance. Ivan tried to chase him but the Pole was away. After the race, Eddie just kept going straight through the pits and out to the stadium car park. Malcolm Simmons beat Ivan in the run-off and somehow England had won the title for a third consecutive season, with Simmo featuring each time.

Ole opened his track at Vojens before he had finished riding. If Foxhall was unwelcoming for visiting teams, then Vojens was positively difficult, well certainly for international meetings anyway. Apart from the fact that it always rained, there was also always the feeling that England, as the Danes' biggest rivals at the time, was picked out for 'special' treatment.

This might well have simply been the attitude of the local pits officials and not part of a deliberate masterplan. It might even have been a figment of my oversensitive imagination, although I do think there were just too many coincidences of petty bureaucracy for that to have been the case, Surprisingly, though, I always seemed to get on well with the Danish team manager of the time, Oluf Pedersen.

You have to admire Ole. Danish team captain, de facto team manager, promoter, main organiser …he used to put in so much effort and energy to the events at Vojens and was never very good at delegating. The words 'control freak' often spring to mind when thinking of Ole.

We came second to the Danes there in the World Team Cup final of 1983. It had been a particularly abrasive meeting and the England boys were very disappointed. We had to endure watching the Danes indulge in over-the-top celebrations – none of them even bothered to give us a second look, never mind the usual handshakes.

Off they went for the victory parade, ignoring us in our side of the pits, with nobody even bothering to suggest to us our presence was needed on the track, although clearly a presentation ceremony was being arranged.

Disappointed, angry and overreacting to being snubbed like this, I suggested to the England riders that they gatecrash the Danish victory party, now in full swing on the track, to shake the Danish riders hands in a show of over-politeness and then withdraw back to the pits.

So that is what we did, even though Olsen, realising his oversight in not inviting us out in the first place, asked us to stay. Turning things around, I would have hoped that had the event taken place in the UK and England been the victors, we would have been a little more thoughtful. But at the end of the day the Danes were entitled to celebrate and not inviting us to the parade was no doubt a small oversight rather than a direct snub.

It was a childish response from me in encouraging the England team to boycott the victory parade and remains one of the few times I think I let England and myself down.

Mind you, Ole was never short of a show of petulance himself. In fact, when things were not going all his own way he could whine like a turbine. Nor was he short of a bit of advice to anyone and everyone. I can't remember a time he ever turned up at Ipswich without telling me what I was doing wrong with the track, or how I could improve things. Sometimes his advice was even sensible!

On the surface, you wouldn't have thought the relationship between Ole and his business manager, Peter Adams, would have worked. Both were smart (in all its meanings), ambitious, single minded and not without a hint of self-interest.

I think Peter was at the stage of still emerging from caterpillar to butterfly at the time of their partnership, and was prepared to sublimate his own strong will to Ole's powerful personality. At the end of the day, though, I reckon they both learned from each other; shades of Ron Bagley and myself.

It has been largely forgotten, but as far back as 1976, these two, Olsen and Adams, had visions of setting up a travelling circus of top stars. Briggs and Mauger had played with the concept of putting together a travelling troupe but they had the good sense to arrange these tours out of the European season, and in far flung places such as Australia, New Zealand and America.

Olsen and Adams had far more ambition. What they had in mind was to set themselves up as the Kerry Packers of speedway. The idea was to put together a full package event, including riders, promotion, meeting operation, the whole works. All a 'promoter' needed to do was the pick up the phone, pay a fee and supply the stadium. Olsen/Adams, and their Masters of Speedway series would supply everything else – at a price! A grand prix series no less.

Given that on the continent, and especially with the lesser speedway nations, most speedways were (are) club-run, and had neither the expertise nor the connections to arrange such prestige meetings themselves, this was an attractive proposition.

As most of these events took place on a Sunday, it was possible to arrange them around the British League, which, at that time, avoided Sunday fixtures. Indeed, many top line British League riders took on their own riding commitments on the continent on Sundays anyway.

But there was unease among the UK promoters. If the 'circus' were to become stronger and stronger, it could easily end up as a serious rival to the virtual monopoly position of the BSPA. However, at that early stage the BSPA decided to look the other way.

Then came a real challenge. Charles Ochiltree, who seemed at that time to have fallen completely under the spell of the charismatic Olsen after signing him from Wolves in 1976, agreed to an approach by the Olsen/Adams partnership to stage one of their events at Coventry.

Clearly this was a direct challenge to the BSPA and they not only refused to allow Ochiltree to effectively sub-lease his track to another (unlicensed) promotion, but they decided it was time to put the boot in.

It is not documented anywhere why the Olsen/Adams Masters of Speedway circus was wound up, but Ole, who was nearing the end of his riding days, had his own Vojens track to play with by then, plus other business commitments in Denmark. Clearly though, Olsen had the vision of setting up a travelling circus even then.

For my money, Masters of Speedway or Speedway Grand Prix, the title makes little difference. It is all about outside players taking the top layer of cream away from the rank and file promoters and leaving them with just the bread and butter stuff (soon to become merely dry crusts). For what it is worth, here are my programme note comments on the concept, taken from the Ipswich programme dated May 17, 1977:

"I congratulate the cricketing authorities for their actions against Tony Greig (in dropping him from the England cricket team). What has this to do with speedway? Only that as the world gets smaller and smaller, in more and more sports we have those who seem to wish to just make a fast buck without putting anything back. Whether it is tennis, golf, football or speedway, if the public are served up with too much instant and very sweet cake, then instead of becoming a treat it becomes sickly, and what is worse, the public will then reject the bread and butter stuff. Without that bread and butter the sport, be it cricket or speedway or whatever cannot thrive, and with no rungs on the bottom half of the ladder to success, new champions will not be produced. As the existing big names die away all that will remain will be a space and through the short sightedness, or worse, the calculated actions of businessmen as opposed to lovers of the sport, it could end up strangled.

"Relating this to speedway, we have more and more big name bonanza meetings, some even at places other than speedway tracks, but aimed directly at attracting the speedway public. The top riders demand not only the cream from the top but a large percentage of the milk as well and so there is less to go round for those at the bottom.

"For those (businessmen) who only use talent that has already been produced by others, the rest of the milk remains theirs. They only use and pay the champions, they do not help to produce them. The cricket authorities have a chance to act before it is too late. For speedway, I fear the time to act has already come and gone."

Personally I think, after the thick end of 30 years, those thoughts still hold good, and have a great deal to do with why the UK has become an irrelevance in world sport, preferring to take the easy option and import sports people from elsewhere rather than develop their own. The relevance to the

Ole and former business partner Peter Adams *(AW)*

current Grand Prix series is also clear.

When Ole retired as a rider and Peter moved on to Cradley Heath their partnership folded and Ole was left with just his Danish commitments. As the Danish team manager he was exceedingly strong-willed. He had always been very patriarchal, to the point of obsession, over all the Danish lads who had followed in his footsteps, even though some of them owed little of their careers to him personally.

Hans Nielsen famously resented what he saw as Olsen's unwelcome attempts to dictate his own particular career path. Erik Gundersen and Tommy Knudsen, on the other hand, decided to keep their noses clean and enjoy Ole's patronage, whilst Nielsen was ostracised. Not that this meant Denmark not using Hans' talents when they needed them, but only when they needed them, and not when they could work around him.

I had my own experiences with this situation of Olsen acting as the 'Godfather' to the Danish boys. Preben Eriksen had to sit out a year's ban before he could go to a track of his own choice and John Jorgensen was within a spit of signing for Ipswich before Olsen stepped in and he ended up at Coventry.

It was refreshing to read somewhere not too long ago that John now considers he might possibly have made the wrong choice way back then.

Ole and I clashed again during this period, not so much on a personal but a 'professional' and international level. Finally for once, as Danish manager, he was holding the trump cards, and he showed just how good a motivator he is. There is little doubt that Erik Gundersen owes him a great deal and that Ole was a great reader of situations and manipulator of events.

It would be interesting to know just how much of the enormous debt Nicki Pedersen owes his manager, Ole's son Jacob, for winning the 2003 world crown against all logic, and how much of that contribution was as a result of the younger Olsen putting his father's teachings into practice. Or perhaps some was also due to Olsen senior's direct input?

The Danish national team enjoyed phenomenal success during Ole's period in charge in the 80s but I suspect that the next generation of Danish riders and officials tired of Olsen treating Danish speedway as entirely his own domain.

Did he step back or was he encouraged to take more of a back seat? Given the subsequent events as they unfolded (the way he seemed to bypass the Danish Motor Union and go direct to Sorber, Vaessen, and the FIM), one had to consider the latter might have been the case, because it certainly seems he still has the enthusiasm for the sport as long as he is doing the leading and organising.

By the time Ole became involved with the Grand Prix in the mid-90s my involvement in speedway had ended. Just as well really, because we would once again have found ourselves on opposite sides. Be assured, the battle would have been fierce!

So let's have a look. Olsen, the speedway rider, was just brilliant, charismatic, professional, reliable, if maybe somewhat dogmatic, and just a bit ruthless at times.

Olsen, the promoter, was excellent. He was typically brusque when he had his 'game face' on, and given the seemingly permanent rain cloud that hung over Vojens, this is no surprise! Any promoter would be the same. He had the good sense to look after the media well and ran a good show. He could also be disarmingly charming when required. If there was a weakness, it was his inability to delegate.

As a team manager, I know of none better. He was a fearsome opponent, being prepared to use every avenue open to him in order to give his team an edge, and able to get the very best out of his riders. The Danish World Team Cup wins at Landshut in 1978, and then seven years later at Long Beach, were largely down to Ole's strength of character.

Olsen, as a man, is very intense, and therefore a little domineering, but as sharp as a tack and always with a valid opinion. Ole's ideas and mine have differed many times over the years but, then again, they have often coincided as well.

Once he had finished with riding, his thoughts about trying to slow equipment down match my own, and he all but committed political suicide during the early days of the Grand Prix over his attempts to force through the use of a less grippy tyre. I think he did the only thing open to him and backed away when he could see it was a battle he was not going to win. At least he tried.

All in all, despite the chequered history between us, I have a huge respect for Ole Olsen.

Michael Lee

...Like a bat out of hell
I'll be gone when the morning comes
When the night is over
Like a bat out of hell I'll be gone
Like a bat out of hell I'll be gone when the morning comes
But when the day is done
And the sun goes down
And the moonlight's shining through
Then like a sinner before the gates of heaven
I'll come crawling on back to you
Then like a sinner before the gates of heaven
I'll come crawling on back to you

I can see myself
Tearing up the road
Faster than any other boy has ever gone
And my skin is rough but my soul is ripe
And no one's gonna stop me now
I gotta make my escape
But I can't stop thinking of you
And I never see the sudden curve until it's way too late
I never see the sudden curve until it's way too late

Then I'm dying on the bottom of a pit in the blazing sun
Torn and twisted at the foot of a burning bike
And I think somebody somewhere must be tolling a bell
And the last thing I see is my heart
Still beating
Breaking out of my body
And flying away
Like a bat out of hell

Isn't it sad that you cannot even think about Michael without also thinking about drugs? I mean, his was a special kind of speedway talent that deserves remembering for its own worth, but sadly that will never really be the case.

By the time this stick insect of a boy – all of 14, coming on 15 – was doing demonstration laps during the interval at King's Lynn in 1974, it was clear he was a child prodigy. I have written before, though, how I believe the amount of dedication he and his father, Andy, put into learning everything about speedway racing, pretty well to the exclusion of anything else, was excessive.

Here, in my opinion, was a classic case of a child with special talents not having the chance to learn about how to cope with life in general, because of over-dedication to those talents at such an early age.

Perhaps we might have seen a true long-term champion if Michael and his father had waited a few years, which would have allowed him to become a bit more worldly wise and fully rounded before becoming a speedway obsessive.

I know Michael is still around, and even claiming to be settled and happy. He might also claim he was victimised but at the end of the day most of that talk is paranoia. Just about all the perceived injustices were brought on by himself. I can only look back on his wasted life with sadness.

Michael believed that the starts of races were a three-way contest between himself, the other riders and the referee - indeed, starts in general had gone in that direction a bit. The Big Daddy of the technique of giving yourself an 'edge' at the starts was Ivan Mauger and many riders subsequently studied and copied Ivan's methods of unsettling the other riders.

I suppose the likes of Michael and Erik Gundersen would claim their methods were their own, but Ivan was the undisputed master when it came to the psychology of starting technique.

Now there are two ways you can look at this practise of disrupting the starts.

Lee/Gundersen/Mauger (and others') supporters might well argue that using gamesmanship was part and parcel of racing, whilst us 'purists', for I count myself in this group, feel the responsibility of a referee is to come up with a fair start which gives everyone a chance to race on equal terms.

Generally, the younger, stronger-minded referees were of the latter view, and began stopping and restarting races if one or more riders gained an unreasonable advantage over the others. Such starts were 'unsatisfactory' as laid down in the regulations. There is a fine line between having faster reactions than the other riders and gaining an unfair advantage, but I would say referees understood the difference. In this respect you can say Michael, among others, was 'targeted'.

The promoters took far too long to introduce the 'no tape-touching' rule, being sucked into the 'my clutch dragged me into the tapes' cop out used so much by the 'rollers'. Admittedly the clutches in those days were not as sophisticated as today, but maybe one instance of tape-touching every 20 or so meetings was down to a clutch malfunction. Once the new regulation was brought in, riders gave themselves and their clutches a little more tolerance.

I was in the vanguard but Peter Adams won the day in getting the no tape-touching rule through general council. He simply pointed out that if we made the tapes out of barbed wire, we would get very few riders rolling into them! By the time this regulation was adopted, I think Michael was nearing the end of his turbulent career but Erik had a hard time making the adjustment.

Michael, though, had other problems.

When the Californians arrived in force in the late 70s/early 80s, they brought with them a drug culture. That is not to say drugs had never been heard of in the UK, or in speedway before that time. Indeed, there are several unproven stories of drug taking incidents in the sport prior to this. In my young day, amphetamines were called 'purple hearts'.

But what the Californians brought along was a completely casual attitude to the using of 'recreational' drugs, specifically marijuana, amphetamines and cocaine. They had grown up with the idea that these drugs were quite socially acceptable. One of the quaint ironies of American law is the extraordinarily strict underage (21) drinking and sex laws, contrasting dramatically with the casual acceptance of the drug culture.

Anyway, many of the less strong-willed UK-based riders found themselves drawn into the drug web. Whilst, by and large, those Americans who partook appeared to keep their drug taking in proportion, Michael became 'hooked'. We can talk about Michael and Mark Courtney in relation to drug taking, because the evidence is in the public domain, but there is no doubting that apart from these two cases the levels of drug use in speedway circles was pretty high during this period.

I don't know if I am now the only adult left in the western world who has never experienced the taking of illicit substances. Sure, I enjoy a drink, and accept what many say in that alcohol is possibly even worse than the other 'recreational drugs', but alcohol is legally and socially acceptable.

I freely admit it isn't a determination not to break the law that stops me from trying these other things. After all, even now I tend to break the law just about every time I drive my car (over the speed limit). No, my reason for not trying drugs is simpler than that. I just do not want to discover I might enjoy it.

I went to a talk given by a police drug squad officer fairly recently. It was an excellent and informative evening, with the police officer being perhaps more scathing about alcohol, in terms of dependency and long term damage to health, than the other 'lightweight' drugs. But he also pointed out that once someone makes the step of taking illegal drugs, it is easy to slip from there into the 'heavy' stuff.

More importantly, the amount of social damage caused by chronic users, and in particular the way in which they get the stuff and the things they do to get the money to pay for it, is just immense.

That little speech hasn't got much to do with speedway but is there to try and demonstrate my thoughts on illegal substances. If riders used them purely to 'unwind', in moderation, and not when they were going to ride speedway, then that is entirely up to them. However, it seems that most of these 'social' drugs linger in the body long enough to be detectable for some time afterwards – and one has to presume that if they are still detectable then they are also still having an effect.

Now in all the time speedway has been operating, I cannot think of an incident when a rider has been 'done' for taking 'performance enhancing' drugs. I recall one or two who have failed alcohol tests or had traces of marijuana but I am sure 'hangovers' are unlikely to be classed as performance-enhancing. Likewise, whilst I have personal knowledge of social drug taking involving speedway riders, I have none involving performance-enhancing stuff.

Michael sticks out a long leg to block Birmingham rider Andy Grahame's inside challenge at King's Lynn. *(CC)*

However, it would take a huge amount of gullibility to assume it hasn't happened. We are not talking steroids or the like here. After all, speedway riders are hardly famous for having Adonis-type muscles. But it would take a mug to think that stuff like amphetamines or 'speed' wasn't being used. After all, although the taking of such reaction-enhancing substances has always been against the regulations, there was no random drug testing until well on into the 80s.

Discussions and gossip within the sport was rife, and circumstantial evidence was always there that some riders were riding under the influence. The finger was pointed many times at some Americans - you may be assured that in my time as England team manager there were several times when the England boys did not believe they were competing on a level playing field.

Things came to a head during the England versus USA Test series of 1982. Kenny Carter was always very outspoken on the subject of drugs in speedway and I have no doubt that this didn't help him with his Anglo-American détente, but the whole of the England team were up in arms at Poole. As it happens, Lee was in the middle of his 'will he, won't he' period at that time and didn't ride in the fifth, and deciding, Test.

Much was made in the press about the Americans' togetherness and camaraderie, a lot of which can be attributed to their upbringing and the fact that they were a long way from home, but on that particular night they were just over the top in the pits, clowning around and playing the fool.

During the racing they were just on a different level. It was as if two sets of riders had been superimposed onto the same track, one pair in slow motion and the other in double time. In virtually every race the Americans' reactions at the starts were so much quicker than the home team, as was their general riding. The two Moran brothers were paired together, and over the years we got used to seeing them do amazing things on speedway bikes, but that night they were just on a different planet.

The only rider who could live with the Americans that night was Kenny. I have never, ever seen a gutsier display by any rider anywhere than the one he put on then. He was so angry but he channelled his anger at what he perceived to be cheating by the Americans into trying to beat them and he rode his heart out for 15 points from six rides in our 39-69 defeat.

I think it is fair to say many of the England team chucked in the towel well before the end of what they felt was an unfair contest that evening. There was also a good deal of talk among the riders on our side of the pits about making some kind of official complaint.

In the event, they left it with me to take up their concerns at the top level. After all, things had been rumbling for some time. I had my say – not on the night but afterwards – and not too much later, random drug-testing was introduced. I am sure it would have been entirely coincidental but over a very short period afterwards quite a number of American riders departed from the British League scene for a variety of different reasons.

Sadly, by then Michael Lee and speedway had also gone in different directions, not long after that Test series in fact. Of course, he blames everyone else but himself. However, that is not the story his ex-promoters tell. Yes, I do think that referees paid more attention to him than many other riders at the starting line – but only because he was forever trying to beat the system.

The new look Lee after a visit to my dentist.

I also believe the SCB finally reached the stage where they decided he was such a liability that it was time for him to take a 'rest', so in that respect I think Michael was correct in thinking he was being victimised. But by then he was out of control.

Do I believe he took drugs to improve his riding? I have no knowledge of that. I will merely say he was using drugs so much by the end of his career, I think it would have been just about impossible for his body to have been drug-free when he did turn up to race, which, towards the end was purely when he felt up to it, or felt like it, or both.

Despite all of this, I liked Michael very much. Just about all of the time the negative stuff only hurt one person and that was himself. Even though he had so much ability, and even though he had more public adoration than he could handle, he had very little respect in himself. A classic example of this was his teeth.

They were in a terrible state, all brown and green mottled. I asked both Michael and his father about this, and they offered the explanation that when he had his appendix (or tonsils, can't remember which) out as a toddler, he was given the wrong mix of gas, which affected the enamel on his teeth.

He has subsequently denied this was the case and says it was simply because he never brushed them, so the wrong gas mix story could easily have been a blind to avoid admitting the truth at that time.

I pestered him to do something about them because it spoiled his whole looks, which were otherwise good, but he told me he had a phobia about dentists. Eventually, I organised for my own dentist, who was also a friend, to come to a speedway meeting at Ipswich when Michael was taking part. He was well used to getting strange requests from me. He had previously filled my Alsatian dog's canine teeth when they had been smashed by a kick from a horse and had then gone bad.

I called Michael into the speedway office after the meeting. The dentist had a quick look and agreed that the only hope was to crown the front six teeth. The deal was, he would do it under full anaesthetic so Michael wouldn't know what was going on.

So we arranged a time when we could do the work whilst the dental surgery was closed. Michael arrived and was immediately put to sleep. The dentist then prepared the front teeth for crowns and tidied up the back ones. I watched whilst all this was happening. I then took the lad back to my house and he had a sleep whilst the crowns (not temps, but the finished articles) were made in a couple of hours by a dental technician who had agreed to assist and had been standing by. Finally, I took Michael back to the surgery and he had the crowns fitted.

They looked tremendous and it made a huge difference to his appearance. I had hoped this would give him a lift and the incentive to take more pride in his appearance but that didn't happen. I don't know if he still has the crowns but the last time I saw him they were looking pretty ordinary anyway.

If I seem to have focussed on the negative side of Michael, then I am sorry. I just hate what happened to him. His racing record stands up for itself. It shows a lad of unbridled talent, dedication and determination to reach the top. Those who saw him at his best simply accept there was nobody like him and that he developed a style entirely his own which has never been copied since.

Those who raced against him have no bad words to say. He won his races purely by going faster than the other riders, not by over-aggressive riding. He was just an outstanding talent with pretty well no enemies among his peers.

Michael took his speedway seriously, especially when he was in his prime, but he knew how to have fun, too.

It was the end-of-season high jinks time at Ipswich. Traditionally, we had called the speedway meeting finished and over at the end of official racing, so as to clear the referee of any embarrassment, or any misunderstanding about the fun part of the evening being mistaken for 'speedway'.

Effectively then, we were releasing ourselves, the riders and the referee from the bit in the programme that said the meeting was being run under SCB regulations. After all, the 'wrong way round race', where the riders raced each other in a clockwise rather than anti-clockwise direction, or the 'two up' race, where each rider carried a pillion passenger (another rider), could hardly be considered as being within the speedway regulations!

The idea of Dennis Sigalos and John Cook doing a 'streak' was not a spur of the moment thing. I had arranged it with them several days earlier. There was no question of payment. It was just a bit of fun, in the manner of the times, when 'streaking' was relatively commonplace and 'fashionable'.

The whole thing was choreographed to get a family-style laugh, and to cause no embarrassment or offence to anyone from kids of six to grandmas of 60.

When Michael Lee found out what was going to happen, he wanted to join in. This part of it was spur of the moment. Up until then, it was to have been a 'match race'.

The riders went to the changing rooms behind the pits area, which was out of bounds to the public. They took off their leathers but kept on helmets, body colours and boots. They emerged straight from the changing rooms and got onto their bikes by the changing room doors. By the time they reached the pits, the bikes had been push-started, so they rode straight through the pits, onto and around the track.

The announcer, John Earrey, had been pre-warned, and in his true professional style, drew attention to the three riders without saying why, as if he couldn't work out what they were up to.

As the riders half-raced, half-rode around, a wave of reaction from the crowd followed them. It was a gasp of disbelief, followed by spontaneous laughter and applause. I suspect most of them were asking each other 'Did they really have nothing on?' because at that distance and with all the movement, there was no chance to tell properly.

The three then rode straight in through the pits gate, through the pits and disappeared back into the changing rooms.

I made only two mistakes. First of all, I pre-warned Dave Kindred, the local newspaper photographer, to get his camera ready. Dave and I were good friends and I knew I could trust him to be discreet.

The second error was to allow Michael to become involved. The young lad was already viewed by the SCB as trouble and the media was, as they do, playing up his bad boy image.

Pictures appeared in the local paper the next day. I hadn't attempted to stop them. I knew I could trust Dave not to allow anything of a crude nature to go to print. Unfortunately, what

Dennis Sigalos (above) lets it all hang out in a fun prank that backfired on me and Michael, though it seemed a good idea at the time.

I had not really considered was that there is one thing on the night, having a blur of indistinct things happening. It was an entirely different thing having those moments frozen in time by a camera, where the whole scenario becomes far more stark and obvious. I should not have pre-warned Dave.

To his credit, when the national 'popular' dailies started telephoning Dave and offering big money for a 'candid' shot of Michael, he resisted the temptation to cash in. He accepted that if I hadn't pre-warned him of what was to happen, the shots would not have been taken and therefore he respected my request to prevent further publication.

That didn't stop the nationals from running the story, though, and the painfully perverse, pedantic and puritanical Dick Bracher of the SCB was alerted.

Had only Siggy and John Cook been involved, it might not have even reached the nationals. Even had it done so, I suspect even Dastardly Dick would have simply dashed off one of his diabolical diatribes, warning of wicked and wanton ways and the consequences of such.

It was one of those fun things that worked beautifully on the night but backfired simply because I got greedy and tried to get extra mileage from it. The Americans were able to laugh it off - but it was another big, black mark against Michael.

Typical of the double standards of the time, Barry Briggs did a photo shoot showing him doing the same thing. It even made the front page of *Speedway Star* – and not one eyebrow was raised.

As a person Michael Lee was impossible not to like, even though he was a bit scatterbrained. There was always a ready smile, and I never had a cross word with him except on the day when, for him, the racing died.

I was at that meeting at King's Lynn when he rode the wrong way along the track whilst a race was in progress. I had tried to talk with him even before that, but he was not prepared to listen to anyone by then. This was the incident that got him banned for a year and effectively brought his speedway life to an end.

Although the idea of him riding into oncoming riders is nightmarish, that is really not what happened. Feeling aggrieved because he had missed the start, he pulled up in the first turn of a race whilst the other riders continued. He then rode back to the start line, going the wrong way but not on the racing line.

He parked his bike on gate position one on the track. It was an act of defiance and calculated to cause a stir but it was not dangerous. It was where a flag marshal would stand to wave his flag at the end of a race

Michael's subsequent actions in visiting the referee, John Eglese, in the referee's box and accosting him were, in my opinion, far more worthy of serious penalty, but it was his riding the wrong way along the track that people all focus on. In any case, had it not been this incident, I am sure there would have been another that would have seen him suspended. By then he really was out of control.

Michael was a breath of fresh air to the sport. He was a really nice, albeit easily led, bloke and in his short reign he served England proud. Some would have it that he damaged the image of the sport, and this might be true, but it seems to me the only one who was ever really seriously damaged was himself.

The England team ready to face mighty Rest of the World at Ipswich in 1977 are (left to right): Dave Jessup, Michael Lee, Malcolm Simmons, John Louis, Gordon Kennett, Peter Collins and Terry Betts.

17 Forty Miles of Bad Road

Well, a good deal more than that really, but King's Lynn and Hackney were our 'local' derby opposition, whilst Mildenhall warrants a special mention by virtue of their proximity and effect on the Witches . . .

Peas and Sweetcorn

I got a brand new combine harvester
An' I'll give you the key
Come on now let's get together
In perfect harmony
I got twenty acres
An' you got forty-three
Now I got a brand new combine harvester
An' I'll give you the key

Peas and sweetcorn? I don't know if it was an original quote, but it came from Ipswich clerk of the course Ray Chinnery. King's Lynn was at Ipswich on a Good Friday. It was the time when the Stars had a good line-up and this drew many of the Lynn faithful to Foxhall in the hope of seeing a rare victory for our Norfolk neighbours.

The Lynn fans were congregated on the exit to the second bend, all decked out in their green and yellow colours. Ray pointed and said: "Look, peas and sweetcorn!" From thenceforth, it was an image I have never been able to get out of my mind. The fact that the area around Lynn is almost all consigned to vegetable growing merely enhances the metaphor.

It has to be said, My speedway relationship with King's Lynn began long before my involvement with Ipswich or as a promoter. On many a Saturday evening we would load up Joe Thurley's speedway bike and head off up the A10 from our north London base to the wilds of Norfolk.

In those days, having a bike rack on the back of the car was a status symbol – you could park the car anywhere with its bike in place and know it wouldn't get touched, especially at the speedway-mad King's Lynn.

We would get to the Saddlebow Road track fairly early and, with the bike on board, would be ushered through to the outer pits car park, from where we would try to sneak into the stadium through the pits. Sometimes it worked, sometimes it didn't. A character called Alec Ford used to hang around and often thwarted our efforts. I was never quite sure of his position at this or other tracks I saw him at but to all intent and purpose you would think he owned them!

After the meeting we would wander into town. It didn't take long to discover the Maids Head in the Market Square was the place to head for. Come closing time, the speedway fraternity who were in the pub would drift upstairs where the landlord would hold court, like Henry VIII. His younger, and very attractive wife, would flirt with the riders and the wannabees equally whilst he looked on with casual amusement. He was a big bloke!

Next day it would be down to the track again for the Sunday training school. Well, training school was a bit of a posh name really. Pay your fiver to Peter, the trackman, get changed, warm the bike up and stick it in the queue. Ride around with two or three others, come back, add fuel and oil, and stick the bike back in the queue again! I suppose most times there would be 20 to 30 lads all expecting to become the next Ove Fundin.

Even at that time the Lynn track was a natural shape to ride and it was well maintained. When the bends were widened a few years later, it really did become a good race track – second, I suspect, only to the Belle Vue Zoo.

I chuckle when I hear that places like King's Lynn and Hackney were such good tracks to ride that they gave no home advantage. What nonsense! The easiest track in the country to ride was Belle Vue – but the home riders just used to ride it better than the visitors.

There never really was any animosity between the King's Lynn and Ipswich promotions for a long, long time. Well, we don't really count Cyril Crane, that walking bundle of little people's disease!

Mighty marvels – Mike Lanham tussling with Ian 'Tiddler' Turner at Saddlebow Road.

In fact, Martin Rogers was a close friend from 1969, when he was a full time journalist just helping out at Lynn and I was just learning the game at Ipswich. At that stage Martin and I had similar views on the sport and its many faults and foibles and actually met socially now and then to put the speedway world to rights.

The lovely Lin, who eventually became Mrs Rogers, was introduced to my then wife and myself before she was launched upon the world of speedway. I think Martin was trying to break her into the speedway scene slowly!

I have already explained the esteem with which I held Maurice Littlechild, who was the active King's Lynn promoter for many years. Even in the early days of the Second Division, though, the competition between the two East Anglian teams was lively.

At that stage, with the first pick of all the kids from their training school, the Starlets should have been a top team but the astute Maurice was never concerned about club glory. He was a true promoter. Maintaining a healthy bottom line, and not setting supporter expectations too high, were more important to him than cups and medals.

Thus, I think, the King's Lynn culture was born and has remained through the years, even though others may have tried to change it.

Certainly, when Lynn was a Saturday track, although the Witches more often than not had their measure on track, it was always the Norfolk promotion that came off best financially. We would take thousands of Witches supporters when we were the visitors, all hopeful of an away victory, whilst not that many Stars supporters normally bothered to come and watch their team get trimmed up at Foxhall.

Terry Betts often made the trip to Ipswich as a spectator on a Thursday night. It was nearer to his Chelmsford home than was Kings Lynn. Terry might well have had something to do with the laid back attitude among the Stars in those early years. Not that he wasn't competitive. Indeed, he was, but he was also a delightful personality who never allowed things to get on top of him and always seemed to maintain a balanced view on life. I expect that is why he was moved over eventually when the Crane/Rogers team brought in Michael Lee, Dave Jessup and a new, competitive edge.

When Martin took over as full time manager of the Norfolk outfit it is fair to say our relationship became a lot more businesslike, but that was bound to happen. Then, when Martin and Lin became promoters themselves in 1983, his attitude and actions changed significantly.

Expediency took over a great deal from idealism. Martin really was never cut out to be a

speedway promoter, though. It changed him completely, even affecting his health. Some people are just not born to take a great deal of pressure on a regular basis.

I had to have some sympathy with him, though. I had one or two riders who were hard work but in Michael Lee, Martin had more than a handful. Such a good rider, but not the most stable of characters and always likely to self-destruct. It would have been interesting to see

Another one for the Lynn faithful to cheer – Tony Davey and Ted Howgeo romp to a Witches 5-1.

if Maurice could have handled the precocious teenager turned paranoid star. I reckon he would have been one of the few people who would, but by then Maurice had passed on.

I used to really enjoy the Ipswich visits to Saddlebow Road. They always had to have a natural edge. It was the old Norfolk versus Suffolk thing; two very rural sets of supporters and both lots of fans were very loyal and committed. Mostly, the riders themselves all knew each other well and rarely had a problem. Nonetheless, we all appreciated a derby is a derby.

Likewise, Ipswich and King's Lynn supporters could enjoy no end of friendly banter without allowing their common sense to desert them. It was never necessary to segregate the two groups and I wonder if, in doing so at football matches, the authorities actually made the problem worse than it was originally.

No chance of Billy Sanders being 'held up' at the gate this time, as he leads Cradley Heath's Erik Gundersen whilst wearing the Stars racejacket.

I used to love setting myself up as an Aunt Sally on our visits to their rustic Saddlebow Road track. Once the two teams were lined up against each other, mateship was put aside as determination took over.

I figured that if the Lynn crowd could become involved a bit, then they would do a wonderful job in winding up my own lads, so I was happy to banter with them, to indulge in a bit of theatrical mime, and to set myself up. Then all I needed to do was to point out to the Ipswich team how the locals were being 'unkind' to 'us' and my job was done!

Ron Bagley and I never missed too many tricks between us and the Lynn fans never expected anything less. Even now, they still talk of the way their team was 'robbed' of a victory one particular year. Ipswich was two points up going into the last race of the match, so all we needed was a 3-3. Either our strike man, John Louis, had to win the race, or he and Kevin Jolly come second and third.

The Lynn pair got away and despite chasing them for two laps, JL was not going to pass them. Kevin, at the back, fell on the first turn of lap three and was unable to clear the track in time to allow the race to continue. It was stopped and rerun, with Louis jumping clear to clinch the 3-3 we needed.

It has to be said, the local supporters were not very happy! Several years later, Kevin finally ended up riding for the Stars, and even now has never said if he fell accidentally or was under orders. It is not for me to break that kind of confidence. All I will say is that no rules were broken! I should add, the regulations were changed shortly after this, allowing referees to award stopped races instead of re-running them.

Billy Sanders was always a fiery lad. When he was still pretty young and we were the visitors at Lynn, he stormed back to the pits after a race. At that time bikes had a lifting handle on top of their rear mudguard and tracks had four assistant starting marshals.

Unlike today's leggy young ladies who parade up and down the start line, these were not there just for show. Their actual duty was to push-start any rider who stalled at the gate. A stalled rider was allowed outside assistance as far as the 30-yard marker. (That, by the way, was the sole reason for the 30-yard marker. The marker had absolutely nothing to do with riders not being able to change 'lanes' before reaching it, as many believed.)

Not officially part of their duties, the starting

Two Witches who found their way to Lynn later in their careers – John Louis and Kevin Jolly.

'assistants' would also help to pull back and disentangle any riders who had rolled forwards into the tapes.

What was the reason for Billy's anger? He claimed that the 'assistant' who was allocated to him had, when the green light came on, got hold of his lifting handle and lifted his rear wheel clear of the track for a moment, causing him to miss the start completely.

Bill was marching along the track to have a 'serious word' with the fellow involved, when I pointed out anyone who could lift bike and rider with one hand needed to be shown some respect!

True enough, like many of the King's Lynn pits and track staff, this man looked like he bit off babies' heads off for fun! He did actually later become the Lynn start marshal, pulling any number of stunts against the Ipswich riders over the years. Ron and I had several run-ins with him but we never let things get physical!

To make this balanced reporting, I have to also point out that long time Lynn team manager, Alan Littlechild (Maurice's son), invariably expressed similar concerns about the neutrality of the Ipswich start marshal. I will tell you this though. Whilst our man paid particular attention to those who tried to cheat, he was never biased. Perish the thought!

It was a shame that eventually the time came when my hate affair with the Lynn fans had to come to an end. Without Maurice's restraining hand, Cyril Crane had become more and more of a loose cannon and the relationship between the two promotions was becoming strained. At one match, as was my way, I started bantering with the fans, but instead of the good-natured booing and catcalling in return, I sensed a much stronger resentment.

Not unusually, a couple of times I over-celebrated a Witches race win or whatever, and the reaction I got was again far more resentful than ever before. Also the diminutive Crane was like a kettle just coming to the boil and ready to do more than just hiss and spit. (I'm sure there is a natural Spoonerism there, but I'll leave that one to you!)

With great sadness, I decided I had better keep my head down for the rest of the meeting, never risking the old wind up again. I missed those moments though, as did, I suspect, most of the crowd, who used to get into the spirit of things. Was it a sign of the times or merely Crane spoiling things? A bit of both I suspect.

Agony 'Awks

Isn't it rich? Aren't we a pair?
Me here at last on the ground, and you in mid-air
Send in the clowns.

Isn't it bliss? Don't you approve?
One who keeps tearing around, and one who can't move.
But where are the clowns? Send in the clowns

Don't you love farce? My fault, I fear;
I thought that you'd want what I want - sorry my dear.
But where are the clowns? Quick, send in the clowns.
Don't bother, they're here.

Strange, isn't it. The two closest same-league tracks to Ipswich, and they were the two the Witches team always seemed to ride best. Was it because, as the King's Lynn and Hackney promoters would have everyone believe, the shape of those two tracks was inviting for visiting riders to have a go on? Personally, I don't think so, although both were 'have a go' places.

I think the promotions from those two tracks relied on putting on good racing and entertainment rather than a win at all costs mentality when constructing their teams, and even in the way those teams were managed. We, at Ipswich, set our stall out in a slightly different manner. We took the attitude that the supporters wanted to see and support a winning team.

I have to say, it was easier for Ipswich to be a little more generous with their riders due to the higher attendance figures but I am not sure this was too significant.

Sandor Levai and Mick Hines are the Witches either side of Hackney's Barry Thomas.

Secretly, I admired the way Hackney boss Len Silver managed to muddle along with a team of, what shall we say, speedway's equivalent to the Crazy Gang? Often they would pull off the most unlikely victories but mainly they would seem to just have fun – win, lose or draw. Yes, they did have the odd one or two very professionally minded riders, like Bo Petersen for instance, but the general atmosphere was pretty lightweight.

I don't know who drew whom into the personal feud that developed between Len and myself. We began happily enough, with lighthearted banter between each other when Ipswich was in the Second Division and raced against Rayleigh, another track where he held a promoting interest. Very early on it became clear that 'Leaping Len' was what he would describe as a showman and performed an act in between races I would describe as that of an old-fashioned circus clown, filling in time between acts.

I was the opposite. I hated being a 'front man' and kept in the background during matches, preferring to pay others to help the show along. There is no doubt also that I had very little charisma and presented a very dour face. I have to say, I have often wished I had Len's ability to go out there and make an arse out of myself in the interests of putting on a show.

The nearest I got to that was one bitter October night at Foxhall in the 80s. It was a dreadful, dragged out meeting. I was cold and bored, and the supporters had to be likewise. So I challenged Steve Bryenton, one of the second half lads, to a foot race around one lap of the track. Steve was in his late teens and proud of his fitness, whilst I was rushing headlong towards middle-age, so on the surface I was being a bit rash. Indeed, I wondered if I could get around a whole lap!

What I had gambled on was that Steve was dressed in his leathers and boots. I just slipped my shoes and heavy coat off. I promise you, that track surface was actually freezing.

Steve went off at the trot, and as the distance between us widened around the first turn I wondered if I might have bitten off more than I could chew, but I hung on about ten yards behind. Down the back straight I could sense the racing boots were taking their toll, and I passed his on the last turn to jog home in front. I didn't look, but I was told he didn't actually finish the lap!

Several lads wanted to take me on after that but I had done my Bobby Rigg bit and retired undefeated.

A 'thing' developed almost from day one between the Rayleigh star man, Geoff Maloney, and several Ipswich riders. Geoff was what is known as a 'wholehearted trier'. In real terms, that meant he seemed to enjoy the physical side of racing. He was the kind of rider who was a hero or a villain, depending if he was riding in your team, or for the opposition.

Incidents between him and several Witches, and in particular a very inexperienced Tony Davey, caused some public verbal sparring between Len and myself, and it just seemed to develop from there. As things developed, programme comments from both Ipswich and Hackney got more and more personal, we ended up simply trying to point-score off each other.

When I was presented with a golden opportunity to get a very cheap laugh about his personal domestic situation, I took it. Of all the provocative comments I came up with in the Ipswich programme over the years, these were the only words I regret putting in, and feel badly about.

By that time, it has to be said, the two promotions were at daggers drawn anyway, so it hardly affected things at a professional level. If anything, it calmed things down, because we were far more publicly circumspect after that, but that cheap gag remains one of very few personal regrets in my speedway life.

Prior to this, I did think that Len left himself a bit open when he decided to compare the Ipswich and Hackney tracks. He described Ipswich as too long and skinny to be a good racetrack and went on to rave about Waterden Road. Well, it is true, the shape and camber of the east London circuit did encourage riders to stick their necks out, but not without taking huge risks.

Particularly coming out of turn one, the riders were encouraged to drift right out to the fence at substantial speed, where solid fence posts and light poles lay in wait for the slightest error or misfortune. The safety record at Hackney was not good. Those solid obstructions claimed more than a couple of lives and plenty of very bad injuries, including the Witches' Kevin Jolly who missed the best part of a season with a broken leg collected there.

Had I been Len, I wouldn't have bragged about the Hackney track but I decided not to have a go back in print and so let his comments go through to the keeper that time.

I think Hackney won at Ipswich three times over the 11-year period. The first was that first ever meeting in the top league, when Davey badly hurt his hand. The last was a genuinely earned League Cup victory in 1983.

The other loss was typical of the pettiness that went on between the two promotions. John Cook failed to front up for the Witches, so we rejigged the team using number eight Andy Hines. Silver convinced the referee that we could not make positional team changes, so we had to put Hines in Cook's team position, which was at number one.

It was something the book was not clear on. Most people would have gone for the commonsense attitude of allowing Ipswich to change their pairings, especially as Cook was withholding his services and we were not even asking for a facility. The referee decided, though, to back Len's view of the way things should be done.

That left the Ipswich pairings badly unbalanced as well as a heat leader down but when Jolly fell in his opening race and effectively played no further part in the meeting, Hackney contrived to fall over the line, by 40-38. Len carried on as if they had won the league title, whilst I was less than amused.

Still, on balance, I think we had the edge over the Hawks overall in that 11-year period. Ipswich won 10 of its visits to Hackney and drew two. That is a greater than 50% success rate, and would have been an even higher percentage if league matches only were counted. Many of our wins at Hackney were by considerable margins, with a 55-23 scoreline in 1976 being the greatest.

One way and another, I think Ipswich came out on top, but I have to say that even for all the bad feeling between the two promotions, I have the utmost respect for Len and his efforts for the sport. When he finally decided to pull the plug as promoter at Hackney at the end of 1983 (he subsequently returned to Rye House), I knew it was time for me to follow.

There was rarely cause for Len Silver to celebrate when the Witches were in town, but I still have the utmost respect for him. (AW)

The Carrot Patch

Where does our love lie?
In the middle of nowhere
Will it soon pass me by?
In the middle of nowhere

Baby, won't you tell me
What am I to do?
I'm in the middle of nowhere
Getting nowhere with you

At Ipswich I knew we drew regular supporters from Cambridge and even further west along the A45. So when I heard of a 'training track' being built in a farmer's field near Mildenhall, only marginally past Bury St Edmunds, my ears pricked up.

The good news was that this would be just another training track for the East Anglian lads to learn their speedway. The bad news was that should the project go further and a league team be based there, we would lose some of our regular clientele to them.

I suppose it could be argued that many new speedway supporters would be produced, some of them adopting Ipswich as their second team. But, far more likely, Ipswich fans who currently travelled long distances for their weekly speedway fix might opt for a much nearer alternative.

So it really was no surprise that, when a licence to enter Mildenhall in the second division was applied for, I objected on behalf of Ipswich. City folk just don't understand that 40 miles in suburban areas is a massive distance, but not so in sparsely populated countryside, especially with a very good road joining the two places. Track to track, it was less than 45 minutes by car. Put another way, supporters from any further than just 20 minutes west of Ipswich found another track closer to their homes.

I was also very aware that, with a team in the lower league and unlimited practice facilities, Mildenhall would have first call on all the youngsters in the area who wanted to become speedway riders. Effectively, the conveyor belt of talent that had been the Ipswich junior policy would be destroyed.

To be frank, I had the feeling that a track set in the middle of nowhere, with no nearby urban area from which to draw support, would struggle for attendance and would need to rely on a proportion of Ipswich (and King's Lynn) supporters. I also knew it would cause us serious problems with our policy of finding local riders.

Many thought us 'lucky' to have discovered John Louis and then Tony Davey and the others. Luck didn't come into it. Nobody suggests Belle Vue was 'lucky' to 'find' Peter Collins, and there is nothing but praise for Eastbourne's conveyor line of talent. Well, excuse me for blowing the Ipswich trumpet here, but we did it without any training facilities and in less time than the others.

It wasn't luck at all. It was a mixture of encouraging local lads to come and have a go, giving them as much opportunity as possible with junior racing in the second halves and after the meetings, persevering with riders and playing the numbers game.

The perception is that every stone we turned over had a ready-made speedway rider underneath. The reality is that we did have quite a high number of lads who never made it. Also, in all honesty, more than one or two of those who did make it, relied more on enthusiasm, character and the Ipswich Speedway culture for their success rather than a great natural talent.

Just to underline the point, here is a list (with apologies for those I expect I missed out) of local lads who had no previous speedway experience and who had their first speedway races in the Ipswich second half programme:

● 1969. Neville Slee*, Bernie Aldridge*, John Louis, Stan Pepper*, Barry Meeks, Bob Jennings, Rex Garrod, Dave Cox, Brian Osborne, Stewart Wallis, Paul Sly, Cliff Wichelo*.

● 1970 Ray Edmunds, Fred Cotton, Clive Noy, Dave Offord, Pat Johnson, Russell Metson, Ian Spencer, Shawn Murtough, D. Sumner, Ralph Waller, Jim Woolford, Adrian Yallop, Les Steward, Len Allum, Dave Winlow, Tony Davey,

● 1971 Denny Barber, Ted Howgego, David Godley, Paul Ward, Paul Scanlon, Ray Watkins, Mick Hines, Mike Lanham, Peter Claridge, Jeff Gale,

● 1972 Trevor Jones, Paul Clipstone, Andy Simms, John Simmons, Ray Ball, Mervyn Cooper

● 1973 Chris Ginn, John Gibbons, D. Lewin, Dave Gooderham, Andy Stebbins, Denny Morter, Paul Mills, Paul Gilbert, Paul Davey, David Emeny, Philip Garneys,

● 1974 Peter Mittell, Colin Cook, Andy Hines, Dick Partridge, Trevor Harvey, Rodney Ward, Edward Miller,

● 1975 Graham Kerry, Kevin Jolly

● 1976 Mike Osborne, Nigel Flatman, Kevin Ross, Graham Steward,

● 1977 Neil Leeks**, Kevin Teager, Dean Newson, Richard Stennett, Steve Grainger, Wayne Greenlaw,

● 1978 Tim Hunt, Andy Hibbs, Carl Squirrel, David Shields, Mark Bilner, Steve Bryenton,

● 1979 Mick Wilde, David Gibbons, Steve Day, Robert Lyons, Gary Cooper

● 1980 Mark Cousins,

● 1981 Roger Dickerson, Andy Harris, Dave Gentry,

● 1982 Andy Nightingale, Adrian Squirrell, Andy Davey, Lawrie Bloomfield,

*Not local riders
**Had ridden at Mildenhall

Now the thing to note is the sudden drop off of riders coming through in 1975. That just happens to be the year the Fen Tigers were born. The Fen track had been running for a year purely as a training track. Kevin Jolly had used it extensively but elected to join Ipswich and go on loan to Mildenhall.

As a training track it was an advantage to Ipswich, and as such it was great to see Mick Hines and Ron Bagley helping the kids out down there. But as a New National League (second division) track, with its training facilities and lower ability entrance level, it was bound to draw away from Ipswich the local youngsters who might be trying to break into the sport.

During a pre-season local radio phone-in at Radio Orwell, based in Ipswich, I deliberately took a swipe at the new set up, describing it, if I remember, as a carrot patch.

Bernie Klatt, the young promoter there, wasn't a bad sort of bloke but the farmer who owned the land and stadium, one Terry Walters, took personal exception to my remarks and the gloves came off!

From that moment on, the relationship between Ipswich and Mildenhall was always at daggers drawn, despite the fact that as the years went on, there was a certain amount of co-operation between the two outfits. That is the nature of speedway. Sworn enemies or not, there has to be a modicum of back scratching.

The situation between Mildenhall and Ipswich, though, on a local level, encapsulated the Macro problem within British speedway. The lower league considered itself a competitor to the British League. It squeezed

Despite competition from Mildenhall, Ipswich still managed to win the Trackstar Junior League in 1984.

away from the senior tracks all the new local talent coming through, forcing them to either pay huge transfer fees or look abroad for an alternative source of riders. In fact, it was the primary reason why I had to look to the likes of Preben Eriksen, Georg Hack and eventually the Americans, Dennis Sigalos and John Cook, to put out an attractive team.

This in turn put the first division promoters at the mercy of the foreign federations and the FIM. Then, when the lower league decided to allow foreign imports into NL, the top league was effectively strangled. They now even had to pay transfer fees for foreign riders.

It was precisely at this stage, after I had mounted a spirited effort to disallow foreign riders in the lower league, and having been accused of xenophobia apart from many other things, that I realised UK speedway was going down a very dangerous road.

The fracture between the two leagues became wider and wider, until it could no longer be papered over. By the 80s, after I had sold Ipswich to Chris Shears, I was asked if I would take over the running of the BSPA in an effort to pull the factions back together. I was flattered, and to be honest, excited about the possibility of trying to get UK speedway back on track, but I was fearful of being able to pull together the various warring factions.

I figured it would require a massive amount of goodwill between promoters to get things to work and it would require something the BSPA had never been able to do – that is to cede some responsibility and day-to-day decision making to a non-promoter. Me!

We were at a BSPA conference abroad, Tenerife as I recall. I was there with Chris Shears, nominally helping represent Ipswich, although Chris by this time had decided he could manage things himself. I was invited to meet with the Division One management committee on the eve of the conference.

Now speedway had been kind to me financially over the years and, to be honest, I would happily have taken on the job, not of being the office manager, but of running the Association for nothing. But I decided to test the resolve of the promoters. I decided to see if they were genuine in their desire for a Brave New World, and so I tossed in two things.

The first was a reasonable remuneration package for the kind of position they required. I asked for a figure of £20,000 per annum. The second was a suitable title indicating the role would be more than that of just a manager.

Again, I point out that neither the money nor the title were important to me. What was important was for the promoters to understand the sea change in thinking that would be required for them to accept decision-making from a non-promoter and get the sport in Britain back on course.

There was much puffing of cheeks and many sideways glances. Neither of my two requirements was accepted there and then. The main objector was Sheffield's Maurice Ducker. If nothing else, Maurice was honest enough to say what he thought. Or at least he was honest enough to give the clear impression that he was not comfortable with me, or the position I was demanding.

Ex-radio disc jockey and speedway announcer, Peter York, had also tossed his hat into the ring. Now I like Peter very much but what he was looking for was the job of BSPA manager. This was not what I thought speedway needed at that time.

Although I was invited to join the chairman and committee at the head of the conference table the next morning, it was plain that full council ratification of the Committee's decision to offer me the position was not going to go through 'on the nod'. It was clear that at least two promotions, Sheffield, and Belle Vue, were less than enthusiastic. This seemed very much like a North/South thing and from their comments these tracks were clearly concerned about my ability to make unbiased decisions. I don't think they were entirely on their own in fearing I would become a biased dictator. You have to believe me, I would not have been biased and resented the implication. As to the 'dictator' part, plainly I wanted to have some executive authority.

Then came a proposition suggesting that, in addition to my own appointment, Peter York should be offered a position as 'Commercial Manager'. Now I think Peter would have been good in the role, and I might well have wanted him on board, but this idea was more about diluting my proposed position than anything else.

The previous BSPA office had closed down and a whole new administration needed to be set up from scratch. The National League was also now clamouring for full autonomy. Up until now, although the name had been changed from the British League Division Two, it was still subservient to the First Division. Mervyn Stewkesbury was leading the revolt, with, in my opinion, his own agenda in mind.

I sat in that conference room for three hours listening to the promoters arguing backwards and forwards about what title I should hold – if I could be impartial with my decision-making, was I the right man for the job? Apart from those promoters who were prepared to voice their concerns, there were others whose support was only lukewarm – and I count Chris Shears among them. On the other hand, the management committee were anything but resolute in my defence.

Long before the lunch recess I had made up my mind. It would have been difficult enough trying to reconcile the differences between the two divisions. I am sure there would have been concerns from the National League about my treating them in a fair-minded way, given my senior league background. Without the full support of all of the Division One promoters my position would have been impossible. Come the very first conflict of interest between promoters of the respective leagues, or indeed the first decision I made that didn't please just one Division One promoter and I would be hung out to dry.

As the meeting was breaking for lunch, I spoke, pretty well for the first time that morning, to say thanks but no thanks. I didn't quite say 'stuff your job where the sun doesn't shine', but that was the gist of it.

Charles Ochiltree, the senior member and president, was sent to talk to me. I have no doubt he was on my side. In his clipped and correct way, he told me the BSPA needed me more than they realised. He listened to my complaints that I felt I would not be given the authority I wanted, and he came back with a very fair argument. He told me that the promoters didn't really know what they wanted and that it was up to me to get my feet under the table and then make the job what it should be.

I wish it could have happened. I really wanted to try and make a difference. And although I know it sounds conceited, I really do believe I could have done a good job for British speedway. Sadly, I knew equally well that I would never be given the chance to prove it. Whatever I tried to do would be undermined and that if I took it on, I would end up soon chucking it all in amidst a mass of bad feeling and recriminations.

I went up to my room and shed actual tears of frustration. But for all of that, I have never doubted my decision to be the shortest holder of the BSPA manager's post of all time was the correct one.

The two leagues went their separate ways during and after that conference. Peter York became manager of the British League at its new office in Rugby, whilst Stewkesbury – in my opinion, the worst thing that has happened to British Speedway – set up a National League administration in Weymouth, putting one of his own people into the NL manager's seat.

As to the relationship between Ipswich and Mildenhall, it got decidedly cooler when Ron Bagley had his short stay there and more than a few people who have tried to work with him questioned the attitude and involvement of the farmer as time went by.

But I grudgingly liked Bernie Klatt and our relationship softened over the years prior to his sad death. The West Row stadium is a pretty little place, even if the access is a nightmare, and in the overall scheme of things it has been a benefit to speedway.

18 No Regrets

I know your leaving is too long overdue
For far too long I've had nothing new to show to you
Goodbye, dry eyes
I watched your plane fade off west of the moon
Then I felt so strange to walk away alone

No regrets, no tears goodbye
Don't want you back
We'd only cry again
Say goodbye again

The ours that were yours echo like empty rooms
But the thoughts we used to share
I now keep alone

I knew halfway through 1980 that something had to be done.

We'd had our fair share of injuries and bad luck early in the season but it was more than that. All of us at Ipswich were stale. Livewire Paul Johnson was forever bubbling around, coming up with ideas, some practical, some not so, and some plain OTT. But something more radical than promotorial gimmicks was needed.

PJ had not grown up with John Louis. He was not aware of how much at Foxhall had been founded on The Tiger's success. John, by that time, was living, if not quite on his well earned reputation, then certainly on cruise control. It is fair to say, the two of them did not get on very well.

Paul had not seen the early years. He could only judge on what he saw then, and at that time he saw a rider with a huge reputation who was patently not putting in the commitment to justify it.

I tread carefully here, because I have a lot of time, respect and care for both John and Pat Louis (now Doncaster) but in order to fully explain things, the relationships within the Louis household need to be considered.

Bear in mind, Pat did not ask for speedway. She had married a storeman who rode moto-cross for fun at weekends. They had the regulation two kids, a three up, two down and a 'normal' life. Pat was several years younger than John, a bit naive but loyal and loving.

Although Pat enjoyed watching speedway, she did not enjoy watching John race. She was typically protective of him and would quickly show her claws if anything was said or done to him or about him she felt was not in his best interests. It mattered not to Pat if these perceived injustices were on or off the track, and one or two other riders' wives could no doubt agree with me when I say Pat would be fiery.

Given that Pat was John's secretary/manager, I sometimes found myself in the firing line, although John always had the final word in the Louis household.

Pat's loyalty and naivety gave John a fairly long leash, and I think there may have been times when 'speedway business' might have been the excuse used once or twice for him to justify his being out and about, although, as I have said, he did enjoy carrying the speedway banner locally in any case.

Corny it might be, but a fact it is, successful sportsmen have opportunities drop in their lap and it is not always easy to do the right thing. Worse, with the attention and notoriety comes a certain resentment about having to return to the 'little woman' and John finally succumbed

Happy days for the Louis family.

John with a young Christopher.

to the attractive alternative of a younger and, at least in his eyes, more attractive model.

This is about where the Louis' were at in 1980. John was in the process of 'shacking up' with this sweet, young thing whose name escapes me. Now when one does this kind of thing, something curious happens. The world seems to become a far more fun place. Boring old responsibilities seem to fly out of the window and life takes on a rosy hue. It's generally described as thinking with your balls instead of your brains.

Robin Williams puts it more succinctly: "God gives men a brain and a penis, but only enough blood to run one at a time". I had been there, done that and knew the feeling well.

This meant that priorities in JL's mind had become a little skewed. Instead of them being speedway, family, enjoying oneself, it had become enjoying oneself . . . with family and speedway an equal but distant second.

Also, we have to remember, despite his Peter Pan impersonations, John was at an age by now when most self-respecting sportsman (and philanderers) are considering retirement.

Not that this meant he had become irresponsible to the extent of not turning up to meetings, or even not looking after himself or his machinery. It was just that there was a distraction that meant his riding had become mechanical, had lost its flair, even lost the team orientation that had been the cornerstone of his, and the team's success.

On the other hand, Billy Sanders always had a far simpler set of priorities. Billy Sanders came first and within that framework, other responsibilities would be given due consideration.

Although there was little between them in riding experience, like it or not, Billy had to demur to John's naturally superior position in the pecking order. It was John who had nursed Billy through his learning period, just as John had learned from Ron Bagley. Also, whereas John had always been a natural skipper, Billy was the shop steward. Billy was also the 'foreigner' and never really tried to hide the fact that personal glory and money were his two main driving forces.

There was also a good half a generation between the two of them.

It comes as no surprise then, that in true pack tradition, when the dominant male started slipping from his lofty position, the younger, stronger, next in line decided to mount a challenge.

Very little unpleasant was said between the pair of them. They had always been team-mates rather than soul-mates, though; happy to work together, but not really drinking partners, and certainly not prepared, for example, to share mechanical expertise.

Previously, their rivalry had only been clearly seen when they had come up against each other in individual events. When representing the team, they had always looked out for each other and had been a formidable duo, which had won many a match with their last race pairing. Now, instead of looking for each other, they had begun looking at each other – and forgetting the opposition.

John's performances were on the wane. Clearly he could not carry the task of being the rock of the team for much longer. Billy was still improving but would never be able to usurp JL's

Public relations – nothing but hard work.

position with the old bull still in the side. There would always be friction within the team from now on as long as both riders were in it.

On the other hand, good a rider as he was, Billy was never a natural leader. Number one and spearhead, maybe, but not leader. In any case, he had already demonstrated his loyalties by having wanted away once, where he had discovered the grass was distinctly not greener.

Billy had also played ducks and drakes every winter, bluffing about not coming back over to England in order to up his deal. He had actually delayed his arrival in England in 1980 until several weeks into the season.

Eastbourne raced on a Sunday. Nothing too surprising about that, except we are talking about the time of the Lord's Day Observance society, and of out of date laws forbidding the sale of certain items – but not others – on a Sunday. In short, the time when Sundays were days when one could not reasonably demand a worker should have to work.

As a sub-plot, it was also a day when the top speedway riders of the era hopped onto planes across to the continent, which did not have these same archaic and arcane Sunday restrictions. There they earned indecent amounts of money racing against the local hopefuls and then wandered back on Monday morning, ready for 'work'. They were not about to give up this lucrative sideline by racing in England for what they regarded as a comparative pittance.

So the BSPA did the time-honoured thing, tried to have two bob each way, and decreed that whilst Eastbourne could stage their home meetings on a Sunday, they could not demand that riders had to attend. Like in Chariots of Fire, riders had to be given the opportunity to opt out, whether it was Church or the pursuit of money they wished to worship.

John Louis' teenage son, Christopher, rode junior grass track. In fact, he was very good at it. He had ridden for some time and, indeed, had appeared in the British Championships. Although very proud of Chris, JL had not been able to share in his son's successes in these Sunday-staged events because he had always been riding somewhere himself. Pat had taken Chris to most events.

Sod's Law decreed that the date of the British junior grass finals in this particular year happened to fall on the day Ipswich were due to race at Eastbourne. Given that John had by now moved out of the family home, he felt obliged to take Chris to this event, and he told me so. I then tried to move heaven and earth to change the date of our visit to Eastbourne.

I could understand why taking young Chris to the junior grass track was important to John, but Eastbourne could not. Slotting in their fixtures around World Championship and other big continental events was a nightmare for them, so they did not consider a junior grass track meeting to be a priority.

I got the same response from the BSPA. After all, they argued, I could always use a guest, knowing or guessing I would not. I was caught in the middle.

In the end, I had no choice but to tell John I could not change the fixture, and that he would have to let Pat take Chris to the junior meeting, as she had done before. Given the new domestic arrangements in the Louis household(s), John was not prepared to let his son down. We had a stand off.

Eventually, I came the heavy. I told John that although the BSPA edict allowed him to miss the meeting, his contract with me did not, and that the consequences of him putting what I regarded as a social event in front of a speedway commitment would be dire.

Remember what part of his anatomy was doing the thinking at the time. He missed the Eastbourne meeting – and I started to consider the direction Ipswich Speedway would go in the following year.

Billy Sanders found Kevin Jolly in his way when he returned to Foxhall in the colours of Birmingham.

The fact that the rest of the Ipswich team, without JL, responded fantastically to the challenge of being without their leader, and only finally succumbed in the last heat after a typically fiery meeting between us and the Eagles, also didn't fail to escape my attention.

I actually made my final decision one miserable night at Swindon, a track where we normally did well but not this time. Neither John nor Billy appeared to have their mind on their work. I had to stand there and watch my twin strikers being headed by a couple of Robins wannabees, whilst the pair of them battled for the odd point at the back, like two old crows fighting over a crust of bread.

The decision was made.

Of course, it is the job of a promoter to know more than just who are the good riders going around, and who are not. He also has to have his ear to the ground so he knows which rider is happy and settled at his home club, and which might well be, or become, available.

Dennis Sigalos, then riding at Hull, was clearly a class act. He was smooth, fast and young, with perhaps something of a reputation for being only a strong front-runner and not a good passer. But he had a silky style, which lent itself to the equipment of the time and would suit the Foxhall track shape and surface. The word was, maybe he was not entirely convinced he would see out his future at Hull.

As a secondary consideration, another American rookie, John Cook, was also riding for the Vikings. He was struggling on slow equipment and was not getting enough rides to be able to make progress. The word was that neither Hull promoter, Ian Thomas, nor Cook was keen to continue their arrangements into the following year.

I dreamed up a filler meeting so that I could book the two Americans into Foxhall for a closer look. They were not aware they were under the microscope at that stage, although general conversation with Sigalos after the meeting indicated he would be looking for a move from Hull for the following year. Siggy again showed his class at the meeting whilst Cook did enough to indicate he would do far better on faster equipment and in a happier frame of mind.

Paul Johnson agreed with me that both Sanders and Louis were not giving their best efforts for the Ipswich cause. It was handy to have someone reinforcing my own views, although the first and last thoughts and decisions were entirely mine.

The dream of an all-conquering, all local side had long since been achieved. In fact, it had now become something of a liability. My long-term plan had always seen John Louis retiring from riding round about this time, in which case I had intended to involve him in the management side. I had hopes of maybe seeing him share running of the speedway with me, with a view to him possibly taking over in the fullness of time.

But John had done three things: He had gone on too long as a rider to fit into my master plan, he had lost the edge that made him such a potent force and he had lost the plot somewhat.

So here was the situation: JL was being paid superstar money and not fulfilling the job. Billy Sanders was costing almost as much but although he was a good number one, was not a ready made replacement for JL in the eyes of the Ipswich public.

I had also grown stale, the team had grown stale, the presentation had grown stale and the supporters who were in at the start were dropping off at a fair rate and not being replaced.

It was, and is, reasonable to expect an active supporter to have a finite time span. You will always get those who are complete speedway freaks, and will arrange their lives around the sport, but they are not the people to be aiming at. You have them already.

As for the others, no matter how loyal they have been, their lives move on and they become passive supporters. Good for sales of the local newspaper and TV ratings, and still, by and large, loyal supporters, but no longer helping to pay the wages.

There are also those who stop coming because they have been offended by something happening of which they disapprove. However, in the vast majority of these cases, those supporters have come to the end of their active supporting period anyway, and more often than not use a particular circumstance or event to break the habit. Maybe the entrance fee went up by 10p; maybe their favourite rider retired or moved on; maybe the team lost a match poorly, or even, the visitors didn't put up much of a show...

Anything can act as the final straw but the truth is, you cannot expect a supporter to keep turning up indefinitely. You have to look to how you are going to replace him. One reason why speedway is a dying sport is that people have failed to answer that question.

Promoters over the years have spent too much time and effort trying to hang on to the supporters they have, or trying to woo back those who have stopped coming, and not enough on trying to attract new support.

Put all of that lot together, and what was I facing? Clearly it was time for some radical changes. Both John Louis and Billy Sanders had to go to make way for new blood.

What about loyalty, you ask? Well, in the case of Sanders, it did not enter the equation. Ours had always been a pretty volatile relationship ever since he had become an adult. I had shown him plenty of loyalty over his formative years and in return he had demanded to leave the Witches, only coming back when he found out the pickings were not as good elsewhere and that he was better off at Ipswich than away from it.

What about loyalty every October, when he developed homesick blues and couldn't be bothered to serve out the season. What about the charade every spring, where he would sit in Sydney until the last possible second (and sometimes beyond) just to try and squeeze an extra sixpence out of the negotiations. And what about the fact that racing for Ipswich was coming further and further second to his personal speedway ambitions.

Worse, what about all the aggro that seemed to follow him around by then? Great for the supporters to have a 'character' in the side, but not much fun for his promoter. Not much fun having to deal with his tantrums and never being certain if one day he would go through with any or all of his bluffs. Not much fun when he got tanked up and wanted to fight everyone, including me. Not much fun when his own wife was frightened of his regular mood swings.

So no, although overall I loved Billy in a prodigal son sort of way, I had no problem with replacing him.

It was a different story with John. If he had not been such a fool to himself, to his wife, to the speedway and to me that year, I'm not sure I could have done it. There were many times in my job, as there are in most management positions, where decision-making comes hard. When you are dealing with other people's lives, it is no fun.

It was not fun having to find alternative homes for the lesser lights when the Ipswich team moved from Division Two to Division One, although I think we managed to keep everyone reasonably happy that time. There was no fun in telling Mick Hines he had to move to Wimbledon in 1976. He had done absolutely nothing to be 'sacked' for. In fact, his only error had been in performing too well. That I knew his speedway would benefit from the move did not make it any easier.

This decision, though, was different. On the one hand, John could expect little more than what happened. Goodness knows I issued enough warnings to him during that 1980 season. On the other hand, this was not something forced onto the team by outside influence. This was a policy decision by me, pure and simple.

Of course, before I could do anything, I needed to check the situation. This meant dealing with Ian Thomas and that would not be easy. We had, for many years, been fierce rivals and whilst I think we quietly respected each other, it has to be said, we were not close buddies.

Having said that, one of the ironies of speedway promoting is that you can be at daggers drawn and wildly in opposition to another promoter, but the whole basis of the sport depends on goodwill between promotions at a business level. You can have been toe to toe the night before, and then have to phone your opposite number to ask if you can use his rider in a meeting next week, or make a fixture change, or whatever.

In this instance, I needed to speak to Ian and ask him if he would be interested in a deal involving Sigalos, Cook, Sanders and money. Always assuming he could do a deal with Billy, and I could do a deal with Sigalos and Cook.

I can't remember if we actually shook hands down the phone on the first such call, or if it involved more than one, but it was quick, easy, businesslike and respectful. It was one of those deals where both parties came out feeling good about it. It says something about old fashioned promoters that we could trust each other, first to honour the over the phone handshake and second, trust each other to work together in the putting together the necessary delicate rider negotiations.

First job for me then was to hop a plane and go chat to Siggy. That was no hardship. It gave me a chance to take in an evening at the Forum watching the Los Angeles Lakers basketball team and an opportunity to see my all-time favourite sportsman, Magic Johnson, in action. That was always my idea of spectating heaven, but it was also valuable education for me. American pro sport knows how to stage a show, so I couldn't help but learn from these visits.

I had flown into LA, driven to the Newport Beach area, where I knew Dennis lived, slept in a decent motel on that famous beachfront and phoned him the next morning. I thought he would say "come on over", but he didn't. He said he would come to me.

I think he was about 20. I was by then fairly experienced in dealing with riders of various nationalities. I didn't know too much about Siggy's background, but I learned fast!

Nearly an hour late, a Ferrari Boxer slid up to the coffee shop, where a very self assured and relaxed young man stepped out. This boy was not riding speedway for the money!

He was polite, well presented and just what I had hoped for. I explained what I wanted from him, that he would be replacing a local legend and that from day one the pressure would be on him to produce the goods. There could be no settling in period. He would be expected to do the business from the outset and must be prepared to cope with a significant backlash from those supporters who were dyed in the wool Louis fans.

He understood, and we both knew where we were. I trusted him to do the job, he trusted me to back him up.

And so on to money. There was no negotiation. Clearly, he didn't need the cash but, by the same token, he had a right to be paid according to the status I wanted him to hold. I didn't mess about. I had done my homework and knew what I could afford. I spelled out the entire package. I didn't hold anything up my sleeve, I put it all on the table. It was pretty much, allowing for inflation, what John Louis had cost me. This was what I could afford, and if he did not accept it, I would have to go to plan B.

Now I don't know how well Dennis had done his own homework. I was comfortably sure my offer would be substantially more than he would have received at Hull. In fact, I was pretty certain it would put him in the top 10, if not in the top handful, of all those who rode in the UK. Perhaps Dennis had spoken with other riders (like friend Bruce Penhall) and perhaps he had even had talks with other promoters. All I know is that he simply accepted the deal.

We shook hands and I scribbled down some details of our discussions and various agreements on my notepad. He took the copy I had made and I kept my original notes. That was our contract, honoured to the letter by both sides throughout the year, and upgraded as easily before the following season. Dennis Sigalos was never anything other than a gentleman and I was pleased and proud to have him on board.

John Cook was not in LA that weekend. He actually came from Sacramento in northern California and might well have been up there. Although I wanted him in the side, he was not essential to it, and as a four point improver could not dictate his own terms.

I spoke to him on the phone later, outlining an incentive deal which would allow him to benefit from any improvement in his scoring over the previous year at Hull, He was happy to get a chance at a place different to the Boulevard, where he had struggled desperately financially, and had not got on particularly well with Ian Thomas. That didn't worry me. I didn't get on particularly well with Ian Thomas either.

Next job was to tell John Louis the bad news. As is normal and correct in these deals, Thomas had spoken to Billy, who had been taken aback but who had struck a deal to go to Hull.

I think it would be fair to say John was gobsmacked when I told him I would be circulating his name as being available for transfer. He promised me the season just gone had been an aberration and that he would be back to his best the following year. He also accepted that he had not represented the club the previous year, on or off the track, in the manner he had done previously, but that would also change.

I believed him when he said this, but two things were clear: First, John's best riding days were behind him and he could no longer play the role of number one and lynchpin. Second, the rest of the deal was now too far down the line to undo. John came back and suggested he would take a cut in earnings and fulfil a lesser role in the team, allowing Sigalos to be the number one and top dog whilst he played the role of 'senior professional'.

This was something I had not expected, considered, or covered for, and it set me back on my heels. I considered this new scenario but it did not work. We never got around to discussing it but I am sure John's idea of a pay cut and my idea of a pay cut would not have been the same. It would also have messed up the balance of the team, forcing me to cut a youngster (or two) to fit him in. Finally, it didn't achieve the plan of changing the direction of the promotion.

Effectively, all I would be doing was swapping Sigalos for Sanders. I had paid a considerable cash balance along with Sanders to get Sigalos (and Cook), and needed a transfer fee for Louis to help balance the books. Also, if John stayed, it meant effectively dropping all of the

Dennis Sigalos – class act and a new crowd favourite to replace the legendary Louis.

blame for the previous season on Billy, which would not have been fair.

Apart from all of these arguments was the deal I had done with Siggy. He was to be the undisputed number one and captain – it would have made his position untenable to have to try and do the job with the star he had replaced still there. It would not be fair to Louis and it would not be fair to Sigalos.

I explained this at length to John but, not surprisingly, he did not see it that way. There was no way we could see eye to eye on the subject and inevitably there was going to be a falling out. How much easier life would have been if JL had not been a Peter Pan and kept going and going!

Just to make the embarrassment all the greater for me, I had been wrong when I had assumed there would be a queue of promoters beating my door down when John's name was released for transfer. Softening the blow (or so I thought would be the case) was the fact that John would be entitled to half of any transfer fee payable. Therefore, a realistic fee of £10,000 would see him pocket a windfall £5,000. This, I reasoned, would at least ease my own conscience.

Americans Dennis Sigalos and John Cook arrived from Hull to herald a new era for Ipswich.

I don't think it entirely worked out that way, though. The only track I was not keen to see snap John up was King's Lynn. Louis fans might decide to follow him there from Ipswich and I was not keen to see that happen. Surprisingly, the Stars didn't make a concerted bid for him, although I had let it be known I would make such a move very difficult.

But no promoter was interested. I had not been the only one to see John's loss of form the previous year and I suspect most had put it down to old age catching up, rather than his domestic situation. Pat and John had not had a reconciliation but at least John was using his head to think with now. Even if he was no longer a 10-point-plus rider, he had at least two more years and maybe more of being a top class heat leader still in him.

By now, the relationship between the two of us had broken down completely. I had given him carte blanche to speak with any promoter (except King's Lynn) and he cobbled together a deal with Halifax. Sadly, fully aware that John's alternatives were limited, the Halifax promoter, Eric Boothroyd, drove a very hard bargain with him, blaming me along the way.

The result was that the money John received as his share of the transfer was not a windfall. It was taken into account as part of his riding deal at Halifax. I cannot blame them, I would probably have done the same thing, but it meant that neither John nor I saw a great deal of return from the eventual reduced fee.

John's bitterness lasted for some time and he did all he could to make life as awkward for me as possible. Only to be expected really and I was as upset as anyone when he damaged his arm during his spell with the Dukes..

The move to Halifax left a sour taste. *(AW)*

Halifax had done very well, getting the use of a world quality rider for two years at cut-price rates, and also getting somebody into their team who could be a voice of reason to the volatile Kenny Carter. I think they might have even made a profit when they sold John to King's Lynn, where Martin Rogers returned to run the show in 1983.

So JL was able to enjoy a couple of respectable seasons with the Norfolk club, during which time bridges between us were rebuilt and I got him back into the Ipswich set up as soon as I could after he finally hung up his leathers at the end of 1984.

19 The Windmills of Your Mind

like a circle in a spiral
like a wheel within a wheel
never ending or beginning
on an ever spinning reel
like a snowball down a mountain
or a carnival balloon
like a carousel that's turning
running rings around the moon

like a tunnel that you follow
to a tunnel of its own
down a hollow to a cavern
where the sun has never shone,
like a door that keeps revolving
in a half forgotten dream,
or the ripples from a pebble
someone tosses in a stream

keys that jingle in your pocket
words that jangle in your head
why did summer go so quickly ?
was it something that you said ?

lovers walk along a shore
and leave their footprints in the sand
is the sound of distant drumming
just the fingers of your hand?

pictures hanging in a hallway
and the fragment of this song
half remembered names and faces
but to whom do they belong ?

when you knew that it was over
you were suddenly aware
that the autumn leaves were turning
And its time I wasn't there.

When I had joined Joe Thurley in becoming a speedway promoter in 1969, it certainly wasn't intended to become my career, my life and my love. It was purely to be a stepping-stone on to a 'proper job'.

From those early days the speedway developed into more than just a money making venture. I had finally found out what I was good at in life. I would never be a front man. I was a natural maker of bullets, not a firer. I was a planner, a schemer, a reader of situations and people. I was a good manager. Some people in this world are born to be doers, and others to be thinkers. I am a thinker.

I loved the logistics of speedway; chess with moving parts. Obviously I refer to team speedway. Individual speedway is merely draughts.

I loved finding the rough pieces of wood and turning them into chess pieces. Some kings (not

Nobody knew that Mick Hines was saying his farewells to Ipswich after the final meeting of 1975.

too many queens!), some knights, some castles and a host of pawns. Even the pieces that had already been moulded needed finishing and painting; they all needed constant care and attention. Some fell on the ground and needed putting back together. Others became lost or broken, so new ones had to be found or swapped.

Then there was the board; the stage on which the games took place. It needed to be kept in top condition so that the pieces could move easily and that the games would be fun to watch.

Finally, the whole thing needed an audience and an army of people to help the supporters and organise the matches. These chess games didn't just happen.

Perhaps the best time for me to have baled out would have been at the end of the 1976 season. You will recall that was the year The Dream was finally completed. Ipswich Speedway was still a highly lucrative business then and had I searched hard enough, I expect I could have found a suitable buyer, someone with a fresh, new angle.

Speedway until then had been predominantly fun. Bloody hard work but fun. Ron Bagley and I fitted well together and covered each other's weak spots. More importantly, we enjoyed what we were doing. We enjoyed putting together a great team – nay, club – and watching it grow.

We were still at that stage more or less the same generation as the riders. We were irreverent to the point of rudeness and we were happy to join in with the madcap fun side of the sport. Although I thought I didn't at the time, I realised later that I also enjoyed the notoriety. I enjoyed the buzz of success. And I enjoyed making things happen.

My favourite picture of the team relaxing before a meeting and not worrying about washing their dirty laundry in public. Back row: John Louis, Trevor Jones, Mike Lanham, Mick Hines, Ted Howgego. Front: Tony Davey, Dave Gooderham, Billy Sanders.

Most of all, everything worked. Whatever we tried, whatever we did seemed to come out right. We were able to either minimise mistakes, or to disguise them so well that even they looked like successes. And we were able to maximise the successes.

As I looked back on the 1976 season, I realised the top of a mountain had been reached. Did I go look for another mountain, or did I accept that even though the only way was down, that down should be comparatively easy going and still fairly rewarding?

In fact, what I tried to do was to grow the speedway forward. First, I made enquiries about the possible purchase of the stadium and Heath.

For those not familiar with Foxhall Heath and its history, when the original consortium of businesspeople came along in the 50s, they bought up the whole of Foxhall Heath, some 120 acres of woodland and scrub. They then cleared enough of it to build the speedway stadium and car park. There are some public footpaths and a bridal path across the Heath but it is still owned by the original speedway company and is not a public open space.

Those first investors more than recovered their outlay but eventually the speedway finished, so they leased the stadium to Spedeworth, a stock car promotion. We subleased the stadium from Spedeworth.

It seemed to me, if I could buy the Heath from the original owners, I could use the income from the speedway and the stock car rent to develop the whole area into an entertainment complex. After all, it was most unlikely planning permission would be granted to change the use of the Heath from amenity to any kind of residential or commercial development. Certainly not in the medium term, anyway.

But I ran into a problem. Most of the original businessmen shareholders of the company that owned the Heath were no more, so the shares were in the hands of second, even third generations. The few bob they received annually from the rental represented a nice drink for them but at that time anyway, if they were to sell, a large percentage of the money would have gone in capital gains tax.

The attitude of the stockholders was, and presumably still is, that eventually the land will become earmarked for building and, as and when that happens, they will get a very nice payday. Until then, they might just as well sit tight. Certainly in my time, they used to routinely submit outline planning applications to the local council whenever the lease came up for renewal (every two years). No doubt they still keep an eye on the situation.

Since my time there, the housing has crept right up to the boundaries of the Heath on two sides, so, given that they have waited 50 years and more, the owners might well presume the majority of the wait is over, especially when one looks at the current condition of the stadium.

Anyway, that attitude put any purchase and expansion of the Heath out of the question, which was a shame really. Even when the stadium was first built there were mutterings about the football club moving up there from Portman Road, and such an idea has a lot going for it.

Then I looked at buying a pub or a nightclub in the area, where speedway people could congregate. At that time, there was very little to do in the evenings, so the idea of the supporters having their own drop-in place seemed to make sense.

I also looked at other spin-off ideas but nothing came of them. I must have been ahead of my time, because a theme pub is one thing I had in mind. Unfortunately, being ahead of my time meant also being too far ahead of the market!

I also tried to purchase the bowling alley, then situated on the corner of the Ipswich ring-road and London Road. Nominally the place was on the market as a going concern. In fact, it had been allowed to run down, and the attitude of the owners to my approaches would lead one to believe the site was worth more in land value than as a business. In any case, it wasn't too long before the Texas hardware store stood in place of the bowling alley.

In truth, though, the speedway was all I could properly cope with. It provided more than enough to put the bread on the table, it was enough to utilise total brainpower and it provided a sense of satisfaction and achievement. I was also doubtful that Ron, although an excellent team manager and confidante, had the all round capabilities to run the show, should I have needed to commit a good deal of my time to another project.

But it has to be said, trying to climb the mountain again, and soon without a close confidante, as Ron had been, was nowhere near as much fun. And all this time Joe was still on 50% of the profits

Most of the fun went when Tony Davey (left) was no longer part of the Witches scene. We all loved Shrimp, pictured (right) showing clever throttle control to keep Michael Lee at bay.

Doing the England job gave me a bit of a challenge but it also caused me to take my eye off my own business. In hindsight, although it gave me some wonderful memories, it was a mistake.

Without going into too many details, by then my domestic life had also become less than ideal.

Next came the break up of the team. Billy Sanders went to Birmingham for a spell and some of the others who had been part of the Dream Team had moved on for various reasons. My close rapport with the riders was breaking down. We were no longer a mob of likely lads all in it together.

Tony Davey's loss, effectively in 1979, when he broke his thigh at Leicester, even though the record books show he rode again in 1980, was a huge blow. Everyone, including myself, loved Shrimp. They admired Billy Sanders, they appreciated John Louis but they loved Shrimp.

He was not the most exciting rider. In fact, since that very first Division One meeting claimed half his hand, we had never seen the real Tony Davey again. He had still been a crucial part of the club though, and his 10-point average in 1978 had been a chance to see something of what might have been.

Somehow, though, his cheeky talk, his strong Suffolk accent and the country boy disarming charm made him a friend of everyone. Even his rolling gait was full of character. I well remember his first time back on a bike after badly injuring his hand. In those days, there was a second half individual competition and many of the public, with work and school the next day, never stayed until the end of a meeting. By the time the last race had been run, those spectators who were left had normally edged towards the exits, which meant any trophy presentations were held in front of empty terraces.

Nothing was announced. I knew Shrimp was going to have a run around after the meeting had finished. I don't think even the rest of the team were aware, though, until he wheeled his bike, with specially adapted handlebars, into the pits as all the other riders except the after-meeting kids were wheeling theirs out the other way.

I really don't know how the word spread but by the time when normally only family and friends remained in the stadium, when Shrimp was pushed out of the pit gates, there were still several thousand people there.

His first two laps were painfully slow. He came back to the pits, and adjusted his bike. Then another couple of slow laps, and finally, he was zipping around again. He did several more laps before coming to a stop. The crowd cheered as if he had just won a world final - and I sent him round on a lap of honour!

But that was history. Now he was gone and, for me anyway, most of the fun days went with him.

The decision to swap John Louis and Billy Sanders for Dennis Sigalos and John Cook was a sensible business decision but losing Tony Davey, followed by those two shortly afterwards, finally finished the fun part of the job for me.

Eventually managing to get Jeremy Doncaster onto a speedway bike in 1982 took away some of the bitterness Cook had left in me after his departure. I was really certain Jeremy would reach the very top.

One of the biggest drawbacks of selling up was missing the opportunity to help Jeremy Doncaster truly fulfil his undoubted potential. He could have gone all the way with the right guidance...

Many might say his third place in the 1987 two-day World Final was getting pretty close to the top but to be honest, I never thought Jeremy reached the levels he was capable of. I'm sure that if he had arrived in the early 70s, and been greeted with the dynamic management duo of that time in a young Berry and experienced Bagley, he would have scaled even greater heights.

Not seeing things through with Jeremy was really the biggest downside to my selling up. I don't mean to be conceited when I say I am sure he had even more to achieve with better guidance.

Jeremy should have been every bit as much of a key man as any of the Big Three. In fact, he was a kind of amalgam of them all. He had the technical riding skills and understanding of the concepts of team speedway of a John Louis. He also had the showboating talents of Billy Sanders, and a fair bit of the party attitude, but he also had Shrimp's unsophisticated, hometown humour and cheek. Even the mums wanted to take him home with them!

It took a while for me to get my man. Young Jeremy originally concentrated on the grass track scene, only moving to speedway when he had become an established grass track star. Maybe even then I might have put a bit too much pressure on him by labelling him the next John Louis, even though he clearly was.

John had been lucky to have had avoided too many tumbles early on in his racing career. In any case, I think moto-cross gives riders a better entry into speedway than grass track. Even so, if Jeremy had managed to steer clear of trouble for the first few weeks, his development would have been so much faster.

As it was, he ran into several back wheels in his first few matches and had the stuffing knocked out of him. Mind you, it didn't affect his down to earth humour.

One of those spills caused quite a nasty cut on the nostril requiring stitches. Only Jeremy could have pulled the stitches out whilst picking his nose – and then bragged about it!

By the end of his first year Jeremy was a heat leader and continued on from there. What a shame, though, he settled for being just 'one of the boys' rather than the superstar he could have been.

It was Jeremy and Richard Knight I hated walking away from. Both of these riders were a pleasure to deal with, although they were absolutely different characters. As much as Jeremy was laid back and relaxed about everything from speedway racing to life in general, so Richard was nervous and uptight.

You would go a long way to find a nicer lad than Richard. His early background had not been without its share of heartbreak, and this perhaps made him a bit intense and lacking in natural confidence, but he made up for this with the most fantastic work ethic.

Perhaps he was always a bit overcritical of himself and this

I hated walking away from Richard Knight and Jeremy Doncaster.

Richard Knight – fantastic work ethic.

Kevin Jolly, Jeremy Doncaster and the unfortunate Mike Lanham.

sometimes had the effect of him not being a natural racer. He was one of those lads who made it through sheer dedication and hard work, although there was a plenty of ability as well.

Telling Richard he was good enough to win races didn't always work and I lost count of the times or the different ways I had to wind him up. Because he was just a nice bloke with no natural aggression towards others, he would often let himself be pushed around by opposition riders of lesser ability but more yap. I would have to get him angry enough to produce his best and most times I did this by being rude to him.

Time after time I would have him one fraction from taking a swing at me, only to come up after a meeting and sheepishly admit I had once again got him to the state where he produced his best! He is a super lad and one of my favourites through the years.

The worst bit about being a boss, I am sure all will agree, is having to 'let people go'. I had my share of parting with riders. I would like to think most understood and there are not many, I hope, who wouldn't stop for a chat if we met in the street.

Of all those who I 'let go', I think the hardest was Mike Lanham. In just about all the other cases, even though not all went happily, I felt in my own mind that it was not a bad career move for them.

I'm sure John Louis would argue against that but when all was said and done, he was able to squeeze an extra few of years of racing in without having the pressures of being expected to continue carrying a team.

Mike, on the other hand, was dumped for no other reason than that the numbers didn't add up. Worse, the only place I could find for him was a track he struggled to ride well.

In the grand scheme of things, the transfer of Mike Lanham seems a relatively mundane decision in the life of a speedway promoter but, for me, it was the single worst job I had to do as the Ipswich promoter.

These things all take a toll every bit as much as the rained-off meetings, the bad losses and the general day to day aggravations. In Mike's instance, in my own mind I felt partly responsible for his subsequent near-fatal injury and loss of use of an arm. What with Shrimp and Mike, that Leicester track has a lot to answer for.

When I was back at Ipswich Speedway a few years ago, I was enjoying a drink with several old friends up on the start line bar, when someone asked why I had decided to sell up. I started coming up with the usual stuff...about speedway going downhill and my wanting to try something different before I became too old.

Pat Doncaster, who was my secretary in 1983, was in the group. Pat, who had been John Louis' wife but who had eventually joined up with and married Jeremy Doncaster after John had moved on, and had proved to be the most

Richard Knight became a star despite his lack of natural aggression.

The stars turned out for Mike Lanham's richly deserved testimonial.

loyal of all my secretaries through the years.

She coughed politely, pulled me slightly to one side and asked in a whisper, if my needing to drink two or three large glasses of Cointreau on the afternoon of a home meeting towards the end might have had some small bearing on things!

I had forgotten just how much of a state I was getting into. I had forgotten how home meetings were no longer challenges but problems waiting to happen. I had forgotten that the sheer enjoyment of putting on a good meeting had gone and been replaced by a responsibility to so many people.

It was no longer us against the rest, but me with the worries of the world, no exciting challenges, an unhappy home environment and nowhere to turn in order to relax and let down what little hair I had left.

Perhaps the happiest event that took place at Ipswich in my time there was not on the track, but in the ambulance room. I have said before, our St John people were mighty efficient and ready to cope with any emergency. In addition to the required ambulance, they also provided a mobile emergency unit (which doubled as a second ambulance) so we were ready for just about any emergency short of an earthquake or an explosion at Sizewell, just along the coast.

On May 6, 1982 Kevin Teager's wife, Julie, was watching the England v USA meeting with the other riders' wives when she felt unwell. Being six months pregnant, she decided she should seek medical attention, and so enlisted the then Pat Louis' assistance in dragging Kevin out of the pits.

Pat walked into the pits and straight into me, in full 'meeting mode'. Pat is made of sterner things than most, though. She wasn't about to be pushed out of the pits – very much a female-free zone in those days – until she had retrieved Kevin. But Kevin's car had been blocked in the car park, so Julie ended up in the mobile accident unit and the track doctor was summoned.

It had been some time since Chris Clarke had been active in obstetrics but, as I said, our intrepid St John staff were equipped for anything. Ann Beeching, one of their number and a midwife by trade, took over from the doc and within very few minutes, out popped a tiny, not quite three pound, three months premature baby boy. A few feet on the other side of the mobile unit window, Michael Lee was being interviewed by Anglia TV!

Now having a baby three months before it is due is not an ideal arrangement, and Baby Teager was rushed to hospital and spent a goodly time in the special baby care unit there. Because of this, and the obvious concern that things could have gone wrong, public comment and celebration at the time was kept to a minimum, so Sean, as he was named later, never got the full publicity he deserved. Also, because of the suddenness and panic involved in the birth, it was a little while before the Teagers came up with a name.

Possibly that was a good thing. A decision made in haste could easily have lumbered the mite with something like 'Sprocket' or 'Lee', or even 'Ryder', who was conducting the interview with Michael!

Have we embarrassed the lad – now 22 and working in a well-known garage in Derby Road, Ipswich – enough? I think so, don't you? I'll bet his face is glowing as he reads this!

Leaving town

. . . But back to my own future and the decision to get out was the correct one. Maybe it was a year or three late.

I didn't want the world to know what I was planning. It would have been bad for morale among staff, riders and supporters. So, unlike other businesses, I could not put a 'For Sale' sign up outside. I quietly put it around among those I could trust that I would not be averse to offers.

Siggy was top of Wolves' wanted list.

Peter Adams came back to me. He wanted to reopen Wolverhampton and put it into the top league. His financial backing came from Belle Vue's Stuart Bamforth.

I liked Peter very much. We got on well and I found him bright, good company, passionate about the sport and meticulous in his organisation and planning. Stuart I found to be a rough diamond. Again, he was very sharp, especially where business was concerned, hard working and very straight. A handshake was a handshake with Stuart for good or bad.

This no doubt stemmed from the business from which he made his money. Apart from being an ex-world champion stock car driver, he was a high-class rag and bone man and scrap metal dealer!

Well, I suppose, the more modern term would be 'recycler'. I think he started out by demolishing some of the many cotton mills that dotted Lancashire, but were left over from the Industrial Revolution and of no use in the mid-20th century. Stuart was also partially responsible for the breaking up of Britain's pride and joy, the Royal Navy. Literally. He bought up old warships, broke them up and sold the scrap.

Such a business no doubt involved a lot of handshake deals and, equally no doubt, a reputation for backing those deals up. Stuart never appeared to be short of work. He wasn't as smooth as Maurice Littlechild but had a lot of The Master's good points. Come to think of it, Maurice made his initial money from transporting horse manure. Put the pair together and they would have been up to their necks in muck and bullets!

Actually it was Stuart, and not Peter, who telephoned me about buying Ipswich. He said simply that they (Wolverhampton) wanted to buy Ipswich from me so as to get Dennis Sigalos, and then sell it on to a third party. They had a couple of people in mind who were keen to take over at Ipswich.

That sounded fair enough to me. I liked Dennis very much but the times when the team was one big family were long gone and Siggy was a professional speedway rider who happened to be riding for Ipswich at that time. Peter Adams was as good a potential promoter as you could find, and with Stuart underpinning the operation, it had to be a good move for the American.

So Stuart and I did a deal, I shook hands with him down the phone. There was nothing in writing but I trusted his word and he trusted mine. Part of the deal was that Stuart would remain in the background, but I figure with him now sadly gone, and Peter no longer the Wolverhampton promoter, that clause can now be lifted.

As time ticked on, those interested in buying the Sigalos-less Ipswich from the Wolverhampton duo were down to one name. I didn't know at that stage but that name was Chris Shears. Stuart, quite rightly, was adopting the attitude that my deal was with him and was settled. What happened after that was not my concern.

But there was a problem with Stuart's next deal with his potential Ipswich buyer (Shears). Deadlines came and went for the matter to be tied up and Stuart decided the buyer was a tyre-kicker who did not have the cash.

I asked what was to happen. Stuart made it clear that a deal was a deal, and that if the worst came to the worst, he would sell off the Ipswich riders Wolverhampton didn't want, strip out and sell off the other speedway assets and pull the pin at Ipswich.

I was left with one of three choices: I could either simply allow things to run their course. In hindsight, that might well have been the best option, because I am sure that when Ipswich was publicly placed on the market, a buyer would have surfaced.

Alternative two was to renege on my deal with Stuart, but that is something I would not have been prepared to do.

So I embarked on a third alternative. I got Chris Shears' name and number from Stuart and established that he genuinely wanted to buy the speedway, but just couldn't put his hands on the cash at that time. I then went back to Stuart, and asked if it were acceptable to him if I just sold Sigalos and Preben Eriksen (who had by now become included in their plans) to Wolverhampton and kept the rest to sell to Shears.

Bamforth was happy with this, so I arranged a drip feed deal with Chris, spread over the next 12 months. This saw me considerably out of pocket on the original agreement with Bamforth and, worse, tied me into staying on until the money had been paid. What it also did, though, was confirm that speedway would continue at Ipswich.

I had a great deal of time for both Peter Adams and Stuart Bamforth. I had some further business dealings with Stuart away from speedway, and greatly admired the speed with which he thought on his feet and the way he backed his own judgement.

I don't know if, when he bought Belle Vue, he saw those history-steeped old stands in terms of so many cubes of quality recyclable timber, or had visions of little brick boxes all over the centre green. Personally, I doubt it, because he spent a lot of money on the place and put huge efforts into the running of the speedway.

But even if his long-term plan was to sell the site for redevelopment, I see little point in 'blaming' him for selling out the greatest speedway in the world. For all of its history, and the fabulous race-track, Belle Vue Stadium was well past its sell by date.

Had it not been Stuart, it would have been someone else who would cash in his chips with a winning hand. For the entire chest-beating of the other promoters, I suspect their main anger was based on jealousy that 'Bammy' had beaten the rush to buy the place when Trust House Forte had unloaded it.

The biggest sadness for me was that for all of his hard work, physical and mental, Stuart Bamforth had only just realised that the making of money was merely a means to an end, and not an end in itself, when he died.

I was also sad that Wolverhampton failed so spectacularly. Sad for Peter Adams that he put so much into it, but a mixture of bad topography (Monmore always seemed to attract any bad weather that was around in the area), bad luck and, finally, a bad domestic situation destroyed his dream.

I am equally as glad that the man was strong enough to rebuild himself and his life, and now finds himself back injecting his own special abilities into the sport, albeit on a casual basis as the Wolverhampton team manager.

Stuart Bamforth (above) and Peter Adams (below) were both involved in my efforts to sell out.

20 Hey, That's No Way to Say Goodbye

Yes, many loved before us
I know that we are not new,
In city and in forest
They smiled like me and you,
But now it's come to distances
And both of us must try,
Your eyes are soft with sorrow,
Hey, that's no way to say goodbye.

I'm not looking for another
As I wander in my time,
Walk me to the corner
Our steps will always rhyme,
You know my love goes with you
As your love stays with me,
It's just the way it changes
Like the shoreline and the sea,
But let's not talk of love or chains
And things we can't untie,
Your eyes are soft with sorrow,
Hey, that's no way to say goodbye.

Now let's start this chapter by saying Chris Shears is one of those people it is very difficult to dislike. Smooth and sophisticated, he is not, but he comes over as genuine and sincere – not thick by any means – and always ready to do a favour or have a laugh.

It should have taken one season to get the balance of my money from him. It took two years – and extracting each and every drip feed payment was like taking a fresh bone from a pack of rottweilers.

I have never known anyone with quite as much bald faced cheek as Chris when it comes to not parting with money, but an hour spent in his coach business office told me all I needed to know about the man.

The coach business is all about massive capital outlays and borrowings. Not only does it cost a fortune to finance and run 30 coaches, but you also need a huge bit of ground to house them on. Huge bits of ground in west London do not come cheap, though Chris had done the right thing and bought the land (although mortgaged up to the hilt) rather than rent it. That land was to be his superannuation.

The coach business is also all about, on the one hand, always being there on time, never letting customers down and being seen to be a well run and reliable business.

On the other hand, it's all about drivers going sick or oversleeping, coaches breaking down or having minor accidents and constant battles with officialdom.

Added to this, his company, Chalfont Coaches, is just a hop, skip and a jump from Heathrow Airport. Given the vagaries of the British weather, it remained a constant possibility for Chris that, at any time of the day or night, he could receive a telephone call from the airlines demanding as many coaches as possible, at a moment's notice and at very acceptable contract rates.

I suppose there are two ways such a coach operation could be run. Either it could be modelled on the Houston base of NASA, or it could be more – casual. I'll leave you to guess which mode represented the Chalfont Coaches HQ.

What all of that meant is that Chris was well used to living on the edge. He was used to making decisions on the run, used to robbing Peter to pay Paul on a daily basis, and used to just making things work. Nothing fazed him. He was pretty much bomb-proof.

My strengths were in my planning and organisation. I was able to operate under pressure and, indeed, did some of my best work at those times. But unlike Chris, who seemed to thrive on it, I hated operating that way, and when under such pressure I was not the most affable bloke around.

It is fair to say, Chris brought out the worst in me. I repeat, though, he was impossible to dislike, or to stay angry at for long. I wouldn't extend those thoughts as far as the hangers-on he surrounded himself with, though.

Not because he is a likeable bloke, but simply because it serves little purpose in this book, I will not go into great detail about my disappointment with the way Ipswich was run under the Shears stewardship.

John Cook (inside) and Preben Eriksen wheel-to-wheel.

I had done what I thought was the right thing by the Ipswich public and it had cost me money and a lot of heartache to do so. In hindsight, I should have called Bamforth's bluff and let him dispose of the speedway. I'm sure a better promoter would have emerged from the woodwork when it had been put on the open market.

The Shears period, though, was a classic case of businessman supporters becoming involved in speedway promotion. By and large, it doesn't work.

That first year of mine as caretaker promoter (1984) was a bit of a blur really. I suppose, on paper, we did well. We won the league and Cup double, anyway, but for me the year contained very few highlights. This was partly due to my domestic situation coming to a head, partly due to trying to work with, and around Chris, and partly due to my looking around for, and dabbling in, new ventures.

Mainly, though, the return of John Cook made managing the team a miserable, soul-destroying experience. The team now became neatly divided. On the one hand, I got on well and could deal with Billy Sanders, Richard Knight, Jeremy Doncaster and Nigel Flatman. On the other hand, there were John Cook, Kai Niemi, and Carl Blackbird.

Blackbird spent the season filling in for Andy Hines, who broke a leg early on. Carl was a nice enough lad, and did well for us, but somehow he and I were never entirely comfortable with each other. I don't know why. Possibly it was because he was a Mildenhall rider.

I expect he had been led to believe I had horns and a tail. Anyway, I think he felt more comfortable with Shears, preferring Chris' laissez-faire ways to my more regimented methods.

Niemi was never openly rude to me but Chalfont Coaches had sponsored him for some time, so he was clearly not going to let me come between him and his milk cow. It is also fair to say I considered Kai to be a taker and an under-achiever.

When Kai first joined White City as a youngster, I saw a massive ability. Every now and then comes along a rider who is simply just a class apart at being able to make a speedway bike go fast. Maybe Ove Fundin had it, I didn't see enough to judge. Maybe Ronnie Moore also had 'it', but not too many more, other than the young Tony Davey, and perhaps Michael Lee.

It's all about getting maximum go forward. Some call it throttle control, others balance, whilst others talk about getting 'drive'. It's a mixture of all those things really, and more. It's the natural instinct of being able to utilise the greatest percentage possible of the bike's power, and turn it into forward movement.

Kai, almost right from the start, was just another heat leader in the British League with White City and Eastbourne but to see him racing

Carl Blackbird and
Nigel Flatman warming up.

I could motivate Richard Knight, but Kai Niemi was his own man.

on the continent was to see a totally different rider. In the UK, he was safe, reliable, unexciting, almost to the point of being boring. On the continent, the Finn was aggressive, spectacular, entertaining and a real crowd pleaser.

In his early days, I drooled at the thought of getting him to Foxhall and unleashing the continental Kai onto the UK public. In the two years he and I were finally joined at Ipswich, and as I got to know him better ... well, let's just say I think Kai was not fair to his talent, not fair to the UK speedway public, not fair to the people around him and, above all, was not fair to himself.

I have no great bone to pick with him on a personal level and, as I said, he was never directly rude to me. But I just hate to see that much talent so badly abused.

Which brings us nicely to the one and only John Cook. I'm still not sure if this character deserves a whole chapter devoted to him, or to be ignored.

I would like to think that most of the lads who rode for Ipswich in my time there would be happy to share a beer with me, and me with them. I'll make an exception with Cook.

It all started so well. After being a four-point-something rider in his first BL season at Hull, he was lucky to get a second chance. California has supplied some top line riders over the years but there has also been some dross. Cook was close to being one of those 'now you see me, now you don't' guys.

But I gave him a second chance on the main stage – and he grabbed it with both hands.

We are not just talking about the points he scored, or even the way he scored them. We are not even just talking about the sheer enthusiasm that spread throughout the team, or the time he showed for the supporters. More than that was his burning desire to improve, the determination to put on a show, and the pure ebullience of his personality in that first season.

Everybody, including me, thought he was an accident waiting to happen with his flamboyant antics. We had already had the pleasure of watching Kelly Moran bring a new style of riding that had little to do with being a neat, compact Dave Jessup-type rider. Brought up on the tiny Californian tracks, this new breed of riders seemed to work on the basis that the less the contact between bike and body there was, the faster the combination went.

Whilst I doubt that was true, a fantastic sense of balance enabled Cook (and the Morans) to pass riders and then worry about how to get themselves out of the mess afterwards. In fact, I have seen Cook (twice) and Kelly Moran actually be so far leaned over as to be effectively crashed, and yet manage to somehow scramble back aboard and continue to race. The art of passing on the inside had become less and less used before these riders came along. They were a breath of fresh air.

What the public did not know was that John listened intently to everything I told him – and put it into practice. If he listened to me, I presume he also did with others. He just wanted to improve, to be as good as the other top Americans. Yes, he still played second fiddle to the classy Dennis Sigalos, in points return, but he certainly stole more hearts.

Although Cook's first year deal was originally modelled on him being a middle order fill in, it

Kai Niemi could beat anyone anywhere when the mood took him.

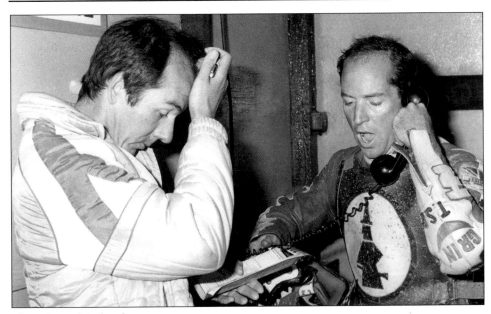

John Cook appeals to the referee.

was also based on his points scores, so he did pretty well financially out of that season. This included additional non-contracted bonuses from me as the season progressed, plus a four figure end of season special handshake. He deserved it. He had been almost too good to be true.

Exit Dr Jekyll at the end of the 1981 season. Enter Mr Hyde at the start of 1982. There had been no indication at all during the winter of what was to come. I had met him in Los Angeles, where we had done the deal for the upcoming season. There had been some negotiating. I gave a bit, he gave a bit and we reached agreement.

As had been my normal practice with all riders, it was done on scraps of scribble pad paper. I gave him a copy and kept one for myself. We shook hands, John asked me to bring back some tins of coffee for a sponsor in the UK, and that was it.

What happened between then and him arriving in the UK for the start of 1982, I shall never know, but something surely did. He sulked and avoided me. He walked away if I approached, would not sign his official BSPA contract, turned his back whenever a photographer was near and generally behaved like a prima donna.

His on track efforts were way, way below what he was capable of and yet when he guested for other teams, or was invited to individual events, he suddenly became his old 1981 self.

Eventually, I managed to pin him down for a conversation. He was surly, unresponsive and difficult. All he would say was that the deal we had agreed in LA had not been officially signed and that he was now not happy with it. Instead of the arrangements being based on high points money, he wanted guaranteed payments.

I was most unhappy about this. We had shaken hands on a deal and that should have been the end of it, but I still treated him with respect, agreeing to change the whole basis of the contract. Because of his efforts the previous year, but against my better judgement, I agreed to pay him a flat per-meeting figure, with the proviso that he gave his best efforts and cooperated in

One of the most spectacular riders in the world, but the fans only saw one side to the troublesome 'Cowboy'.

An altogether different John Cook in 1981.

all team functions and affairs.

He had got his own way but continued to avoid contact with me whenever he possibly could. He continued to turn his back on photographers, pressmen, supporters (except a select few) and team-mates. He ceased pretty well all the crowd-pleasing, on-track antics of the previous year. And his scoring plummeted.

Now came the crunch. Because his average dropped so much, he became very popular as a guest. And when he rode as a guest, everyone saw the real John Cook, complete with high scores and crowd-pleasing efforts.

By now, we were well into the season. I tried – goodness, I tried – to get that man to do the right thing. It was a waste of time. Finally, I told him the situation was not working. He was not keeping his part of the contract because he was patently not putting in his best efforts.

I gave him a new deal based on performance. If he were to score more than his then current (and reduced) average, he would be considerably better off than with his previously agreed fixed payments, depending by how much he exceeded the figure. If he equalled his average, the return to him would be the same as the fixed rate. If he failed to reach his average, his return would be lower than the fixed rate.

For the first four weeks, I think, his points returns were higher, so he took home more than the fixed amount he had been on before. Then one week, his return, and therefore his pay cheque, was lower.

He failed to turn up for our next match and when I discovered he was making plans to leave the country, I sent someone around to retrieve his loaned vehicle, short of several of the non-bolted down bits like spare wheel and back seat he had 'disposed of'.

I tried and tried to fathom what had caused this huge personality swing compared to the previous year. I wondered if it had been me, or something I had said or done. Whatever it was, and regardless of the disappointment of a large proportion of the supporters, we were better off without him.

When I sold out to Chris Shears, he decided to re-sign Cook. I warned him it would be difficult, outlining the difficulties I had gone through. But Chris decided to go ahead. I won't say Cook re-wrote his contractual arrangements with Chris on a weekly basis. That would be an exaggeration. It would not be an exaggeration, though, to say that he gave Chris the constant run-around when it came to financial arrangements.

Now Chris was a bit of an oddball character himself where money was concerned, so was prepared to put up with this. Meanwhile, as team manager, I was faced with managing six riders of a seven-man team. Cook never spoke to me. On pre-meeting team walks around tracks, he would either not go, or hang back away from the group. He got on well with some of the riders but that is all. He was never able to reproduce the magic of that first year, remaining totally unpredictable from meeting to meeting.

As I said, I don't remember too many highlights in that double-winning year of 1984, although in truth, there had to have been some. The one match I do recall stands out like a beacon. We had won the league by then and faced a mighty strong Belle Vue in the KO Cup final. It was October and before the first leg in Manchester there had been some bad frosts.

Frost and shale are not good friends. Ice crystals get trapped between the clay type particles and if the track top then melts, the surface becomes swampy. This happened to Stuart Bamforth, so he put on a surface of fresh, dry shale, then packed it down. It's a job to explain but doing such a thing on a wet top surface and a frozen base turns the whole lot into spongy plastecine.

When you walk on it, you bounce, leaving imprints, although the surface is only damp and not wet to the touch. On such surfaces, instead of cutting through the top and causing the rear wheel to break away, the tyre just grips, making turning very, very difficult. It can often make world class speedway riders look extremely silly.

Normally a meeting would not start on such a surface but this was late October, with no certainty of an improvement in the weather, so we in the Ipswich camp decided to give it a go. As league champions, the Witches were pumped up and boosted by a huge banner that was unfurled by the Ipswich travelling faithful, declaring us champions. When I say huge, I am talking maybe 50 yards long by three-feet tall!

When we said yes, we would race, the Belle Vue team had no alternative but to agree. They probably wished they hadn't. With Billy Sanders as strong as an ox; Kai Niemi, as I said above, one of the all time great motorcyclists, when in the mood; John Cook, whatever his character, still a great motorcyclist; Jeremy Doncaster, European Grass Track champion; and Richard Knight, another strong lad; we simply rode all over them.

The records show the Ipswich Witches were given a civic reception at the end of the season. I suppose I must have been there but I don't recall it too well. I suspect I spent the evening hiding up at the back.

That year should have been my last one. It was supposed to be my last one. At least it would have seen me depart on a high note but I still had monies outstanding. I was left with the choice of either suing Chris for the outstanding money, and in doing so causing bad publicity and bad feelings in the team, or staying on and ensuring I was close enough to ensure the money was eventually paid. I decided to stay on.

Once again, in the early part of the 1985 season, Cook gave Shears the run around. This time it was generally hushed up - and the loss of Billy Sanders affected everything that year - but even though Shears had made Cook captain (against my advice), he remained a nightmare to deal with. Not just for me as team manager, but also for Shears on the financial front.

There were high spots, though, particularly in the shape of Jeremy Doncaster and Richard Knight. They were two contrasting personalities: Richard was uptight, unsure of himself, always nervous of making mistakes or letting people down; Jeremy, laid back, seemingly self-assured, certainly prepared to drop his social guard and very much a 'people person'.

Both took their speedway very seriously, so it was a delight to try to help them. Billy Sanders had matured a lot by then and, apart from his usual world championship obsession, was a lot easier to work with. Possibly my not being the overall boss at that stage might have helped our relationship.

Nigel Flatman was . . . just Nigel! He tried hard, was very loyal and a nice bloke. In terms of speedway riding, though, he was simply one paced. To be more precise, he rode in the same manner on every track he arrived at. If track shape and condition on that night suited his style, Nigel would do well; otherwise he would not. He was pretty fearless, though, and managed to get under the skin of a few opponents. Well, if 1984 had been a bad year for me, there was plenty of trouble still sitting there waiting to appear in 1985.

John Louis had finally hung up his leathers that winter, so I managed to get him involved in a management role, back at his track. Clearly, with Chris busy running his coach company and only managing to turn up on the afternoon of race days, he would need a local manager, and John was the obvious choice. I figured that the 1985 season would give me the opportunity to hand things over gradually.

After Billy had gone, and with Cook having been made captain against my wishes, I quite deliberately moved to as near the back seat as I could to concentrate really on Jeremy and Richard, who both enjoyed quite good seasons. I didn't like the way things were going at Foxhall. I didn't like the fact that the reputation of Ipswich Speedway, built up over many years, was beginning to suffer. And I didn't like not having the authority to do anything about it.

In the final race of the KO Cup final, second leg at Oxford, Ipswich needed a 5-1 to take the trophy. For two laps, Cook and Jeremy Doncaster were way out in front, side by side, and under no pressure at all. The Cup was ours...

Then Cook just rode into the side of Doncaster, sticking him into the fence. There was no reason for it – Cook was certainly a good enough rider not to have simply lost control. Was it a genuine accident or something more sinister? Well, Ipswich lost the Cup and, given all of the previous history, I couldn't accept it as 'just one of those things'.

I had several long chats with Shears. This was to be my last year of involvement at Ipswich, and anything I said or did might affect the 1986 season negatively so I had to be very careful.

I asked Chris if he intended persevering with Cook for the following year. He said there was no way he would consider it. I then asked if, given that was the case, he minded my saying what I thought about Cook in the local media. Chris was pleased. He told me that it would help the Ipswich people understand why he was not going to have the bloke back the following year. So I went ahead and said what I thought.

This amounted to the fact that Cook had been a nightmare to deal with all year, had destroyed my enthusiasm for speedway, and that I could not accept the incident at Oxford as 'just one of those things'. The local newspaper decided the angle to use was that I was saying Cook had driven me out of Ipswich. Plainly, I had reached the end of my official time at Ipswich anyway. What I might have suggested was that if Cook was to be around in future, then I would not be. Certainly, in anything but a spectating role anyway.

Shears then totally distanced himself from every word and accused me in the press of stirring up trouble! Nothing like being hung out to dry and then leaving under a cloud.

Surprise, surprise! After the usual 'contract problems' at the start of 1986, Cook finally walked out on the club for the last time. He might well have been a very good rider and showman, but after that first season he was a promoter's nightmare. He made the last couple of my years associated with the club a misery.

The final crunch came at the traditional end of season supporters' club dinner and dance. A function, I should point out, that my new partner, Linda Gould, in her long-term role as supporters' club secretary, and I had put together countless times in the past.

Not only did I find us not on the top table that evening but during the course of the night – through all of the speeches, the presentations to riders and others and all the general back-slapping – there was not one single reference to Linda or myself standing down. In our different ways, we had done quite a lot for Ipswich Speedway over the years.

I felt like a corpse at its own wake.

I slunk off to the bar in the next room and had a few drinks, pretty much on my own. I was about to shoot through when Andy Archer, the Radio Orwell presenter and good friend over several years, called the dance to order. Of all people, my ex-long time girlfriend Denise had been horrified at the way I had been treated. between them, she and Andy stopped the proceedings, presented me with a bottle of Cointreau and said a few kind words of public appreciation. That meant a great deal to me, as did the warm reception from the supporters.

Other than that, it was a pretty sad way to sign off on 17 years of my life.

1984 League and Cup winners.

21 Hotel California

...Mirrors on the ceiling
Pink champagne on ice
And she said
We are all just prisoners here
Of our own device
And in the master's chambers
They gathered for the feast
They stab it with their steely knives
But they just can't kill the beast
Last thing I remember
I was running for the door
I had to find the passage back to the place I was before
Relax said the night man
We are programmed to receive
You can check out any time you like
But you can never leave...

I had been 'retired' from speedway for a couple of years. I had tried several very diverse business ventures, with varying levels of success, and other ways to fill in the gap left where speedway had been. I still wandered down to Foxhall for my weekly 'fix' but more often than not found the evenings very frustrating. Other than that, my main pre-occupation was trying to get my golf handicap down.

After the 1986 season Wimbledon Speedway was about to close but a group of supporters were going to try and save it. Somehow I got invited to go along to an exploratory meeting in order to pass on advice. As I recall, Phil Rising had thrown my name into the mix. Ego forced me to attend but that didn't stop me from telling the group of bodies what the score was.

I told them that it would be just about impossible for them to make a go of it. I told them they would lose money, patience and love of the sport. I pointed out that just about all of the good promoters of the past had walked out of the speedway door and the sport was destined to go only in one direction.

There's none so blind as those who will not see.

Despite all of my warnings, there were enough people at that meeting prepared to put their hand in their pockets in order to get the Dons back and running. As I recall, there were about a dozen who kicked in some financial promises of help and of those, five or six individuals (or couples) who were prepared to chip in with time and expertise as well as potential ongoing financial commitment.

This core group set about forming a limited company, Wimbledon Speedway 1987 Ltd. I was flattered by their invitation to act as 'consultant'. They were a motley group who had only two things in common. One was their love of (Wimbledon) speedway, the other was their lack of any working knowledge of the sport.

Speedway Star boss Phil Rising had promised them as much support as his available time and position could offer but they needed more than that. Peter Brown had been involved with the former Wimbledon Speedway regime in a largely honorary but time-consuming role propping up a well-loved Cyril Maidment. Peter was another of those people who was far too intelligent

The Wimbledon Dons from 1987 – my last full season in British speedway. Left to right: Neville Tatum, Jeremy Luckhurst, Kevin Jolly, Peter Brown, Mark Fordham. Front: Terry Mussett, Roger Johns (on bike), Nathan Simpson. *(AW)*

and resourceful to fall under speedway's dubious spell but had managed to do so.

All the stranger was that this immensely likeable and highly successful bloke was an ex-touring, and, by then, highly respected club golf professional. Why he needed to move into a different sporting sphere for his fun was beyond me. All I wanted was to talk golf, whilst he preferred to talk speedway!

Peter was firm friends with Roger Johns, who was to be the new Dons' captain, and initially said he would restrict his involvement to helping Roger. Needless to say, Peter became more and more involved again and was the major positive to come out of the whole Wimbledon experience. His enthusiasm is boundless and his intellect huge. He is the kind of person it is impossible to dislike. He kept me going when I was getting frustrated and remains a firm friend today.

The first thing was to guide this disparate group of supporters come speedway promoters through the fun process of becoming accepted into the Second Division (by now under the title of National League). They had sorted out a deal with the stadium management that would see them provided with the use of Plough Lane for one night a week on a walk in/walk out basis.

This meant the stadium provided everything from track preparation to turnstile operators and stadium cleaning – for a price. The speedway promotion was responsible only for the team, the programme production, advertising and race night track staff.

The positive side to this meant that all the physical work side of promoting was taken care of. The downside was that they had no control over anything at the stadium and were subject to the political intrigues involved in its operation. In the minds of both the stadium owners, GRA, and the workforce, the speedway promotion's place in the pecking order came just below pond life. And the 'rent' was anything but cheap.

Because of this arrangement, it was simple to operate the speedway without having to be on hand at the stadium during the week, so, like a mug, I agreed to look after the actual team and speedway management side of things, provided others took care of the promotional aspects. All I would get in return was help with petrol, telephone and postage costs.

Next, we needed permission to join the National League. Because of the group's lack of experience, I became the licensed promoter. Even at the very first general council meeting where we made our application, Mervyn Stewkesbury and I took an immediate dislike to each other. He was everything I dislike in people. A middle aged Jack-the-lad who considered himself

God's gift, he treated the rest of the promoters as sheep with himself as the shepherd. This time, though, my knowledge and understanding (especially on speedway) was far in advance of his and there was no way in the world I was going to have him throw his weight in my direction. I suspect this immediate clash of personalities did not help Wimbledon Speedway.

That first season at Wimbledon was one of absolute frustration. I was used to having the last word. I was used to making decisions and then making those decisions work. But this wasn't my bat and ball. Every slightest decision went to a directors' meeting. These board meetings seemed to take place every two minutes. That is not meant as a dig at the people involved. It was their money and they were entitled to have their say. Making the speedway operation financially viable was always going to be difficult. It was not for me to spend their money for them.

By the end of that first season we had all done money. I don't know what the directors' losses were, but I reckon I was the best part of ten grand the poorer for my involvement. More importantly, I found it very difficult to cope with the stadium people, the NL promoters' association (aka Stewksbury), and the collective board of Wimbledon Speedway 1987.

Individually, the members of the board were nice people but I simply found it difficult to cope with having each of them responsible for specific areas of operation. Organisation by committee never works well.

And so I decided to hunt around for a better candidate than myself to be the Wimbledon Speedway manager for 1988. I had a huge respect for Dave Lanning and it seemed his son, Russell, was beginning to show the Lanning Senior traits in terms of journalism and speedway promotion. He had appeared to have performed a useful role at Eastbourne Speedway and so I recommended him for the job, with me retaining the promoter's licence but moving to my original position as 'consultant'.

What I discovered was that Russell was good at managing the day-to-day things but I came to the conclusion that Dave was very much the guiding hand behind many of the things Russell did.

Still, the directors, and specifically, managing director, Don Scarff, was happy with Russell and that was the important thing. I was already making my own plans for the future.

I was finding that living in Ipswich was not easy any more. The speedway had spoiled me and I could muster no enthusiasm for the various other business ventures I had become involved with. Instead of being on top of these operations, I was leaving both the work and the decision-making to other people – and finding, to my cost, how much of a mistake that was. I have to be honest and also admit, although I thought I hated having a high profile around town as the Ipswich promoter, I missed the kudos. I missed not being able to drive into the VIP car parks and not being telephoned for advice every five minutes. The speedway had also been my social outlet but now I felt an outsider there.

I had decided way back in 1976 that Perth, Western Australia, and its people, had captivated me. It had always been my intention to finish my days there and I had spent many a winter break in the company of my new friends down under.

Had my new partner, soon to become wife, Linda, not come into my life, I think I would have moved to Perth a couple of years earlier. But she is an Ipswich girl, born and bred, and was reluctant to leave family and friends.

We had also, by then, discovered the delights of Florida, and both fancied the idea of a place there, but we knew nobody in America and were not sure if we could get a visa. Also, we saw Perth as very much England in the sun, whereas Florida was a different culture entirely.

Anyway, eventually Linda agreed to make the move, and my putting in Russell at Wimbledon had been one of the loose ends I was tidying up.

Sadly, the situation at Wimbledon went sour. Knowing I was planning to emigrate, and being

Mervyn Stewkesbury (right) seen here talking to BSPA manager Peter York. *(AW)*

aware that the consortium were happy enough with Russell, I generally kept my own reservations about him to myself. I think he had realised what my own thoughts were but also understood where the power was in the set-up, so he concentrated hard on keeping Don Scarff happy.

I have mentioned the 'personality clash' between myself and Stewkesbury. Things had not improved between us but there was no point in developing a feud I had no interest in maintaining. Then, out of the blue, during the 1988 season, I received a call from the National League manager, Alan Hodder. Now I quite liked Alan, even allowing for the fact that he was a Stewkesbury acolyte, but I didn't like what he told me.

He alleged that there was an 'irregularity' with the BSPA contract Russell had lodged for Ray Morton, who had been on loan from King's Lynn for 1987 but who we had arranged to sign on full contract for 1988. It appeared that Stewkesbury and Morton had 'just happened' to be discussing Morton's future, even though he was riding in the Wimbledon team, when Morton claimed he had not signed that year's contract but a further loan agreement. This had caused Hodder to check the files.

I telephoned Russell to check what had happened. I pointed out to him that, admittedly with a loss of face, I could resolve the situation if indeed there had been an irregularity. Russell swore to me there was nothing untoward and so, taking him at his word, I ripped into Hodder, who stood his ground and agreed to send me photocopies of the documents.

It was clear from the moment I saw the photocopies that things were not all they should have been.

If Russell had been up front with me, I could have saved the situation, albeit with some personal discomfort, but because I had gone out on a limb for him, I found myself hung out to dry.

So that left me as the sacrificial lamb. I handed in my promoter's licence, no doubt much to Stewkesbury's delight. Russell was disciplined by the NL management committee and Ray Morton became a 'free agent' at the end of the year, even though, ironically, he carried on riding at Wimbledon.

It was time for me to leave Wimbledon and speedway, and it improved my humour none to be told by one of the other Wimbledon Speedway directors, some distance down the line, that Russell's indiscretion had never been raised at Board level even though the managing director, Don Scarff assured me it had..

One of that original consortium had worked for a stock broker. He got me into share trading – which ultimately cost me a lot of money in the 1988 crash. Another of the group worked in Lloyds of London and introduced me to his agency there. My joining them became a major error of judgement and some years further down the track this was to cost me a good deal more than share trading ever did!

One way and another, you can say my involvement at Wimbledon did not turn out very well although I met some great people and enjoyed being back in the rough and tumble of the sport.

It was actually twelve months later, July 4th 1989, American Independence Day, when Linda and I finally stepped on the plane to Perth, return tickets in hand. Why return tickets? Because I had promised Linda we would come back for a visit within twelve months.

We did so again the following year, and it would be lying to say part of us didn't miss the UK. But after Alexander John was born in 1992, Linda's parents came out for a trip, and have done so most years since. It is also rare for us not to have at least one and often more sets of family or friends out during our summer, so we hardly have the opportunity to miss people. We've been back a few times, but with Alex very much an Australian I think we now safely call Australia home. We still miss some things. I miss the speedway, but Aussie Rules is a great spectator sport: Linda misses Bisto. (Not really – her mum brings supplies with her!)

We discovered Australia is not England in the sun, but the lifestyle is great, and as technology continues to cause the world to contract, we can still enjoy keeping up with the exploits in Coronation Street and Albert Square and the speedway Grands Prix but sit in shorts and tee shirts holding a cold beer whilst doing so. Like most thing in Australia, they are a little late in arriving, but that suits the laid back lifestyle.

All in all, life is good.

22 Please Don't Tell Me How the Story Ends

Never's just the echo of forever
Lonesome as a love that might have been.
Let me go on lovin' and believin' 'til it's over
Please don't tell me how the story ends.

So where to now?

No, not for me! I think my future is pretty well mapped out. At 60, I've been qualified for 'mature persons' housing for the last five years. Mind you, I don't know how they would cope with my wife Linda, still in her first flush (nod, nod, wink, wink) of middle age, or a full on, full-time, barely reached double figures but thinks he's all grown up, number one and only son Alexander.

Yes, I know, I left things a bit late! The trouble is, there are some things that being the world's best spectator do not exactly qualify you for!

No, I was thinking more of where to now for speedway? I've not exactly been quiet on the subject. Bits of my thoughts are scattered around the odd speedway magazine, Internet newsgroup and many personal correspondents' hard drives.

It is strange really. I tend to drift through life in general without any great visions on how to save the world. I shrug my shoulders at the latest war and who was right and who was wrong to cause it. Politics is only a game designed to keep the worst of the legal profession busy anyway. Labour, Conservative, Liberal . . . it matters not. The world is really run by Humphrey Applebys and the spruikers are just a sideshow.

Admittedly, I do get a bit steamed up when watching sport. The spectator in me never lurks far below the surface but the only thing I feel qualified to talk about with any authority is speedway. Even now, 12,000 miles and 14 years away, I feel my opinions are valid, although this might not be universally accepted.

I was lucky enough to become involved in the sport at the beginning of the end of the last cycle of The Golden Years. Will there ever be another cycle? Frankly, I have my doubts. Speedway, as we know it (Jim) is dead. Sadly, nobody has told it.

I take some responsibility for the demise myself. It was the likes of me (and Joe Thurley) and Ian Thomas (and Geoff Brownhut) who bashed on the doors of the incestuous cartel that was speedway in the late 60s. And it was us, and those who followed through those opened doors, who pushed through all manner of changes.

Elsewhere, I touched on the question of the BSPA opening its doors up to outsiders, with the resultant collapse of the pillars of salt on which many of the cornerstones of the British League had been laid.

I saw no wrong in bringing new professionalism into the sport. I saw no wrong in trying to get the sport onto some kind of level playing field basis. I did not understand why the tired, old, unambitious and badly run promotions should be propped up by the better ones.

I understand now.

Call it what you like. Call it living by market forces, call it evolution, call it survival of the fittest, but us 'new boys' brought a new era into speedway – the dog-eat-dog era.

When the British League Division Two was first formed in 1968, it was initially run entirely by Division One promoters and it was openly called a training league. It was there to utilise all the riding talent floating around that couldn't get a ride in the top league. Riders, when they were trained up to the required standard in the training league, were moved on to the same promoter's Division One team.

When the Second Division was entirely run by Division One promoters it was as simple as that, and along the way those promoters earned themselves a few bob staging racing at their 'training tracks'.

But as soon as the Second Division started expanding and letting in new boys, the surplus pool of riding talent started to dry up and the new promotions had to pay a bit over the odds to encourage old hands out of retirement. It was either that or offer new, young riders incentives to sign for them rather than the team down the road that could offer a direct route into the top league.

Those new promotions, like us at Ipswich, still relied on Division One promoters loaning out their junior riders, though. Indeed, Coventry's John Harrhy and Pete Bailey were vital to the Witches' early days.

Eventually the penny dropped regarding riders being loaned to the lower league by the big boys. As soon as the Division One loanee, who had been trained to be a Division Two heat leader, was good enough to hold down a team place with his senior club, off he went.

The senior team received a ready trained up rider - but the Division Two track was left with a big gap in their team and no compensation. In contrast, if the same rider had started his speedway life with the Second Division club, then that club could dictate, to a certain extent, where and when the rider went up into the senior league, and could also negotiate some nice 'compensation'.

So now it was important for the Second Division teams to find and train their own talent – and the easiest way to do this was to refuse to take any loaned riders from the senior league. Faced with this, the junior riders became reluctant to sign for the Division One clubs. If they signed for the Division Two team, first, they might get better initial treatment and faster entry into team racing. Second, they were not tied to the one Division One track when the time came to move up. Third, they stood to benefit from receiving a percentage of any transfer fee when the step up was made.

Even though many of the Division One promoters still had interests in Division Two tracks, the newcomers were always eroding their authority in the lower league. Finally, the fact that the two leagues were now actually in competition was crystallised in 1975 when BL Division Two decided it was not second class at all, but 'alternative', and changed its name to the New National League.

Not enough alarm bells rang at that time within British Speedway. After all, the Division One clubs still controlled the sport, didn't they? Didn't they?

Already the senior league promoters had begun dipping back abroad for their ready-made replacement riders. The difference this time, though, was, without work permit restriction for many of the EEC lads, and with the Speedway Riders' Association now dead and buried in all but name, the 'ready made' bit was replaced by 'no initial cost'. Effectively, Division One conceded virtually all of the domestic newcomers to the New NL, and looked overseas for its new, untapped talent.

As if that wasn't bad enough, the FIM (or the part of it called the CCP, which was responsible for oval circuit racing) had no BSPA representative at all. The British representation on that committee came from grass track interests in the Auto Cycle Union.

Historically, the largely amateur grass track organisers and the professional speedway people did not see eye to eye. UK speedway received no favours from these Sunday Afternoon Czars, and it helped not that the manager who was foisted upon the SCB by the RAC hierarchy, Dick Bracher, appeared to have no love at all for the sport he was supposed to be managing.

So the BSPA simply ignored the FIM. They had done a deal with Sweden and Poland, the only other genuine speedway nations to share the individual World Finals on a three-year rotation. In the years when the UK did not have an individual World Final, it had either a World Team Cup or Pairs final.

The attitude of the BSPA was purely head in sand. Meanwhile the CCP was being taken over by people from fringe speedway nations. The movers and shakers came from such well-known speedway countries as Italy, Germany, Norway and so on.

These representatives from minnow nations started coming up with all sorts of weird competitions, such as the European Grass Track Championships, which was effectively a second division World Long Track Championships. Another was the Under-21 speedway championship, which has changed its name over and over again but remains an excuse for getting young lads to ride all over Europe for next to nothing.

Now don't kid yourselves. These competitions were not about anything other than getting attractive meetings for oddball speedway nations on the cheap. Drop a title onto an event, and riders will travel all over the world for a pittance. The meeting organisers got a titled prestige meeting full of foreign stars for next to nothing, the CCP got a nice little income in licence fees, and the Sunday Afternoon Czars got their all-expenses paid trips to exotic locations. This happens now more than ever.

The ones who miss out are the riders, who are not only prepared to subsidise these events out of their own pockets, but are also happy to miss meetings to do so. Also, these riders' promoters (mainly UK) have to manage without their services whilst they are away and also cope with their pre-trip distraction and post-trip blues.

Meanwhile, the Danes, who had, since rape and pillage was taken off the international sporting calendar, settled for badminton as their major international sporting success story, decided to adopt Ole Olsen as their national hero.

We'll gloss over the fact that he learned just about all his speedway knowledge by riding in the UK. The fact is, starved of sporting success, the Danish youngsters all wanted to be the next Ole Olsen. Speedway mania swept that little Scandinavian country.

Bless 'em, they all want to play golf now. Far less dangerous, and a good deal more lucrative, so speedway in Denmark is fast following hoola-hoops, pogo sticks and Pokemon cards into oblivion. But we are talking about the mid-70s and 80s here and speedway was the latest craze then.

Olsen had his own dream: a World Final at his little country track at Vojens in Denmark. But to achieve that, he needed to muscle in to the Big Three nations' cosy triopoly.

Gunther Sorber was a speedway man through and through in Germany, where speedway historically provided nothing more than a training and practice area for long track riders. Gunther also had his own visions.

Olsen and Sorber was a dangerous duo for the Swedish-Polish-UK alliance and these two could be assured of support from countries like Italy, Australia and the USA (or more particularly, Harry Oxley, who was the de facto head of US speedway) who all had their own agendas.

Then the worst thing happened. The management at Empire Stadium, Wembley changed and the new boys no longer wanted to play with speedway. The SCB was happy to take the first reaction from Wembley that their deal with the Football Association prevented the laying of a track around the soccer pitch. At least, that is what they broadcast to the world.

The good, old RAC had appointed a new chairman to the SCB in Michael Limb. He fitted in well with the incumbent manager. Neither knew, or indeed seemed to care too much, about speedway, its history, or its traditions.

Old school ties akimbo, they set UK speedway down the road towards that great big ex-open cut coalmine hole in the ground called Odsal, up in the centre of that spiritual home of speedway, Bradford! The SCB then played its trump card by actually directing the ACU representative on the CCP to vote against retaining the Big Three's hold on the World Finals.

That was, without doubt, the biggest ever stab in the BSPA's back, from Bracher, who never ever, in my opinion, had the remotest interest in UK speedway.

Et tu Brute!

And then came along a quixotic character from another famous speedway nation, Holland.

It really is difficult to see how and where he sprung from, but Jos Vaessen was a heavyweight career mandarin who, I believe, was very high in the Transport Ministry in Holland. I think one of his briefs was to oversee motor sport in that country. Somehow he found his way into a CCP conference.

He must have liked what he saw, because in no time at all he had moved in and taken control. What an operator! They call them number-crunchers in Australia; maybe clever operators might be a better term, or even Mr Fixits. Whatever name you give him, Mr Vaessen seemed to be able to lobby delegates in such a way as to always conjure anything he wanted.

In the first instance, this turned out to be the presidency and control of the CCP. The next

Gunther Sorber *(AW)*

objective was the disastrous two-day world individual final in Amsterdam in 1987. Now if ever anyone should have been shown the door after that shambles, it was him. But, as I have said, he was some kind of operator.

The whole of the FIM set up must have been the easiest of touches for someone of Vaessen's capabilities, because his next two objectives followed in what appeared to be no time. Backed up by Gunther Sorber, who had finally found someone on whose coat tails he could cling, and Ole Olsen, who he had aided to his Vojens World Final, our Josh set to changing the World Championship from a knockout event into a grand prix system, whilst personally aiming for the very top post in the FIM.

I'm sure that if I were Danish (or American, or German, or Norwegian, or Italian...), I would resent the theory that the (speedway) world at that time revolved around the UK. Olsen surely did and he is a Danish patriot. Good on him.

We all know that the road to becoming world champion was not a straight and narrow one. The theory behind the World Championships was that everyone should have a chance at reaching the goal. It was like golf's Open Championships or soccer's FA Cup. It had honour, tradition and great heritage. It was also a British speedway initiative that was hijacked by the FIM after it had become a success.

A knockout competition always comes up with surprises. It is the very beauty of the contest. Most times, the one who finishes at the top of the pile fully deserves his success but on the way there are plenty of hard luck stories and heartbreaks.

I don't think it was the possibility of a rider being knocked out of the contest by bad luck that Olsen disliked; just the opposite really. What Ole hated more than anything was the underhand manipulating of finishing orders so as to aid riders, who might otherwise have fallen by the wayside, to sneak through to the next stage.

I'm breaking no great secrets here. If you want to blame anyone, blame Bruce Penhall, who, in 1982, decided to spend a vital race of the Overseas Final half a lap behind the other contestants, doing wheelies for the crowd at White City, instead of at least pretending to be trying against his three fellow Americans; or Simon Wigg, who was happy to provide plenty of ammunition to a stranger who turned out to be an investigative reporter from the Sunday People.

Team-mates, countrymen, friends . . . whatever the reason, come the last round of races in a World Championship qualifier and you could be sure that, nine times out of 10, there was some chicanery and all was not what it might seem on the track. Sadly, this open secret painted speedway in a very poor light, provoking suggestions that it is little more than wrestling.

This is not true. There are very few professional sports that, in my opinion, could stand up to close scrutiny.

But Ole just hated any collusion at all. I can see why he likes the grand prix idea. In theory at least, select the best riders, put them in many races spread over the whole season and you should be able to eliminate a touch of bad luck from ruining one's title chances. You should be fairly sure the winner at the end has got there on his own merits.

Even just the introduction of the grand prix idea, of course, does not guarantee such things, because if scores are still tight at the end of the series there remains room for collusion. In fact there were rumours about a group of riders 'ganging up' against another early in the grand prix days. This is why the formula was changed to the current diabolical affair (soon to be changed again, we hear).

Anyway, for what it's worth, I believe Olsen's devotion to the GP format, in preference to the sudden death, was based on a mixture of wanting to ensure that the best riders possible were in the competition, that the best overall rider won it and that the promotorial benefits of staging the events were spread over a broad range of countries and not limited to a select few.

Equally, I have no doubt Ole could foresee a clash between the BSPA and the Speedway GP. Blind Freddy (but not, it seems, the British promoters themselves) could see the two competitions were mutually incompatible. The GP, should it reach its intended conclusion, will cause the world's top riders to stop competing in the British League altogether. I don't think such an outcome would have bothered Ole for one moment.

Let's get back to the split between the two British leagues. After just one season the New National League had decided it was no longer really 'New' and had dropped the prefix from its title. It then did something that, in the context I suppose of European law, was inevitable sooner or later, but which I thought should have been later. It allowed the use of foreign riders.

I felt this was a very backwards step, and said so, only to be accused by *Speedway Star*, among others, of xenophobia. I did not, nor do not, see things in quite the same way. It seemed to me that by introducing yet another level of foreign imports, over which whose comings and goings the promoters had no control, was merely asking for trouble.

However, for the UK promoters in both leagues it was a short-term, shortsighted option, which allowed them to abdicate responsibility for the finding, training and encouraging of local talent.

The web was tightening. The UK promoters had no voice at the FIM, the two leagues were at war with each other and by virtue of relying more and more on oversees riders, they were ceding increasing power to the FIM and overseas interests.

By this time, just about all the promoters who had been operating when I joined the BSPA had, one way or another, seen the light and were jumping ship. Finally, when Len Silver called it a day (before his subsequent return to Rye House), I could clearly see the writing on the wall.

So began the era of the 'gentleman promoters' in British speedway. These are people who do not rely on speedway for their daily bread. In general, they are self-made men who are attracted to the sport and the chance for a bit of glory. Soccer had been afflicted with these types for years. Now they were taking over speedway.

Some were in it for the glory, others for the 'glamour' and maybe one or two were attracted to the cash and carry nature of the business. One way or another, the era of the professional speedway promoter was fast coming to an end.

It was time for me to go.

If the FIM had Vaessen inflicted on them, then British speedway had a similar problem in the shape of Mervyn Stewkesbury, a builder by trade and Poole Speedway promoter for fun and maybe pocket money.

This builder of houses obviously preferred to build castles in the air and tried to turn them into empires. With his egotistical, bullying manner he quickly took over control of the lower league, which by then had become a mix of those who had no interest in anything but their own show and those who had neither the wit nor wisdom to play a leading role. He did so to such an extent that he installed his own man, Alan Hodder, as the league's manager and set up office in his own Weymouth back yard.

This established Stewkesbury as the unchallengeable Emperor who people crossed at their peril. It was claimed that the lower league was better managed than the top league at the time. Some might argue that perhaps the top league was merely more democratic.

When Stewkesbury foisted his Grand Plan onto British speedway, he really excelled himself. Some might imagine it was engineered merely to get Poole Speedway into the top flight without having to pay a premium. Others might be a little kinder and suggest that Napoleon Stewkesbury really believed His was the Light and the Way.

It was doomed to fail, and fail it did, leaving the Emperor, whose new clothes had finally been recognised for what they were, to take his bat and ball, and return from whence he came.

Is it any wonder then, that speedway in the UK had contracted further and further, with just about no cohesion, little promotional experience and no leadership at all? Nobody could doubt that Stewkesbury's successor, Middlesbrough boss Tim Swales, was well meaning, but he carried neither the forethought and stature, nor the support to be anything but a caretaker.

With British speedway in such a mess, who could blame Olsen for working on the basis that if UK speedway was in such a self-inflicted state of decay, then frankly, it didn't deserve special consideration.

I reckoned it would take between five and 10 years for the grand prix series to become another full-time sporting circus, like the tennis, the golf, or Formula One racing, and that UK speedway would be reduced then to being a sport for semi-professional enthusiasts.

I hadn't planned on two things. First, I had assumed that, having gone as far as they had, the gang of three (Vaessen, Olsen and Sorber) would go the extra few yards and ensure the GP shows were properly staged. Also, I didn't imagine that Olsen would allow himself to get sidetracked by a particular hobbyhorse of his, which also happens to be one of mine.

I refer to the question of speedway bikes becoming too technically advanced for the tracks on which they race. This problem has always existed with the F1 circus, whose biggest task from day one has been to contain the speed of its cars. Each year, as the most financially able teams introduce great technical innovations, so the organisers have to find ways of reducing the power output. It leads to an often stormy relationship between the competitors, manufacturers and the organisers - but it needs to be done.

Olsen chose the question of tyre traction on which to make his stand and introduced a tyre with far less grip for grand prix events. The logic was sound, but logic and speedway are not always happy bedfellows. It was a huge miscalculation, brought about by Ole's own ego, and it set back the fledgling GP by some distance.

It also cost Sorber his long-held position of power and authority within the CCP, although, having served his purpose, I expect Olsen felt him expendable and a reasonable sacrificial lamb.

You could also argue it was this same tyre dispute that cost Vaessen the position to which he had now risen, which was that of president of the FIM itself - although it is my opinion the man just stood on far too many fingers on his mercurial climb to the top. As tends to happen with all such organisations, I suspect the tyre thing caused him to turn his back on those he had elbowed out of the way on his way up, allowing the knives to strike.

No bad thing really. What speedway needed was someone of Vaessen's ability to wheel and deal, but with a lot more insight into what is good for the sport rather than good for the people within it.

The second reason for the GP not being an overnight success is typical of speedway throughout the world. Whilst Olsen was trying to put together a good on-track product, utilising the best riders and trying to inject some semblance of professionalism into them, nobody thought to do the same for the events themselves.

The total inadequacy of the FIM was there for all to see. When it came to blowing all those inscription fees for events around the world, the Sunday Czars were great. They could organise

New World Champion Jason Crump on his way to winning the GP crown at Hamar, Norway in October 2004. *(MP)*

a piss-up in any brewery on this earth, and the more far flung, expensive and exotic the better. The annual FIM conference was/is a junket *par excellence*, worthy of any monopoly organisation in the world.

Unfortunately, injecting the same amount of professionalism into staging the various GPs was asking too much, so each federation that stuck its hand up to stage a round was left to do its own thing.

Well. Not entirely. There was the list of the Sunday Afternoon Czars as long as your arm to be wined and dined, transported, feted and fawned over, but who had little or no impact on the show. In fact, they were almost certainly more nuisance than they were worth, and certainly a drain on the staging budgets.

Now given that even the elite speedway nations around the world had latterly failed miserably to put on a decent show for the annual one-off World Final, what chance was there that minnow nations would do any better with their mini finals?

Still, at least what each country put into staging its GP directly reflected what it got out of it in terms of financial gain.

British speedway had one of two choices: It could either wring the infant GP's neck by refusing to cooperate, refusing to stage a UK round and telling the riders to choose between racing in England or racing in the GPs, which I am sure would have been the chosen option of the 70s promoters. Or it could throw in its lot with the GPs, accept that sooner or later they would lose the top riders to the circus, but could at least grab a sizeable piece of the GP action.

In true BSPA tradition, it did neither.

Where were all those professional promoters who used to make such a success of staging the World Finals at Wembley? Gone!

So why didn't the BSPA itself recognise that an ageing and out of touch Charles Ochiltree could no longer do a reasonable job promoting the UK round of the new Grand Prix series at Coventry when, for him, it was just another in a season of events?

Why didn't they consider employing a person – Peter Adams, for instance – or a company to take on the staging of the event and make it special?

But they didn't. Meanwhile, Poland, free from the shackles of communism, was enjoying rampant capitalism. Every bright-eyed, bushy tailed entrepreneur only had to set up a stall and customers would overwhelm him, and there were enough such likely lads to jump on the speedway bandwagon. Instant riches!

Now let's change the subject a little. Let's look at pay TV and its effect on sport. The banning of tobacco advertising and sponsorship had presented a serious problem for many sports throughout the world but the introduction of pay TV had suddenly given those sports a whole new market place.

Well, when I say suddenly, I don't mean overnight. Certainly, the power of sport on TV had become well recognised in the US, where cable TV arrived many years before it did around the rest of the world. The big four sports over there, baseball, football, ice hockey and basketball, had already cashed in on the TV dollar. No longer were they prepared to give their product away to the TV companies in the hopes of making a few bob from sponsors. They could auction their sport among the TV people and give their sponsors all the coverage they wanted.

Certainly, even well before pay TV, the power of sport to television ratings was recognised here in Australia, resulting in the Packer circus in cricket – an event that changed the face of cricket worldwide for ever.

I had been a part of UK speedway's negotiations with TV in the past. Even when British speedway had events like a near sell out Wembley World Final on offer, the cost to TV was a slap up lunch, a couple of bottles of wine and what was, for the TV people, a bit of petty cash, whilst the likes of Dave Lanning constantly reminded us how lucky we were that we got anything at all.

To be fair, UK speedway did contract several agencies to help sell itself, but none either understood, or made any attempt to advise the sport on how to dress itself up. Nor, I suspect, would anyone within the sport have taken any notice if they had.

But multiple 24-hour-a-day TV sports channels chew through an awful lot of material, even allowing for repeats, and those fringe sports quick on their toes realised there was an opportunity to grab a slice of the action. They tailored their products to the telly and came up with a sensible packages.

Suddenly, American-style wrestling became huge business, then the likes of the 'extreme' sports got their acts together, to be joined by all sorts of fringe activities and way out stuff. Along came monster truck racing, strong man contests . . . anything to put on the screen between adverts.

The Speedway GP was attempting to cash in on that opportunity but not too many realised the kind of money potentially involved. Clearly, the individual federations should have clarified that if they were staging a GP round, then all the rights to that round, including TV, sponsorship and advertising, should go along with it.

The federations seemed to have overlooked this. Maybe the FIM did, too. It seemed that they were just happy to get speedway onto the small screen at any price, without considering the possible financial return to be had.

Now I know speedway hardly carries the same charisma and appeal as The Olympics, soccer's World Cup and FA Cup final, baseball's World Series or the Superbowl, but give or take a nought or three at the end of the cheque, the same principle applies. At the highest level, sport now makes its real money from flogging the media and sponsorship rights, not from turnstile admissions.

In the SGP, was the potential to package a purpose-made for TV series. Although such a series would inevitably damage domestic speedway, and in particular the UK scene, it was difficult for a neutral to attack the logic.

UK speedway would have to try to work around the GP and it would have to accept the eventual loss of its top stars. But in return it could expect a reasonable hand out from the money the series generated, which could be ploughed back into the grass roots of the sport.

I must admit, I don't know the detail of how it happened, but I suspect Olsen, possibly Vaessen before his demise, and others were punting around for someone with the expertise to take "their" GP along the next step. They needed someone familiar within the corridors of TV deal making, and who might be able to open the right doors.

They needed a company like BSI, who made its money by selling content to television. They also needed someone to take the show from being the equivalent of a 'B' grade 50s movie and turn it into a Harry Potter success.

So far, so good. But then, in my opinion anyway, the plot goes horribly wrong, at least from speedway's point of view.

If you came from a Formula One background, you would be aware of just how much money is involved in the sport and what a pathetic return on investment the punters (be it those who turn up on the day to watch or the TV armchair experts) get for their money in terms of entertainment.

But F1 supremo Bernie Ecclestone took a rich man's play toy, dressed it up in new clothes and turned what has become increasingly the most boring two hours of high speed procession into a massive, massive revenue-earner that countries, never mind promoters, scrap over for the rights to stage a round of.

And then there is speedway. Logistically far easier to organise, with its small oval configuration enabling spectator and camera alike to keep the action in view the whole time. A series of explosive one minute bursts which don't last long enough to become boring and around which can be put so much window dressing and so much time for TV adverts. Finally, but just as importantly, from a visual point of view, far more chance of crashes and close-up views of blood, snot and gore. Also, an opportunity for lively interaction between riders on and off the track.

It just had to be a winner!

So never mind about showing them how to sell what they have and earn a small commission, how about if BSI, like the man from Remington, could buy the product? Unlike Omar Kyam, though, this man, who had no doubt read the Bernie Ecclestone story very carefully, could get his hands on the product for nothing up front except a few promises, and a pay-as-you-go drip feed of very little. All he needed was plenty of nerve.

Can you imagine the Sunday Afternoon Czars at the FIM? They had been running around, cap in hand, trying to get TV interested in their product. Suddenly, here was a chance to give the FIM some real clout, some real finance and some real power. Just think of the number of representatives they could now send scuttling around the world, business class, puffing out their chests and looking important, whilst someone else did all the work and took all the chances.

What about the individual federations? Millions of pounds, dollars, kronor, zlotties... would come flooding into the sport. And guaranteed TV.

This looked like a real gift horse, so nobody bothered to open its mouth and take a look inside.

Ever since the deal was struck, I've been asking the same two questions: How much money is actually involved, and where does that money go? After years of BSI involvement in the sport, I have yet to have found an answer. However, a glance at BSI's annual returns, even allowing for the usual smokescreens, indicates someone is doing very well out of it!

None of the federations, it seems, receive anything at all by way of a direct share of the supposed millions paid to the FIM by BSI, whether they actually stage a round or not. So far as I can ascertain, whatever money is paid goes into the black hole called the FIM and simply disappears in a haze of jobs for the boys and 'administration expenses'.

When BSI was first presented to the speedway world after they had struck the deal with the FIM, everyone was impressed with the BSI principal, John Posslethwaite's 'can do' approach. He was young, brash and used all the mediaspeak words that speedway had been crying out for.

Nobody even stopped to think about what was being 'given away'.

Remember, BSI's expertise is in flogging airtime to TV companies, and in finding and servicing sponsors. Put yourself in their position. Or should I say 'his' position. For all of its high profile image, effectively BSI revolves around one man, and effectively there is no great difference to using the term 'BSI' or 'John Posslethwaithe' – except that one is a good deal easier to type!

If they could rent the rights to the GP series for a relatively small amount, then sell on the individual events to gullible promoters for enough to pretty well recoup the outlay, out pops potentially the most lucrative parts of all – the transmission and commercial rights, for next to nothing.

For the FIM, which, when all said and done, should be nothing more than an administration working for the federations, this was a chance to establish itself with a firm and independent line of finance. This represented a real opportunity to empire build.

Suddenly then, the stagers of the individual rounds, be it individual promoter or federation, had to pay for the pleasure of putting them on - and we are not talking small numbers. Where previously a staging federation had paid no staging fee, now there was a hefty charge. Also, they had to cede the commercial rights. I described all of this when the BSI deal was first announced as being 'all smoke and mirrors'. I see no reason so far to change my thoughts.

For the riders, plenty of talk of jam tomorrow; plenty of encouragement to commit huge amounts of money into making themselves seem more professional and, for the top few, a chance to maybe earn enough to cover the outlay. The great majority, though, face a loss of earning opportunities over the weekends they commit to the GPs, costs well above those they are likely to recover in the medium term and an actual loss on the day.

For the federations, in return for 'lending' their riders to the GP series, with all the inherent uninsured risks (in terms of asset loss) and loss of use of the riders themselves, a big fat zero. This is fine for minnow nations, with no real domestic speedway structure and no professional organisation, but a serious problem for those federations and promotions that supply all of these riders with opportunities to make regular and good money from the sport.

For the actual promoters of league teams, who pay transfer fees for these riders, who ferry them all over the world, who supply, directly or indirectly, all of the racing and back up equipment, and house and support them . . . nothing.

Nothing for losing the use of these riders whenever SGP feels like it, nothing in compensation when riders are injured whilst taking part in the GPs, nothing towards bringing the far flung riders to Europe to race in the GPs, and nothing towards the supply and maintenance of equipment for use in the GPs.

So, let's backtrack to the bit where the GP series had been introduced, when the federations had the opportunity to share in its success. That has now gone. The potential blue sky profits, which are the transmission rights, have been stripped out.

It is also becoming more and more difficult to find promotions prepared to pay a large up front fee, take on huge staging costs and run the risk of potential disaster, such as happened at Gothenburg in 2003 where the temporary track wasn't laid properly, or of Sydney, where the shortfall for the staging promoter was in six figures.

So ... back to the original question: where to now?

Ironic, isn't it, having 'given away' the TV rights to the Speedway Grand Prix, The Elite League in England seems to have gone to enormous lengths to have domestic speedway on the box.

I think it is quite wrong that the most influential promoter, BSPA president, Terry Russell, receives a huge commission on the TV income. It is argued that he 'earned' this commission by putting in the lion's share of the work to get the TV interested and, after all, it's claimed the league would have been happy enough to pay the commission to an outside agency.

I view this in two ways: First, as president of the BSPA, I feel Russell was representing the BSPA rather than himself in his negotiations with the television companies. Far more important, I think large sums of money paid, dependent upon performance, to an active promoter must run the risk of clouding decision-making and create conflicts of interest.

Add to this, we are not talking any old promoter, but the most influential and highest ranking office holder. As I see it, a real danger exists for a conflict of interests.

I just cannot understand why the BSPA rolled over as soon as the GP came along when they could easily have either killed it off or taken a stake. As it stands, they have given up the best fixture dates and times of the year, they have given up their rider assets without so much as insurance cover against loss of use through injury, and they have juggled their regulations and fixture planning so as to fit around the riders and not around the paying public.

The same can be said of the domestic TV coverage now provided by Sky. Other than the obvious financial benefit to the promoter who cops the commission, I wonder if anyone has actually worked out the net benefit of the Sky deal.

Staging promoters on nights their matches are televised take a huge hit in attendance revenues. The other promotions that would normally operate on that night have the choice of changing their regular race night, or also taking a hit. Those supporters who do turn up find themselves messed about by the TV requirements. Riders, aware of the money coming in from TV, inflate their own demands, diluting the return to the tracks considerably. As with the GP stagings, fixture lists are turned upside down and regulations changed – or so it seems – to suit the TV coverage ...

In theory, apart from the money aspect, TV exposure is supposed to allow speedway to showcase itself. It is supposed to convert people into becoming active supporters and it is supposed to bring in additional sponsorship revenues. This doesn't not seem to have happened.

In Poland, the bubble appears to have burst for many of the promotions. No doubt, those entrepreneurs who did so well out of the glory years are off to find the next 'good thing', leaving behind riders who have become used to big money living and will find a chill wind blowing through their lifestyles.

Sweden continues to happily pay its way because of its club-run style of operation and because it has such a limited and strange Tuesday night fixture list. But if riders found themselves restricted to trying to exist purely on Swedish returns, even augmented by GP earnings, their pickings would become very slim.

All of the rest of the speedway staging nations are largely amateur, or at best, semi-professional.

And the Grand Prix? At best, I would say it is in limbo. As long as it remains propped up by the goodwill of the Big Three nations, I think it can be maintained, but I am sure the owner must, by now, be getting nervous. When BSI arrived, with a great explosion of fireworks, loud music, air horns and start-line girls with the hint of professional presentation, everyone decided this was it. Now I am not so sure.

The debacle of Sydney, which was always on the cards because the costs involved in bringing the 'circus' over, was never going to work without some huge financial assistance from BSI. Clearly, more than one GP round in Europe must be losing money, whilst the queue of replacement venues waiting to jump in seems to have dried up. I suspect that BSI has discovered it is not easy to maintain momentum.

I don't know what the TV rights return to BSI but I would think they are substantial. Already, they stage three rounds themselves. Maybe those rights return enough for BSI to effectively take on all of the rounds, or maybe they will have to encourage more interest from prospective promoters by dropping their staging fees and costs.

To move forwards, the GP has to stage more rounds, but more rounds means more disruption to the British calendar, bringing forward the possibility of further confrontation with the UK promoters over rider availability.

BSI must find at least four more rounds to risk that confrontation and give the GP riders enough to keep them loyal - adding just one or two rounds will merely cause confrontation with no certainty the riders will abandon their bread and butter racing for what, at this stage, is little more than glory.

British speedway, on the other hand, just has to make its own decisions. And soon. Does it accept that sooner or later its star men will move on to the 'circus' (augmented by other leagues on the Continent) full time, and bite the bullet now in the hopes of minimising the damage, or does it simply accept the inevitable and try to work around it?

Had it not been for Sky TV, with its reasonably lucrative contract payments and the desperation of Terry Russell, I really think crunch time would have already come and gone.

The way forward

So that lot begs the question: what would I do, if I was a British promoter today, to get things back onto a firmer footing?

Well, like the village idiot said when asked directions by the tourist, I wouldn't have started from here.

It is not with the benefit of hindsight that I come up with these thoughts. Obviously with some small modifications to allow for events in between, my basic opinions have not changed greatly since the original idea of the GP was floated.

First of all, I do not place the problems associated with British speedway on the introduction of the GP series. Rather, it was because of the state the BSPA had got itself into that the GP was allowed to happen. A strong and capable group of UK promoters would have seen the dangers looming and stamped the thing out before it was born. Or taken control of it.

Going right back to my promoting time, the death of Charles Foot had a huge impact. He was the only promoter who had the respect of the federations around the world. Even at the time of his untimely demise, he was working towards a union with Sweden and Poland that would have allowed for those 'professional speedway' nations to work alongside, but not be entirely deferential to, the FIM.

Alas, it didn't happen because there was nobody left in British speedway with Foot's authority or universal respect to see things through. It should be appreciated, at that stage the oval racing division of the FIM (the CCP) was really of no consequence.

Generally, the BSPA made its own rules, and within a year or so the FIM copied them. Apart from a couple of junkets each year, and rubber stamping the way the Big Three nations had divided up the various World Championship staging dates and venues, there was not much else to do except for the delegates to puff their chests out and look important.

Many of the BSPA 'hotheads', like Len Silver and myself, were all for having the UK pull out of the FIM altogether. At that time the only place where riders could earn a living was in the UK. I was confident that those foreign riders employed in Britain, when put to the test, would continue to race there, even if it meant being disowned by their own countries. The only bargaining tool the CCP held was the 'World Championship' title.

Would riders have foregone their chance in that competition whilst the UK promoters (who had set up the original championship) established a rival competition? Also, profits from the staging of the World Final when it was held in the UK were substantial, so promoters were reluctant to gamble that money away.

Ironic, isn't it, that those profits now go into the coffers of the FIM and/or BSI?

So the original promoters got out, leaving the BSPA organisation to its egotists and the inexperienced. What was desperately needed then, as it is now, is an independent and experienced controlling authority. I tossed my hat into the ring many years ago but it was tossed back out again. If there is one thing the speedway promoters will not do under any circumstances is to allow any 'outside' interference. This has been their fundamental problem for many years.

Even now, if the UK promoters were prepared to sort out their structure right from the top down, they would be able to claw back much of the ground they have lost. But as it stands, just one or two dominant personalities with their own agendas are preventing any kind of forward progress.

The FIM, using the money they receive for renting out the world championship tag, however much that might be, continues to grow into a true Applebyan bureaucracy – but only at the expense of British speedway. Until, and unless, that situation is redressed, I have grave concern for the future of speedway in the UK, as we have known it. Even now, top riders are thinking twice about maintaining their British racing commitments,

As in most things these days, Britain has already fallen from being the Mecca of speedway and is fast becoming an also-ran.

Events in speedway move fast. The situation might well already have changed since I wrote these words. Somehow, though, I doubt it.

As things stand, I do have a detailed strategy I believe would give speedway in the UK a fighting chance of survival. There is no point in filling several pages with those ideas, though, because the promoters in the UK would rather go out of business than take steps to regain control of their sport.

Reg Fearman suggested some radical ideas when he was the BSPA chairman but his fellow promoters showed no interest. Even at that time speedway was becoming unviable as a professional sport for many of the promotions.

Reg simply made the observation that promoters were not yet desperate enough to take action. I can think of very few, if any, of those promoters who sat around that table in the early 80s who are still involved today. OK, you can allow for the odd few retirements and untimely deaths, but the vast majority of us simply got out of the sport.

Some managed to leave with dignity, some lost their shirts, but collectively they were never desperate enough to take the hard decisions needed. They left the sport rather than do that.

The same situation exists today. Nobody seems to be desperate enough to make the toughest decisions. They simply fall by the wayside, one by one.

The optimists make the point that the pessimists have been predicting the demise of speedway, as we have known, it, for the last 50 years, and argue that it is still around. It might well be, but it is certainly not the speedway of 20 years ago.

And although I accept that some kind of speedway racing will continue in the UK into the future, I have my doubts it will be as strong as it is even now.

The top three in the 2004 Speedway GP – Jason Crump flanked by Tony Rickardsson (left) and Greg Hancock. *(DF)*

Acknowledgements

It is normal practise to put acknowledgements at the front of a book, but here would seem a more sensible place to me.

My wanting to put something down in print has been around for most of the nearly 20 years since I was directly involved in the sport. Originally Martin Rogers, who, at that time was still a promoter, and possibly had a vested interest, put me off the idea!

Also, computers were in their infancy then and my typing so bad, I could not have afforded the Tippex. Printing techniques at that time also made 'niche' publishing difficult.

But to be interesting, the 'book' would need to rely heavily upon photographs to cover for the inadequacies of the author, and I was lucky to have as friends from the very early days at Ipswich Speedway, Anne and Dave Kindred.

Dave was the long-time head of the East Anglian Daily Times Ltd photographic department, before recently branching out on his own. He is a brilliant photographer who adjusted easily to the difficulties of taking speedway photos, and was responsible for programme pics as well as supplying the 'Anglian' and 'Star' with superb speedway photo coverage over many years.

Dave immediately offered to assist with the book even before my having to resort to threats! Thank you, Dave (and Anne, his child-bride, who would have been responsible for the threats being carried out!).

Not every photo in the book is Dave's. One of the pleasures of the sport though, is the people in it, and many other photographers in the speedway family have helped fill in the gaps, and receive credits where the photos can be identified to them. You will find (AW) under many photos, and I am sure the others will not mind me giving Alf Weedon, an emperor amongst kings, a special mention.

Intermixed with my collection of old shots taken by Dave were those taken by Owen (Ollie) Hines and, later, Ken Rivers. I cannot identify individually who was responsible for which.

Whilst most of the cover shots were Dave Kindred's, a big thanks goes to Ken Rivers for his 'Foxhall By Night'. A framed copy of the picture is the only thing speedway that survives on show in my house (apart from the 1978 World Team Cup, and that only because it is the perfect shape and size to hold two spare toilet rolls I also like the positioning, tucked alongside the throne in the 'small room', a testament to my conceit of years gone by.) Thank you very much gentlemen.

The next thing I need to do is to list all of those who deserved to feature in this book, but by reason only of space, could not be accommodated. I could say I should apologise, but perhaps not all would have been thrilled with a mention!

All of the race night track staff, who gave up their time, and put up with my histrionics, for little more than washers, deserve a special thanks. Meeting after meeting, year after year, the same people were there to help with the show.

Of those, John Earrey, the announcer, was a huge part of the Ipswich success. Of all our so-called 'luck' at Ipswich, falling across John was by far the best of it. A whole passage about his brilliant work lies on the cutting room floor for want of space. He and John Bennett, the timekeeper and spin-doctor (PA and music controller) made the show what it was.

Many gave far more than the minimum, and John Booth, Jill Cotton and Trevor Seymour need mention from the early days. Then there was Mike Horne, Ray Chinnery, Brian Messenger, Ted Howgego, Clive Noy, Bryan Seery, Keith Barton, Fred Cotton, John Bloomfield, Ray Walters, Pat and Jeremy and so many more . . .

We had the undisputedly best St John team in speedway, and every one of our track doctors were great, but especially Chris Clarke, who lasted the longest and also had to cope with being my own GP. Also, a section dealing with Physiotherapist Brian Simpson did not survive the editor's blue pencil.

Another chapter, treated in the same manner by the blue pencil brigade, was devoted to the riders' wives and parents. Sometimes we loved them, and sometimes not, but I give credit to all of them for their general patience and fortitude.

A special mention also to Anita, John Simmons' mum. She has been his rock over more years than we care to count.

I also need to recognise the enormous part the local media, and the two papers, the morning *East Anglian Daily Times* and evening *Ipswich Evening Star* played in helping the speedway succeed.

Many times I was too quick to react to the odd negative comment, and many times I was either patronising or too secretive. Nevertheless, I sincerely thank the East Anglian Daily Times Company, its management, and in particular Mike Horne from the early days and Elvin King from the time Mike moved on until now. Needless to say, the same applies to the whole of the photographic department.

We were really lucky that the new, exciting local Radio Orwell more or less had the same timeline as the speedway. It was new, it was young, and it was full of local issues, including the speedway.

Orwell played an important part, and I want to thank in particular Tim Ewart and Pete Barraclough, who both went on to better things, and Pete Slater, who took over from the other Pete and did a fine job until the sports department was downsized. Such a shame that, for Orwell, the thanks are posthumous.

Especially, a mention to Andy Archer, who was the best presenter on Orwell by a country mile, a firm personal friend, and a great ambassador for the Ipswich Speedway.

At the end of the day though, speedway racing is about the riders. I have concentrated on many over the previous chapters, but some obvious names were not given full appreciation, simply through space constraints.

Dennis Sigalos deserved more words. He was a great rider and a true professional. Kevin Jolly could also have had his own chapter. He was a great character, really good bloke, and someone I liked very much. Kevin and I got on really well when he rode at Wimbledon during my time there. Tim Hunt. A strong character who quickened the pulse with his daring deeds and was as much a gentleman off the track as he was determined on it. Clive Noy, Stan

Pepper, Dave Gooderham, Nigel Flatman, Colin Cook, Andy Hines, all deserved more mention than they received, as did a host of fringe and junior riders.

There are also plenty of other people who had varying influences on myself and Ipswich Speedway. Sections on Reg Fearman, Martin Rogers and James Easter in particular found themselves cut.

On a personal level, thanks go to my wife, Linda, and son, Alex (AJ) for putting up with my moods and the hogging of the computer whilst this was being written, and a special thanks to

To you, goodbye . . . from Linda, Alex and I.

Tony McDonald, who has kept my enthusiasm going 'till the end, and has been daft enough to put his money where my mouth is!

Thanks also go to Elvin King, Mike Bacon and Richard Clark for wading through the manuscript and supplying positive encouragement and nice quotes, along with help in launching the book.

Finally, thanks to those people in the UK who have been so supportive, especially Bob Radford, John Chaplin, Dave Feakes, Colin Barber, Ray Walters, James Easter, Pat Doncaster and just so many others. I am lucky to have such good friends.

To those whom I have left out, I am very sorry. Put it down to the way those little grey cells are dying off at an alarming rate.

And speaking of dying, have you noticed, we never get any older. It's everyone around us! I saw Sean Connery on *Parkinson* the other night. Is that really the man I watched with Ursula Undress in *Dr Who* such a short time ago?

Sadly, the years come at a cost. Almost every week it seems another friend has wandered off to that great speedway track in the sky. Many of those I have mentioned in this book have gone down that path. Probably even more of them than I know about. I have not referred to them as 'the late' or dwelt upon their passing. I promise you, this is not a lack of respect on my part. I wrote about them as they were, and I prefer to remember them that way, full of life.

And so it remains simply to say thanks if you have stayed awake and got this far. I hope you enjoyed reading these bits and pieces. I find that whenever I have read an autobiography (and this is as near to one as I will ever get), I have been left with a series of questions I would have liked to put to the author. Well, if you have any thoughts or opinions you would like to pass on to me, feel free to email me on berry11@bigpond.net.au. I will be pleased to hear from you.

Yesterday when I was young,
The taste of life was sweet as rain upon my tongue,
I teased at life as if it were a foolish game,
The way the evening breeze may tease a candle flame;
The thousand dreams I dreamed,
The splendid things I planned I always built, alas,
on weak and shifting sand;

I lived by night and shunned the naked light of day
And only now I see how the years ran away.

Yesterday
When I was young,
So many drinking songs were waiting to be sung,
So many wayward pleasures lay in store for me
And so much pain my dazzled eyes refused to see,
I ran so fast that time and youth at last ran out,
I never stopped to think what life was all about
And every conversation I can now recall concerned itself with me,
and nothing else at all.

Yesterday the moon was blue,
and every crazy day brought something new to do,
I used my magic age as if it were a wand,
and never saw the waste and emptiness beyond;

The game of love I played with arrogance and pride
and every flame I lit too quickly, quickly died;

The friends I made all seemed somehow to drift away
And only I am left on stage to end the play.
There are so many songs in me that won't be sung,
I feel the bitter taste of tears upon my tongue,
The time has come for me to pay
for Yesterday When I was Young.

Ipswich Speedway Major Honours 1969-1985

British League Division One

League Champions – 1975, 1976, 1984
League Runners-up – 1981, 1983

Knockout Cup Winners – 1976, 1978, 1981, 1984
Knockout Cup Runners-up – 1974, 1985

League Cup Runners-up – 1982
Inter-league Knockout Cup Winners – 1977

British League Division Two

Knockout Cup Winners – 1970, 1971

Season-by-Season League Record

British League Division Two
1969   11th (16 teams)
1970   6th (17)
1971   3rd (17)
British League Division One
1972   6th (18)
1973   5th (18)
1974   3rd (17)
1975   1st (18)
1976   1st (19)
1977   4th (19)
1978   6th (19)
1979   15th (18)
1980   7th (17)
1981   2nd (16)
1982   3rd (15)
1983   2nd (15)
1984   1st (16)
1985   5th (11)

Discography

Key:
Chapter Title
Song title (if different)
Writer
Original hit version
My preferred artist version

Introduction
For the Good Times
Kris Kristofferson
Perry Como
Kris Kristofferson

We've Only Just Begun
Paul Williams
Carpenters
Carpenters

Happy Days
Norman Gimbel + Charles Fox
Happy Days crew

The Way We Were
Marvin Hamlisch, Alan Bergman, Marilyn Bergman
Title song from the movie
Barbara Streisand
Elaine Paige

The Impossible Dream
Mitch Leigh and Joe Darion
From Man of La Mancha
Various
Mathis

Climb Every Mountain
Rogers and Hammerstein
From the Sound of Music
Various

I Can See Clearly Now
Johnny Nash
Johnny Nash
Johnny Nash

It Takes Two
Sylvia Moy, William Stevenson
Marvyn Gaye & Kym Weston

The Silver Tongued Devil and I
Kris Kristofferson
Kris Kristofferson
Kris Kristofferson

19th Nervous Breakdown
Mick Jagger/Keith Richards
Rolling Stones
Rolling Stones

Land of Hope and Glory
Pomp and Circumstance
Edward Elgar
Various
Band of the Coldstream Guards

Love is All Around
Reg Presley
The Troggs
The Troggs

It's All In the Game
Charles Dawes and Carl Sigmon
Cliff Richard
Tommy Edwards

Take it to the Limit
D. Henley, G. Frey, R. Meisner
Eagles
Eagles

The Kid, The Shrimp and The Tiger
Traces (of love)
Buddy Buie, James Cobb, Emory Gordy
Various
Mathis

Didn't We
Jimmy Webb
Richard Harris
Mathis

The Way We Were
Marvin Hamlisch, Alan Bergman, Marilyn Bergman
Gladys Knight
Mathis

Alone Again (naturally)
Gilbert O'Sullivan
Gilbert O'Sullivan
Johnny Mathis

Three Great Riders
The Rose
Amanda McBroom
Bette Midler
Elaine Paige

Oh Lord, It's hard to be humble
Mac Davis
Mac Davis
Mac Davis

Bat Out of Hell
Jim Steinman
Meat Loaf
Meat Loaf

Forty Miles Of Bad Road
Duane Eddy and Lee Hazelwood
Duane Eddy
Duane Eddy

The Combine Harvester
Melanie Safka and Brendan O'Shaughnessy
The Wurzels
The Wurzels

Send In The Clowns
(From *A Little Night Music*)
Stephen Sondheim
Judy Collins
Judy Collins

The Middle of Nowhere
Buddy Kaye and Bea Verdi
Dusty Springfield
Dusty Springfield

No Regrets
Tom Rush
The Walker Brothers
The Walker Brothers

Windmills of Your Mind
Marilyn and Alan Bergman and Michel Legrand
Noel Harrison
Mathis

Hey, That's No Way to Say Goodbye
Leonard Cohen
Leonard Cohen
Roberta Flack

Hotel California
Don Felder, Don Henley, Glenn Frey
Eagles
Eagles

Please Don't Tell Me How the Story Ends
Kris Kristofferson
Kris Kristofferson
Kris Kristofferson

Yesterday When I Was Young
Charles Aznavour
(English Lyrics: Herbert Kretzmer)
Charles Aznavour
Charles Aznavour

Index

If you have enjoyed reading 'Confessions', then you can read more of **JOHN BERRY'S** superb, incisive writing in every issue of...

BACKTRACK

The new retro speedway magazine

The bi-monthly, 40-page, retro speedway magazine packed with exclusive interviews and features on riders and personalities from the 70s & 80s. Where are they now?...defunct tracks..magic memories...pure nostalgia all the way...we catch up with former stars and find out what they are doing today. If you watched speedway anywhere in the 70s or 80s, you won't want to miss **Bactrack Magazine**.

On sale around the tracks for £3.00 per issue – or avoid the frustration of rain-offs and have your copy delivered direct to your door...

Subscribe now for just £16 for 6 issues per year by phoning our Credit Card Hotline:

01708 379 079

You can also subscribe online at: **www.retro-speedway.com**

Or write, enclosing your cheque/postal order (payable to Retro Speedway) to: **Backtrack (Subs), Unit 4, Ashton Gate, Ashton Road, Harold Hill, Romford, Essex, RM3 8UF.**

Backtrack is produced by the publishers of *Confessions of a Speedway Promoter*